Managerial Accounting
Study Guide and Selected Readings

Managerial Accounting
Study Guide and Selected Readings

Henry R. Anderson
University of Central Florida

Edward H. Julius
California Lutheran University

Houghton Mifflin Company   **Boston**

Dallas   Geneva, Illinois   Palo Alto   Princeton, New Jersey

Cover photograph by Ralph Mercer.

Library of Congress Catalog Card Number 88-81318

ISBN: 0-395-32466-1

ABCDEFGHIJ-WC-9543210/89

Contents

Appendixes

vi

To the Student

This self-study guide is designed to help you improve your performance in your first accounting course. You should use it in your study of *Managerial Accounting,* by Anderson, Needles and Caldwell.

Reviewing the Chapter

This section of each chapter summarizes in a concise but thorough manner the essential points related to the chapter's learning objectives. Each Integrated Learning Objective is restated and its page reference given for easier cross-referencing to the text. All key terms are covered in this section or in the Testing Your Knowledge Section.

Testing Your Knowledge

Each chapter contains a matching quiz of key terms, a completion exercise, true-false statements and multiple-choice questions to test your understanding of the learning objectives and vocabulary of the chapter. Approximately every second chapter includes a crossword puzzle to test your knowledge of key terms.

Applying Your Knowledge

An important goal in learning accounting is the ability to work exercises and problems. In this section of each chapter, you can test your ability to apply two or three of the new principles introduced in that chapter to "real-life" accounting situations.

Readings

Most chapters include one or two current readings to provide you with a broader understanding of the accounting profession, careers in all fields of accounting, and current issues in managerial accounting.

The Study Guide concludes with answers to all questions, exercises, problems, and crossword puzzles.

H.R.A.
E.H.J.

CHAPTER 1 INTRODUCTION TO MANAGEMENT ACCOUNTING

REVIEWING THE CHAPTER

Objective 1: Describe the field of management accounting (p. 4).

1. **Management accounting** consists of specific types of information gathering and reporting functions and related accounting techniques and procedures. The management accounting discipline aids the decision-making process by providing management with pertinent financial information. The types of information that management seeks are (a) product costing information, (b) information to assist in planning and controlling operations, and (c) special reports and analyses to support management's decisions.

Objective 2: Distinguish between management accounting and financial accounting (pp. 5-8).

2. Management accounting focuses on accounting for internal operating activities and results. Financial accounting is primarily concerned with recording and reporting practices as they relate to the preparation of external accounting reports.

3. Management accounting can be distinguished from financial accounting by looking at (1) the primary users of information, (2) the types of accounting systems required, (3) restrictive guidelines, (4) units of measurement, (5) the focal point of analysis, (6) frequency of reporting, and (7)

degree of reliability in the information reported.

Objective 3: Compare the information needs of a manager of: (a) a manufacturing company; (b) a bank; and (c) a department store (pp. 8-11).

4. The manager in a manufacturing company has special information needs that center around production of a product. Product costing information, including costs of materials, labor, and factory overhead, must be controlled. Operating efficiency must be sustained. Production planning and scheduling, product-line management and development, cash management, capital expenditure decision analysis, and selling and distribution expense analysis are all areas where the manufacturing manager requires information.

5. The bank manager must maintain an accurate internal information recording and reporting system because surprise inspections by federal and state officials are a common occurrance. In addition to using a cash balancing and monitoring system, bank managers use budgets and service-line analysis reports extensively. Cash management for internal use is also important. Captial expenditure decision analyses are also part of a bank manager's duties. Recently, bank managers have begun to

rely on product costing procedures as applied to bank services. Operating efficiency and cost effectiveness are the objectives of the move.

6. Department store managers need much of the same information required by both manufacturing managers and bank managers. Budgets, cash management reports, product sales analyses, capital expenditure analyses, and product selling cost analyses are examples of such needs. However, department store managers have a special need for information. Their organizations deal directly with the consumers of products. Information to monitor customer traffic flow, product display, advertising campaigns, and delivery of merchandise are all important areas to department store managers.

Objective 4: Identify the important questions a manager must consider before preparing a managerial report (pp. 11-13).

7. The four W's, **Why? What? Who?** and **When?** are important questions that must be answered before preparing a managerial report. **Why** is the report being prepared? **What** information should the report contain? **Who** is the report being prepared for? **When** is the report due? Once these questions have been answered, the report can be prepared.

Objective 5: Prepare analyses of nonfinancial data (pp. 13-18).

8. The management accountant is often called upon to prepare analyses of nonfinancial data. Most people associate the accounting discipline with analyses of monetary matters. Although management accountants do prepare analyses expressed in dollars, they also confront problems requiring solutions formulated around such items as labor hours, machine hours, units of output, number of employees, and number of requests for a service.

Objective 6: State the differences between accounting for a manufacturing and a merchandising company (pp. 18-20).

9. Merchandising companies purchase goods in finished form and resell them. Manufacturing companies, on the other hand, produce the goods that they sell. To find product costs and inventory valuation, the merchandiser just uses the purchase cost figures. The manufacturer, however, must add together the costs of production.

10. Manufacturers use management accounting systems to determine the costs of their manufactured products. Accurate cost data are necessary to produce reliable financial statements. Thus the manufacturing company must accumulate the costs of materials, labor, and factory overhead for its products. The cost of goods that are sold appears on the income statement as Cost of Goods Sold. The ending inventory accounts in the balance sheet contain period-end costs of materials, work in process, and finished goods, which are a manufacturing company's three kinds of inventory accounts.

11. Materials are the substances used in manufacturing a product. Work in process consists of the costs attached to all goods that have been started but are still unfinished. Finished goods are products that are ready for sale.

Objective 7: Describe a Certified Management Accountant (CMA) and state the requirements one must satisfy to attain this designation (pp. 20-23).

12. The designation of Certified Management Accountant (CMA) was established in 1972 to recognize professional competence in the field of management accounting. To become a CMA, one must pass the CMA exam and satisfy certain professional and educational requirements. The CMA exam consists of the following five parts: (a) economics and business finance, (b) organization and behavior, including ethical considerations, (c) public reporting standards, auditing, and taxes, (d) internal reporting and analysis, and (e) decision analysis, including modeling and information systems.

Testing Your Knowledge

Matching

Complete the chart below by writing the appropriate letter in the blanks under each column.

	Financial Accounting	*Management Accounting*
1. Primary users of information	_____	_____
2. Types of accounting systems	_____	_____
3. Restrictive guides	_____	_____
4. Units of measurement	_____	_____
5. Focal point of analysis	_____	_____
6. Frequency of reporting	_____	_____
7. Degree of reliability	_____	_____

a. The business entity as a whole
b. No guides or restrictions: only criteria is uscfulncss.
c. Various levels of internal management
d. Demands objectivity; historical in nature
e. Persons and organizations outside the business entity
f. Whenever needed; may not be on a regular basis
g. Double-entry systems
h. Various segments of the business entity
i. The historical dollar

j. Heavily subjective for planning purposes but objective data are used when relevant; futuristic in nature
k. Periodically on a regular basis
l. Not restricted to double-entry system; any useful system
m. Adherence to generally accepted accounting principles
n. Any useful monetary or physical measurement, such as—labor hour or machine hour; if dollars are used, may be historical or future dollars

Completion

Use the lines provided to complete each item.

1. Compare the users of financial accounting data with those who use management accounting reports.

_____

_____

_____

_____

2. What is the primary difference in the area of units of measurement when contrasting financial and management accounting?

_____

_____

_____

_____

Introduction to Management Accounting

3. What reports do both the manufacturing manager and the bank manager require in their daily managerial duties?

_____

_____

_____

_____

4. Identify information needs that are unique to the manager of a department store.

_____

_____

_____

_____

5. Give three examples of reports based on nonfinancial data that are useful to a bank manager.

_____

_____

_____

_____

6. Show how cost of goods sold is computed for the merchandise company.

_____

+ _____

= _____

− _____

= _____

7. What kinds of costs are charged to the Work in Process Inventory account of the manufacturing company?

_____

_____

_____

_____

8. When planning a special report, what should the who question provide to the accountant?

_____

_____

_____

_____

True-False

Circle T if the statement is true, F if it is false.

T F **1.** The function of the management accountant is to make the important decisions for the company.

T F **2.** A merchandiser's goods that are for sale are called finished goods.

T F **3.** Management accounting exists primarily for the benefit of people inside the company.

T F **4.** An accountant for a company or government organization relies more on financial accounting principles than management accounting principles.

T F **5.** The business entity as a whole is the focal point of analysis in financial accounting.

T F **6.** The degree of reliability in data supporting management accounting reports is often subjective.

T F **7.** Financial accounting has no guides or restrictions: the only criterion is usefulness.

T F **8.** Management accounting reports may be prepared monthly, quarterly, and/or annually on a regular basis, or they may be requested daily or on an irregular basis.

T F **9.** In addition to using the cash balancing and monitoring system, manufacturing managers use budgets and service-line analysis reports extensively.

T F **10.** Report preparation depends on the four W'S: Who? What? When? and Where?

T F **11.** Analysis of nonfinancial data is common for the financial accountant.

T F **12.** Analysis of nonfinancial data is more common for a manufacturing company than it is for a bank.

T F **13.** Computing ending inventory values is more complex for a manufacturing company than for a merchandising concern.

T F **14.** The Certified Management Accountant (CMA) designation is awarded to a person who has worked ten or more years as a management accountant.

Multiple Choice

Circle the letter of the best answer.

1. Management accounting and financial accounting do not differ with respect to
a. primary users of information.
b. supplying timely data.
c. restrictive guides.
d. unit of measurement.

2. Which of the following reports is used by managers in manufacturing companies, banks, and department stores?
a. Budgets
b. Work in Process inventory analyses
c. Make or buy decision analyses
d. Service-line management analyses

3. The primary users of financial accounting information are
a. journalists.
b. engineers.
c. stockholders.
d. middle managers.

4. Management accounting principles and procedures normally rely on
a. the double-entry system.
b. generally accepted accounting principles.
c. usefulness as a guide.
d. the historical dollar.

5. Management accounting reports and analyses are usually heavily subjective, which means that
a. much of the data has been estimated.
b. developed based on guess work.
c. the data is verifiable.
d. the reports use historical-dollar information.

6. Cash management analyses are useful for managers of
a. banks, primarily.
b. banks and department stores.
c. banks and manufacturing companies.
d. banks, department stores, and manufacturing compaines.

7. Which of the following is not based on non-financial data?
a. Analysis of deliveries
b. Operating budgets
c. Survey of customers served
d. Analysis of labor hours worked

8. Accounting for a manufacturing company differs from that of a merchandising company in which one of the following?
a. Balance sheet presentation only
b. Income statement only
c. Determination of cost of goods sold
d. Use of double-entry accounting system

Applying Your Knowledge

Exercises

1. Nonfinancial data analysis.

Tony Nelson is the owner of Tony's Pizza Palace in upstate New York. Over the years, Tony has developed measures of efficiency for his employees.

Number of Pizzas Served Per Hour	Employee Rating
Over 20	Excellent
17-19	Good
14-16	Average
10-13	Lazy
Under 10	The Pits

During March, the following labor-hour information was generated for the month's servers:

Employee	Hours Worked	Number of Pizzas Served
P. Porter	130	2,860
S. White	140	2,520
R. Shach	145	1,885
E. Butterfield	136	2,176
B. Kirby	168	3,192
B. Worrell	154	2,310
G. Johnson	150	1,350

Evaluate the performance of these employees.

2. Report Preparation.

John Madd has been asked to prepare a report of parking-lot usage at the Melbourne plant of Sirrah Corportation. He has determined that the report will be prepared for Denise Crosby and that its purpose is to determine usage patterns and traffic flow.

Is John ready to gather the data and prepare the report? If not, what else needs to be done before he proceeds?

Is it Managerial Accounting or Management Accounting?

Managerial accounting is alive and well! Or is it the discipline of management accounting that is thriving? Recently I had the privilege of dining with two respected teachers and writers in this difficult-to-title area. They live hundreds of miles from one another, so I took advantage of the moment by asking each of them, "Is there a difference between managerial accounting and management accounting?" Their responses were similar to many I have received during the past few years. One stated, "They are similar in nature, covering virtually the same topics." The other looked at the first and in a joking fashion said, "I always thought that managerial accounting was studied at the undergraduate level."

These two statements illustrate the difficulty we have in distinguishing managerial accounting from management accounting. The term "managerial" has concerned me for some time. I believe that the title "managerial accounting" came into use several decades ago to describe all accounting transactions related to the actions of management. It is a generic term used to cover all such accounting-management-related actions. Over the past ten to fifteen years, a discipline known as "management accounting" has evolved. This discipline includes a special certification, the Certified Management Accountant. The CMA has gained recognition rapidly and is now a respected professional designation. The CMA examination is almost as long and *just as difficult* as the CPA examination.

The second reason that I prefer the term "management accounting" is closely related to the first. Management accountants are responsible for accounting for the *internal* operations of any enterprise. Far too often, only manufacturing-related accounting practices and procedures are associated with "managerial" accounting. Management accounting, however, is useful within every type of venture including manufacturing, service, not-for-profit, and governmental organizations. Some of this information generated by management accountants may be filtered through the accounting system and become part of the external financial statements, but the vast majority of the management accountant's work will never be viewed by people outside the enterprise. In fact, much of this data is considered confidential and in some cases, *top secret*. (This is one reason why it is more difficult to get real-world examples for use in the management accounting section of a *Principles of Accounting* textbook.) Good internal management accounting systems make a company more competitive and profitable by contributing to the product or service pricing mechanism and by helping to conserve costs and resources.

The reason that we base much of the management accounting discussion on manufacturing accounting is that all three cost elements--materials, labor, and overhead--play a part in the analysis. For service-related industries such as banks, hospitals, and hotels, only labor and overhead costs come into play. There is no "product" and therefore no need for direct materials. Once students understand accounting for manufacturing operations, they should be able to apply those same concepts and procedures to the service business environment.

During the past couple of years, much discussion has centered on the overuse of manufacturing company problems in the management accounting sections of *Principles of Accounting* texts with little emphasis on the service industries or not-for-profit organizations. The fact that almost 70 percent of our economy is non-manufacturing oriented justifies this concern. There is a definite need to limit instructors' dependence on examples with only manufacturing underpinnings.

But did we ever resolve the issue of "is it managerial accounting or management accounting?" The Management Accounting Practices Committee of the National Association of Accountants has defined "management accounting" as

. . . the process of identification, measurement, accumulation, analysis, preparation, interpretation, and communication of financial information used by management to plan,

Source: Article by Henry R. Anderson. Reprinted from the Spring 1987 issue of *Accounting Instructors' Report.*

evaluate, and control within an organization and to assure appropriate use of and accountability for its resourses.[1]

Doesn't this statement cover the knowledge that we are trying to instill in those future accountants and managers out there in our classrooms? Could we do the same thing under the guise of the title, managerial accounting, too?

[1] "Objectives of Management Accounting," National Association of Accountants, Statement Number 1B, New York, N.Y., June 17, 1982, page 1.

CHAPTER 2 OPERATING COSTS: TERMS, CLASSIFICATIONS, AND REPORTING

REVIEWING THE CHAPTER

Objective 1: State the differences between the three manufacturing cost elements: (a) direct materials costs; (b) direct labor costs; and (c) factory overhead costs (pp. 41-42).

1. Manufacturing costs are classified as direct materials, direct labor, or factory overhead costs.

2. A **direct cost** is any cost that can be conveniently and economically traced to a specific product or cost objective. An **indirect cost** is one that cannot.

3. **Direct materials** are materials that can be conveniently and economically traced to specific products. Direct materials used in producing a desk are the wood used as legs, drawers, and desk top. However, the cost of nails, glue, and screws used to build the desk are too insignificant to assign as part of its direct materials cost. These materials are called **indirect materials,** and their costs are classified with other indirect costs as factory overhead.

4. **Direct labor** costs are all labor costs that can be conveniently and economically traced to specific products. Wages for machine operators are an example of a direct labor cost. On the other hand, wages of maintenance workers are called **indirect labor** and are classified as factory overhead.

5. **Factory overhead** is all manufacturing-related costs that are not classified as direct materials or direct labor. It is also called manufacturing overhead, factory burden, or indirect manufacturing costs. Examples of factory overhead costs are depreciation, insurance, utilities, and all indirect materials and labor costs associated with the manufacturing operation.

Objective 2: Identify the source documents used to collect information on manufacturing cost accumulation (pp. 42-47).

6. To ensure an efficient system of materials purchases, certain documents should be used. A **purchase requisition (purchase request)** is used by a production department to request that the company purchase certain materials. The materials are purchased when the purchasing department sends the supplier a **purchase order.** When the ordered goods are received, a **receiving report** is prepared, indicating the quantity and conditions of the goods. When materials are needed for production, a **materials requisition** form is prepared and presented to the storeroom clerk.

7. **Time cards** are used to keep accurate track of the number of hours worked by employees. **Job cards,** on the other hand, record

labor hours per job and help to verify the time recorded on the time cards.

8. **Gross payroll** equals all wages and salaries earned by the employees and is used in computing manufacturing costs. **Net payroll** is the amount paid to the employees after all payroll deductions have been subtracted from the gross payroll. **Labor-related costs** that arise from direct labor costs and can be conveniently traced to such costs should be accounted for as direct labor costs. Otherwise, they are considered part of factory overhead. One example of a labor-related cost is employee fringe benefits such as paid vacations, sick pay, and pension plans. Another example is the payment of employer payroll taxes, such as unemployment taxes and the employer's share of social security contributions.

9. Manufacturing costs may be classified as variable, fixed, or semivariable depending on the way the cost changes with changes in production. **Variable manufacturing costs** go up or down in direct proportion to the number of units produced. Examples are direct materials and direct labor. Costs such as insurance, rent, and supervisory salaries that do not vary with units produced are called **fixed manufacturing costs.** Semivariable costs, such as those for telephone use, are part variable and part fixed.

Objective 3: Compute a product's unit cost (p. 47).

10. A product's unit cost is comprised of direct materials, direct labor, and factory overhead costs. To compute a unit cost, the total materials, labor, and factory overhead costs incurred must be divided by the number of units produced during the period. This unit cost is used for inventory pricing of Finished Goods Inventory and as a basis for determining the price of the product.

Objective 4: Distinguish between product costs and period costs (p. 48).

11. **Product costs** are made up of the three cost elements—direct materials, direct labor, and factory overhead—that are included in the cost of a product. A product cost is inventoriable and can remain an asset as part of the Work in Process or Finished Goods Inventory. This same product cost becomes an expense in the year that the associated product is sold.

12. **Period costs (expenses)** do not benefit future periods, so they are classified as expenses in the period in which they are incurred. In other words, any costs that cannot be inventoried, such as selling and administrative costs, are considered period costs.

Objective 5: Describe the nature, contents, and flow of costs through the Materials, Work in Process, and Finished Goods Inventory accounts (pp. 49-53).

13. Under the **periodic inventory method,** manufacturing costs are recorded in the general ledger but are not assigned to specific inventory items. At the end of the accounting period, the beginning inventory balances are updated by actually taking a physical inventory of the items on hand. Interim inventory balances cannot be determined without a physical count.

14. Under the **perpetual inventory method,** manufacturing costs are recorded in the general ledger and are assigned to inventory accounts as materials are received and production takes place. Therefore, inventory account balances are continually being updated, and they can be determined at any point in time without a physical count. However, a physical count should be taken periodically to verify the account balances.

15. The manufacturer maintains three separate inventory accounts, **Materials Inventory, Work in Process Inventory,** and **Finished Goods Inventory.** The Materials Inventory balance represents costs of all purchased but unused materials. The Work in Process Inventory balance contains costs attached to partially completed products. The Finished Goods Inventory balance represents the cost of products completed but not yet sold.

16. Product costing and inventory valuation rely on a structured flow of manufacturing costs. **Manufacturing cost flow** begins when materials are purchased and other manufacturing costs are incurred. Once incurred, these costs are classified as direct materials, direct labor, or factory overhead, and are transferred into the Work in Process Inventory account. When the goods are complete,

their cost is assigned to the Finished Goods Inventory account. Finally, costs associated with goods sold are transferred to the Cost of Goods Sold Inventory account.

Objective 6: Prepare a statement of costs of goods manufactured (pp. 55-58).

17. The manufacturer's income statement is much like the merchandiser's. The two differences are that the manufacturer used the heading Cost of Goods Manufactured instead of Merchandise Purchases, and Finished Goods Inventory instead of Merchandise Inventory.

18. The manufacturer prepares a **statement of cost of goods manufactured** so that cost of goods sold can be computed in the income statement. Three steps are involved in preparing this statement, as follows:

a. First, the cost of materials used must be found. Arbitrary numbers will be used to aid understanding

Materials Inventory, beginning of period	$100
Add materials purchased	350
Cost of materials available for use	$450
Less Materials Inventory, end of period	200
Cost of materials used	$250

b. Second, **total manufacturing costs** must be computed.

Cost of materials used (computed in section a)	$250
Add direct labor costs	900
Add factory overhead costs	750
Total manufacturing costs	$1,900

c. Third, **cost of goods manufactured** must be computed.

Total manufacturing costs (computed in section b)	$1,900
Add Work in Process Inventory, beginning of period	400
Total cost of work in process during the period	$2,300
Less Work in Process Inventory, end of period	700
Cost of goods manufactured	$1,600

19. When the figure for cost of goods manufactured has been found, it can be transferred to the Cost of Goods Sold section of the income statement, as follows:

Finished Goods Inventory, beginning of period	$1,250
Add cost of goods manufactured (computed in section c)	1,600
Total cost of finished goods available for sale	$2,850
Less Finished Goods Inventory, end of period	300
Cost of goods sold	$2,550

20. The objective of the statement of cost of goods manufactured is to translate manufacturing cost data into usable information for inventory valuation, profit measurement, and external reporting. However, a cost accumulation system is first needed for day-to-day activities.

Objective 7: Prepare an income statement for a manufacturing company (pp. 58-59).

21. A manufacturer's income statement is identical to that of a merchandiser's, with the exception of the way cost of goods sold is calculated (see Learning Objective 6).

Objective 8: Apply cost classification concepts to a service-oriented business (pp. 59-61).

22. When you shift from a manufacturing environment to a service-oriented environment, the only major difference is that you are no longer dealing with a product that can be assembled, stored, and valued. Services are rendered and cannot be stored up or placed in a vault. Of the three manufacturing cost elements, direct materials cost is no longer applicable to the pricing mechanism. Service costing is made only up of direct labor and service overhead costs. Service projects can be in process at period end, so some of the service costs are inventoriable. For the most part, service costing is for cost control and pricing purposes.

Operating Costs: Terms, Classifications, and Reporting

Testing Your Knowledge

Matching

Match each term with its definition by writing the appropriate letter in the blank.

___ 1. Time card

___ 2. Factory overhead

___ 3. Direct materials

___ 4. Indirect materials

___ 5. Direct labor

___ 6. Indirect labor

___ 7. Variable manufacturing costs

___ 8. Fixed manufacturing costs

___ 9. Product cost

___ 10. Period cost (expense)

___ 11. Periodic inventory method

___ 12. Perpetual inventory method

___ 13. Cost of goods manufactured

___ 14. Total manufacturing costs

a. Materials that cannot be conveniently and economically traced to specific products

b. Materials that can be conveniently and economically traced to specific products

c. All indirect manufacturing costs

d. Wages, salaries, and related costs that cannot be conveniently and economically traced to specific products

e. Total costs charged to completed units during the period

f. A cost that will not benefit any future period and is expensed in the period incurred

g. Wages, salaries, and related costs that can be conveniently and economically traced to specific products

h. A record of the number of hours worked by an employee

i. The system that updates inventory account balances only when a physical count is taken

j. Costs that vary proportionately with units produced

k. Costs that do not vary with units produced

l. The system that keeps a continuous record of inventory account balances

m. A cost that is assigned to a specific job

n. Total costs charged to production during the period

Completion

Use the line provided to complete each item.

1. Manufacturers have three types of inventory. Name them.

   _____

   _____

   _____

2. What are the three chief components of manufacturing costs?

   _____

   _____

   _____

3. When is a cost considered to be a direct cost?

   _____

   _____

4. What three types of information does management receive from the management accountant?

   _____

   _____

   _____

5. Show how cost of materials used is computed.

   _____

   +_____

   =_____

   −_____

   =_____

6. Show how total manufacturing costs are computed.

   _____

   +_____

   +_____

   =_____

7. Show how cost of goods manufactured is computed.

   _____

   +_____

   =_____

   −_____

   =_____

8. Show how cost of goods sold is computed for the manufacturer.

   _____

   +_____

   =_____

   −_____

   =_____

9. Distinguish between gross payroll and net payroll.

   _____

   _____

   _____

True-False

Circle T if the statement is true, F if it is false.

T F 1. A product cost should not appear in the income statement until the period in which the product is sold.

T F 2. The Work in Process account does not contain any period costs (expenses).

T F 3. Direct labor data for a particular job can be found on a time card.

T F 4. Factory burden is another term for factory overhead.

T F 5. Factory rent is considered a fixed manufacturing cost.

T F 6. An inventoriable cost is one that can be associated with a specific product.

T F 7. Direct labor is an example of a variable manufacturing cost.

T F 8. Under the periodic inventory method, the trial balance will show beginning-of-period figures for its inventory accounts.

T F 9. Under the perpetual inventory method, material purchases are debited to a separate Purchases account.

T F 10. The statement of cost of goods manufactured must be prepared after the income statement.

T F 11. For the manufacturer to compute cost of goods sold under a periodic inventory system, the beginning finished goods amount must be known.

T F 12. Cost of goods manufactured minus total munufacturing costs equals the change in Work in Process during the period.

T F 13. Cost of goods manufactured must be computed before total manufacturing costs.

T F 14. Cost of materials used must be computed before cost of goods manufactured.

T F 15. Under a periodic inventory system, all three inventory accounts of a manufacturer are debited for their beginning balances in the cost of Goods Manufactured column of the work sheet.

T F 16. Advertising is included in the computation of cost of goods sold.

T F 17. All beginning inventory accounts are closed with credits.

Multiple Choice

Circle the letter of the best answer.

1. Which of the following is considered a direct product cost?
   a. The cost of glue used in making a bookcase
   b. The janitor's salary
   c. The cost of legs used in making a chair
   d. The cost of rags used in cleaning a machine

2. Documents relating to materials must be processed in a specific order. Which of the following lists those documents in their proper order?
   a. Materials requisition, purchase requisition, purchase order, receiving report
   b. Purchase order, purchase requisition, receiving report, materials requisition
   c. Purchase requisition, purchase order, receiving report, materials requisition
   d. Receiving report, purchase order, materials requisition, purchase requisition

3. Which of the following would probably be considered a period cost?
   a. Salaries paid to the salespeople
   b. Wages paid to an assembly-line worker
   c. Freight in
   d. Materials used in the manufacture of a product

4. A document sent to the vendor to buy goods is a
   a. purchase requisition.
   b. materials requisition.
   c. receiving report.
   d. purchase order.

5. Before materials can be issued into production, which form should be presented to the storeroom clerk?
   a. Materials requisition
   b. Purchase requisition
   c. Job card
   d. Purchase order

6. Which of the following is a variable cost?
   a. Rent
   b. Insurance
   c. Electricity
   d. Property taxes

7. Which of the following is computed last?
   a. Total manufacturing costs
   b. Cost of goods sold
   c. Cost of materials used
   d. Cost of goods manufactured

8. Which of the following is least likely to appear in the manufacturer's income statement?
   a. Total manufacturing costs
   b. Cost of goods sold
   c. Cost of goods manufactured
   d. Finished Goods Inventory, beginning of period

Applying Your Knowledge

Exercises

1. Corbin Corporation has provided the following data for 19xx:

Cost of Goods Manufactured	$450,000
Finished Goods, Jan. 1	75,000
Finished Goods, Dec. 31	80,000
Materials, Jan. 1	92,000
Materials, Dec. 31	70,000
Work in Process, Jan. 1	55,000
Work in Process, Dec. 31	64,000

In the space provided, compute Cost of Goods Sold.

2. Given the following accounting data, complete the statement of cost of goods manufactured for Spencer Company in the form provided.

Depreciation, Factory Building and Equipment	$ 31,800
Direct Labor	142,900
Factory Insurance	2,300
Factory Utilities Expense	26,000
Finished Goods Inventory, Jan. 1	82,400
Finished Goods Inventory, Dec. 31	71,000
General and Administrative Expenses	163,000
Indirect Labor	42,800
Net Sales	855,100
Other Factory Costs	12,600
Materials Inventory, Jan. 1	8,700
Materials Inventory, Dec. 31	32,600
Materials Purchased	168,300
Selling Expenses	88,500
Work in Process Inventory, Jan. 1	34,200
Work in Process Inventory, Dec. 31	28,700

3. Classify each of the following costs as direct materials, direct labor, or factory overhead by using the letters DM, DL, or OH.

____ a. Sandpaper
____ b. Worker who assembles the product
____ c. Worker who cleans and sets up machinery
____ d. Steel plates used in production
____ e. Glue and nails
____ f. Worker who sands product before painting
____ g. Wheels attached to product
____ h. Depreciation of machinery
____ i. Paint used to touch up finished product
____ j. Overtime for factory worker (½ time of 1½ time rate)

Spencer Company Statement of Cost of Goods Manufactured For the Year Ended December 31, 19xx		

Crossword Puzzle
for Chapters 1 and 2

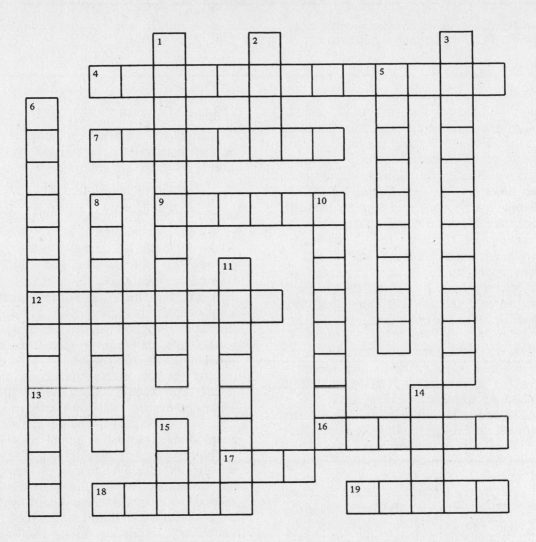

ACROSS

4. Document sent to a supplier (2 words)
7. Not traceable to specific products
9. ——— goods manufactured
12. Inventory method
13. Management accounting expert
15. Traceable to specific products
17. ——— materials
18. Cost that doesn't vary with changes in output
19. ——— manufacturing costs (DM + DL + OH)

DOWN

1. Expenditure that can be traced to goods (2 words)
2. Predetermined overhead ———
3. Purchase request
5. ——— report (prepared when goods arrive)
6. Goods partially complete (3 words)
8. Indirect manufacturing costs
10. (Goods) ready for sale
11. Labor document (2 words)
14. Example of 18-Across
15. Payroll deduction

Women in Management Accounting: Moving Up . . . Slowly

How successful are women working in the field of management accounting? Are they satisfied with their profession? Do they expect to occupy positions in senior management?

To answer these questions, *Management Accounting* editors surveyed 500 of NAA's female members who hold the position of manager, controller, treasurer, chief financial officer, chief executive officer, and president/owner.

Today more women than ever are attracted to the career opportunities in accounting and finance. A recent survey by the AICPA disclosed the percentage of female accounting graduates with bachelor's and master's degrees has increased from 28% in 1976-77 to 49% in 1985-86. At NAA, women now account for approximately 30% of the Association's total membership. Our survey represents NAA's first effort in documenting this exciting new trend.

Our study revealed that 69% of the women are in the 31 to 50 age group—the peak managerial and earning years for executives. They tend to work in manufacturing, service, and financial industries. (See Figures 1 and 2.)

Most are married, and almost half are mothers. The compensation they receive for the substantially more than 40 hours per week they work is good but not extravagant—42% earn $40,000 or more per year. This compares favorably with what members of the American Woman's Society of CPAs earn. According to a recent survey the AWSCPA conducted, 27.7% earn $40,000 or more annually.

Only 32% of our respondents have an accounting certificate (CPA, CMA, or CIA), and approximately 85% of all certificate holders are 40 years old or younger. Eighty percent have baccalaureate degrees or higher.

Source: Article by Susan Jayson and Kathy Williams. Reprinted from the June 1986 issue of *Management Accounting*.

"I Love My Work!"

Women in management accounting are optimistic that their goals are attainable through extra effort. An assistant controller working in the construction industry wrote: "I can go as far as *I* want to, although I still have to work harder than my male colleagues to get there."

As women management accountants advance up the corporate ladder they are enjoying many personal and professional rewards. In fact, more respondents mentioned the positive and satisfying aspects of their job rather than the problems faced in their career.

Bonuses and good salaries are considered important rewards. At every job level, however, women view the opportunity to work in a challenging environment, status in the profession, respect from senior management, being part of a decision-making team, and being in a position to influence the growth and development of the people they supervise as important also.

"The expanding responsibilities of my job, the opportunity to play the role of mentor to the people I supervise, and the realization that my success in a conservative company is based solely on my abilities and achievements is gratifying," explained Linda Nellis, general accounting manager.

A CPA and manager of financial reporting earning more than $40,000 per year happily reported: "The pay is high enough to travel and own a home. At work I have the freedom to make decisions and help initiate changes."

"Being with a company that has grown and being a part of its growth is exciting," reports the treasurer of a medium-size manufacturer.

Getting Ahead

According to the survey, in the next five years 13% see themselves remaining in a management level position. More than 60% expect to be corporate controllers, treasurers, and chief

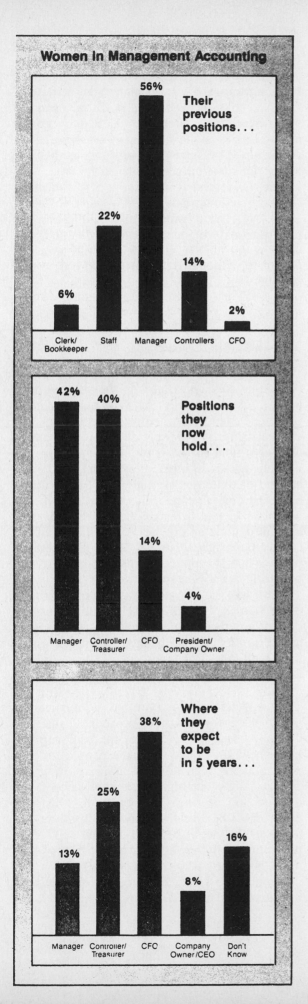

Women in Management Accounting

Their previous positions...

- Clerk/Bookkeeper: 6%
- Staff: 22%
- Manager: 56%
- Controllers: 14%
- CFO: 2%

Positions they now hold...

- Manager: 42%
- Controller/Treasurer: 40%
- CFO: 14%
- President/Company Owner: 4%

Where they expect to be in 5 years...

- Manager: 13%
- Controller/Treasurer: 25%
- CFO: 38%
- Company Owner/CEO: 8%
- Don't Know: 16%

financial officers. Eight percent have ambitions to be a CEO or company owner.

To help them achieve their career goals, more CFOs than managers or controllers have or had an advisor (52% vs. 36% vs. 30%). Usually the advisor is a male. As CFO, Judith L. Englund commented, "I couldn't have made it this far in the organization without the support of the owner who is male. Women still need men's support." About half the president/owners had an advisor during their career, most of whom were male, and 90% now help other women, mainly through on-the-job opportunities and some career counseling.

In addition to long hours spent at the office, women in management accounting participate in outside activities that they believe will help them to advance in their careers. CFOs, controllers, and managers report that continuing their education is the number one outside activity, followed by professional affiliations and membership in a women's organization. Slightly more CFOs than managers are involved in these activities (86% vs. 76%), and controllers rank third (67%). Company owners, however, place professional affiliations first.

The company owners have worked hard to reach the point where they are on their own and can be their own boss. "I enjoy the respon-

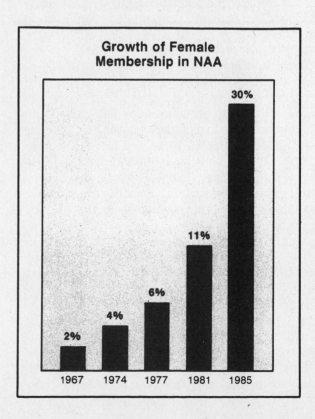

Growth of Female Membership in NAA

- 1967: 2%
- 1974: 4%
- 1977: 6%
- 1981: 11%
- 1985: 30%

19

sibility, challenge, flexibility, and recognition," says Katherine Westover from Neenah, Wis., who puts in about 75 hours a week as president of a small wholesale/retail company and who previously has been a staff accountant and a corporate controller. Sally Ann Parks, owner of a personnel agency in Waterville, Maine, for eight years, agrees. "It's great being able to manage my own company," she says. Most of the respondents in this category held various financial positions such as manager, auditor, accounting manager, vice president, general manager, or controller before reaching their goal as president, owner, or partner.

If they own their company, their main goal is to expand, and no one wants to leave her current job. If she could be tempted to change, it would be to further career goals or earn more money. A whopping 82% of this category would choose the same career path. Only one would not, and one is undecided.

Although they are content now, their careers have not been without problems. Take Ana Prince, for example. She has owned a company for about a year. This is her second business; she had owned another company for 15 years, ending in 1972, and has made a couple of changes in the last five years. She's delighted with her success now, but recalls she "was asked to type and take shorthand with her master's degree and men were not, even with an associate degree." Mrs. Prince, incidentally, holds three college degrees in addition to her master's in accounting.

Kate Farley Moynahan, owner of a financial services business for the past seven years, and who has been in accounting for 14 years, notes: "I worked for an insurance company and was openly discriminated against. I left the job because the situation was intolerable." She also says that, in hindsight, "I would have been stronger and more assertive during my first five to ten years in business." Now she serves as a mentor to other women.

Jean Barnett, a 30-year veteran of the business world, has been president of a small computer installation/sales/support company for the past five years that she considers a "progressive group" that accepted her on merit. Previously she "was not always accepted as part of the team when other women managers were not present."

One management consultant and owner of her own firm who has been in accounting more than 20 years and self-employed for eight re-

marked, "There was no work in my small southern town for women in management eight years ago so I had to open my own business. I still have to outperform men to be accepted."

On the other side, Judy Thompson, president of an executive search firm in San Diego for nine years, says she has experienced no career problems: "I've never accepted sex as being a reason for discrimination against me."

Anne C. Ransdell, controller of a printing company and nominee for NAA vice president, notes: "If I as a woman had been given the opportunities women are today when I began working for NASA in 1945, I would be at the top of the corporate ladder in a Fortune 500 now. I worked very hard to be where I am today."

Fair and Equal Treatment

How do women view the work performed by their male colleagues, and do they believe they have the same chances as their male counterparts for advancement within the company they work for? Their opinions depend on what job they now hold in the corporate hierarchy.

When asked whether they spent the same amount of time as their male counterpart did in preparing for his career, the CFOs overwhelmingly (86%) reported that they spent the same amount of time as the men. More than half the other groups agree, but a significant percentage believe that they have devoted more effort to preparing for their career.

When asked if they put the same amount of effort into their work as their male colleagues do, the groups differed. While managers (57%) and controllers (55%) believe they work harder than men, the same percentage of presidents and CFOs say that it's an equal amount of effort.

When it comes to opportunities for advancement, managers are more pessimistic than the CFOs. Almost half (46%) of the managers believe they don't have the same chance for promotion as the men do, and 17% are uncertain.

More CFOs are optimistic that gender has nothing to do with advancement, but 57% either don't believe they have the same opportunities as men or don't know. Sixty-five percent of the controllers, however, believe they have the same chances to advance.

According to Linda Ellis, "Opportunities have increased at the middle management level, but

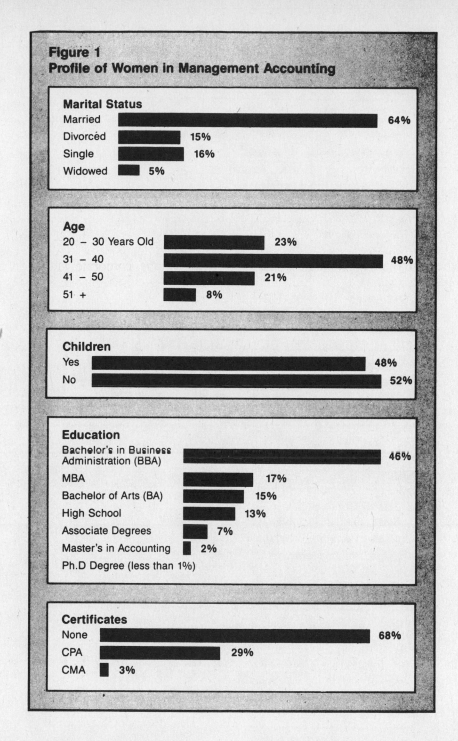

Figure 1
Profile of Women in Management Accounting

Marital Status
- Married 64%
- Divorced 15%
- Single 16%
- Widowed 5%

Age
- 20 – 30 Years Old 23%
- 31 – 40 48%
- 41 – 50 21%
- 51 + 8%

Children
- Yes 48%
- No 52%

Education
- Bachelor's in Business Administration (BBA) 46%
- MBA 17%
- Bachelor of Arts (BA) 15%
- High School 13%
- Associate Degrees 7%
- Master's in Accounting 2%
- Ph.D Degree (less than 1%)

Certificates
- None 68%
- CPA 29%
- CMA 3%

access to upper management seems to be almost as restricted as ever."

I Quit!

Instances of discrimination or sexual harassment were noted. A concern for many respondents was denial of a deserved promotion and uncertainty as to how far up the corporate ladder they could advance. For example, a highly paid controller was passed over for a promotion and after pursuing the reason in-house filed discrimination charges. The manager involved was fired, and she has moved up.

Francine M. Gaie, manager of an accounting department, said: "I was earning less than my male counterpart who had the same responsibilities as I did. After confronting management I was promised equal pay. I achieved parity in three years."

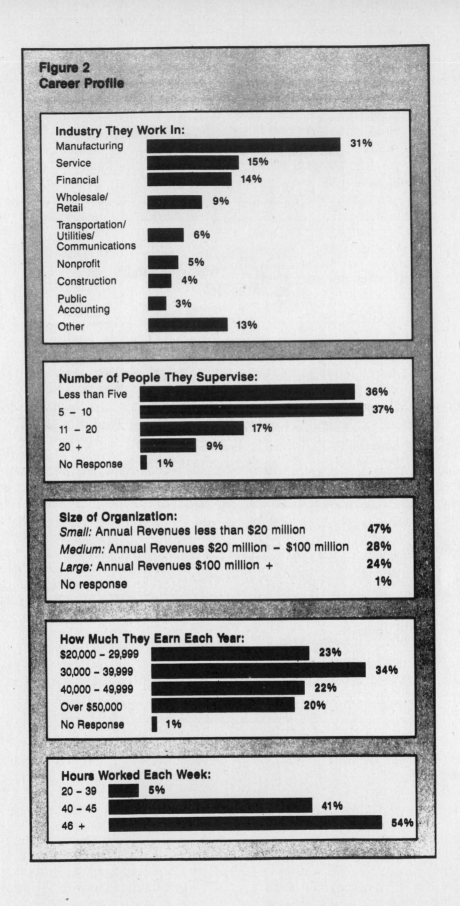

Figure 2
Career Profile

Industry They Work In:

Manufacturing	31%
Service	15%
Financial	14%
Wholesale/Retail	9%
Transportation/Utilities/Communications	6%
Nonprofit	5%
Construction	4%
Public Accounting	3%
Other	13%

Number of People They Supervise:

Less than Five	36%
5 – 10	37%
11 – 20	17%
20 +	9%
No Response	1%

Size of Organization:

Small: Annual Revenues less than $20 million	47%
Medium: Annual Revenues $20 million – $100 million	28%
Large: Annual Revenues $100 million +	24%
No response	1%

How Much They Earn Each Year:

$20,000 – 29,999	23%
30,000 – 39,999	34%
40,000 – 49,999	22%
Over $50,000	20%
No Response	1%

Hours Worked Each Week:

20 – 39	5%
40 – 45	41%
46 +	54%

Although the women surveyed believe that progress has been made in eliminating the stereotypical perceptions of women in business, they also believe it still exists to some degree in corporate America. Judith Englund, a CFO of a civil engineering firm, reported that "male managers don't have as much confidence in my financial judgment as I think they would have in a man. I am left out of telephone discussions involving major decisions."

A manager of internal audit who also is a certified internal auditor told of her difficulties in proving to the male vice presidents that she is capable and qualified to handle the company's audit. "What makes my work more difficult are the many sexist remarks that often are made during closing meetings when everyone is feeling pressured."

A controller notes, "Even though I have been controller three years, I am still referred to by some people (including the owner on occasion) as a bookkeeper." Two others reveal: "Women are still stereotyped as secretaries or bookkeepers," and "management thinks women make wonderful clerks but nothing else!"

How are women coping with these problems? Some quit. Others discuss the problems with senior management or ignore the situation, hoping that performing their responsibilities in a professional manner will resolve the problem.

"The biggest opposition to women in management accounting are men in their 40s and 50s," said Michaela I. Thompson, cost accounting manager. "I was in a job where I could not advance any further than a cost accounting manager. The reason or most of the reason was that I was a woman—I changed jobs," she said.

A CPA and financial analyst reported that she was her superior's "little girl." "We discussed the problem and I tried to be more professional—in other words, more masculine," she said.

A small minority were irritated that women themselves are overly concerned with the issue of discrimination. "I think women seldom encounter problems with male employees unless they're looking for them."

Very few problems with managing home and family responsibilities were reported, which is unusual considering the amount of time women are dedicating to their work and the high percentage of married women with children. Either these women are managing their households successfully or they are accustomed to not revealing this as a career problem for fear

that it would be a deterrent to further promotions.

One general accounting manager did express concern that her husband was not understanding about the demands of her job and the fact that she had to travel from time to time. Another revealed that her husband's refusal to relocate when she was offered a transfer resulted in her eventually losing her job. A controller said she wished she could find a company that demanded less overtime so she could spend more time with her children.

Moving On

The average number of job changes in the past five years for women in management accounting was once or not at all. We asked them to tell us which of the following reasons would motivate them to make a job move: to further personal career goals, more money, less travel, less overtime, new location, a better opportunity for promotion, increased travel, new challenges, spouse transferred, or other.

Among the managers earning the lowest salary, $20,000-$29,999, more money was the most important factor for a job change followed closely by the opportunity to further personal career goals. As salary levels increase, the importance of more money decreases. At the $50,000 level it ranks third, with a better opportunity for promotion being the number one reason to change positions; furthering personal career goals is second. For those earning between $40,000 and $49,999 the most important reason is to further personal career goals.

For those in the CFO category, "earning more money" is number one until the salary range reaches $50,000 and more per year. At that salary level it is the desire for new challenges and to further personal goals that would prompt a CFO to leave her current position. "New challenges" and "to further personal career goals" rank second and third to the CFOs in the other salary ranges. Controllers at all salary levels, however, list new challenges first, furthering career goals second, and more money third.

Almost half the CFOs have either a master's degree in accounting or an MBA. One has a law degree. Only one CFO did not attend college. Forty-eight percent have an accounting certificate (CPA, CMA, or CIA). Most work in manufacturing, nonprofit, or the service industries, in small organizations (annual revenues under $20 million), supervising fewer than five

PROFILE OF THE WOMAN MANAGEMENT ACCOUNTANT

Company Owner/President

Company presidents/owners represent 4% of the NAA sample responding to the survey. Also included in the category are partners of public accounting firms. Some statistics for the group are:

- 18% are 20 to 30 years old, 55% are 31-40, 27% are 41-50, and none are older than 51
- 45% are married
- 45% have children
- 45% earn more than $40,000 a year
- 73% work more than 46 hours a week
- 55% hold college degrees, 36% hold undergraduate business degrees, and 36% hold advanced degrees. Only one person did not attend college.

Forty-five percent hold accounting degrees: 36%, CPA, and 9%, CMA. All work in small businesses (annual revenues under $20 million), mainly public accounting or service businesses, and most supervise fewer than five people. The presidents have been in the business world 10-15 years and in their current position a median of five years. Eighty percent belong to other professional organizations in addition to NAA.

Chief Financial Officers

CFOs represent 14% of the total respondents. Also included in this group are vice presidents of finance and directors of finance. Some statistics for this group include:

- 23% are between 20 and 30 years old, 45% are between 31 and 40, and 31% are over 40 years old.
- 73% are married
- 57% have children
- 87% earn more than $40,000 annually
- 70% work more than 46 hours per week

people. The CFOs have worked in accounting/finance a median of 10 years.

Controllers

Controllers represent 40% of the respondents. Included in this group are division controllers, corporate controllers, treasurers, directors of finance, and assistant vice presidents. Some statistics for the group are:

- 17% are between 20 and 30 years old, 48% are 31-40, 21% are 41-50, and 14% are 51 and over
- 62% are married
- 55% have children
- 38% earn $30,000-39,999 a year, and 41% earn more than $40,000
- 54% work more than 46 hours a week
- 60% hold college degrees, 45% with business degrees; 15% hold advanced degrees; 11% hold associate degrees; and 16% attended high school but not college.

Twenty-two percent hold accounting certificates: 21% are CPAs, and 1% are CMAs. Most work in small manufacturing or service companies and supervise 5-10 people. They have been in the business world 10 to 15 years, in their current position a median of 12 years, and have made very few job changes other than promotions in the last five years. Fifty-two percent have professional affiliations in addition to NAA.

Managers

Managers represent 42% of the total respondents. Also included in this category are plant accountants, assistant controllers, and internal auditors.
Some statistics for this group:
- 75% are 40 years old or younger
- 67% are married
- 43% have children
- 32% earn between $20,000 and $29,999 annually, 37% earn between $30,000 and $39,999, and 31% earn $40,000 or more.
- 40% work in manufacturing
- 50% work more than 46 hours per week.

How well educated are the managers? Thirteen percent did not go beyond high school. Fifty-one percent have a bachelor's degree in business, and 17% have an MBA. There are 34 CPAs, three CMAs, and one CIA among the managers. Sixty-eight percent have 6-15 years' experience in accounting and finance.

Any personal reasons for a job change less travel, less overtime, and spouse transferred are minor considerations for all groups. No group would change jobs in order to travel less often. Although 28% of the managers and 24% of the controllers would relocate if their spouses were transferred, only 18% of the CFOs indicated that this would prompt them to leave their current employment. Although 27% of the presidents would change jobs if it meant less overtime, only 11% of managers and 1% of the controllers would, and this reason is not a consideration for any of the CFOs.

More Responsibility for Women

Do these women believe the general business environment has changed since they started working, and have women been able to influence any changes in the corporate world?

All groups agree that increased responsibility for women and more career opportunities for women to advance in their careers are the most noticeable changes. The third most obvious change witnessed by CFOs is an increase in salary for women. Owners, controllers, and managers disagree. For them the change in stereotypical perceptions of women in business was more noticeable. They see no major trend of women advancing into senior management.

When it comes to influencing the corporate working environment, all groups concur that today's working women are succeeding in eliminating the perceptions of women in traditional roles. An increased number of available child care services and more flexible work schedules to accommodate working mothers also are indications of how women are influencing the workplace.

Women management accountants indeed are making strides in their careers, and many feel there's nowhere to go but up. The controller of a medium-size manufacturing company summed up the climate: "Women in management are modern business pioneers. There are no rules and no role models. The situation is just as we ourselves create it."

CHAPTER 3 PRODUCT COSTING: THE JOB ORDER SYSTEM

REVIEWING THE CHAPTER

Objective 1: Identify the differences between job order costing and process costing (pp. 80-81).

1. The main reason for having a cost accounting system is to find the unit cost of manufacturing a company's products. Unit cost information aids a business in (a) determining a proper selling price, (b) forecasting and controlling operations and costs, (c) determining ending inventory balances, and (d) determining Cost of Goods Sold.

2. The two basic approaches to cost accounting systems are job order costing and process costing. The kind of production process a company has will dictate which of the two approaches it uses.

3. A **job order cost accounting system** is used in companies that manufacture one-of-a-kind or special-order products such as ships, wedding invitations, or bridges. In a job order cost system, the following conditions exist: (a) All manufacturing costs are assigned to and accumulated for specific jobs. (b) Emphasis is placed on job completion periods rather than on weekly or monthly time periods. (c) One Work in Process Inventory account is used. Its balance is supported by the job order cost sheets of jobs still in production.

4. A **process cost accounting system** is used when a large number of similar products are being manufactured. Companies producing paint, automobiles, or breakfast cereal would probably use some form of a process costing system. The following conditions exist in a process cost system: (a) Manufacturing costs are accumulated by department with little concern for specific job orders. (b) Emphasis is placed on a weekly or monthly time period rather than on the completion period of a specific order. (c) A Work in Process Inventory account is used for each department in the manufacturing process.

Objective 2: Describe the concept of absorption costing (p. 82).

5. Product costing may be accomplished only when the costing method being used specifies the types of manufacturing costs to be included in the analysis. The most common product costing methods are based on **absorption costing,** in which direct materials, direct labor, variable factory overhead, and fixed factory overhead are assigned to the products. Job order costing generally uses absorption costing.

Objective 3: Compute a predetermined overhead rate, and use this rate to apply overhead costs to production (pp. 82-84).

6. **Predetermined overhead rates** are useful for product costing, price determination, and

inventory valuation. The rate is determined at the beginning of the accounting period by dividing total estimated overhead for the period by some logical basis. The most common bases used are (a) estimated direct labor hours, (b) estimated direct labor dollars, (c) estimated machine hours, and (d) estimated units produced. After the rate has been determined, it is multiplied by the actual amount of the basis (hours, dollars, et cetera) for each job or product to obtain the overhead that should be applied.

Objective 4: Dispose of underapplied or overapplied overhead (pp. 84-88).

7. If estimated figures for overhead costs and the allocation basis equal the actual amounts for the period, then total overhead applied to jobs will equal actual overhead incurred during that period. Because estimates and actual amounts will seldom be equal, there will usually be an under- or overapplication of overhead. When actual overhead is more than applied overhead, overhead has been **underapplied.** When the reverse is true, overhead has been **overapplied.** The only way to assure that actual overhead will equal applied overhead is to wait until the end of the year to apply the year's actual overhead to the jobs worked on during the year. However, this is not done because interim cost figures are usually necessary, and a small under- or overapplication of overhead must therefore be tolerated.

8. At the end of the period, an adjustment must be made for the difference between actual and applied overhead.
   a. If the difference is small or if all items worked on during the period have been sold, the entire amount can be added to or subtracted from Cost of Goods Sold. When overhead has been underapplied, Cost of Goods Sold and Factory Overhead Applied are debited and Factory Overhead Control is credited. The entry is the same when overhead has been overapplied, except that Cost of Goods Sold is credited.
   b. Another method is used when the difference is large or when the costs of the items worked on during the period are still in Work in Process and Finished Goods, as well as Cost of Goods Sold,

at the end of the period. In such a case, the difference should be divided among these three accounts proportionately.

Objective 5: Explain the relationship between product costing and inventory valuation (p. 88).

9. Product costing is very important for income statement and balance sheet purposes. Only those manufacturing costs assigned to units sold should be reported in the income statement (as Cost of Goods Sold). The manufacturing costs assigned to goods in ending inventory should appear on the balance sheet, and should be transferred to the income statement only in the period in which the goods are sold.

Objective 6: Describe cost flow in a job order cost accounting system (pp. 88-92).

10. In a job order cost system, there is a specific procedure for recording materials, labor, and factory overhead. Basically, a perpetual inventory system is used. Costs flow through the Work in Process and Finished Goods Inventory accounts to Cost of Goods Sold. The costs are connected with specific jobs by means of **job order cost cards.** One job card is maintained for each job to accumulate its cost. The cost cards for all uncompleted jobs make up the Work in Process subsidiary ledger (detailed records to support the **control** or **controlling account**).

Objective 7: Journalize transactions in a job order cost accounting system (pp. 92-99).

11. The journal entries in a job order cost system reflect the actual flow of costs during production. Note from the following analysis that costs are tranferrred into an account with a debit, and out of an account with a credit.
   a. The purchase of materials is recorded by debiting Materials Inventory Control and crediting Cash or Accounts Payable.
   b. When materials or supplies are issued into production, Work in Process Inventory Control is debited for the direct materials portion, Factory Overhead Control is debited for the indirect materials portion, and Materials Inventory Control is credited.

c. The factory payroll and actual overhead costs are recorded by debiting Factory Payroll and Factory Overhead Control, respectively, and crediting Cash or some other appropriate account.

d. To distribute the payroll to the production accounts, Work in Process Inventory Control is debited for the direct labor portion, Factory Overhead Control is debited for the indirect labor portion, and Factory Payroll is credited for the gross payroll.

e. Factory overhead is applied to specific jobs by debiting Work in Process Inventory Control and crediting Factory Overhead Applied.

f. Upon the completion of a specific job, Finished Goods Inventory Control is debited, and Work in Process Inventory Control is credited.

g. When the finished goods are sold, two entries must be made. First, the sale is recorded by debiting Cash or Accounts Receivable and crediting Sales for the total sales price. Second, Cost of Goods Sold is debited and Finished Goods Inventory Control is credited for the cost attached to the goods sold.

h. At the end of the period, an adjustment must be made for under- or overapplied overhead.

Objective 8: Compute product unit cost for a specific job order (pp. 99-100).

12. The first step in computing unit costs in a job order cost system is to total all manufacturing costs accumulated on a particular job order cost card. Then, this amount is divided by the number of units produced for that job to find the unit cost. Finally, the unit cost is entered on the job order cost card and used for inventory valuation.

Testing Your Knowledge

Matching

Match each term with its definition by writing the appropriate letter in the blank

___ **1.** Absorption costing

___ **2.** Overapplied overhead

___ **3.** Underapplied overhead

___ **4.** Process cost accounting system

___ **5.** Job order accounting cost system

___ **6.** Job order cost cards

___ **7.** Control (controlling) account

___ **8.** Subsidiary ledger

a. The result when actual overhead exceeds applied overhead

b. The accounting method used by a manufacturer of one-of-a-kind or special-order products

c. The product costing method that includes all manufacturing costs

d. Records of the accumulation of job costs

e. The result when applied overhead exceeds actual overhead

f. The accounting method used by a manufacturer of a large number of similar products

g. Individual accounting records that support the corresponding control account

h. A ledger account that represents the accumulation of several related individual account balances

Completion

Use the line provided to complete each item.

1. If estimated overhead costs equal actual overhead costs for the period, could an underapplication of overhead occur? Explain.

_____

_____

2. What are the three components of Work in Process Inventory?

_____

_____

_____

3. What two methods are used to adjust for under- or overapplied overhead?

_____

_____

_____

_____

4. List three products for which a job order cost system should be used.

_____

_____

_____

True-False

Circle T if the statement is true, F if it is false.

T F 1. If the predetermined overhead rate is based on direct labor hours, and actual direct labor hours equal estimated direct labor hours for the period, then overhead will be neither underapplied nor overapplied in all cases.

T F 2. A small underapplication of overhead should be charged to cost of goods sold.

T F 3. A large under- or overapplication of overhead should be divided among Materials, Work in Process, and Finished Goods Inventories.

T F 4. A large toy manufacturer would probably use a process cost system.

T F 5. A job order cost system uses a Work in Process Inventory account for each department.

T F 6. Indirect manufacturing costs bypass Work in Process Inventory and are charged directly to Finished Goods Inventory.

T F 7. If a company determines a job's selling price by taking 120 percent of its computed cost, then the company will not make the desired profit when overhead has been underapplied.

T F 8. The subsidiary ledger for Work in Process Inventory consists of job order cost cards for uncompleted jobs.

T F 9. As soon as work begins on a job, its sale should be recorded.

T F 10. The factory payroll is distributed to production with a debit to Work in Process Inventory (for direct labor), a credit to Factory Overhead Control (for indirect labor), and a credit to Factory Payroll.

T F 11. When overhead costs are applied to specific jobs, Work in Process Inventory is debited and Factory Overhead Applied is credited.

T F 12. When goods are shipped to the customer, Cost of Goods Sold should be debited and Work in Process Inventory credited.

T F 13. A manufacturer of custom-made clothing would probably use a job order cost system.

T F 14. A job order cost system normally uses a periodic inventory system.

T F 15. The cost information needed in computing product unit cost may be found on the job order cost cards.

Multiple Choice

Circle the letter of the best answer.

1. Which of the following represents an overapplication of overhead?
   a. Estimated overhead exceeds actual overhead.
   b. Actual overhead exceeds estimated overhead
   c. Applied overhead exceeds estimated overhead.
   d. Applied overhead exceeds actual overhead.

2. A job order cost system would most likely be used for the manufacturer of which of the following?
   a. Paper clips
   b. Gasoline
   c. Supersonic jets
   d. Electric typewriters

3. When overhead is underapplied, and many of the goods worked on during the period are still in Work in Process and Finished Goods Inventories, then
   a. net income is overstated before the adjustment is made.
   b. Cost of Goods Sold is understated before the adjustment is made.
   c. the entire underapplication should be charged to Cost of Goods Sold.
   d. ending inventory is understated before the adjustment is made.

4. Which of the following does not require a debit to Factory Overhead Control in a job order cost system?

   a. Indirect material

   b. Applied overhead

   c. Depreciation expense

   d. Indirect labor

5. Factory Payroll is recorded as a

   a. debit when paid.

   b. debit when distributed to production.

   c. credit when paid.

   d. none of the above.

6. Absorption costing

   a. includes direct materials, direct labor, and variable factory overhead only.

   b. includes direct materials and direct labor only.

   c. may not be used with a job order cost system.

   d. includes direct materials, direct labor, variable factory overhead, and fixed factory overhead.

Applying Your Knowledge

Exercises

1. Parkinson Manufacturing Company estimates that overhead costs for 19xx will be $720,000. It also estimates that 450,000 direct labor hours will be worked during the year, with all workers receiving $4 per hour.

   a. What is the predetermined overhead rate, assuming that the application basis is direct labor hours? $_____

   b. What is the predetermined overhead rate, assuming that the application base is direct labor dollars? $_____

   c. If a job required 150 direct labor hours, how much overhead cost should be applied to the job, assuming a direct labor hour basis? $_____

2. The King-Size Shoe Company manufactures shoes of unusual lengths and widths on special order. For each of the following sets of facts, prepare the journal entry in the journal provided on the next page. Assume that the company uses a job order cost system.

Dec. 23 Purchased (on credit) materials costing $2,950.

     26 Issued materials costing $850 into production. Of this amount $50 was for indirect materials.

     26 Paid the following bills:

            Utilities $350

            Rent $700

            Telephone $150

     27 The week's gross payroll of $1,500 was distributed to production accounts. Of this amount, 80 percent represents direct labor. (Do not prepare the entries when the payroll is *paid*.)

     27 The week's overhead costs are applied to production based upon direct labor dollars. Estimated overhead for the year is $165,000, and estimated direct labor dollars are $55,000.

     29 Goods costing $3,900 were completed.

     30 Finished goods costing $2,000 were shipped to a customer. The selling price was 70 percent greater than the cost, and payment for the goods is expected next month.

31 Applied overhead for the year was $150,000, and actual overhead was $130,000. The difference is divided among Work in Process Inventory Control, Finished Goods Inventory Control, and Cost of Goods Sold in proportion to their respective ending balances of $30,000, $10,000, and $160,000.

General Journal				
Date		Description	Debit	Credit

The High Tech Challenge to Management Accounting

Technological change and so-called high tech organizations and their products and services are increasingly important factors in the U.S. economy. One might expect that high tech would make an imprint on accounting, much as the rise of the service firm had an impact on accounting. Indeed, a recent publication is titled *Technological Change: Its Impact on Accounting*.[1] Unhappily, that work ignores management accounting. My purpose is to fill that gap: what are the implications of high tech for management accounting?

To appreciate the major impact of high tech, recall the purposes of management accounting. The very first sentence of a leading text identifies three purposes for management accounting: ". . . (1) planning and controlling routine operations; (2) nonroutine decisions . . . ; and (3) inventory valuation and income determination."[2] In short, two of those purposes are significantly restricted in the high tech environment. Much as is the case with service firms, inventories are of minimal importance. And, routine operations also are of much less interest.

The notion of product life cycle is used here to illustrate high tech's impact on management accounting. But first, high tech should be given some definition. A high tech organization is ". . . built for continuous technological change, growth, and fast reaction time. . . ."[3] Similarly, high tech products and services have a basic applied science characterized by complexity and rapid change.

Product Life Cycle

The notion of a predictable life cycle for a product or service is a robust tool in marketing and strategic planning. Traditionally, the pro-

duct life cycle includes four stages: start-up, growth, mature, and decline. Most manufactured goods—and many services—spend most of their lives, often a decade or more, in the last two stages. And, not surprisingly, the mature and decline stages are the domain of many management accounting tools.

High tech products, by contrast, spend comparatively little time in that domain. Such products by definition come from organizations that are designed for continuous change, for growth, and for fast reaction time. High tech products spend most of their lives in the start-up and growth stages and pass through the mature and decline stages comparatively rapidly.

Most management accountants are familiar with the mature and decline stages with their characteristics of stability, long production runs, and cost control emphasis. But few management accountants appear to focus on the start-up and growth stages, the domain of high tech organizations. If fact, a recent NAA-sponsored study of management accountants reports that less than 20% of management accountants feel they influence new product decisions, and 43% say they are not consulted at all about new products.[4]

Table 1 shows the key activities of the start-up and growth stages by organizational function. The breakdown follows logically from the definition of high tech organizations and should provide management accountants with a basic understanding of the stages. Note that Table 1 omits the mature and decline stages on the premise that high tech organizations continuously operate almost exclusively in the start-up and growth stages of the product life cycle.

From the marketing function, probably the biggest impact on management accounting arises from marketing preceding production. That is, there is considerable pressure on the high tech firm to get into the market as early as possible so as to capture a large share of the

Source: Article by Earl K. Littrell. Reprinted from the October 1984 issue of *Management Accounting*.

[1] U. Galil, "The Impact of Technology on Industrial Organization," in E. L. Summers, editor, *Technological Change: Its Impact on Accounting*. The Council of Arthur Young Professors, Reston, Va., 1983.

[2] Charles T. Horngren, *Cost Accounting: A Managerial Emphasis*, 5th ed., Prentice-Hall, Englewood Cliffs, N.J., 1982.

[3] Galil.

[4] G. H. Lander, *et al.*, *Profile of the Management Accountant*, NAA, New York, N.Y., 1983.

TABLE 1
Start-up and Growth Implications for Management Accountants

Key activities	Start-up stage	Growth stage	Implications for management accounting
Marketing:	1. Selling ideas and concepts before the actual product is available. 2. Making initial penetration of markets.	1. Responding adequately to unsaturated demand for products. 2. Assessing future customer needs as a key input to R&D.	1. Product is costed and priced before actual data are known. 2. Controlling inventory comparatively unimportant.
R&D + Production:	1. Designing & refining prototype product. 2. Designing & refining pilot production capacity. 3. Building production capacity.	1. Expanding production capacity. 2. Supplying product on time and in quantity. 3. (R&D) Finding next product for start-up stage.	1. Data to build standard costing system not available. 2. Relevant range in Cost-Volume-Profit analysis keeps moving. 3. Application of fixed overhead is complicated by capacity changes. 4. Inventory control and costing is comparatively unimportant.
Financial:	1. Obtaining initial financing.	1. Obtaining additional financing. 2. Designing and implementing financial management system. 3. Generating positive operating cash flow from growth stage product.	1. Cash budgeting and capital budgeting are most important. 2. Growth stage management is crucial.
General management:	1. Grasping the technology and business opportunity at hand. 2. Building management team.	1. Adding structure to informal organization. 2. Continuing importance of adaptive management style. 3. Coping with steep part of learning curve.	1. Integrative management techniques (efficiency cost control, etc.) are perceived to be relatively less important. 2. Management accountants should emphasize adaptive talents. 3. Standards need to be flexible to reflect learning curve effects.
Management accounting:	1. Cash Budgeting. 2. Projecting costs and revenues. 3. Preparing pro forma statements to support financing requests. 4. Capital budgeting.	1. Cash Budgeting. 2. Projecting costs and revenues. 3. Preparing pro forma statements to support financing requests. 4. Capital budgeting. 5. Recording actual revenues and costs. 6. Designing and implementing systems and procedures.	Note what is missing or of reduced importance: 1. Control of routine operations. 2. Inventory valuation. 3. Standard costing. 4. Cost variance analysis.

market. Selling the product before it exists provides a considerable time advantage over the more customary design-produce-sell sequence. This strategy tends to force the establishment of a price for the product before any actual data are obtained on the costs associated with that product. Thus, the crucial pricing decision must be made on the basis of cost estimates and projections, not on actual cost experience. The comparative importance of cost estimation and projection—and the difficulty of that task—are further enhanced by that nature of high tech products: they tend to be in new areas where one cannot look to similar products for cost data.

Another effect of the sell-produce sequence on management accounting is that inventory levels, at least for successful products, are quite low. A direct result is that inventory control and inventory costing become relatively less important tasks for the management accountant. To grasp the significance of this change, recall the introductory quote that claims that inventory valuation is one of the three major purposes of management accounting.

R&D Merges with Production

Moving on to the next organizational function, note that continual operations in the start-up and growth stages force a merging of the research and development function with the production function. High tech firms just don't have the long production runs and long lead times for product development that permit the separation of production and R&D in firms with more traditional product life cycles. A direct result of this characteristic on management accounting is that it becomes difficult or impossible to put together the body of data necessary for setting standards. And without standards, standard costing with all of its control and performance evaluation features is precluded.

In the production area, the growth stage has two notable effects on management accounting. One effect is that the familiar notion of the relevant range of activity, one of the keys to effective cost-volume-profit analysis, keeps changing. That means that the common assumptions about linear cost (and revenue) behavior become less tenable and require more frequent review. It also means that the line between variable costs and fixed costs, another of the keys to effective cost-volume-profit analysis,

becomes blurred. Or, to put it differently, fixed costs tend to fade into semi-fixed or even variable status.

A second effect of rapidly growing production capacity is on the application of fixed overhead. Most fixed overhead application schemes rely on reasonably stable measures of production capacity, often the so-called "normal capacity." But when capacity is changing rapidly, it is likely to be tough to construct workable application rates for fixed overhead.

In the financial management function, the chronic needs for ever more financing have the most predictable effects on management accounting. Cash budgeting and capital budgeting techniques assume even more importance. In fact, one could argue that high tech firms do tend to resemble the old saw about a firm being nothing more than a collection of capital budgeting decisions taped together.

But there is another important issue in the financial management area, one that is much less obvious. The customary experience is that growth stage products, with their needs for increased levels of working capital and plant assets, soak up cash. In contrast, products in the mature and decline stages are expected to be net generators of cash. In fact, the notion of mature products feeding cash to growth products is a fundamental part of product portfolio theory. High tech products spend little time in the mature stage, or don't go through it at all. If so, where does the internally generated cash come from?

Growth stage products are the only viable candidate high tech firms have for the role of internal cash generator. To fill that role, growth stage products must bring in early cash—deposits, prepayments, and so forth—and this fits nicely with the sell-produce sequence discussed earlier. The products also must command prices robust enough to cover the inefficiencies and scale problems of growth style production as well as to provide large margins. The impact of these factors on management accounting is clear: the growth stage is the high tech firm's main game, and it must be taken seriously. There just isn't the opportunity to lay back, planning to sort things out during the mature stage.

In the general management function, there is a very important implication for management accountants. It stems from the distinction between adaptive and integrative management activities. Briefly, adaptive management activities help the firm cope with its environment and change in significant ways. Marketing, R&D, and strategic planning are examples of adaptive activities, and they are frequently perceived as the strengths of the firm most pertinent to the start-up and growth stages. By contrast, integrative activities help a firm to become more efficient, more systematic, more organized. Production and accounting are frequently perceived as mainly integrative activities. The perception continues that these activities really become important in the mature stage of the product life cycle. But, if there isn't a mature stage, it becomes critical for management accountants to counter these perceptions, or misperceptions. Management accountants need recognition for the genuine adaptive contributions they can make in the start-up and growth stages.

A final observation from the general management area: the firm continually operates on the steeper portions of the learning curve. Recall that it takes the mature stage with its long production runs and relative stability in order to obtain the cumulative production experience necessary to get out to the flatter portions of the learning curve. (The "steeper" and "flatter" terms here assume the curve is plotted on standard graph paper, not the customary log-log paper.)

Traditionally, management accountants prefer to assume that they are operating in the flat portions of the learning curve. But continually coping with the steep portions of the curve has pervasive implications, especially for budgeting and standard-setting. Assuming, for example, that the data problems mentioned earlier are overcome, the standard-setting process must still cope with significant production experience effects, probably through flexible standards.

In sum, then, two of the three major purposes of management accounting are comparatively unimportant in the high tech setting. Control of routine operations and inventory evaluation, in spite of their historic importance as the functions of cost accounting, are simply swamped by the importance of the nonroutine functions in the high tech setting.

Comparison with Service Firms

Can management accounting adapt to the high tech environment? There are good reasons to be optimistic about management accounting making that transition. One reason, of course, is that some major management accounting tools, notably cash budgeting and capital budgeting, are already well adapted to the high tech setting. Another reason for optimism comes from considering how well management accounting, with its roots in manufacturing, has adapted to service firms.

Compared with manufacturing firms, service firms exhibit these major differences:

• Little or no inventory,
• Difficulties in measuring output quantities and quality, and
• Labor intensive nature.

Still, management accounting has been able to cope with these differences and adapt well. The focus on key variables pertinent to services—such as the billed time ratio for professionals — and the use of project-function matrix evaluation schemes are just two examples of successful adaptation to the service environment. And, given that the service sector of the U.S. economy has been larger than the manufacturing sector for a considerable time, successful adaptation to the service setting was vital for management accounting. Successful adaptation to the high tech setting is likely to prove just as vital to management accounting.

CHAPTER 4 PRODUCT COSTING: THE PROCESS COST SYSTEM

REVIEWING THE CHAPTER

Objective 1: Explain the role of the Work in Process Inventory account(s) in a process cost accounting system (pp. 122-123).

1. A process cost system is used mainly by companies that produce large quantities of identical products and have a continuous product flow. The objectives of such a system are to determine (a) product unit costs and (b) ending balances for Work in Process and Finished Goods Inventories. Whereas job order costing is concerned with the cost of a particular batch or job, process costing deals with production cost over a certain period of time.

2. The process costing analysis revolves around (a) the schedule of equivalent production, (b) the unit cost analysis schedule, and (c) the cost summary schedule.

Objective 2: Describe product flow and cost flow through a process cost accounting system (pp. 123-124).

3. Before a product is completed, it usually must go through several departments. For example, a bookcase might go through cutting, assembling, and staining departments. In a process cost system, a separate Work in Process Inventory account is maintained for each department. Each Work in Process Inventory account contains costs of materials (if any), direct labor, and manufac-turing overhead for that department plus any costs that have been transferred in from the previous department.

Objective 3: Compute equivalent production for situations with and without units in the beginning Work in Process Inventory (pp. 124-130).

4. **Equivalent units** (also called **equivalent production**) produced equals the sum of (a) the number of units started and completed during the period, and (b) an amount for partly completed units. Because production flows in a first-in, first-out manner in operations utilizing a process cost system, a **FIFO product and cost flow** is frequently assumed for product costing. An alternative method, called the average costing approach, is slightly less accurate than the FIFO approach but is easier to apply. Under average costing, it is assumed that all items in beginning work-in-process were started and completed during the current period. Equivalent unit figures for both materials and **conversion costs** (direct labor plus factory overhead) must be computed in the **schedule of equivalent production**.

Objective 4: Compute product unit cost for a specific time period (unit cost analysis schedule) (pp. 130-131).

5. The unit cost for materials, direct labor, and factory overhead make up the product unit cost for a department.
   a. The unit cost for materials is found by dividing total material costs by the equivalent units for materials.
   b. The unit cost for direct labor and overhead equals direct labor and overhead costs (also called conversion costs) divided by equivalent units for direct labor and factory overhead.

6. The purposes of a **unit cost analysis schedule** are to (a) add all costs charged to the Work in Process Inventory account of each department and (b) compute the cost per equivalent unit for both materials and conversion costs. The schedule is divided into a total cost analysis part and a computation of equivalent unit costs part.
   a. The total cost analysis consists of beginning inventory costs plus current period costs for both materials and conversion costs. The result is total costs to be accounted for.
   b. Equivalent unit costs equal the current period's materials and conversion costs divided by equivalent units for materials and conversion costs from the schedule of equivalent production.

Objective 5: Prepare a cost summary schedule that assigns costs to units completed and transferred out of the department during the period, and find the ending Work in Process Inventory balance (pp. 131-134).

7. The **cost summary schedule** distributes total costs accumulated during the period to units in ending Work in Process Inventory and to units completed and transferred out of the department. Data for the cost summary schedule are taken from the schedule of equivalent production and the unit cost analysis schedule. When figures for ending Work in Process Inventory and cost of goods transferred out of the department are determined, they are totaled and compared with total costs to be accounted for in the unit cost analysis schedule. If the figures do not agree, then there has been an error in arithmetic.
   a. Ending Work in Process Inventory is arrived at as follows: (1) Multiply equivalent units for materials in ending Work in Process Inventory by the unit cost as computed in the unit cost analysis schedule. (2) Multiply equivalent units for conversion costs in ending Work in Process Inventory by the unit cost as computed in the unit cost analysis schedule. (3) Add the two amounts together.
   b. The cost of goods transferred out of the department is arrived at as follows: (1) Multiply units started and completed by the total unit cost as computed in the unit cost analysis schedule. (2) Determine the cost connected to units in beginning inventory (same as ending inventory of preceding period). (3) Figure the costs necessary to complete the units in beginning inventory by using unit cost and equivalent unit figures. (4) Add the amounts together.

Objective 6: Make the journal entry(ies) needed to transfer costs of completed units out of the Work in Process Inventory account (pp. 134-136).

8. Once the figure for cost of goods transferred out of the department has been found, it can be journalized to record the transfer of goods to the next department. Then Work in Process Inventory (next department) is debited and Work in Process Inventory (this department) is credited. When goods are completed, the debit is transferred to Finished Goods Inventory.

9. Product cost information is important not just for inventory pricing. It also helps companies set selling prices. Cost-based pricing is only a starting point, however. Other factors are usually considered before the selling price is finally established.

Matching

Match each term with its definition by writing the appropriate letter in the blank.

____ 1. Process cost system

____ 2. Schedule of equivalent production

____ 3. Unit cost analysis schedule

____ 4. Cost summary schedule

____ 5. Equivalent units (equivalent production)

____ 6. Conversion costs

a. The schedule used to distribute costs during the period to ending Work in Process Inventory and transferred units
b. Direct labor plus overhead
c. The schedule in which equivalent unit production is computed
d. The accounting method used when large quantities of identical products are being produced
e. Whole units produced, taking into consideration partially completed units
f. The schedule that computes a cost-per-unit figure

Completion

Use the lines provided to complete each item.

1. What three schedules are prepared in a process cost system? List them in their order of preparation.

_____

_____

_____

2. Show the computation for equivalent units, under the average costing approach.

_____

\+ _____

\+ _____

= _____

3. What two items are computed in the cost summary schedule?

_____

_____

4. Show the computation for cost of goods transferred out of the department.

_____

\+ _____

\+ _____

= _____

True-False

Circle T if the statement is true, F if it is false. For all questions, assume a process cost system.

T F 1. Because process costing is used where large quantities of identical items are being produced, only one Work in Process Inventory account is ever needed.

T F 2. Factory overhead must be applied to production for the period.

T F 3. The finished units of one department become in effect the materials input of the next department.

T F 4. Product unit cost is made up of cost elements used in all departments.

Product Costing: The Process Cost System

T F 5. Equivalent units produced equal the number of units that were started and completed during the period.

T F 6. Conversion costs equal direct labor plus factory overhead.

T F 7. A separate unit cost figure is normally computed for direct labor and for factory overhead in the unit cost analysis schedule.

T F 8. In computing equivalent production under the average costing approach, beginning inventory is multiplied by the percentage completed as of the beginning of the period.

T F 9. In the schedule of equivalent production, units to be accounted for must equal equivalent units for materials plus equivalent units for conversion costs.

T F 10. The unit cost analysis schedule must be prepared before the cost summary schedule.

T F 11. Ending Work in Process Inventory is determined by multiplying total units by total cost per unit.

T F 12. When goods are completed in Department 1 and transferred to Department 2, Finished Goods Inventory is debited and Work in Process (Department 1) is credited.

T F 13. Units completed minus units in beginning inventory equals units started and completed (assuming that all units in beginning inventory have been completed).

T F 14. The computational check for total costs to be accounted for is made in the unit cost analysis schedule.

T F 15. In most manufacturing operations that use a process cost system, production flows in a LIFO manner.

Multiple Choice

Circle the letter of the best answer.

1. A certain department started and completed 10,000 units during the period. Beginning inventory of 5,000 units was 60 percent complete for conversion costs, and ending inventory of 7,000 units was 30 percent complete for conversion costs. What is equivalent production for conversion costs for the period, under the average costing approach?
   a. 4,000 units
   b. 14,100 units
   c. 15,000 units
   d. 17,100 units

2. Which of the following is not a schedule prepared under a process cost system?
   a. Cost summary schedule
   b. Schedule of equivalent production
   c. Schedule of conversion costs
   d. Unit cost analysis schedule

3. Which of the following is not a component of cost of goods transferred out of the department in the cost summary schedule?
   a. Costs necessary to complete units in beginning inventory
   b. Costs attached to units in beginning inventory
   c. Costs of units started and completed
   d. Costs necessary to complete units in ending inventory

4. On which of the following schedules will no unit costs appear?
   a. Schedule of equivalent production
   b. Unit cost analysis schedule
   c. Cost summary schedule
   d. None of the above

5. A certain department began the period with 5,000 units that were 80 percent complete, started and completed 12,000 units, and ended with 2,000 units that were 30 percent complete. Under the average costing approach, equivalent units produced would equal
   a. 13,600.
   b. 14,400.
   c. 17,600.
   d. 19,000.

6. Conversion costs represent the sum of
   a. materials and direct labor.
   b. direct labor and factory overhead.
   c. factory overhead and materials.
   d. materials, direct labor, and factory overhead.

7. The cost of ending Work in Process Inventory is computed in the
   a. schedule of equivalent production.
   b. cost summary schedule.
   c. unit cost analysis schedule.
   d. income statement.

8. The cost of goods transferred to Finished Goods Inventory is computed in the
   a. schedule of equivalent production.
   b. cost summary schedule.
   c. unit cost analysis schedule.
   d. balance sheet.

Applying Your Knowledge

Exercise

1. Data for Department 1 of the Morris Manufacturing Company for the month of May
are as follows:

Beginning Work in Process Inventory
Units = 2,000
Materials = 100% complete
Conversion costs = 30% complete
Materials costs = $12,000
Conversion costs = $3,000

Ending Work in Process Inventory
Materials = 100% complete
Conversion costs = 30% complete

Operations for the month of May
Units started = 24,000
Materials costs = $114,000
Conversion costs = $30,750
Units completed and transferred to the next de-
partment = 19,000

Assuming an average costing approach, complete the three schedules that follow. Round off
unit cost computations to three decimal places.

		Morris Manufacturing Company Schedule of Equivalent Production For the Month Ended May 31, 19xx		

| Units—Stage of Completion | Units to Be Accounted For | Equivalent Units | |
		Materials	Conversion Costs

Morris Manufacturing Company
Unit Cost Analysis Schedule
For the Month Ended May 31, 19xx

	Total Costs			÷	Equivalent Unit Costs	
	Costs from Beginning Inventory	Costs from Current Period	Total Costs to Be Accounted For		Equivalent Units	= Cost per Equivalent Unit
Materials						
Conversion Costs						
	————	————	————			————
Totals	========	========	========			========

Morris Manufacturing Company Cost Summary Schedule For the Month Ended May 31, 19xx		
	Cost of Goods Transferred To Next Department	Cost of Ending Work in Process Inventory
Beginning Inventory		
Units Started and Completed		
Ending Inventory		
Computational Check		

Crossword Puzzle
for Chapters 3 and 4

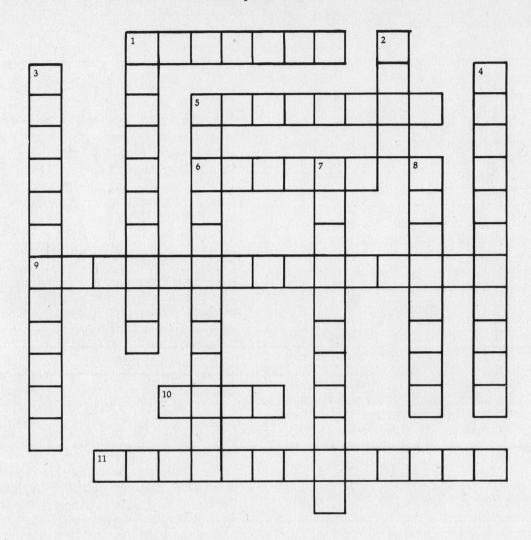

ACROSS

1. Account supported by subsidiary records
5. Outlay per manufactured item (2 words)
6. Cost that can be traced to a specific job or product
9. Productive output of 4-Down (2 words)
10. Product and cost flow assumption
11. ——— overhead rate

DOWN

1. Direct labor and factory overhead costs
2. See 8-Down
3. Accounting system for batches of products (3 words)
4. Accounting system for homogeneous units (2 words)
5. Misallocated overhead
7. Schedule used in 4-Down (2 words)
8. With 2-Down, denominator in computing 11-Across

Cost Accounting in the Age of Robotics

Generations of management accountants have been brought up to: compute product costs as the sum of direct labor, burden and material, and compute burden as a percentage of labor; assume that direct costs vary with production; allocate indirect costs based on direct labor; and record historical cost depreciation and exclude interest from the cost of production.

While these tenets have served manufacturing companies well for years, their utility wanes in an age where machines replace labor, burden rates skyrocket, direct labor costs become fixed, control shifts from line supervisors to manufacturing technologists, and historical costs no longer reflect current values. The old arithmetic falls apart. Costs no longer reflect reality, and uneconomic decisions are made as a result of misleading information.

Traditional cost accounting, therefore, must change to accommodate the age of robotics, where automated factories replace labor-intensive production lines. To adapt their cost accounting systems to the age of robotics, management accountants should consider:

- Replacing the concept of labor and burden with conversion;
- Re-examining the notion of direct costs;
- Restructuring the bases for allocating indirect costs;
- Focusing their control systems on investment and inventory management decisions rather than on cost center operating costs; and
- Establishing an equipment cost center that "rents" machinery and equipment to productive departments.

Let us look at how manufacturing companies may apply these techniques to gain more reliable product cost information so they can manage the factory of the future more effectively.

Source: Article by Allen H. Seed, III. Reprinted from the October 1984 issue of *Management Accounting*.

The Concept of Conversion

The traditional arithmetic for determining product cost is straightforward: Direct labor costs are determined by multiplying man-hours by a labor rate per hour. A burden rate is determined by dividing all elements of overhead for a cost center by direct labor. This rate is multiplied by direct labor to calculate burden. Labor, burden, and material are added together to calculate total manufacturing cost.

The traditional approach works well in a labor-paced manufacturing environment where machines function as tools to assist production workers. It often provides unsatisfactory results in an automated environment, however, where the work is machine-paced.

An automated factory feeds work into the cost center, processes it with one or more machines, and removes it from the cost center without human intervention. One person may tend a system of a dozen or so machines, and this person tends to spend more time dealing with trouble than operating the machines.

In such circumstances, burden rates based on direct labor may approach infinity, and production costs bear little relation to the amount of work the machine operator does.

With the exception of new plants, factories usually do not become totally automated in one stroke. Machine-paced equipment and robotics gradually replace old, man-paced machinery. Plant modernization programs often take several years. Thus a firm's cost accounting system should accommodate both man and machine-paced environments at any one time and provide meaningful comparative cost data between automated and nonautomated production processes.

Management accountants can solve this problem by replacing the concept of "labor and burden" with the concept of "conversion." The steel, paper, chemical, and food processing industries have used this technique for some time, but many manufacturing companies still struggle to develop burden rates and compile direct labor and burden costs.

The distinction between direct labor and burden often is blurred. Some companies, for example, classify overtime premium pay, payroll taxes and benefits, set-up, and waiting time as direct labor, while others treat some, or all, of these elements as burden.

Conversion costs need not distinguish between direct labor and burden. They may consist of: Direct and indirect labor, labor fringe benefits, energy, operating supplies, repairs and maintenance, supervision and support services, machinery and equipment costs, and building occupancy.

Conversion costs may be man-paced or machine-paced. If costs are man-paced, the most appropriate unit of production is usually the standard direct labor hour. If costs are machine-paced, the most appropriate unit of production is either: a unit of measure such as tons, pounds, or gallons for homogenous products or engineered machine center hours for products of different sizes, shapes, and complexity. Depending on the circumstances, conversion costs may be expressed as a cost per ton, pound, gallon, or engineered machine hour.

An engineered machine center hour measures the total, normal, productive capacity of a machine center in one hour of operation. While this measurement may be developed primarily for scheduling purposes, the accountant also can use it for cost finding. To illustrate: If a machine center can produce five castings of a given type per hour, each casting would use 0.2 engineered machine center hours. However, if two large castings consumed 60% of the machine center's capacity and three small castings consumed 40%, the large castings each would use 0.3 engineered machine center hours and the small castings each would use 0.133 hours.

The New Meaning of Direct Cost

While the concepts of variable and fixed costs still have relevance in an age of robotics, the concepts of direct and indirect costs take on new meanings. In a man-paced environment direct costs typically consist of direct labor, fringes, direct supervision, material handling, quality control, operating supplies, energy and, sometimes, repairs and maintenance. Because these costs generally vary with the volume of production, direct costs also are referred to as variable costs. Indirect costs consist of plan services and administration, building occupancy, rent, insurance, taxes and depreciation. Because

these costs do not vary with production in the short term, such indirect costs also are referred to as fixed or period costs.

The neat parallels between "direct" and "variable," and "indirect" and "fixed," however, unravel in a machine-paced environment. As illustrated in Figure 1, "machine" costs become "direct" costs, but these machine costs are largely fixed in nature. Direct machine costs, for example, may consist of rent, insurance, taxes, depreciation, and repairs and maintenance, in addition to operator labor, fringes, and energy.

Definitions of which elements constitute direct and indirect costs vary and are the subject of debate. I suggest that direct costs be defined as costs that can be assigned directly to a cost center or product irrespective of their behavioral characteristics. Indirect costs are those costs which must be allocated to cost centers or products.[1]

Applying this definition, the depreciation and maintenance of machine center equipment is a direct production cost, but the depreciation and maintenance of tool room equipment is an indirect cost. The wages and fringes of the personnel who operate the machine center are a direct cost while the wages and fringes of the personnel in the production scheduling or industrial engineering department are indirect. Quality control may be a direct or indirect cost depending on whether or not the activity can be directly associated with a machine center or product.

Many firms recognize two kinds of indirect costs: Service costs and administrative costs. Service costs typically include such cost centers as maintenance, data processing, and material handling, which can be charged directly to production cost centers based on services rendered.[2] Under these circumstances, such service costs may be considered direct costs and only unassigned service costs remain in the indirect category.

The difference between service and administrative costs is also unclear. Some argue that all indirect manufacturing operations are service centers. Moreover, if maintenance and repair is

---

[1] The National Association of Accountants' Management Accounting Statement Number 2, "Management Accounting Terminology," defines indirect costs more fully as "costs common to a multiple set of cost objectives and not directly assignable to such objectives in a specific time period. Such costs are usually allocated by systematic and consistent techniques to products, processes, or time periods."
[2] Statement Number 2 defines service departments as "those departments that exist solely to aid the production departments by rendering specialized assistance with certain phases of the work."

FIGURE 1
Conversion Costs: Man-paced and Machine-paced Environments

| | Conversion Costs | | | | | |
| | Man-paced environment | | | Machine-paced environment | | |
	Direct	Indirect	Total	Direct	Indirect	Total
Variable costs—both environments						
Energy	$ 300		$ 300	$ 800		$ 800
Operating supplies	600		600	500		500
Overtime premium	200		200	100		100
	$1,100		$ 1,100	$1,400		$ 1,400
Variable costs—man-paced environment						
Fixed costs—machine-paced environment						
Direct labor operations	$5,000		$ 5,000	$ 500		$ 500
Labor fringe benefits	1,900		1,900	400		400
Setup labor	500		500	1,000		1,000
Material handling labor	400		400	--		--
Quality control labor	500		500	500		500
Repairs and maintenence	300		300	1,000		1,000
	$8,600		$ 8,600	$3,400		$ 3,400
Fixed costs—both environments						
Supervision		$ 800	$ 800	$	$ 400	$ 400
Production support services		1,800	1,800		1,800	1,800
Building occupancy		700	700		500	500
Insurance		100	100	300		100
Property taxes		300	300	1,000		1,000
Depreciation—machinery and equipment		600	600	3,000		3,000
		$4,300	$ 4,300	$4,300	$2,700	$ 6,800
Total cost of operation	$9,700	$4,300	$14,000	$9,100	$2,700	$11,600
Standard man-hours			1,000 hours			
Cost per standard man-hour			$ 14.00			
Engineered machine center hours						100 hours
Cost per engineered machine center hour						$116.00

a service why not classify building occupancy costs the same way? Building occupancy costs, for example, can be assigned directly to cost centers on a square footage basis.

I suggest that these definitions are largely irrelevant. Ultimately, all manufacturing costs should be assigned to products and it makes no difference whether they are called "direct," "indirect," "service," or "administrative" costs. Such terms refer to how the cost was determined rather than the behavioral characteristics of the cost element. While product cost data should be aggregated to identify variable and fixed costs, the distinction between direct and indirect, and service and administration is not useful for product cost and profitability analysis.

Modern, computer-based manufacturing resource planning (MRP II) systems easily accommodate the compilation of variable and fixed conversion costs. Several systems can maintain two or more standards, update costs on line and reflect the impact of engineering and machinery and equipment changes. These systems can help a management accountant to apply appropriate cost-finding techniques to a manufacturing environment where machines are gradually replacing men.

Cost Control and Behavior

Direct costs are sometimes referred to as the resources that are assigned to a machine center over which the manager of the center has "control." The term "control," however, should be used in its most limited sense in a machine-paced environment. Machine center managers seldom determine the investment in their machine center and are responsible largely for controlling output rather than cost. Moreover, even output is determined by schedulers, and most breakdowns and work stoppages lie beyond the control of the machine center manager. Thus, control—and the focus of control reporting—shifts from the plan floor to the engineering, planning, scheduling, and maintenance functions. Investment and inventory management decisions become the focal point of the control system; labor and operating expense control become relatively less important. In a machine-paced environment manufacturing technologists, rather than line supervisors, are the real "controllers" of manufacturing costs.

Automation increases fixed costs and investment, and reduces variable costs. It also increases overall profit margins, improves the return on investment, and moves breakeven points upward. This shift in the product cost structure provides an incentive to operate at close to full capacity. The experience of the paper, steel, chemical, and airline industries suggests that firms will continue to respond to these incentives in order to maximize the return on investment.

Indirect Cost Allocations

Factory automation complicates cost allocations. In a man-paced environment, indirect costs are largely incurred to support the work force, while in a machine-paced environment such costs tend to be unit-of-production oriented. In the former case, indirect costs are assigned to cost centers based on direct labor. A machine-paced environment, however, requires more sophisticated methods. Five methodologies for assigning indirect costs to cost centers and products include:

1. *Unit of production.* This method can serve as a basis of indirect cost allocation for factories producing homogeneous units. Paper mills, for example, commonly assign general mill production costs to end products on a per-ton basis.
2. *Investment.* Industrial engineering and other plant administrative costs may be assigned to cost centers on an investment basis on the premise that such costs are a function of the investment managed. Investment management firms, for instance, base their fees on the size of the investment under management.
3. *Standard direct conversion cost.* This method reflects the value added by production. As previously discussed, the concept of conversion costs applies to both man- and machine-paced environments. Accordingly, many companies consider this method the most reasonable basis for allocating indirect costs.
4. *Standard material cost.* Materials manage-

ment costs, such as purchasing, receiving, incoming inspection, inventory control, and material handling are viewed as a function of material cost, particularly in firms where materials compose a major component of costs. In such cases, indirect materials management costs often are assigned to products as a percentage of standard materials.
5. *Total standard direct costs.* Because total standard direct costs reflect all the costs directly assignable to products, residual indirect costs may be appropriately assigned to products on this basis. This approach is useful especially where components are purchased from others and the distinction between conversion and material has little meaning.

An Approach to Equipment Rental

As in an automated factory, equipment forms an important element of cost in the construction industry. Construction firms invest millions of dollars in cranes, graders, trucks, and other tools. Some construction managers believe that each job should provide both a "construction profit" and an "equipment profit." The construction profit is a function of labor, and the equipment profit is a function of the equipment used. A few firms have established equipment subsidiaries and rent the equipment from the subsidiary for the job. This practice enforces the discipline of obtaining an equipment profit as well as a construction profit from each job.

Why not apply the equipment rental concept used in the construction industry to automated manufacturing companies? To implement this approach, a firm would set up a cost center for equipment the same way many do for building occupancy. The equipment cost center would "rent" machinery and equipment to production cost centers. The center would base the rental charge on the current rental value of the equipment, including repairs and maintenance, thus ensuring that the firm obtains an equipment profit as well as a manufacturing profit.

The equipment rental charge could be a flat monthly amount or it could be based on units of production. Because the rental charge would include a profit, the difference between the rental charge and historical cost may be included in product costs for evaluation, but it should be excluded from product costs for inventory valuation purposes.

The equipment rental approach offers several

advantages. It focuses product profitability analysis on costs that reflect current values and includes an appropriate return on capital employed. The equipment rental approach also may help overcome educational hurdles. Unlike the concepts of residual income, charging for the cost of capital, and current cost (value) depreciation, the idea of renting equipment is easy to explain and easy for nonfinancial production and marketing managers to understand. Managers understand what "renting" means because they encounter it in their day-to-day lives. In essence, however, the arithmetic of renting equipment from an equipment cost center amounts to the same thing as applying the more sophisticated concepts of current value and residual income.

Facing the Realities

Automation in the age of robotics calls for new approaches to cost accounting, new definitions of terms, and new allocation techniques. The concept of conversion cost should replace the concepts of direct labor and burden. Direct cost does not mean the same thing as variable cost and is seldom useful for cost analysis. The focus of cost control in an automated factory shifts from the factory floor to manufacturing technologies. Other bases, such as units of production, investment, direct conversion costs, material costs, and total direct costs, should be considered for allocating indirect costs to cost centers and products in a machine-paced environment. Finally, the notion of "renting equipment" can serve as a painless way to introduce the concepts of current value and residual income in an age of inflation and robotics.

CHAPTER 5 COST BEHAVIOR AND ALLOCATION

REVIEWING THE CHAPTER

Objective 1: Explain the concept of cost behavior as it relates to total costs and costs per unit (pp. 156-157).

1. For an organization to be successful, it must institute an effective system to plan and control costs. This kind of integrated cost planning and control system is called **budgetary control.** Several management accounting techniques, based on the concepts of cost behavior and cost allocation, help achieve effective cost planning and control.

2. **Cost behavior** refers to how costs change in relation to volume (units of output). Understanding cost behavior is useful in analyzing past cost performance and estimating future costs. Normally, a cost can be classified as either variable or fixed. There are certain costs, however, that exhibit characteristics of both variable and fixed costs.
   a. **Variable costs** are costs that vary (in total) in direct proportion to volume. On a per-unit basis, however, variable costs remain constant as volume changes.
   b. **Fixed costs** are costs that remain the same as volume changes. On a per-unit basis, however, fixed costs vary as volume changes.

Objective 2: Identify specific types of variable costs and compute changes in variable costs caused by changes in operating activity (pp. 157-160).

3. In dealing with variable costs, we assume that a linear relationship exists between cost and volume, even though such a relationship actually might not exist. Examples of variable costs are direct materials, direct labor, operating supplies, sales commissions, and the cost of merchandise. Although productive output is the most common measure of volume, a cost can vary with other activity bases, such as miles driven or hours worked. The activity base chosen should be the one that relates most closely to the cost under consideration.

4. Operating capacity is the maximum a company can produce with existing facilities. In discussing cost behavior, we assume that volume will not exceed operating capacity.

5. Many costs vary with operating activity in a nonlinear fashion. Examples of nonlinear variable costs are the costs of computer usage and power consumption. Here, cost behavior can be approximated within the relevant range using a linear approximation technique. The **relevant range** is the vol-

ume range within which actual operations are likely to occur.

Objective 3: Identify specific types of fixed costs and describe the impact of changes in the level of operating activity on fixed costs (pp. 161-163).

6. Within the relevant range of activity, and within a limited time period, fixed costs remain constant. Examples of fixed costs are depreciation, insurance, rent, and supervisory salaries. Fixed costs are classified as either committed or discretionary.
   a. **Committed fixed costs** (property taxes, insurance, rent) are costs that must continue for the company to maintain its existing level of operations.
   b. **Discretionary fixed costs** (research and development, advertising, employee training) are costs that are much more subject to change by management than are committed fixed costs.

7. **Step-variable costs** are costs that increase in steps within a wide range of volumes. For example, one maintenance worker might be needed for up to 10,000 units produced, while a second worker must be hired until 20,000 units are produced, and so on.

Objective 4: Differentiate between a semivariable cost and a mixed cost, and apply methods used to separate their variable and fixed cost components (pp. 163-169).

8. A **semivariable cost** acts like both a variable cost and a fixed cost. Telephone expense, for example, includes a fixed monthly service charge plus variable charges for long-distance calls. Other utility costs typically behave in a semivariable manner.

9. **Mixed costs** are a combination of fixed and variable costs charged to the same general ledger account. For example, mixed costs would be found in an account like Repairs and Maintenance.

10. It is important to be able to break semivariable or mixed costs down into their fixed and variable components. The cost separation techniques commonly applied are the scatter diagram technique, the high-low method, and the least squares method.

   a. A **scatter diagram** is a graph containing plotted points that represent the relationship between the cost item and the related activity measure. If a somewhat linear relationship appears to exist, a cost line can be drawn through the points to approximately represent their relationship.
   b. The **high-low method** is a mathematical technique used to fit a line through plotted points. That is, a line is drawn mathematically between the high and low points of those observed, with the assumption that the line does an adequate job of representing the plotted points.
   c. The **least squares method** is a statistical technique to fit the best line through plotted points. This technique employs simple linear regression analysis and relies on the use of two formulas. The objective is to obtain an equation in the form of $y = a + bx$, where y represents total cost, a represents fixed cost, and bx represents variable cost per unit times the volume.

Objective 5: Define cost allocation and describe the role of cost objectives in the cost allocation process (pp. 169-171).

11. Many manufacturing costs apply to more than one segment of a company. A system of **cost allocation** or assignment must be used to assign the costs to the segments in a logical manner.
   a. A **cost center** is any segment of a business for which costs are accumulated.
   b. A **cost objective** is anything (such as a department or a product) that receives an assigned cost.

12. Direct costs are costs that can be conveniently and economically traced to a specific product or cost objective. Direct materials and direct labor are direct costs. Indirect costs, such as factory depreciation and maintenance, cannot be traced easily.

Objective 6: Identify specific uses of cost allocation in corporate accounting and reporting practices (pp. 171-173).

13. Accounting reports are prepared for all levels of management, from the president

down to the department manager or supervisor. In addition, reports must be prepared for all cost centers, including the company as a whole, each division, and all departments within each division. Often it is difficult to trace costs to specific cost objectives, especially when the cost objective decreases in size (is further refined). Here, it becomes necessary to allocate indirect costs using an allocation base, such as direct labor hours or square footage.

Objective 7: Assign costs of supporting service functions to operating departments (pp. 173-174).

14. A **supporting service function** assists the production departments. Its costs must be allocated to the production departments in a logical manner. Examples of supporting service departments are repair and maintenance, production scheduling, and inspection. Examples of allocation bases are labor hours, kilowatt hours, and number of service requests.

Objective 8: Allocate common costs to joint products (pp. 176-179).

15. Joint products (such as petroleum or beef) are produced from common input or raw material. They cannot be identified as separate items throughout much of the production process. It is not until the **split-off point** that separate products emerge. A **joint cost** is a cost that relates to a joint product. Joint costs are allocated to the specific products by either the **physical volume method** or the **relative sales value method**.

Matching

Match each term with its definition by writing the appropriate letter in the blank.

_____ 1. Cost behavior

_____ 2. Variable cost

_____ 3. Fixed cost

_____ 4. Relevant range

_____ 5. Semivariable cost

_____ 6. Cost center

_____ 7. Cost objective

_____ 8. Split-off point

_____ 9. Joint cost

_____ 10. Cost allocation

_____ 11. Budgetary control

_____ 12. Supporting service function

_____ 13. Committed costs

_____ 14. Discretionary costs

_____ 15. Scatter diagram

a. A cost that remains constant within the relevant range of volume

b. Where a joint product becomes two or more products

c. Fixed costs that are flexible within a relatively short time period

d. The process of assigning a cost to a cost objective

e. Anything that receives an assigned cost

f. How costs change in relation to volume

g. A department that assists the production departments

h. Any segment of a business for which costs are accumulated

i. The volume range within which actual operations are likely to occur

j. Fixed costs that must continue in order to maintain current operations

k. A cost that varies in direct proportion to volume

l. A graph of plotted points that represent observed costs

m. An integrated system to plan and control costs

n. A cost that is common to two or more products

o. A cost with both fixed and variable components

Completion

Use the lines provided to complete each item.

1. List three examples of semivariable costs.

a. _____

b. _____

c. _____

2. Briefly explain the purpose of the high-low method.

_____

_____

_____

3. State two reasons why it is important to understand a cost's behavior.

a. _____

b. _____

4. In the space below, draw a graph depicting a step-variable cost. Label both axes.

5. What is the difference between tracing a cost to a cost objective and allocating the cost?

_____

_____

_____

True-False

Circle T if the statement is true, F if it is false.

T F **1.** On a per-unit basis, variable costs remain constant with changes in volume.

T F **2.** On a graph, fixed costs can be represented by a straight horizontal line.

T F **3.** A fixed cost can change when it is outside the relevant range.

T F **4.** Factory insurance is an example of a variable cost.

T F **5.** Property taxes are an example of a fixed cost.

T F **6.** Joint costs include all costs incurred before and after the split-off point.

T F **7.** Cutting costs by 10 percent is an example of a cost objective.

T F **8.** It is easier to assign a division's costs to its departments than it is to do the reverse.

T F **9.** A mixed cost is one in which both variable and fixed costs are charged to the same general ledger account.

T F **10.** Under the relative sales value method, joint production costs could be allocated based on pounds of each joint product produced.

T F **11.** Factory depreciation is an example of a committed fixed cost.

T F **12.** In applying the least squares method, the objective is to solve for the variables x and y.

T F **13.** When applying regression analysis, the point at which the regression line intercepts the y axis is equal to the fixed cost.

T F **14.** A company's factory is a supporting service function.

T F **15.** As a segment of a company is broken down into smaller components, indirect costs tend to become direct costs.

Circle the letter of the best answer.

1. Taxi fares with a certain base price plus a mileage charge would be an example of a
   a. fixed cost.
   b. variable cost.
   c. semivariable cost.
   d. standard cost.

2. Which of the following is *not* an example of a supporting service department?
   a. Building and grounds department
   b. Health center
   c. Factory cafeteria
   d. Assembling department

3. The physical volume method
   a. results in a more realistic gross profit percentage than the relative sales value method.
   b. ignores revenue per unit of volume.
   c. is applied to costs incurred after the split-off point.
   d. allocates joint costs in proportion to the revenue that each product can generate.

4. Which of the following is an example of a direct cost?
   a. Factory depreciation
   b. Janitorial wages
   c. Assembly line worker's wages
   d. The cost of nails

5. Which of the following is an example of a discretionary fixed cost?
   a. Advertising
   b. Insurance
   c. Rent
   d. Property taxes

6. As volume decreases,
   a. variable cost per unit decreases.
   b. fixed cost in total decreases.
   c. variable cost in total remains the same.
   d. fixed cost per unit increases.

7. In defining a cost as variable, each of the following can act as an activity base *except*
   a. hours worked.
   b. cost incurred.
   c. miles driven.
   d. units produced.

8. In applying the high-low and least squares methods, the slope of the line obtained represents the
   a. total cost.
   b. fixed cost.
   c. mixed cost.
   d. variable cost.

9. The most accurate method for dividing a semivariable cost into its fixed and variable components is the
   a. high-low method.
   b. physical volume method.
   c. least squares method.
   d. scatter diagram method.

10. The most logical basis for allocating to production the cost of a company's central power department is
    a. direct labor hours worked.
    b. kilowatt hours used.
    c. direct labor dollars incurred.
    d. square footage occupied.

Applying Your Knowledge

Exercises

1. The following vehicle repair figures were assembled for Chess Cab Company for the first four months of 19xx.

Month	Activity Level	Cost
January	10,000 miles	$3,400
February	12,400 miles	$3,900
March	11,200 miles	$3,550
April	9,600 miles	$3,200

a. Using the high-low method, produce a total cost formula for the company that describes its cost behavior for vehicle repairs.

b. Using the answer to 1a above, approximately what repair cost would the company expect to have at an activity level of 16,000 miles?

2. Before a certain process reaches the split-off point, $36,000 has been expended. After the split-off point, three separate products are manufactured:

24,000 units of X, which will sell at $.50
8,000 units of Y, which will sell at $1
16,000 units of Z, which will sell at $5

Compute the portion of the $36,000 joint cost that should be allocated to each of the products, using the physical volume method and relative sales value method.

Physical Volume Method	Relative Sales Value Method
X = $ _____	X = $ _____
Y = $ _____	Y = $ _____
Z = $ _____	Z = $ _____

3. Raymer Manufacturing Company has four production departments that share a maintenance department. Maintenance department costs are allocated to the production departments on the basis of their square footage:

Dept. 1: 2,500 sq. ft.
Dept. 2: 4,000 sq. ft.
Dept. 3: 2,000 sq. ft.
Dept. 4: 1,500 sq. ft.

How much of November's $50,000 maintenance department cost should be allocated to

a. Dept. 1? $ _____

b. Dept. 2? $ _____

c. Dept. 3? $ _____

d. Dept. 4? $ _____

4. During the first five weeks of 19xx, Topanga Manufacturing Company incurred the following maintenance costs at the following levels of production:

Week	Direct Labor Hours	Maintenance Cost
1	100	$350
2	120	400
3	90	320
4	110	370
5	80	300

a. Using the least squares method, obtain a total cost formula in the form $y = a + bx$. Use the equations provided in the text, and do your calculations in the space below. If necessary, round amounts to the nearest cent.

b. Using the answer to 4a above, approximately what maintenance cost would the company expect to incur at an activity level of 150 direct labor hours?

The Controller's Role in Corporate Planning

The implementation of the strategic planning process is a natural extension of the control aspect inherent in the controller's function.

The scope of the modern controller's responsibilities is expanding in more and more companies to encompass coordinating the planning activities associated with the annual planning cycle. Strategic planning is becoming recognized as the most effective way to manage as we move into the turbulent 80s. Strategic planning is a conceptual exercise that establishes a framework for strategic management decisions that will affect the future of the company.

The controller is uniquely positioned to capitalize on this opportunity to expand his horizons considerably. In major corporations the controllers who have been able to administer effectively the strategic and operating planning cycles have gone on to participate in management of some of the new businesses that evolved out of the strategic planning process. In addition, the controller involved in planning is positioned to assess the financial viability of embryonic strategies in terms of their long-term financial requirements thanks to his intimate knowledge of the financial structure of the organization.

Strategic planning is an iterative integrated managerial accounting exercise. It is financially fine tuning the organization by establishing a discipline of constantly measuring performance against the short-term annual budget, as well as the strategic milestones and their related capital expenditures that are built into the operating plan, which evolves out of the strategic plan. Let's explore how the controller gets involved.

The Start of Real Planning

The greatest contribution the controller can make to the planning process is in providing financial education to line managers.

Source: Article by Robert M. Donnelly. Reprinted by permission from the September 1981 issue of *Management Accounting*.

In most companies strategic planning gets started by the chief executive officer getting bit by the "planning bug." This can happen in a variety of ways: the CEO can read about it in a magazine, can be introduced to it by one of his peers at lunch or the club, can attend a seminar on strategic planning, or can simply decide that if other companies have used it successfully maybe his company should try it, too. In any case, the first step in the process is to identify an administrator, or coordinator, of the planning process. Because planning concepts have to be financially quantified before any decision can be made, and if implemented then have to be controlled—who is better qualified to do both than the controller? In addition, the controller manages the budgeting and is the keeper of all of the historical management information critical to starting the strategic planning process.

It almost becomes a natural extension of the controller's duties for him to become the administrator of the planning cycle. In order to do this the controller has to be one of the first members of the management team to familiarize himself with the fundamentals of strategic planning. In most cases, the controller assumes the position of being the right hand of the CEO in the implementation of the strategic planning exercise. It is a natural extension of the control aspect inherent in the controller's function.

Strategic planning starts with the introduction of the concept to senior management, or those who report directly to the CEO, which would include the controller. At that introductory session it should be made clear to those present that the controller will be available for consultation on the process, with the financial support to analyze strategies, and will function as the coordinator of the exercise.

The formalized strategic planning process starts at some agreed-upon time shortly after the initial presentation, and usually begins with the management team getting back together for about two days, when each member of the team presents his individual perceptions of the internal and external strengths and weaknesses of the business.

As this kind of presentation unfolds, it usually becomes obvious that there is a divergence of perceptions as to the overall strengths and weaknesses of the organization. Sometimes these perceptions differ from the CEO's. But strategic planning's basic thrust is to bring the management team together by enabling team members to identify with the same problems and opportunities to work toward the same common goals and objectives.

Out of this first formal planning session should come either a dictated set of strengths and weaknesses by the chief executive officer, or the management team's consensus of the same. In any case, the assignment for the team at the end of this first session is to take the agreed-upon strengths and weaknesses and develop strategies which will emphasize the organization's strengths and improve, or overcome, its weaknesses. The assignments are then given to each member of the management team as they relate to his or her expertise and area of responsibility. The controller should plan to give financial guidance to each respective manager.

The second formal session should take place after a reasonable period of time is allowed to get all the work done (which in most cases is about a month to six weeks), and should be at least a two-day session during which all of the proposed strategies are thoroughly discussed by the management team. Out of this discussion will come tentative viable strategies, some that will be discarded as unachievable, and others as modified "group" strategies.

This session's function is to produce a set of achievable strategies that the group agrees can be accomplished with existing resources and that appear to be economically attractive. Then the respective managers must "price-out" these strategies with the help of the controller's staff. In other words, analyze: how much will the strategy cost? Who will be accountable for getting it done? How long will it take? And what will be the projected results of implementing these plans?

This second session analysis necessitates involvement of subordinate management and is usually a longer process because of the level of detail required in planning the best possible moves. And, as a result, this detailed preliminary analysis may result in some strategies being scrapped.

The third session is spent reviewing the second session's analytical results. And the number of strategies to be reviewed will determine the length of the third session—usually not more than two days because not too many strategies survive to this phase. The surviving strategies coming out of the third meeting will constitute the basis for developing the mission statement of the company and the strategic planning document.

The last phase consists in putting the strategic plan document together and writing a cohesive narrative of the combination of strategies. This document is then communicated to management and becomes the basis for developing operating plans and budgets.

It is now up to the management team to implement the strategic plan, measure its performance, and periodically update the plan and organization as business conditions warrant. Strategic planning sets the parameters for a company's long-term growth by identifying opportunities and setting in motion a series of chronological planning activities to exploit them. The process constitutes setting futuristic goals and objectives and working back in time to plan for the specific subsets of the overall plan. These subsets are generally referred to as operating plans and are usually three-year periods of time.

Contained in the first year of the operating plan is the budget or the month-by-month tasks that must be accomplished to make the operating plan a reality.

The strategic plan identifies opportunities in a prioritized fashion, with the most important heading the chronological order of action plans or strategies to be implemented. Those deemed lower priority strategies have a longer implementation schedule and may, or may not, be dependent on the success or failure of higher priority action plans. The strategic plan encompasses all of these strategies and is based on the assumption that the total plan is achievable.

The operating plan is developed from the most important action plans and coordinated by the controller. It is important to understand that the life of a strategy can range from a few months to several years. The operating plan contains all of the strategies for the first three years of the strategic plan and their respective time-phased capital expenditures.

Some strategies may begin and end in the budget year, start at the beginning of the budget year and end in one of the operating plan years, or begin and conclude in the operating plan years.

The development of the operating plan initiates the detailed planning process of fitting the plan's conceptual framework into a more specific set of action objectives with timetables. This is where the controller's real involvement as an administrator and financial planning consultant begins. The process is begun by laying out the chronological order of strategies and their respective time frames.

Operating Plan

Once the operating plan has been developed, it can be folded into the budgeting activity and the preparation of the overall operating plan. To reemphasize: the operating plan provides the control mechanism to measure progress against strategic milestones. In addition, this process allows for the identification of capital expenditures for the planning period so that prudent financing can be arranged. Arraying these strategies guarantees the opportunity for human resources planning and development of organizational structures in advance of implementation.

After these jobs have been done, the budget year then becomes the most detailed month-by-month set of goals and objectives crucial to an effective operating plan and, finally, the strategic plan. As this process becomes the managerial discipline it should be, one operating plan flows into the next, and the whole exercise becomes a tremendously valuable managerial activity.

Operating plan strategies should be evaluated on a quarterly basis. Because of their independency and the significance of the capital expenditures associated with each action plan, it is critical that the performance of each strategy be carefully synchronized with the overall operating plan. The interaction of the budget with the operating plan determines the future impact of the present business conditions. This kind of futuristic barometer is an integral part of sound business planning.

Moreover, budget and operating plan interaction produces a continuing demand for contingency planning. Good budgets are developed on a range of potential business situations of pitfalls and opportunities. Well-done budgets contain scenarios ranging from the most optimistic to pessimistic forecasts, and project

Figure 1

Interaction of Strategic Planning with Operating Plans and Budgets

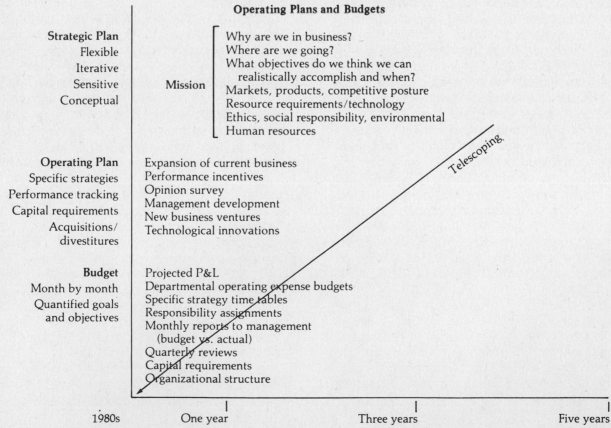

financial results. In turn, these potential situations each have an impact on planned strategies, and management should be made aware of them by the controller. Figure 1 illustrates the interaction of strategic planning with operating plans and budgets.

The Controller as Planning Coordinator

The major problem controllers have in taking on the responsibility of planning coordinator is that it represents a major change in "image." Controllers are thought of as bean counters, accountants, and are generally considered to be dealing with the past (historical data). Planning is futuristic. In addition, controllers keep talking that funny language which no one else in the company really understands, and if we can't understand what the controller is trying to tell us about the financial results now, how are we ever going to understand planning?

Unfortunately, in many companies the controller is misunderstood because he does not take the time to educate the rest of the management team about the financial ramifications of different business decisions. However, planning is a great opportunity for the controller to overcome that image problem because planning has to be explained. The process of planning requires other managers to become more financially oriented because all plans have to eventually be financially quantified. This exercise has to involve the controller and in the process the controller and the manager should work together as a team.

So the best way for the controller to start out as the planning coordinator is to have a planning orientation session to explain the purpose of the exercise. This orientation session has to be attended by the CEO and the CEO *must* support the process.

The second major problem controllers have as planning coordinator is the schedule and getting everyone to adhere to the schedule. Unfortunately, again, in too many companies, controllers send out "budgeting" schedules in the form of a schedule stapled to a bunch of forms with a note that says, "Please fill these forms out and get them back to me according to the attached schedule." This approach will get an equally impersonal response in the form of haphazardly completed forms, or no forms at all. This scenario creates part of that image problem because everyone mentally concludes: here come those damn forms again and the controller will be bugging me if I don't do something.

The right way to solicit cooperation in the planning process is to explain to managers why it is important to get their best input, how to fill out the forms, and to offer to be helpful and available for consultation. When the controller takes on the responsibility of planning coordinator it becomes a natural extension of the budgeting exercise into a more conceptual and futuristic process. Scheduling is an integral part of planning. The controller has to be the enforcer and work with management to help it meet the planning schedule.

The third problem controllers have when they first take on the responsibility of planning coordinator is that they have to summarize all of the respective managers' plans into the overall company plan. This summary also requires evaluation, which means that the controller has to become familiar with all aspects of the business. In reality this is a great opportunity for the controller but also represents a delicate political needle to thread. The controller is faced with making an evaluation of an operating manager's plan and comparing all of

Table 1
Key Performance Indicators

	Jan	Feb	Mar	Apr	May	Jun	Jul	Aug	Sep
Sales reps productivity									
Average revenue product									
Months-on-hand (inv.)									
Days-of-sales outstanding									
Mean time between product failure									
Absenteeism									
New Accounts									

Table 2
Typical Set of Instructions

Interoffice Memo

TO: Divisional CEO's, General Managers, (etc.)

FROM: Corporate CEO

RE: Annual Operating Plan Schedule and Guidelines

This package includes the forms to be completed for our annual operating plan exercise. You are also expected to develop a narrative on your respective operations that addresses:

- Summary & Highlights (this year vs. next)
- Key Problems & Opportunities
- Marketing Summary with Product Line Profit & Loss discussions
- Strategies: (by strategy)
  Description of the strategy.
  Why it is necessary.
  Who will be responsible for it.
  How long will it take to implement.
  How much will it cost.
  What is the expected return on the investment.
- Asset Management, including strategies in the capital spending projection.
- Organization, with manpower comparisons.

We would also like to know of all of your planning assumptions with as much rationale as possible. Please discuss this with your budget coordinator if you have any questions. For planning purposes use the following overall guidelines:

Compensation: Exempt—Cost of living 7% across the board
                                Meritorious 10% avg. by department
                 Nonexempt—Cost of living 7% across the board
                                Meritorious 9% avg. by department
Inflation factors: Materials and utilities 15%
                    All other expenses   10%
Financial Returns: On capital expenditures (investments) 15%
                    Profit on sales   10%

In addition, we expect to receive projections for your respective businesses as follows:

Sales by product	September 30
Standard cost by product	October 31
Expenses	November 30

Your complete operating plan is due in my office by the end of the first week in December. We will begin operating plan review meetings in the second week in December, and you should be prepared for at least a three-hour meeting on your plan. The schedule of these review meetings will be sent to you later this year. As in the past you should plan to make a presentation of this year's plan highlighting the key performance indicators and your contingency plans for greater than or less than plan performance.

After your respective operating plan has been approved, you should also be prepared to discuss individual compensation plans to accomplish the goals and objectives set forth in the operating plan.

those plans to the financial criteria necessary for the overall profitable growth and stability of the company.

Perhaps the greatest contribution that the controller can make to the planning process is providing financial education to line managers so that they have a better appreciation for how their actions impact the company. This learning experience also contributes to the team concept of good planning and the controller acts as the facilitator in this educational process.

The next key phase of team planning is management reporting, which also falls under the controller's responsibility. Most controllers produce the standard financial statements and each month there is an agonizing management meeting where the controller "goes over" the financial results line-by-line.

Unless the management team has a financial background this process literally leaves them cold, unsure as to what actually happened as a result of their individual actions last month. Good planning creates a slightly different way of looking at results by concentrating on trends and the analysis of the impact of those trends in the future. A planning technique that is particularly effective is looking at *key performance indicators* every month (Table 1).

Key performance indicators are those volume-related six or seven factors that drive the business—those most significant results that impact everything else in the business and act as barometers for the future. The controller is the keeper of this data and is responsible for producing the key performance indicators' report. When constructed properly, this report will summarize all of the pertinent information the management team really needs to react to short-term problems and opportunities. More important, the constant use of key performance indicators focuses management's attention on the interactions of all aspects of the business, and each component clearly has an inter-relationship with the others. So the controller should blend the concept of key performance indicators into the introduction and explanation of planning. These indicators represent trends that have a significant impact on future planning.

Another important problem for controllers when they first take over the planning responsibility is that they, themselves, often are unfamiliar with planning. If, in turn, they don't have the right level of authority to implement

their new-found responsibility it becomes an even greater challenge.

In the case where the controller is unfamiliar with planning there are two quick solutions: attend a seminar and get some good books on planning. A third alternative might be to visit other controllers who are involved in planning to get their advice.

Even with this knowledge, however, the only way the controller can be effective is to have the authority to command a response to the planning guidelines, schedules, and forms. The controller should clearly control the process.

The Coordination Process

The planning cycle begins with the controller developing the planning guidelines in a memoranda format for signature by the CEO (Table 2). The guidelines should include: an overall statement of the inherent responsibility of managers to plan and budget, the corporate planning assumptions, financial return expectations for individual businesses, the planning timetable, and forms with explanations on how to complete them. The next step should be a brief meeting to go over the memo with all respective operating unit managers and their planning coordinators (usually divisional budget analysts) to resolve any questions about the schedule, assumptions, or how to complete the forms.

Then the controller becomes both the counselor and the policeman. The forms are collected when due and the controller begins to array all the data from the respective business units and compares them for reasonableness and growth, or decline, from historic patterns. This comparative data analysis process is best done by the controller and his group so that it can present the overall corporate consolidated planning results.

The controller's group also should be responsible for scheduling the planning review meetings between the business unit manager team and the corporate management group, which should include the controllers and respective divisional budget analysts. Minutes of those meetings are usually kept by the controller.

Once the plan has been approved, it has to be seasonalized, calendarized, or spread-by-month. The controller then begins the second phase of becoming the planning coordinator by producing the monthly management reports to commence the *control* phase of the process.

Controlling the Strategic Plan

Monthly management reports should contain:

☐ A one-page narrative on the nature of the business (Table 3).
☐ The Key Performance Report.
☐ Several Charts or Graphs of the Most Important Indicators.
☐ The Financial Statements.

This format allows for a fairly thorough discussion of operations so that when the financial statements are reached they represent the results of the business trends discussed in the narrative, portrayed by the key performance indicators, and illustrated on the charts and graphs. The controller should present this report to management, attend the management meeting, and follow up on any "action items" for the next meeting.

The next step in the process is the First Quarter Review. The First Quarter Review is a mini-budgeting activity that requires the controller to develop a quarterly review memo and forms with instructions. The controller has to monitor the quarterly data collection process, prepare the presentation, and attend the quarterly review meeting.

Monthly management reports are developed for the next three months. The First Half Review is similar to the First Quarter Review with comparisons of the first six months actual to the same six months of last year, and the six months budget. The last six months of last year, the budget, and a projection of the balance of the year make up the review package. A nine-month review is not required because you are back in the planning cycle for the next operating plan.

Developing, Monitoring, Updating

The Quarterly and First Half Reviews also require the controller to develop reports on capital expenditures and progress against the strategic milestones represented by those expenditures. The progress, or lack thereof, of strategies can cause a realignment of strategic priorities, which is usually decided at these quarterly review meetings. The controller is responsible for monitoring these changes and incorporating these decisions in the upcoming annual planning process.

So the role of the controller as coordinator of the planning process encompasses: developing the initial plan, monitoring progress against that plan, and updating the plan based upon management's ability to make the plan happen.

```
┌─────────────────────────────────────────────────────────┐
│                      Table 3                            │
│               Monthly Management Report                 │
│                                                         │
│                    ABC Division                         │
│     Management Report for the Month of _____      │
│                      ($000's)                           │
│                                                         │
│    Actual sales for _____ of $X were 97% of plan,  │
│  but 105%                                               │
│  of _____ last year. Especially good performance   │
│  was                                                    │
│  accomplished with our new line of Y products. On a     │
│  year-to-date                                           │
│  basis, we are 95% of plan and 101% of last year.       │
│    Cost for _____ were on budget, which brings     │
│  year-to-date                                           │
│  cost to 98% of plan. Slow-moving inventories are being │
│  analyzed and                                           │
│  special promotions are being planned to dispose of     │
│  those products by                                      │
│  the end of the quarter.                                │
│    Expenses for _____ were 4% over budget          │
│  primarily due to                                       │
│  accelerating promotions for Y products that were       │
│  budgeted for later                                     │
│  periods. This brings year-to-date expenses to 101% of  │
│  budget. Total                                          │
│  full year expenses are expected to be only 95% of      │
│  budget as a result                                     │
│  of planned reductions in travel and sales meetings in  │
│  the second half.                                       │
│    Profits for _____ were 5% below budget, which   │
│  brings                                                 │
│  year-to-date performance to 97% of plan. Full year     │
│  profitability is still                                 │
│  expected to come in on budget.                         │
│    Total manpower for _____ is still six below     │
│  plan, two in                                           │
│  production and four in the field sales force. Active   │
│  recruiting is under                                    │
│  way.                                                   │
│    Collection of receivables is slightly behind plan,   │
│  but this has been                                      │
│  identified as a timing problem and not a collection    │
│  issue. About $X                                        │
│  of inventory has been determined to be obsolete and    │
│  will be written                                        │
│  off in the next accounting period.                     │
└─────────────────────────────────────────────────────────┘
```

CHAPTER 6 COST-VOLUME-PROFIT ANALYSIS

REVIEWING THE CHAPTER

Objective 1: Explain how changes in cost, volume, or price affect the profit formula (pp. 198-201).

1. **Cost-volume-profit (C-V-P) analysis** is used primarily as a planning and control tool. Among the uses of C-V-P analysis are projecting net income at different activity levels, measuring the performance of a department within a company, and assisting in the analysis of decision alternatives. Based on the notion of cost behavior, C-V-P analysis helps management by making use of a number of techniques and problem-solving procedures. A simple application of C-V-P analysis is the computation of **break-even volume,** the sales volume at which there is no profit or loss. Other applications include assistance in product pricing, sales mix analysis, adding or deleting a product line, and accepting special orders.

2. A conceptual overview of basic C-V-P relationships can be obtained by preparing a C-V-P graph. At this point, we recommend that you refer back to figures 6.1 and 6.2 of the text to be sure that you fully understand all the components of a C-V-P graph. The break-even point, for example, is the point at which the total revenue line crosses the total cost line.

3. Operating capacity refers to maximum productive output and related costs, given an assumption about operating efficiency. **Theoretical (ideal) capacity** is the maximum productive output possible over a given period of time. **Practical capacity** is theoretical capacity reduced by normal, anticipated work stoppages. **Normal capacity** is the average annual operating capacity needed to satisfy expected sales demand. It realistically measures what will be produced rather than what can be produced. **Excess capacity** refers to extra machinery and equipment available when regular facilities are being repaired or when expected volume is greater than actual.

Objective 2: Compute the break-even point in units of output and in sales dollars (pp. 201-202).

4. The **break-even point** is the point at which sales revenues equal the sum of all variable and fixed costs. A company can earn a profit only by surpassing the break-even point. The break-even equations are $S = VC + FC$ or $S - VC - FC = O$. In these equations, S represents sales, VC represents variable costs, and FC represents fixed costs.

   a. The break-even point in units can be computed algebraically, or as follows:

$$\frac{\text{Fixed costs}}{\text{Unit selling price} - \text{variable cost per unit}}$$

b. The break-even point in dollars is computed as follows:

Break-even units X selling price per unit

Objective 3: Prepare a break-even graph and identify its components (p. 202).

5. A standard break-even graph has five parts: (a) an x axis representing volume, (b) a y axis representing dollars of cost or revenue, (c) a horizontal fixed cost line, (d) a sloping line beginning at fixed cost and representing total cost, and (e) a sloping line beginning at the origin and representing total revenue. The variable cost line, which typically is not separately identified on a break-even graph, differs from the total cost line by beginning at the origin. The area below the break-even point represents a loss; the area above it represents a profit.

Objective 4: Define contribution margin and use the concept to determine a company's break-even point (pp. 203-204).

6. The **contribution margin** equals sales minus total variable costs. The contribution margin per unit equals selling price minus variable cost per unit. The break-even point in units equals fixed costs divided by contribution margin per unit. It is the only point at which the contribution margin equals the fixed costs. In addition, for every unit sold, the company's income increases, not by the selling price, but by the unit's contribution margin.

7. Below is the calculation of net income using the contribution format:

Sales	$XX
− Variable costs	XX
= Contribution margin	XX
− Fixed costs	XX
= Net income	XX

Notice that under this format, production, selling, and administrative costs are divided into their fixed and variable components.

Objective 5: Apply contribution margin analysis to estimate the levels of sales that will produce planned profits (pp. 204-205).

8. To determine the number of units that must be sold to produce a certain net income, fixed costs plus the target net income are divided by the contribution margin per unit. Alternatively, we can set up an algebraic equation to solve for target units.

9. The contribution approach is very useful for planning purposes. For example, it can be used to calculate projected income given a change in one or more of the income statement components. Changes in production costs, selling and administrative costs, variable costs, fixed costs, product demand, and selling price can drastically alter projected net income.

Objective 6: Prepare an analysis that shows the effects of changes in sales mix on a company's profits (pp. 212-216).

10. **Sales mix** refers to the combination of product sales in a company that is producing more than one product. Sales mix analysis is used to find the most profitable combination of product sales. In general, where possible, a company should shift toward those products that produce the highest contribution margin percentages. It is important, however, for management to know the effects of a shift in product sales mix on the company's contribution margin (and therefore net income). It is possible, for example, for a shift in sales mix to reduce sales dollars while increasing net income.

11. To calculate break-even sales dollars when more than one product is being manufactured, total fixed costs are divided by the average contribution margin percentage. The sales mix percentages then can be multiplied by this figure to produce the total sales dollars needed from each product to break even.

12. To make use of C-V-P analysis, six assumptions must be made.
   a. The behavior of variable and fixed costs can be measured accurately.
   b. Costs and revenues have a close linear relationship.
   c. Efficiency and productivity will hold steady within the relevant range.
   d. Cost and price variables will hold steady during the period being planned.
   e. The product sales mix will not change during the period being planned.
   f. Production and sales volume will be about equal.

Testing Your Knowledge

Matching

Match each term with its definition by writing the appropriate letter in the blank.

_____ 1. Cost-volume-profit (C-V-P) analysis

_____ 2. Break-even point

_____ 3. Contribution margin

_____ 4. Sales mix

_____ 5. Theoretical (ideal) capacity

_____ 6. Practical capacity

_____ 7. Normal capacity

_____ 8. Excess capacity

a. The operating level needed to satisfy expected sales demand
b. The sales volume at which overall net income is zero
c. The maximum productive output possible over a given period of time
d. A method of determining net income at different levels of volume
e. Extra machinery and equipment available on a standby basis
f. Sales minus total variable costs
g. Ideal capacity minus normal work stoppages
h. The combination of product sales

Completion

Use the lines provided to complete each item.

1. In the space below, write the break-even formula.

2. On the five lines below, show how net income is calculated using the contribution format.

_____

− _____

= _____

− _____

= _____

3. Distinguish between the concepts of sales and contribution margin.

4. State the six assumptions underlying C-V-P analysis.

a. _____

b. _____

c. _____

d. _____

e. _____

f. _____

5. In sales mix analysis, what strategy will produce an overall increase in net income?

True-False

Circle T if the statement is true, F if it is false.

T F **1.** The most realistic plant capacity measure is practical capacity.

T F **2.** At the break-even point, sales equal variable costs.

T F **3.** At the break-even point, the contribution margin equals fixed costs.

T F **4.** The break-even point in dollars can be determined by multiplying break-even units by the selling price.

T F **5.** Theoretical capacity refers to the maximum productive output possible.

T F **6.** A contribution margin cannot be realized until the break-even point has been surpassed.

T F **7.** On a break-even graph, the *x* axis represents dollars of cost or revenue.

T F **8.** The contribution format income statement does not contain a line for cost of goods sold.

T F **9.** An assumption of C-V-P analysis is that the product sales mix will not change during the period being planned.

T F **10.** A reduction in sales dollars also reduces the contribution margin percentage.

T F **11.** On a break-even graph, the variable cost line starts at the orgin.

T F **12.** The best product to sell is the one with the highest selling price.

T F **13.** An increase in the variable cost per unit lowers the contribution margin percentage.

T F **14.** The average contribution margin percentage of three products being sold equals the sum of the products' individual contribution margin percentages divided by 3.

T F **15.** The contribution margin percentage measures the contribution margin per unit in relation to the selling price.

Multiple Choice

Circle the letter of the best answer.

1. When fixed cost is $10,000, variable cost is $8 per unit, and the selling price is $10 per unit, the break-even point is
   a. 1,000 units.
   b. 1,250 units.
   c. 5,000 units.
   d. 10,000 units.

2. When volume equals zero units,
   a. fixed cost equals zero.
   b. variable cost equals zero.
   c. total cost equals zero.
   d. net income equals zero.

3. At the break-even point,
   a. the contribution margin equals fixed cost.
   b. sales equal variable cost.
   c. total cost equals contribution margin.
   d. net income equals total cost.

4. In graph form, the break-even point is at the intersection of the
   a. total revenue and variable cost lines.
   b. total cost line and vertical axis.
   c. variable cost and fixed cost lines.
   d. total cost and total revenue lines.

5. The operating capacity that is required to satisfy anticipated sales demand is
   a. normal capacity.
   b. excess capacity.
   c. practical capacity.
   d. theoretical capacity.

6. The break-even point can be determined by
   a. dividing fixed costs by the variable cost per unit.
   b. multiplying the contribution margin per unit by the selling price.
   c. dividing fixed costs by the contribution margin per unit.
   d. dividing the contribution margin per unit by the fixed cost.

7. When both the selling price and the variable cost per unit are increased by $5,
   a. more dollar sales are needed to break even.
   b. fewer units need to be sold to break even.
   c. the contribution margin per unit also increases by $5.
   d. the break-even point remains the same.

8. Product X has a selling price of $50 and a variable cost per unit of 70 percent of the selling price. If fixed costs total $30,000, how many units must be sold to earn a profit of $45,000?
   a. 900
   b. 1,500
   c. 2,143
   d. 5,000

9. Product Y has a variable cost per unit of $10 and requires a fixed investment of $40,000. If sales are anticipated at 10,000 units, what selling price must be established to earn a profit of $26,000?
   a. $16.60
   b. $14
   c. $12.60
   d. $6.60

10. A company has the opportunity to sell 100 units of A, B, or C. The product that will contribute the most to net income is the one that
    a. has the highest selling price.
    b. will produce the highest total contribution margin.
    c. has the highest contribution margin percentage.
    d. has the lowest variable cost per unit.

Applying Your Knowledge

Exercises

1. Leisure Manufacturing Company is planning to introduce a new line of bowling balls. Annual fixed costs are estimated to be $80,000. Each ball will be sold to the retailer for $13 and requires $9 of variable costs.
   a. The break-even point in units is

   _____ .

   b. The break-even point in dollars is
   $ _____ .

   c. If 12,000 balls are sold per year, the overall profit or loss is
   $ _____ .

   d. The number of balls that must be sold for an annual profit of $50,000 is

   _____ .

2.

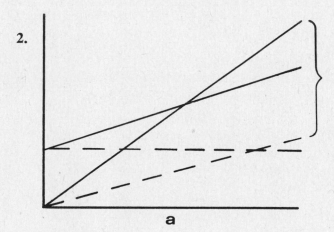

a

Using the letters that correspond with the labels listed below, identify the elements on this break-even graph. "Volume" has already been indicated.
   a. Volume
   b. Cost or revenue
   c. Break-even point
   d. Profit region
   e. Loss region
   f. Fixed cost
   g. Variable cost
   h. Total cost
   i. Contribution margin
   j. Sales

3. Evans Corporation sold 20,000 units of Product Z last year. Each unit sold for $40 and had a variable cost of $26. Annual fixed costs totaled $300,000. This year, management is thinking of reducing the selling price by 15 percent, purchasing less expensive material to save $2 per unit, and spending $50,000 more on advertising. It is expected that sales will double with the proposed changes.
a. What was the company's profit or loss last year? $ _____
b. In the space below, prepare a projected contribution format income statement, assuming that the proposed changes are instituted and that sales do double.

Evans Corporation
Projected Income Statement
For the Year Ended December 31, 19xx

4. Doherty & Sons produces three products: A, B, and C. The operating results for last month are shown below.

Product	Unit Sales	Dollar Sales	Dollars of CM	CM%
A	500	50,000	10,000	20
B	300	60,000	24,000	40
C	900	90,000	27,000	30

In addition, fixed costs totaled $36,600.
a. Calculate the average CM ratio for the given sales mix. Do not round off your answer.

b. Calculate the break-even point in sales dollars for the given sales mix.

c. Calculate the sales of each product (in dollars) at the break-even point.

Crossword Puzzle
for Chapters 5 and 6

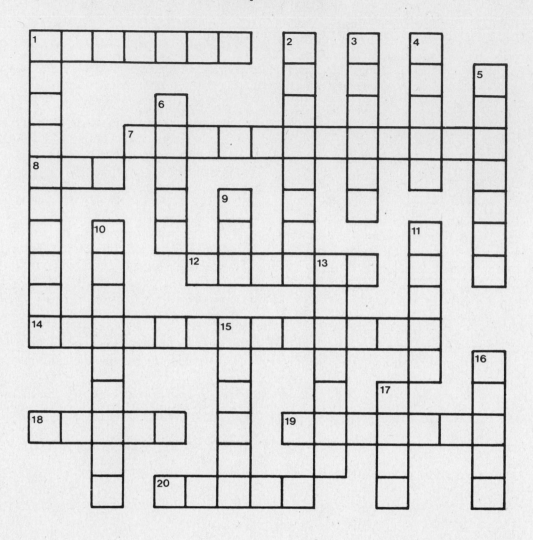

ACROSS

1. Budgetary ——
7. —— margin
8. —— analysis
12. —— capacity (additional equipment available)
14. Probable activity level (2 words)
18. With 17-Down, point of no profit
19. Supporting —— function
20. Relative —— value method

DOWN

1. Business segment that accumulates expenses (2 words)
2. Cost that changes with activity level
3. Physical —— method
4. —— -off point
5. Justification for cost allocation
6. Cost that relates to several products
9. Sales —— (combination of products sold)
10. Behaving in other than a straight line
11. Cost comprised of fixed and variable costs
13. —— diagram (graph with plotted points)
15. —— capacity (anticipated sales demand)
16. Theoretical (capacity)
17. See 18-Across

Multidimensional Break-Even Analysis

We are all familiar with break-even analysis that takes a two-dimensional approach and determines the sales quantity at which total revenues equal total costs. In this article, Roger A. Camp *illustrates a "multidimensional" break-even approach used in profit analysis of his company's trucking operations. The author is the CFO of The Motor Convoy, Inc., a Georgia-based common carrier operating primarily in the southeastern United States.*

The chart below illustrates a typical break-even analysis at The Motor Convoy for a relevant range of trips—from about 100 to 450 miles. The rate and cost per pound are graphed along the Y axis, while the length of the trip (in miles) is charted along the X axis. The following curves are plotted:
□ Motor Convoy's rate curve.
□ A competitor's rate curve.
□ Motor Convoy's cost curves at various volumes.

Graphing the rates charged by each competitor illustrates the competitive forces that the company must confront and the competitive constraints affecting analysis of profit margins. (Information for plotting this curve is obtained from the marketing department.)

Source: Reprinted with permission from the *Journal of Accountancy,* Copyright © 1987 by American Institute of Certified Public Accountants, Inc.

Within the range of the chart, the fixed costs per unit increase or decrease while the variable costs per unit remain constant. The slope of the cost curves stays the same, producing a series of curves at different volumes parallel to each other. As volume increases, total costs per pound decrease by the reduction in fixed costs per unit.

In the chart the cost curve is plotted for volumes of 2,000, 2,500, 3,000 and 3,500 pounds. Motor Convoy's break-even points for the above volumes are trip lengths of approximately 190, 260, 320, and 410 miles, respectively.

The interrelationship of such factors as volume, trip length and competitors' rates are extremely important, requiring careful study so that strategies for increasing profits can be developed. To examine these interrelationships, let's discuss four cases at Motor Convoy, which are charted on the opposite page. In each case, volume is 2,000 pounds for the range of trips illustrated.

Case 1. The competitor's rate curve is parallel to Motor Convoy's cost curve and both rate curves cross at 110 miles. At this volume Motor Convoy's business should be concentrated on trips between 110 and 190 miles. On shorter trips, the competition is cheaper than Motor Convoy, while on longer trips Motor Convoy is losing money.

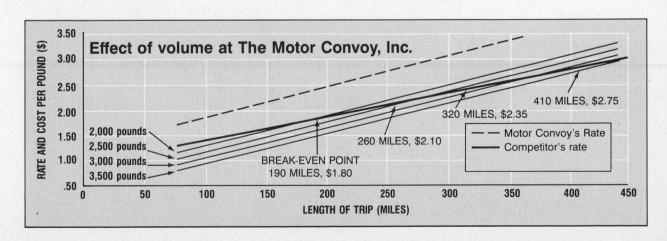

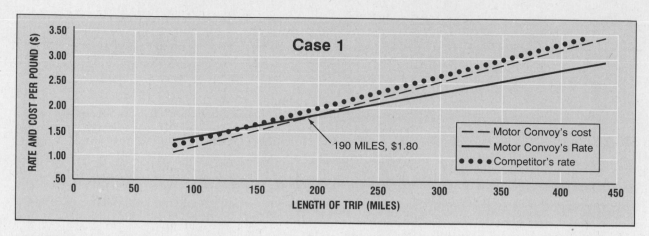

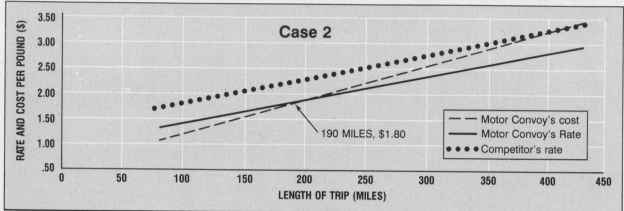

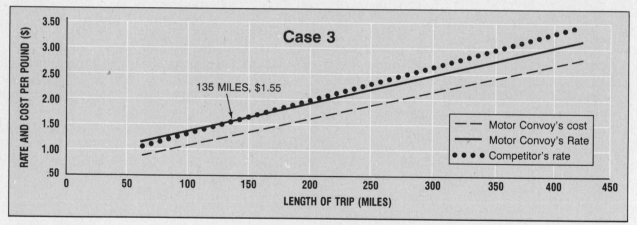

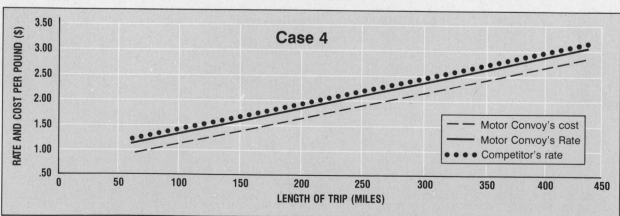

Chapter 6

Case 2. The competitor's rate curve is parallel to and above Motor Convoy's rate curve. Motor Convoy's cost curve crosses its rate curve at 190 miles (the break-even point at this volume). Although Motor Convoy is more competitive at all levels, it should direct its sales effort toward obtaining shorter trips of less than 190 miles, since it is unprofitable above this level.

Case 3. Motor Convoy's rate and cost curves are parallel. The competitor's rate curve crosses Motor Convoy's rate curve at 135 miles. Although Motor Convoy is profitable at all levels, it should probably place more effort on obtaining trips greater than 135 miles, since below that level the competition has lower rates.

Moreover, in this case, if Motor Convoy obtains its competitor's short business, it could probably eliminate that competition—not an unhappy scenario.

Case 4. Although highly unlikely, this is the ideal environment to operate in because the competitor's rate curve is parallel to and above Motor Convoy's rate and cost curves. There is no competition at any point and Motor Convoy is profitable at all levels.

In each of the above cases, volume changes and trip lengths outside the illustrated range could significantly alter strategies. Furthermore, such analysis can highlight those areas in which a company is not competitive and provide guidance for changing the company's rate structure to improve its performance and competitive position.

A Must for Survival

Financial analysis of profit margins must take into consideration underlying cost and rate structures, competitors' rate structures, volume and patterns of business. This type of analysis is a must for survival because of the tight profit margins in most industries.

Breaking Through the Breakeven Barriers

Frustrated Chief Executive: "You say our break-even point is now 60% of our capacity, but how much better or worse is that than what we did in the past? And do our plans project improvement or deterioration?"

Apologetic Controller: "We can draw you break-even charts for every product and for every past and planned year, but we have no way to boil it down to one consistent picture that shows all past and future analyses."

CEO "Find a way!"

There are many practical and theoretical barriers to consolidating standard breakeven analyses. Nevertheless, our company found it worthwhile to break through these barriers with some nonstandard analysis. The result was the development of a single graph that portrays an entire company's breakeven history and plans with two curves. Mobay Chemical calls this "profit geometry." (See Figure 1.)

Barriers to Breakeven Analysis

In developing this profit geometry type of breakeven analysis and graphical presentation, we had to cope with the following obstacles that often deter management accountants from using breakeven charts:

1. Inflation smears year-to-year comparisons.
2. Product variety makes aggregating totals of questionable value.
3. Capacity additions change the chart's dimensions.
4. Fixed costs are often actually variable over time.
5. Measures of statistical significance are difficult, if not impossible, to apply.
6. Inventory change and one-time charges distort comparisons of historical with planned periods.
7. "True" breakeven (including cost of capital) is often ignored.

Source: Article by Howard Martin. From *Management Accounting,* May 1985. Reprinted by permission.

Consolidating standard breakeven analyses enables the controller, financial analyst, or planning professional to answer questions like:

- How did last year's profit compare with the last time we experienced this level of capacity utilization (actual production levels relative to maximum possible production levels)?
- How much have our so-called fixed costs actually increased with volume over recent years?
- What level of profitability as a percent of sales and/or investment can we expect at "full" utilization of capacity?
- What confidence level can we have that a recent actual or forecast future change in profitability is really significant (i.e., more than just normal variability)?

As shown in Figure 1, the profit geometry diagram displays data as a percent of sales revenue vs. utilization of capacity. Inflationary influences are removed by allowing revenue dollars per unit of capacity to act as a deflator. The position of each year's data point is thus comparable with every other point.

In other words, the question of how each year's profits compare with those of prior years can be answered directly from this graph. For example in 1983, both gross margin and operating margin were well above the fitted line, roughly 2% of sales better than what historical experience would have indicated for this level of capacity utilization.

The first fitted line follows the equation: gross margin equals sales minus variable costs minus fixed costs adjusted for capacity utilization. The process of fitting the curve (i.e., correlation) determines A, an average incremental margin (sales minus variable costs), and B, a figure for fixed costs as a percent of sales at capacity. In other words, these two factors (the coefficients of the correlation equation) are held constant over the full period to see how well this equation fits the historical data. The equation may be written: Gross Margin = A−B/U.O.C., where U.O.C. = utilization of capacity = 1.0 @ 100%.

Creeping Costs

"Creeping Cost" is the problem of selling prices not keeping up with the inflating cost of goods sold. The operation depicted in this example is not affected by creeping cost. If it were, the data points would have shown a different pattern. The more recent points would have been below the fitted line and the earlier data would have been above. It also should be noted that sufficient data points are necessary to ensure a distribution of high and low utilization years in both recent and earlier periods. Otherwise, it would be necessary to analyze operating costs for a representative year on a line-by-line basis for variable and fixed components and generate from this analysis the incremental margin and fixed costs. A curve generated from these components inserted in the equation noted above will show whether or not the profits in recent years have been suffering from creeping cost.

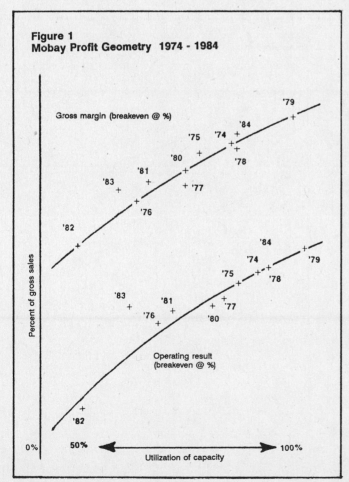

Figure 1
Mobay Profit Geometry 1974 - 1984

The lower fitted line is derived from the gross margin equation given above minus sales, administrative, and research expense (SARE). We actually found that from year to year, these overhead expenses are almost directly variable, even though we know that from month to month they are largely fixed. Further analysis showed that fixed expenses became mostly variable after a lag of several months.[1] In other words, we have—at least in the past—increased and decreased SARE in response to capacity utilization such that less than 20% of our overhead can be considered truly fixed.

The timing and severity of the 1982 recession led many chief executives to question whether present capacities would ever produce adequate profits. Such concerns often can be answered satisfactorily using standard breakeven charts that plot dollars versus capacity. On the other hand, the profit geometry chart, will show the potential profit as a percent of sales. This can make it easier to compare current performance with more distant periods (such as the peak year 1979) or with industry competitors, whether larger or smaller. For example, our chief executive likes to measure our performance against the chemical industry giants who are five or ten times our size.

Increasing the use of statistics in accounting analyses may not be the wave of the future, but here is one case where the combination proved to be interesting. It is visually obvious from Figure 1 that 1983's performance was substantially better than the fitted line would have forecast. Moreover, the simple statistical technique of multiple correlation allows one to determine the standard deviation of the historical data. The 1983 point in both gross margin and operating profit is roughly three standard deviations above the curve. Therefore, there is less than a 1% chance that the improvement is merely a predictable random event and management can say we accomplished something significant. Unfortunately, we can also see that the gain largely disappeared in 1984.

Breaking Down the Barriers

Using sales dollars as the inflation adjustment, multiple correlation against constant fixed costs, and incremental margin and statistical

[1]The equation for a six-month lag reads: SARE (% of sales) = Variable portion (% of sales) + Fixed portion (% of sales) divided by the sum of U.O.C. (current year) + ½ of the increase in U.O.C. vs. prior year.

significance via actual vs. standard deviations are the techniques we used to produce the profit geometry. However, other techniques that we found necessary to use include: dollar-averaging capacity utilization, absorbing capacity additions, normalizing distorted history where applicable, and adding in the cost of capital.

The dollar-averaging method used to calculate capacity utilization also handles capacity additions. However, it is important to determine the potential sales revenue at 100% capacity utilization. In other words, calculate each unit's capacity times its average selling price and sum these dollar amounts. The average utilization is simply the actual sales total divided by this potential revenue figure.[2] Incidentally, for resale products or other small segments where capacity is not readily measurable, we assigned an average utilization equal to that of the major, measurable units. Naturally, when capacity additions (or deletions) occur, this method automatically adjusts utilization by an appropriate amount.

The technique we use for normalizing distorted figures is a side calculation plus an arrow. Specifically, the particular period's profit is recalculated excluding the abnormal factor and then the data is plotted on the graph with an arrow. The tail of the arrow indicates the reported figure and the head of the arrow shows where that period's point would fall under "normal" circumstances. Typical abnormalities we have handled in this manner include: inventory change (i.e., production out of balance with sales), inventory revaluation, startup expense, one-time sales programs, etc.

Finally, the profit geometry graph permits more flexibility in adding the cost of capital. No single cost of capital figure actually can tell how much a business should be asked to earn. The correct cost of capital depends rather on whether the business is expected to continue as is, or to expand aggressively, or to be considered for liquidation. In addition, cost of capital depends on interest rates and debt-to-equity ratios. The profit geometry format adapts to these variables by allowing space for a family of curves.

In Figure 2, we show cost of capital as a profit goal. For the particular debt-to-equity ratio, income tax, and asset turnover rates used

in this example, this operation was above the 8% "cost of capital" curve only one year, 1979. Even then, it was just equal to the cost of capital implied by the 9+% interest rate on long-term U.S. government bonds which was the average for 1979.[3] The impact of rapid growth on both profitability and capacity utilization was clearly substantial. Also, the importance of the profit improvement such as that shown in 1983 becomes more dramatic. Assuming we could stay on that new, higher profit geometry curve, then we would have the potential to reach the higher "cost of capital" breakeven curve generated when government bond rates are 12% as they were in 1984. The two "cost of capital" curves shown in Figure 2 represent only one of at least three families of such curves including "cost of replacement capital," and "cost of actual assets at net book value."

[3]It should be noted that these curves assume all debt is paying current interest rates. No benefit or penalty from fixed rate debt acquired at lower or higher than current interest levels is included.

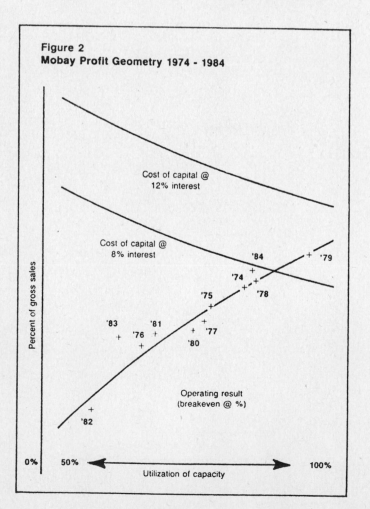

Figure 2
Mobay Profit Geometry 1974 - 1984

[2]The choice of dollar-averaging is seen to be logical when one realizes the purpose is to relate utilization to profit margin, which is also a dollar-averaged figure.

Chapter 6

The cost of replacement capital curves show what profit rate is necessary to pay the cost of expanding this business aggressively (assuming new capacity will match the replacement cost of existing facilities).[4] These curves are the highest hurdles for a company. Cost of replacement capital is probably an unrealistic target for a total company, but not for fast-growing product lines.

Second highest are the curves that measure the cost of actual assets at net book value. These curves show what utilization of capacity will produce the profit necessary to cover the depreciated value of the assets actually shown on the books of this business.

The lowest hurdle rates are generated for those businesses considered for liquidation. These curves indicate the likelihood of the business generating enough profits to justify

---

[4]These calculations require, of course, that allowance also be made in the cost of capital for the change in annual depreciation charges resulting from revaluation of depreciable assets.

foregoing the cash (including tax credits) that would be generated if the current and fixed assets were disposed of.

The profit geometry approach to breakeven analysis opens the way for management accountants to gain interesting insights into a business' profit performance. Current results can be more effectively compared with past performance and with future plans. Both gradual and abrupt changes in margins that are not explained by capacity utilization can be identified and measured. Products of widely varying sales value can be summed and thus statistical analysis, including the benefits of offsetting deviations, can be incorporated. Profit potentials not only can be calculated, but can be compared to competitors' performance and to various definitions of cost of capital.

Perhaps you have a chief executive who likes to say, "Find a way!" If so, maybe you should try the profit geometry approach to breakeven analysis for your company or various segments of it.

CHAPTER 7 RESPONSIBILITY ACCOUNTING AND PERFORMANCE EVALUATION

REVIEWING THE CHAPTER

Objective 1: Define responsibility accounting and describe a responsibility accounting system (pp. 231-235).

1. Responsibility accounting is an information reporting system that (1) classifies financial data according to areas of responsibility in an organization and (2) reports the activities of managers by including only revenue and cost categories that are controllable by a particular manager.

2. A responsibility accounting system focuses on the *reporting* of information, not the *recording* of information. Using data that has already been recorded by the management accounting system, the responsibility accounting system simply reclassifies the information according to a manager's defined area of responsibility (responsibility center) and reports the information in a form tailored for each manager.

3. The corporate organization chart is important to a company's responsibility accounting system because that chart determines the flow of the reports. Each manager will be given a report containing only those revenues and/or costs that he or she controls. A condensed version of a lower manager's report will be included in each supervisor's report.

Objective 2: Identify the cost and revenue classifications that are controllable by a particular manager (p. 235).

4. A manager's controllable costs and revenues are those that result from his or her actions, influence, and decisions. For costs and revenues to be controlled and profits maximized, the system must identify the origin of the cost or revenue item and the person responsible for it. Problems in identifying controllable costs often arise at lower management levels. These managers usually have only partial authority to acquire and control resources or must share resources with another department. To counteract cost-control problems, individual managers should help identify their controllable costs and revenues.

Objective 3: Distinguish between a cost/expense center, a profit center, and an investment center (pp. 236-238).

5. The activity of a particular responsibility center dictates the extent of its manager's responsibility. The three types of responsibility centers are (a) cost/expense centers, (b) profit centers, and (c) investment centers.

6. Any organizational unit, such as a department or division, whose manager is responsible only for costs incurred by that unit is

known as a **cost/expense center.** Cost/ expense centers provide important support services but usually do not have direct connection with the sale of a company's final product. These centers' inputs (costs) are measurable in dollars but their outputs (product or service) cannot be easily measured in dollars. The Repair and Maintenance Department of a manufacturing company is a good example of a cost/ expense center.

7. When the manager of an organizational unit is responsible for revenues, costs, and resulting profits, the responsibility center is known as a **profit center.** The profit center is treated like a separate minibusiness and its manager is expected to run the business as if it were an autonomous unit. Profit centers are a means of controlling large, diverse companies. Through decentralized organization, control is delegated to profit-center managers. The cosmetics department of a large department store is an example of a profit center.

8. An **investment center** is a profit center whose manager can make significant decisions about the assets used by the center. In addition to revenue generation and cost control, an investment center's manager is evaluated on the effective use of assets employed to earn profits. **Return on investment,** which is computed by dividing net income by the dollar value of the assets employed to generate income, is the means used to evaluate the manager of an investment center.

Objective 4: Identify and describe the behavioral principles of performance evaluation (pp. 239–240).

9. Performance evaluation is the application of appropriate financial measurement techniques designed to compare actual results with expectations so that performance can be evaluated and judged. Performance evaluation is important because it helps management control operations and achieve goals. In order for an evaluation system to be successful, certain behavioral and operational principles must be followed.

10. **Managers should have input into the standards and goals set for their areas of responsibility.** This process is called par-

ticipative goal setting. When a manager is involved in setting his or her goals, the goals are more realistic to the manager, and thus the manager's incentive to reach those goals is greater.

11. **Top management's support of the evaluation process should be evident.** This support is shown by communicating plans and goals clearly. Clear communication accomplishes two important objectives. First, each manager has a very good idea of the targets to work toward. Second, top management demonstrates that it is deeply involved in the performance evaluation process and will support managers in their efforts to reach targets.

12. **Only controllable cost and revenue items with significant variances should be the focus of performance reports.** Holding someone responsible for what he or she does not control decreases the effectiveness of the evaluation system and generates negative feelings. In addition, when there are several cost and revenue items under the control of one manager, designing the report to focus directly on items needing immediate attention saves the manager valuable time.

13. **Opportunity for manager response should be a part of the evaluation process.** Top management should praise good performance. If performance is substandard, the manager who is responsible should be given an opportunity to defend his or her actions. There may be a good reason for the variance.

Objective 5: State the operational principles of performance evaluation and explain how they are interrelated (pp. 240–242).

14. Making a performance evaluation system operable requires that a set of operational principles be followed. The operational principles are closely linked with the behavioral principles, and the operational principles are all supported by the behavioral principles.

15. **Provide accurate and suitable measures of performance.** A suitable measure of performance is one that results in a realistic and attainable goal. Examples include predetermined budgets and standards, perfor-

mances of other people in comparable jobs, and past performances in the same job classification. Nonfinancial measures, such as labor hours or units of production, can be as useful as dollar measures.

16. **Communicate expectations to appropriate managers and segment leaders to be evaluated.** The system of communication should run both up and down the organization hierarchy, providing feedback that is essential to the success of a performance evaluation system.

17. **Identify the responsibilities of each manager.** A manager cannot legitimately be held accountable for actions that were not his or her specific responsibility. Identifying specific responsibility occurs when the responsibility accounting system is devised.

18. **Compare actual performance with a suitable base.** In order to evaluate performance, it is important to compare what actually happened with a measure of what was anticipated.

19. **Prepare performance reports that highlight areas of concern.** If there are twenty or more controllable cost and revenue items, highlighting items that are significantly over or under budget leads to an efficient review of operations.

20. **Analyze important cause-and-effect relationships.** Determining a budget variance is only the beginning of the performance evaluation process. It is equally important to identify the reason(s) behind the variance. For example, the purchase of inferior materials may explain sudden high labor costs. Much of this information must come from the manager being evaluated.

Objective 6: Prepare a performance evaluation report for (a) a cost/expense center, (b) a profit center, and (c) an investment center (pp. 243-253).

21. Implementation of a performance reporting system to generate the performance report requires the following eight steps:
   a. Develop a responsibility accounting system. This process begins with the creation of a detailed organization chart of the company, so that all managerial positions that will become part of the performance reporting system can be identified.
   b. Determine adequate performance measures.
   c. Identify and communicate each manager's duties and performance expectations.
   d. Establish a system of communication that involves each manager in setting his or her goals.
   e. Develop a performance report that contains only cost and revenue items under a manager's control.
   f. Allow manager input on the causes of significant budget variances, once budgeted and actual amounts have been measured and compared.
   g. Work out with the manager corrective measures for problems.
   h. Create a strong system of manager rewards and feedback.

22. For a cost/expense center, the performance report should distinguish between the controllable and uncontrollable costs of the manager. The report for the manager of a profit center should distinguish between controllable and uncontrollable revenues and costs. The report for the manager of an investment center adds return on investment data to the report of the manager of a profit center.

Testing Your Knowledge

Matching

Match each term with its definition by writing the appropriate letter in the blank.

____ 1. Responsibility center

____ 2. Return on investment

____ 3. Behavioral Principle #4: Opportunities for manager response to any part of the evaluation process.

____ 4. Performance evaluation

____ 5. Profit center

____ 6. Cost/expense center

____ 7. Operational Principle #3: Identify the responsibilities of each manager.

____ 8. Operational Principle #2: Communicate expectations to appropriate managers and segment leaders to be evaluated.

____ 9. Investment center

a. Any organizational unit, such as a department or division, whose manager is responsible only for costs incurred by that unit.

b. Where the manager of an organizational unit is responsible for revenues, costs, and resulting profits.

c. A profit center whose manager can make significant decisions about the assets used by that center.

d. Mr. Brown is manager of the data processing department. Determining Mr. Brown's responsibilities is an example of this operational principle.

e. Allowing Ms. Smith, manager of the welding department, to explain significant budget variances is an example of following this behavioral principle.

f. Carefully explaining to managers what is expected of them is an example of following this operational principle.

g. The application of appropriate financial measurement techniques designed to compare actual results with expectations so that performance can be evaluated and judged.

h. The measure used to evaluate managers of investment centers.

i. Defined responsibility areas of specific managers or management positions.

Completion

Use the lines provided to complete each item.

1. Name the three responsibility centers.

_____

_____

_____

2. The cafeteria in a manufacturing plant would be what type of responsibility center?

_____

3. What type of responsibility center would the women's clothing section of a department store be?

_____

4. What type of responsibility center would the molding department in a manufacturing plant be?

_____

5. The formula for return on investment is

_____

6. List the four Behavioral Principles of Performance Evaluation.

_____

_____

_____

7. List the six Operational Principles of Performance Evaluation.

_____

_____

_____

_____

_____

_____

True-False

Circle T if the statement is true, F if it is false.

T F **1.** Responsibility accounting centers on the recording, not the reporting, of cost and revenue data.

T F **2.** If the manager cannot control a cost or revenue item, that item is either not included in his or her performance report or it is separated from the controllable items.

T F **3.** Managers themselves should help to identify costs and revenues that they will be held accountable for in their performance reports.

T F **4.** If a cost is allocated to a department, it can still be considered controllable by the manager of that department.

T F **5.** A profit center must be directly involved with sales of the company's product or service in order to be accounted for as a profit center.

T F **6.** Since an investment center is a profit center carried one step further, the manager of an investment center must be responsible for cost, revenues, and resulting profits.

T F **7.** Listing only items with significant budget variances focuses attention on factors needing immediate action, thus saving valuable manager time.

T F **8.** According to the operational principles, the system of communication should be two way in order to communicate top management's expectations to managers and to provide feedback from managers to top management.

T F **9.** Identifying the responsibilities of each manager is the last step in the performance evaluation process.

Multiple Choice

Circle the letter of the best answer.

1. Which of the following is not a characteristic of a controllable cost?
   a. The cost can be regulated or influenced by the manager of the department.
   b. The cost is allocated based on direct labor hours of the department.
   c. The cost can be directly traced to a department or cost objective.
   d. The decision to incur the cost is made by the manager.

2. Which of the following fixed costs is controllable by the manager of a cost/expense center?
   a. depreciation
   b. property taxes
   c. fixed cost of supervision
   d. none of the above, since all fixed costs are considered uncontrollable by the manager of a cost/expense center

3. Which of the following is a characteristic of a cost/expense center?
   a. Input is measured in dollars, output is measured in units.
   b. The center usually does not have a direct connection with the end product.
   c. Its manager is charged only with producing a good quality product at an acceptable cost.
   d. All of the above

4. Which of the following costs are not controllable by the manager of an investment center?
   a. corporate costs assigned to the center based on the value of the center's assets
   b. property taxes on property that is under the manager's control
   c. depreciation on the center's assets
   d. the center's fixed supervision costs

5. Involving the manager in the budget-setting process reflects which of the following performance evaluation principles?
   a. Top management support of the evaluation process should be evident.
   b. Managers should have input into the budgets and targets set for their areas of responsibility.
   c. Only controllable cost and revenue items with significant variances should be the focus of performance reports.
   d. Opportunity for manager response to poor performance should be a part of the evaluation process.

6. Manager Jones worked her department very hard to achieve the 12 percent return on investment wanted by top management. Her performance was not praised. Instead, top management criticized her for slightly decreased employee morale and did not allow Manager Jones to explain the reason for the decrease. What behavioral principle has not been followed?
   a. Managers should have input into the standards set for their areas of responsibility.
   b. Top management's support of the evaluation process should be evident.
   c. Only controllable cost and revenue items with significant variances should be the focus of performance reports.
   d. Managers should be given opportunities to respond to any part of the evaluation process.

7. Accurate and suitable measures of worker performance do not include which of the following?
   a. Performances of other people in comparable jobs
   b. Past performances in the same job classification
   c. Targets developed by the workers
   d. Predetermined budgets

8. The performance report for the Marketing Department has been prepared. However, no one can decide whether the numbers shown on the report represent good or bad results. Which of the following operational principles needs to be applied?
   a. Identify the responsibilities of each manager.
   b. Analyze important cause and effect relationships.
   c. Compare actual performance with a suitable base.
   d. Communicate expectations to appropriate managers and segment leaders to be evaluated.

9. A large unfavorable labor variance in the Molding Department was reported on the performance report. The reason for the high labor cost is poor quality materials acquired by the Purchasing Department. This fact was not noted, and the manager of the Molding Department was criticized. What operational principle has not been followed?
   a. Identify the responsibilities of each manager.
   b. Analyze important cause and effect relationships.
   c. Compare actual performance with a suitable base.
   d. Communicate expectations to appropriate managers and segment leaders to be evaluated.

10. Which of the following is a step in implementing a performance reporting system?
    a. Devise a reporting format that will contain only cost and revenue items under a manager's control.
    b. Identify specific duties and operating expectations and communicate to each manager.
    c. Design a strong system of rewards and feedback for managers.
    d. All of the above.

Applying Your Knowledge

Exercises

1. Analysis of organizational hierarchy.

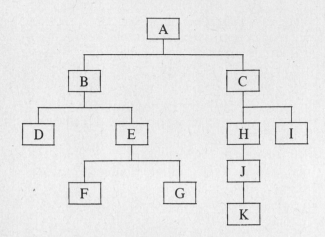

For each department identified below, list the other departments that would contribute information to its performance report.

Department	Contributing Departments
B	_____
C	_____
H	_____

2. The following cost and revenue information relates to Department X of Company Y.

Inventment in plant assets, $800,000.

	Actual	Budgeted
Revenue from sales	$900,000	$870,000
Cost of Goods Sold	750,000	700,000
Storage expenses	3,000	49,000
Selling expenses	1,000	900
Depreciation*	500	500
Property tax*	1,000	1,200
Corporate costs*	4,000	3,500

*Allocated to department

a. Prepare a performance report, treating Department X as a profit center.
b. Prepare a performance report, treating Department X and an investment center.

How to Construct a Successful Performance Appraisal System

In this, the first installment of a two-part article, the authors examine why performance appraisal systems fail.

Few would argue that the design and implementation of an effective performance appraisal (PA) system for an entire organization, a department, or a work unit is one of the most difficult tasks faced by managers and human resource development (HRD) professionals. Surveys consistently indicate user dissatisfaction and recurring costly revisions. Expectations are so low that a "good" performance appraisal system is often viewed as one in which managers simply complete the forms, after considerable prodding, and forward them to the personnel department to be filed. In a "poor" performance appraisal system, the forms are seldom even completed!

The frustration (and loss of credibility and power) of those in HRD over performance appraisal is matched by that of the users. Managers required to complete the ratings often see performance appraisals as another time-consuming, personnel-paperwork requirement, having little utility in solving such "real" managerial problems as meeting deadlines, containing costs, improving productivity, or deciding whom to promote. Subordinates being rated often view the performance appraisal system as yet another indication of management's capricious decision-making, subjectivity, and prejudice. They see few rewards given to those receiving the highest ratings withheld from those rated as merely average. In fact, almost everyone receives high ratings! Finally, neither raters nor ratees use the performance appraisal system as a tool to provide feedback and improve performance.

In short, even if the performance appraisal forms are completed, do the results matter? Is the performance appraisal system actually used to make managerial decisions or solve manager's problems? Is it used to manage performance?

The key to improve the effectiveness of performance appraisal systems is not to design

Source: Article by Craig Eric Schneier, Richard W. Beatty, and Lloyd S. Baird. Reprinted from the April 1980 issue of *Training and Development Journal.*

another form or fine-tune an existing form, but to design a performance management (PM) system. Such a system not only enables managers to solve performance problems, but also enables HRD specialists and staff to provide a useful tool and a successful program.

Deciding What to Appraise

Appraisals systems fail for a variety of reasons (see Figure 1). For all but the most elementary jobs, identifying appropriate appraisal criteria is difficult. We legitimately can evaluate an assembly-line worker on the number of units which meet quality control standards, or a typist on accuracy, and we can measure their performance with agreed-upon methods. But what about initiative, appearance, tact, or organization skills? Should they be included, and if so, how should they be measured? When considering professional or administrative positions, or any positions with a variety of tasks, unprogrammed work, and complex requirements, the measurement problem becomes acute. Even if we can determine what ought to be measured, we must still determine how well people must perform. That is, performance standards themselves must be set. Exactly how many errors is the typist allowed to make per page? Or, how effective at leading group discussion must the manager be? Answers can vary across raters, across units within a single organization, and over time.

Many appraisal systems stress "objective" measures. Typically, these end up as easily quantified indices or deadlines that may not capture the essence of the work. The aim of appraisal systems is not to quantify everything, but rather to avoid arbitrary, capricious, or biased measurements (see Figure 2). Between objective and arbitrary measures are many based on sound judgment, agreed upon by raters and ratees, illustrated and defined fully, and related to job success. Expecting all measures to be "objective" is unrealistic and often irrelevant. Appraisal requires judgment.

Managers need to make informed, accurate, data-based judgments—some may be quantifiable, some not—about performance. The role of HRD staff is to provide the tools to help managers make these judgments and to monitor accuracy, consistency, and defensibility. To take out of appraisal the legitimate roles of observer, measurer, and judge under a guise of objectivity dooms the system to failure.

Judgment Problems

The second set of performance appraisal problems comes from the raters. No matter how conscientious and well-meaning a rater may be, human judgment is subjective. We understand relatively little about observing behavior, recalling it, interpreting its causes and effects, evaluating its desirability, and ultimately rating an employee on an appraisal form. The manner in which the raters process information about rate behavior may affect the results more than the ratee's behavior itself. Performance appraisal means judgment and information processing, not merely completing forms.

One manager might observe a subordinate performing well and attribute it to high ability. Another manager who views the same subordinate might feel the task was not very difficult. The first manager, attributing behavior to an internal cause (the subordinate's own aiblity) might give a high rating. The second manager, attributing behavior to an external cause (the nature of the task), might give a lower rating. People use their own conditioning, perspectives, values, expectations, philosophies, experiences, biases, prejudices, and interpersonal styles when making ratings. Due to judgment problems, performance appraisal become quite difficult, with lenient and otherwise less-than-accurate ratings common, regardless of the type of form used.

Few performance appraisal system users enjoy the prospect of setting standards. Managers can judge how well a person is doing in three ways (see Figure 3). People are successful in jobs because of what they achieve (results), what they do (behaviors), and/or what they are (personal characteristics).

Managers work with subordinates to determine what specific achievements, behaviors, and characteristics lead to successful performance

---

Figure 1 – Performance Appraisal (PA) System Problems, Symptoms, and Potential Cures

The Measurement Problem: Deciding What to Evaluate	The Judgment Problem: Appraising Performance	The Policy Problem: Using the Results of the Appraisal	The Organization Problem: Recognizing How Managers Work and the Organization Culture
Symptoms: Ambiguity in roles and resibilities of each job	**Symptoms:** Disagreement on ratings	**Symptoms:** Top management fails to reward managers who are excellent in staff assessment and development	**Symptoms:** Appraisal forms not completed
Job performance is difficult to quantify	Reviewing official changes ratings	Marginal performers receive promotions or salary increases	Managers complain about time requirements
No clear statement of overall objectives of units or organization	Appeals, grievances, accusations of bias, discrimination		System perceived to belong to designers, not users
Appraisal contains only numerical indices			Personnel/human resource specialists take "enforcer," not "advisor" role
			System revised frequently
Potential Cures: Job analysis and credible position description	**Potential Cures:** Observable, behaviorally based criteria	**Potential Cures:** Top management actually uses PA itself	**Potential Cures:** Implement PA using the Performance Management (PM) Model
Outcomes for each job identified	Performance documented over time	Policies governing use of PA consistently applied	
Overall goals of units and of organization set	Rater training and practice	Performance-contingent reward system in operation	
Train managers to make documented judgments	Effective communications of of performance expectations		

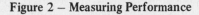

Figure 2 – Measuring Performance

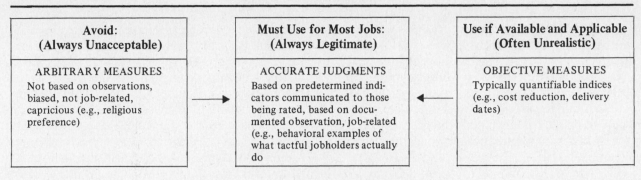

Avoid: (Always Unacceptable)	Must Use for Most Jobs: (Always Legitimate)	Use if Available and Applicable (Often Unrealistic)
ARBITRARY MEASURES Not based on observations, biased, not job-related, capricious (e.g., religious preference)	ACCURATE JUDGMENTS Based on predetermined indicators communicated to those being rated, based on documented observation, job-related (e.g., behavioral examples of what tactful jobholders actually do)	OBJECTIVE MEASURES Typically quantifiable indices (e.g., cost reduction, delivery dates)

Figure 3 – Simplifying Appraisal Judgments

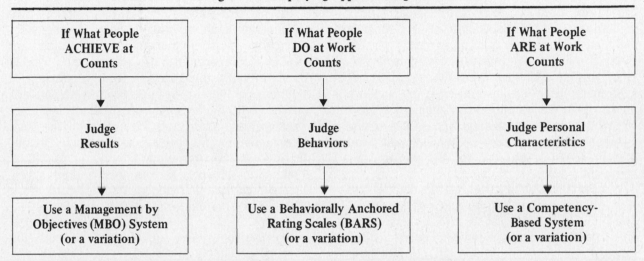

If What People ACHIEVE at Counts	If What People DO at Work Counts	If What People ARE at Work Counts
↓	↓	↓
Judge Results	Judge Behaviors	Judge Personal Characteristics
↓	↓	↓
Use a Management by Objectives (MBO) System (or a variation)	Use a Behaviorally Anchored Rating Scales (BARS) (or a variation)	Use a Competency-Based System (or a variation)

and, with the assistance of HRD staff and the performer, develop viable standards. While there are innumerable varieties of methods for determining performance standards, the method used must be relevant in the context in which it will be used. That is, performance standards must be helpful in setting and communicating performance expectations, directing effort toward successful performance, providing performance-related feedback, solving performance problems, and linking performance to rewards. Skill and practice are needed, but setting standards gets easier when manager and subordinate begin to describe achievements, behaviors, and characteristics required.

Performance appraisal standards and judgments (ratings) must pass certain legal tests. Specific job-related descriptions of performance are appropriate. Rating personnel characteristics—what people are—is neither illegal nor invalid, despite the problems typically associated with trait-based rating systems. The laws do not say personal characteristics such as initiative, dependability, interpersonal skill, or tact do not help determine success—managers know they do and use them—but rather that these characteristics require unambiguous, consistently applied, well-communicated, job-relevant illustrations and definitions. Developing a set of competencies is often a useful approach, as well as a valid one!

Policy Problems

Even in organizations where careful attention has been given to identifying measures, setting performance standards, and reducing subjectivity and bias in human judgment, the performance appraisal system may be ineffective if its results are not used or are applied inconsistently (see Figure 1). Solutions involve policies that mandate the use of performance appraisal results as a rationale for reward administration, promotion, job assignment, and training. Those workers given the highest evaluations must receive certain performance-contingent rewards. Just as important, those managers who assess and develop their subordinates effectively, using the performance appraisal system as a tool, should be considered successful managers and rewarded appropriately. If human resource decisions are not tied to the results of the appraisal through a set of well-articulated and enforced policies, the performance appraisal system becomes a relic, not a management tool.

Reality Problems

The measurement and judgment problems discussed above can be alleviated through various techniques relating to design of performance appraisal formats and training of raters, respectively. (Specific suggestions are offered in Part II of this series.) However, the policy issues associated with the transition from performance appraisal to performance management require forceful, committed management, trust in the accuracy of performance appraisal results, and a clear sense of purpose for the performance appraisal system.

What remains as a considerable deterrent to performance appraisal system effectiveness, however, does not relate to psychometric properties of scales, information-processing characteristics of raters, or clarity of policies governing the system, but rather to failure to recognize the realities of managerial work and organizational culture or environment. Performance appraisal systems often clash with the way managers perform their tasks on a day-to-

day basis, what degree of control they have, and other realities related to organizational life (Figure 1).

As Figure 4 indicates, performance appraisal systems typically require managers to plan extensively (e.g., setting objectives), interact formally with others (e.g., in formal performance review sessions), adhere to prescribed systems (e.g., completing forms at a certain time each year), and take specific actions (e.g., promotion, pay increase). Performance appraisal also requires managers to relinquish the "superior" role to some extent in order to accept the "coach" role or to allow for participation in goal-setting or performance feedback discussions. Managers may not view their role as including such administrative or personnel functions as performance appraisal; there are HRD staff specialists for these activities. In conflict with these performance appraisal requirements, studies of managerial work indicate that most managers prefer the nonroutine, possess less than complete control over such decisions as promotions, and engage in activities of short duration. It is no wonder they seldom embrace a performance appraisal system—it clashes with the realities of their work and what they enjoy about their jobs.

Figure 5 shows that the effective operation of an appraisal system often conflicts with the typical organization's culture. Variance in performance levels decreases as we move up the hierarchy. A "natural selection" process, while certainly not foolproof, allows the best performers to reach the top. Yet performance appraisal systems may not be very useful if

---

Figure 4 – Performance Appraisal (PA) Systems Fail to Recognize the Realities of Managerial Work*

The Reality of Managerial Work Is:		Performance Appraisal (PA) Systems Require:
• Numerous Activities of Short Duration • *Ad hoc,* Informal Interactions • A Penchant for the Nonroutine and for Variety • Interest in Taking Decisive Action • Effectiveness Due to Legitimate Authority and Supervisory Role • Low Priority and Little Importance Attached to Administrative or Personnel Tasks and Systems	?	• Advance Planning • Formal Sessions, Meetings, Interviews • Prescribed Systems, Schedules, Forms • Impact of PA Results Questionable, Indirect • Take Role of Coach or Counselor and of Equal Participation in Discussions • Sponsored and Designed by Administrative/ Personnel/Human Resource Development Staffs

Chapter 7

Figure 5 — Performance Appraisal (PA) Systems Fail to Recognize the Realities of Organization Culture

The Reality of Organization Culture Is:		Performance Appraisal (PA) Systems Require:
• Ever-Smaller Variance in Performance Levels for Upper-Level Positions • Little Time and Resources Available for Administrative Tasks • Seniority and Loyalty Rewarded • Success (and Failure) Often a Function of Numerous, Complex Interdependent Relationships • Definitions of Success (and Failure) Difficult to Develop and Subject to Disagreement • Performance Expectations, Levels, and Priorities Change Rapidly in a Dynamic Job Environment	?	• Variance in Performance Levels Necessary for Reward Allocation • Considerable Time and Resources • Performance Rewarded • A Single Individual's Evaluation is Sought • Accuracy, Consistency, Equity, and Relative Objectivity Necessary • Current Information in Order to Retain Credibility

*Figures 4 and 5 are adapted from M. W. McCall and D. L. DeVries, *Appraisal in Context: Clashing with Organizational Realities* (Center for Creative Leadership, 1977). See also L. S. Baird, R. W. Beatty, and C. E. Schneier, *The Performance Appraisal Sourcebook* (Human Resource Development Press, 1982).

everyone receives high ratings. How can people be rewarded differentially? A seniority system rewards long tenure and loyalty, while performance appraisal rewards performance. Much success or failure in organizations cannot be traced to a single individual. Yet performance appraisal typically evaluates a single person. Further, objective measures of desired performance and/or those easily agreed upon often do not exist. Yet performance appraisal requires agreement on the definition of successful performance and its indicators. In short, performance appraisal often clashes with the way organizations actually work; no wonder performance appraisals often don't work.

Towards Performance Management

An examination of performance appraisal system problems, symptoms, and potential cures provides many answers as to why performance appraisal seldom works. What those designing, implementing, evaluating, and using performance appraisal systems in organizations must realize is that such systems cannot be successful unless they are consistent with the realities of managerial work and organizational environments. They must be "user-friendly" and "customer-driven." They must be integrated into the day-to-day activities of managers to help them solve real problems.

An increasing number of organizations have found that appraisal systems are effective if they enhance the superior-subordinate relationship by allowing for frequent communication, specification of expectation, accurate evaluations, and problem solving. It is a *management* cycle, not an appraisal cycle, that facilitates high performance.

References

1. Schneier, C. E. & Beatty, R. W. (1984). Designing a legally defensible performance appraisal system. In M. Cohen and R. Golembiewski (Eds.), *Public Personnel Up-date.* Marcel Deliker.
2. Mintzberg, H. (1973). *The nature of managerial work.* Harper and Row.

CHAPTER 8 THE BUDGETING PROCESS

REVIEWING THE CHAPTER

Objective 1: Describe the structure and contents of a budget (pp. 278-281).

1. Unlike many of the areas studied in accounting, there is no standard form or structure for a budget. A budget's structure depends on what is being budgeted, the size of the organization preparing the budget, the degree to which the budgeting process is integrated into the financial structure of the enterprise, and the amount of training the budget preparer has in his or her background.

2. A budget should contain enough information presented in an orderly manner to communicate its purpose to the budget's user. Targets should be defined and identified. The amount of information should be limited so that the document does not lose its meaning. The contents should be clearly labeled.

Objective 2: Identify the five groups of budgeting principles, and explain the principles in each group (pp. 281-284).

3. The principles of effective budgeting are (a) long-range goals principles, (b) short-range goals and strategies principles, (c) human responsibilities and interaction principles (d) budget housekeeping principles, and (e) follow-up principles.
   a. Before annual operating budgets can be developed, top management must communicate their long-range goals for the company to those who will prepare the budgets. The expected quality of products or services, company growth, and profit expectations are three examples of long-range goals.
   b. The short-range yearly operating budget turns the long-range goals into detailed plans for the coming year. The budget director is responsible for developing the annual budget and its timetable.
   c. The budget director should bring all levels of management into the budgeting process. This effort leads to **participative budgeting.** Budget implementation tends to be less effective if top management simply dictates its goals to lower-level management or displays little support for the participants' input.
   d. Budgets should be based on realistic, not inflated, goals, and deadlines for their development should always be met. In addition, they should be flexible enough to deal with changes in revenues and expenses during the period.
   e. Finally, follow-up principles are part of budgetary control. The budget should be checked at all times to assure that operations are going as planned. Performance reports should be prepared for each operating segment so that problem areas can be identified, analyzed, and handled in the next period's budget.

Objective 3: Define the concept of budgetary control (pp. 284-285).

4. **Budgetary control** means planning future company activities and controlling operations to help achieve those plans. The planning function should consist of projecting a long-term plan covering five to ten years and a short-term plan covering one year at a time. Long-term plans are general in nature and must be translated by management into specific goals for the year. Short-term plans, which are expressed in a **period budget,** consist of a forecast of operations as well as specific planned activities for segments of the company.

Objective 4: Identify the components of a master budget, and describe how they are related to each other (pp. 285-289).

5. The **master budget** is a combined set of departmental or functional period budgets that have been consolidated into forecasted financial statements for the whole company. Preparation of the master budget consists of preparing (a) detailed operating or period budgets, (b) the forecasted income statement, and (c) the forecasted balance sheet.

6. The detailed period budgets mentioned above normally include the (a) **sales budget** (in units), (b) **production budget** (in units), (c) **selling expense budget,** (d) **revenue budget,** (e) **materials usage budget,** (f) **materials purchase budget,** (g) **labor hour requirement budget,** (h) **labor dollar budget,** (i) **factory overhead budget,** (j) **general and administrative expense budget,** (k) **capital expenditure budget.** These budgets are interrelated, and must be prepared in a certain order (for instance, the sales budget must always be prepared first). At this point, a thorough review of Figure 8-1 is recommended.

7. Budget implementation will be successful if there is (a) proper communication of budget targets to all key operating personnel and (b) support and encouragement from top management.

Objective 5: Prepare a period budget (pp. 289-291).

8. Responsibility accounting, together with the concepts of cost allocation and cost accumulation, are cost accounting tools that are very helpful in preparing the period budget (one-year budget).
   a. When a responsibility accounting system is used, budget preparation begins with the communication of annual sales and production plans from top management to the various managerial levels. This information then allows the segment managers to develop detailed operating budgets for their areas of responsibility. Finally, these managers submit the detailed budgets to the budget director, who puts together the operating budget for the entire company.
   b. When unit sales have been forecast, cost-volume-profit analysis can be used to determine associated costs and to predict net income for the period.

Objective 6: State the purpose and makeup of a cash budget (pp. 291-295).

9. A **cash flow forecast (cash budget)** is a summary of all planned cash transactions found in the detailed period budgets and in the forecasted income statement. For example, cash receipts may be predicted mainly from the sales budget. The main objectives of a cash budget are to (a) show the projected ending cash balance and (b) allow management to anticipate periods of high or low cash availability. An expected period of low cash availability, for example, would alert management that short-term borrowing may be necessary. Care must be taken to include only cash inflows and outflows that are likely during the period.

Objective 7: Prepare a cash budget (pp. 295-297).

10. The cash budget consists of (projected) cash receipts, cash disbursements, beginning cash balance, and ending cash balance.

Testing Your Knowledge

Matching

Match each term with its definition by writing the appropriate letter in the blank.

_____ **1.** Budgetary control

_____ **2.** Period budget

_____ **3.** Participative budgeting

_____ **4.** Master budget

_____ **5.** Cash budget (cash flow forecast)

_____ **6.** Sales budget

_____ **7.** Budget director

_____ **8.** Production budget

a. The basis for all other operating budgets

b. A combined set of departmental or functional period budgets that have been consolidated into forecasted financial statements for the whole company

c. The planning of and control over future company activities

d. The basis for the materials, labor, and overhead budgets

e. The involvement of all levels of management in the budgeting process

f. The person in charge of the budgeting process

g. The budget prepared after all period budgets and the forecasted income statement

h. Yearly operating plans for a segment of the business

Completion

Use the lines provided to complete each item.

1. List the five groups of effective budgeting principles.

_____

_____

_____

_____

_____

2. Which five budgets can be prepared immediately after the production budget?

_____

_____

_____

_____

_____

True-False

Circle T if the statement is true, F if it is false.

T F **1.** Budgetary control refers only to the control of operations.

T F **2.** A long-term plan is called a master budget.

T F **3.** A period budget refers to planned activities for a segment of the business only.

T F **4.** A projection of sales must be made before the production budget can be devised.

T F **5.** The sales budget is expressed in sales dollars, whereas the revenue budget is expressed in unit sales.

T F **6.** Monitoring the budget is considered a follow-up principle of effective budgeting.

T F **7.** Depreciation expense would be listed as a cash disbursement in the cash budget.

T F **8.** Establishing long-range goals should go on before establishing short-range ones.

T F **9.** The capital expenditures budget concerns purchases of facilities and equipment.

T F **10.** Total sales for a period would be included in that period's cash budget as part of cash receipts.

T F **11.** The materials usage budget must be prepared before the materials purchases budget.

T F **12.** Cost-volume-profit analysis is very helpful in budget preparation.

T F **13.** Information must be provided from the cash budget in order to prepare the general and administrative expense budget.

T F **14.** The labor hour requirement budget must be prepared before the labor dollar budget.

Multiple Choice

Circle the letter of the best answer.

1. The first step involved in preparing a master budget is preparing
   a. a forecasted income statement.
   b. a general operating budget.
   c. a forecasted balance sheet.
   d. detailed period budgets.

2. Which of the following components of the master budget must be prepared before the others?
   a. Labor dollar budget
   b. Cost of goods sold forecast
   c. Production budget
   d. Materials purchases budget

3. The period budgets should begin with a forecast of
   a. overhead.
   b. production.
   c. sales.
   d. direct labor.

4. The cash budget is prepared
   a. before all period budgets are prepared.
   b. after the forecasted income statement but before the forecasted balance sheet.
   c. as the last step in the master budget.
   d. only if the company has doubts about its debt-paying ability.

5. Integrating realism and flexibility into budget preparation is a
   a. human responsibilities and interaction principle.
   b. follow-up principle.
   c. short-range goals and strategies principle.
   d. budget housekeeping principle.

6. Which of the following budgets would not be a source of cash disbursements in the cash budget?
   a. Sales budget
   b. Capital expenditure budget
   c. Selling expense budget
   d. Labor dollar budget

7. Budget preparation
   a. should be done entirely by independent professionals hired by the company.
   b. should involve all levels of management.
   c. should be done entirely by the budget director.
   d. should be done entirely by top management.

8. The following budget information is provided for Schramm Company:

Quarter	1	2	3
Sales in units	20,000	25,000	23,000
Production in units	23,000	24,000	21,000

Each finished unit requires three pounds of material. The inventory of material at the end of each quarter should equal 10 percent of the following quarter's production needs. How many pounds of material should be purchased for the second quarter?
   a. 71,100 lb.
   b. 72,000 lb.
   c. 74,400 lb.
   d. 75,000 lb.

Exercises

1. E & J produces and sells a single product. Expected sales for the next four months are:

April	10,000 units
May	12,000
June	15,000
July	9,000

   The company needs a *production budget* for the second quarter. Experience indicates that end-of-month Finished Goods Inventory must equal 10 percent of the following month's sales in units. At the end of March, 1,000 units were on hand. Compute production needs for the second quarter.

E & J Company
Production Budget
For the Quarter Ended June 30, 19xx

---

2. Rensch Enterprises needs a cash budget for the month of June. The following information is available:

a. The cash balance on June 1 is $7,000.

b. Sales for May and June are $80,000 and $60,000, respectively. Cash collections on sales are 30 percent in the month of the sale, 65 percent in the following month, and 5 percent uncollectible.

c. General and administrative expenses are budgeted at $24,000 for June. Depreciation represents $2,000 of this amount.

d. Inventory purchases will total $30,000 in June, and totaled $40,000 in May. Half of inventory purchases are always paid for in the month of the purchase. The remainder are paid for in the following month.

e. Office furniture costing $3,000 will be purchased for cash in June, and selling expenses (exclusive of $2,000 in depreciation) are budgeted at $14,000.

f. The company must maintain a minimum ending cash balance of $4,000, and can borrow from the bank in multiples of $100. All loans are repaid after 60 days.

In the space provided, prepare a cash budget for Rensch Enterprises for the month of June.

Rensch Enterprises
Cash Budget
For the Month Ending June 30, 19xx

Crossword Puzzle
for Chapters 7 and 8

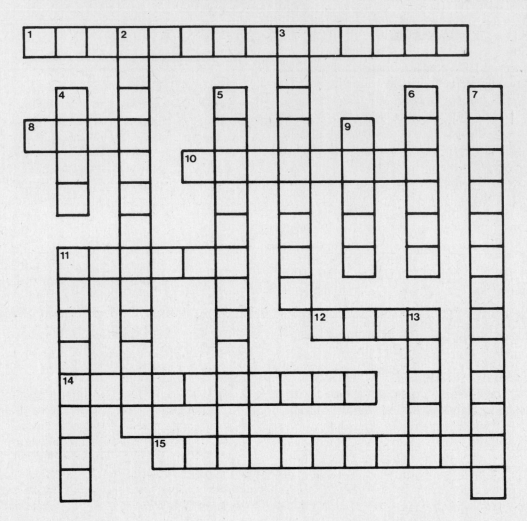

ACROSS

1. Accounting system that assigns costs to managers
8. Business expenditure
10. Cash flow projection
11. See 15-Across
12. One of last budgets prepared
14. Return on ——
15. With 11-Across, document disclosing budget variances

DOWN

2. Budgeting involving all levels of management
3. Relating to a financial plan
4. Business target
5. Business unit responsible for both revenues and costs
6. That which is compared with "budgeted"
7. Consisting of autonomous segments
9. First budget prepared
11. Cash budget section
13. —— responsibilities and interaction principles

"What Supervisors Don't Like About Budget Evaluations"

One of the primary methods used by top-level managers to motivate subordinates is to relate organizational rewards to performance. Given the proper reward system, individuals tend to engage in behavior that they feel will improve their performance or, more specifically, their performance evaluations. The emphasis here is on evaluations because rewards are generally tied to them rather than directly to actual performance. Evaluations should reflect performance, but subordinates react to several aspects of the evaluation.

First, the subordinate acts or reacts in accordance with the particular measure or data used. For example, accounting data representing actual results of operations are commonly compared with budget information in evaluating a supervisor's performance. Other measures may pertain to such factors as dependability, initiative taken on the job, and ability to plan and control operations.

If accounting data are used as a measure of performance, the supervisor will tend to take actions designed to improve the evaluation. While many aspects of an accounting system promote desirable behavior, other aspects of the same system may result in behavior which is undesirable. Consideration must be given to this important aspect in selecting evaluation measures.

Second, a subordinate's behavior may be shaped also by the way the data are used. If budget variances are used as a measure of performance, they should be used to identify areas for analysis. In this way the supervisor may be able to spot a problem and take appropriate action. On the other hand, if the variances are used rigidly as the measure of performance, the supervisor may be encouraged to initiate short-term fixes to the detriment of long-term productivity.

Moreover, the subordinate may not react to the actual use of the measure. He is more likely to react to the way in which he perceives that the data are used. Individuals react to perceptions, not necessarily to reality. If the subordinate's perception of the way data are used conflicts with the actual use of the measure by his superior, the resultant behavior is probably the same as if the superior did in fact use the data in the perceived manner.

Bearing these observations in mind, we undertook a study to identify measures frequently used in industry to evaluate performance, to identify the relationship between the measures, to determine how the measures were perceived to be used, and to draw some conclusions or implications from the findings.

How Research Was Designed

The research project was designed to identify different ways in which accounting and non-accounting-related data were perceived to be used for performance evaluation in actual business settings. Eight industrial companies agreed to distribute a questionnaire to their supervisors and provided a cover letter, signed by an upper-level manager, to encourage supervisors to respond. Only supervisors in charge of a budget unit were surveyed, and the questionnaires were returned directly to us to assure their confidentiality. This procedure resulted in 177 usable responses representing 61% of the total questionnaires distributed.

The questionnaire consisted of a list of 26 statements composed from the literature relevant to performance evaluation of supervisory personnel (Table 1). Supervisors were asked to indicate the extent to which they agreed with each of the statements on a five point scale, ranging from "strongly agree" to "strongly disagree."

Factor analysis was performed on the responses to identify the relevant measures and to provide a description of the manner in which

Source: Article by Paul J. Carruth, Thurrell O. McClendon, and Milton R. Ballard. Reprinted from the February 1983 issue of *Management Accounting.*

TABLE 1

The Questionnaire

Read each item carefully.

Indicate the extent to which you agree with each of the following statements concerning the manner in which your immediate superior evaluates your performance.

DRAW A CIRCLE around one of the five letters (A B C D E) following the statement to show the answer you have indicated.

A = Strongly agree   C = Somewhat agree   È = Strongly disagree
B = Agree   D = Disagree

1. Factors more significant than budget-related information are used in my evaluation.   A B C D E

2. Cooperation with colleagues receives high importance in my evaluation.   A B C D E

3. Budget-related information is the most important factor in my evaluation   A B C D E

4. My superior tends to use budget variances as a pressure device, by emphasizing "meeting the budget."   A B C D E

5. Ability to handle my subordinates is a very important factor in my evaluation.   A B C D E

6. My superior knows that at times budget variances can be confusing and misleading for evaluation purposes.   A B C D E

7. Dependability receives high importance in my evaluation.   A B C D E

8. I feel free to discuss budget variances with my superior.   A B C D E

9. My superior is more concerned with showing favorable short-term reports than with longer term effectiveness.   A B C D E

10. My superior questions budget reports, and uses them carefully in my evaluation.   A B C D E

11. Planning ability is a very important factor in my evaluation.   A B C D E

12. My superior listens to my problems in budget matters.   A B C D E

13. Budget variances are frequently mentioned to me during performance evaluation interviews.   A B C D E

14. Effort put into the job is a very important factor in my evaluation.   A B C D E

15. Budget-related information is rigidly used in evaluating my performance.   A B C D E

16. My superior mentions budgets while talking to me about my efficiency as a manager.   A B C D E

17. Knowledge of the work is a very important factor in my evaluation.   A B C D E

18. My superior holds me personally accountable for budget variances.   A B C D E

19. My superior is likely to ask about variances beyond my control.   A B C D E

20. Initiative on the job receives high importance in my evaluation.   A B C D E

21. My explanation of a variance is generally rejected on the grounds that the variance is simply unfavorable.   A B C D E

22. My superior believes that budget-related information must be supplemented by other sources of information.   A B C D E

23. Getting along with the boss is a very important factor in my evaluation.   A B C D E

24. My superior generally views an unfavorable budget variance as an indicator of poor managerial performance.   A B C D E

25. Attitude towards the work and company is a very important factor in my evaluation.   A B C D E

26. My superior expresses dissatisfaction to me when the budget has not been met.   A B C D E

supervisors perceived that accounting and non-accounting-related data are used in evaluating their performance. Factor analysis is a multivariate statistical technique used to examine the interrelationships among a large number of variables, to group the variables according to their common, underlying dimensions or factors, and to explain the variance in the responses in terms of these factors.

Several alternative models can be used. However, we used principal factoring with iteration (common factor analysis) using the varimax criterion for factor rotation. Factor significance was established by the eigenvalue greater than one criterion. Further details on the computational aspects of factor analysis can be found in other sources.[1]

Factor loadings represent the correlation between the statement and each factor identified in the solution. They are also the key to understanding the nature of a particular factor. For example, the solution value may range from 0.00 to ±1.00; the larger the absolute value the stronger the relationship that exists between the statement and the factor. The sign is also important. While a positive value represents direct correlation, a negative value indicates an inverse relationship; e.g., the statement may take on an opposite meaning in relation to that particular factor.

Through this technique, we identified four factors that explained 90.4% of the total variation in the responses to the survey. These factors were labeled (1) Budget-Rigidity (explained 45.1%), (2) Nonaccounting Style of Evaluation (27.8%), (3) Personal Accountability (8.9%), and (4) Budget Flexibility (8.6%). Budget-rigidity was characterized by supervisors who perceived that budget-related information was the most important element in their evaluations and that the data were used in a rigid or inflexible manner. The measures included in personal accountability also related to budgets, but emphasized individual responsibilities rather than the data. In addition, budget-flexibility uses accounting-related data, but implies a completely different approach. It is characterized by an awareness on the part of the superior that

budget variances can be confusing and misleading and that accounting information should be used with care during performance evaluations. The nonaccounting style of evaluation factor contained such measures as initiative, knowledge of the work, and effort put into the job.

What Do the Data Mean?

The factor—budget-rigidity—explained 45.1% of the total variance in responses to the questionnaire. This figure is almost twice as high as that for any other factor. Supervisors in this category perceived that budget-related information was the most important element in their evaluations and that the data were used in a rigid or inflexible manner. Both of these statements received exceptionally high factor loadings (0.756 and 0.791, respectively) as shown in Table 2. Supervisors also believed that they were evaluated by a superior who placed a major emphasis on "meeting the budget" and used budget variances as pressure devices.

Also related to the budget is factor three—personal accountability (Table 3). It explained another 8.9% of the total variance. While factor one—budget rigidity—focused on the budget data, this factor focused on personnel and reflects the idea that ultimately a particular supervisor must be held responsible for budget variances. Supervisors in this classification felt that their superiors did in fact hold them personally responsible for departures from the budget and that the superiors expressed dissatisfaction to them when budgets were not met. The dissatisfaction extended even to variances beyond their control. Combined, these two closely related factors accounted for 54% of the total variance in the responses.

Factor four—budget flexibility—also uses accounting-related data, but it implies a completely different approach. This factor (Table 4) is characterized by an awareness on the part of the superior that budget variances can be confusing and misleading and that accounting information should be used with care during the performance evaluation process. Thus, supervisors in this category felt free to discuss budget variances with their superiors and believed that their superiors actually listened to their budget-related problems. However, this factor explained only 8.6% of the variance in the responses to the questionnaire.

Factor two—nonaccounting style of evaluation—

[1] Many sources exist on factor analysis. However, an excellent choice would include Harry H. Harman, *Modern Factor Analysis*. The University of Chicago Press, Chicago, 1976; R. J. Rummel, *Applied Factor Analysis*. Northwestern University Press, Evanston, Ill., 1970; N. Nie and others, *Statistical Package for the Social Sciences*. McGraw-Hill, New York, 1975.

TABLE 2

Questionnaire Statements Associated With Factor One—Budget Rigidity

Statement		Factor loading
1	Factors more significant than budget-related information are used in my evaluation.	−0.546
3	Budget-related information is the most important factor in my evaluation.	0.756
4	My superior tends to use budget variances as a pressure device, by emphasizing "meeting the budget."	0.634
10	My superior questions budget reports, and uses them carefully in my evaluation.	0.417
13	Budget variances are frequently mentioned to me during performance evaluation interviews.	0.721
15	Budget-related information is rigidly used in evaluating my performance.	0.791
16	My supervisor mentions budgets while talking to me about my efficiency as a manager.	0.594
24	My superior generally views an unfavorable budget variance as an indicator of poor managerial performance.	0.523

TABLE 3

Questionnaire Statements Associated With Factor Three—Personal Accountability

Statement		Factor loading
18	My superior holds me personally accountable for budget variances.	0.650
19	My superior is likely to ask about variances beyond my control.	0.540
26	My superior expresses dissatisfaction to me about results when the budget has not been met.	0.693

TABLE 4

Questionnaire Statements Associated With Factor Four—Budget Flexibility

Statement		Factor loading
6	My superior knows that at times budget variances can be confusing and misleading for evaluation purposes.	0.613
8	I feel free to discuss budget variances with my superior.	0.756
12	My superior listens to my problems in budget matters.	0.491

as defined in Table 5, explained 27.8% or slightly over one-fourth of the variation in the response. This factor represented the second most prevalent style of evaluation as perceived by the supervisors. Only budget-rigidity surpassed it. Initiative, knowledge of the work, and effort put into the job were the most important elements in this factor as evidenced by high factor loadings. These loadings were 0.784, 0.694, and 0.683, respectively. Other significant elements included dependability, ability to plan and to handle subordinates, and attitude toward the work and the company. Of course, these factors are important. However, the exclusive use of personality traits or attitudes does have shortcomings because of a lack of objectivity.

As noted earlier, these four factors explained a cumulative total of over 90% of the variation in the responses. Other factors accounted for the remaining variance. It is interesting to note that the accounting-related factors make up approximately 66% of the variations in the responses.

What Are the Implications?

This study focused on performance evaluations of supervisors in charge of budget units within industrial organizations. Given an adequate reward system, effective evaluations should motivate the supervisor to engage in desirable behavior. The system may fail to achieve this result for several reasons, such as inaccurate or irrelevant data provided by the system, mis-interpretation or misuse of the data by the evaluator, or misperception of how the data are in fact used.

Naturally, some implications exist for the supervisors surveyed during this research, but implications also exist for the supervisor's superiors and for accountants.

SUPERVISOR'S CONCERNS

The factor analysis identified four significant factors which represented specific types of data classified by the manner in which the data were perceived to be used. Three of the four factors pertained to accounting-related information which explained about two-thirds of the total variation in the responses to the survey. The supervisor is concerned with two aspects of this data. First, he must have confidence that the data are relevant, accurate, and timely in order to be used effectively in appraising his performance. Second, he is concerned with the manner in which the data are used.

Management accountants have long been aware of the problems associated with preparing reports used in performance appraisals. The task is particularly difficult when supervisors do not exercise control over all items reported under their jurisdiction or when the accounting system does not reflect organizational goals and objectives. Complex relationships of interdepartmental activities are hard to reflect accurately within the accounting framework. For example, a supervisor may produce an inferior product

---

TABLE 5

Questionnaire Statements Associated With Factor Two—Non-accounting Style of Evaluation

Statement		Factor loading
5	Ability to handle my subordinates is a very important factor in my evaluation.	0.454
7	Dependability receives high importance in my evaluation.	0.522
11	Planning ability is a very important factor in my evaluation.	0.432
14	Effort put into the job is a very important factor in my evaluation.	0.683
17	Knowledge of the work is a very important factor in my evaluation.	0.694
20	Initiative on the job receives high importance in my evaluation.	0.784
25	Attitude towards the work and company is a very important factor in my evaluation.	0.428

by using less than the standard quality or quantity of materials or labor. This action will appear as a favorable budget variance even though the inferior product may result in the loss of future sales. The results of the lost sales may eventually materialize in the overall accounting report as reduced revenue, but they may not be reflected in the report of the supervisor responsible for the inferior work.

Other problems such as overemphasizing departmental results can exist and cause supervisory decisions which are inconsistent with the goals of the organization. Under these conditions, the concept of responsibility accounting becomes more important to the supervisor. It ensures that reports appraising performance contain only those items of costs and revenue that are considered to be under the control or significant influence of the person being evaluated. It seeks to identify the one person in the organization with the most decision-making authority over the variance in question. In other words, it seeks to pinpoint responsibility.

Thus, the problems of being held personally accountable for items beyond the control of the supervisor (factor three—personal accountability) may be avoided. Given this situation, the supervisor should react favorably to the accounting-related data used in his performance evaluation.

If long-run, organizational goals are to be realized, however, the accounting-related data must be properly used. Flexibility in the manner in which it is used for performance evaluations is essential. Supervisors should feel free to discuss budget problems with their superiors and be justified in believing that their input is effective. This statement implies some degree of participation by supervisors in budget matters such as setting goals and defining the manner by which these goals will be achieved. Research has shown that participation by supervisors contributes to budget acceptance, to improved morale, and to greater personal commitment to the organization. All of these are desirable results. Unfortunately, only 8.6% of the total variation in the survey responses was explained by factor four—budget flexibility—which mirrors these concepts. The apparent limited application of these important concepts identifies a significant shortcoming in actual business settings.

Another shortcoming identified in our study is that factor one—budget rigidity—explained

almost one-half of the variations in the responses. Chris Argyris published a landmark study concerning the use of budgets in manufacturing plants in 1952.[2] He observed that budgets were being used to bring pressure on supervisors and other workers. Argyris concluded that using budgets this way resulted in unfavorable behavioral relations such as increased hostility, tension, fear, and mistrust. Although such a threatening system of management may provide short-term benefits, it can lead to a deterioration of positive company attitudes, motivation, and communications in the long run. The resulting behavioral and attitudinal changes may increase turnover, lower product quality, and decrease productivity.[3]

Other researchers have reported the tendency of supervisors to "pad" their budgets in order to report favorable variances.[4] Accordingly, it appears that too much emphasis on accounting-related data is not consistent with organizational interests. Our study found that a large segment of the supervisors within the industrial companies surveyed perceived that accounting-related data were used rigidly in their evaluations. No attempt was made here to determine if the perceptions were in step with reality. If so, then the implications would place the solution on the supervisor's superiors. If not, better communications are needed between the two groups.

At best, accounting-related data represent an incomplete source of information for performance appraisals. Accounting systems do not provide information on all the dimensions relevant for performance evaluations. The maintenance of equipment or the development of human resources both represent important aspects of a supervisor's job. Yet, these factors may be omitted from accounting reports in some cases, and in others they may be judged against inadequate standards.

Further, a significant group of the supervisors surveyed in this study felt that nonaccounting-

---

[2]Chris Argyris. *The Impact of Budgets on People*. The Controllership Foundation, Inc., New York, 1952.

[3]L. S. Rosen and R. E. Schneck, "Some Behavioral Consequences of Accounting Measurement Systems," *Cost and Management*, October 1967.

[4]For example, A. E. Lower and R. W. Shaw, "An Analysis of Managerial Biasing Evidence from a Company's Budgeting Process," *Journal of Management Studies*, October 1968. Rosen and Schneck, *Cost and Management*.

related data were more important than accounting-related data to their evaluations. Factor two—nonaccounting style of evaluation—explained approximately 27% of the total variation in the survey responses. Undoubtedly, these factors are very important, but it must be kept in mind that appraisals based on personal traits are subjective in nature. If a supervisor is congenial, cooperative, and somewhat industrious, the superior is likely to be favorably impressed, and this impression may result in a higher evaluation that is justified by the supervisor's performance. The opposite may occur also—that is, the superior may have a negative bias toward an individual.

Just as accounting-related data represent an incomplete source of data for performance evaluations, appraisals that concentrate on personality traits or characteristics alone offer little guidance to the individual supervisor for identifying specific behavior that will improve his productivity. Evaluations should include a follow-up designed to benefit the supervisor being evaluated. Supervisors should be provided with behavioral guidelines that are goal oriented and that have the possibility of improving their evaluations and their potential as managers.

A balanced approach is needed. Nonaccounting data should be merged with the accounting-related data, and a proper emphasis placed on each. The supervisor, however, should never lose sight of the fact that accountability is an important management concept. Responsibility accounting can lend a high degree of objectivity to the process, but it should not be used only to place blame. Rather, it allows for attention to be directed toward a supervisor who should be asked to explain the variance. In this fashion problems can be identified and solved.

SUPERIOR'S CONCERNS

Most of the implications discussed above may apply also to the superior. Superiors who are aware of the problems of accountability and of the complex relationships of interdepartmental activities are more likely to carefully interpret accounting reports. Supervisors should be evaluated on the basis of their controllable performance, and subjectivity should be tempered with sound, professional judgment. Objectivity

is demanded if the reward system is to accomplish its desired results. Accounting-related data, if used properly and not abused, can lend itself to this purpose.

ACCOUNTANTS' CONCERNS

Notwithstanding the difficulties discussed above, many managers place major emphasis upon accounting-related data. Therefore, accountants must develop systems that produce relevant and accurate information to meet this demand. The accountant's relationship with supervisors could be affected if he produced anything less. Pearson, Seiler, and Weiss found "that an impressive number of accountants in industry perceive something less than a pleasant attitude from operation personnel."[5] This phenomenon was more prevalent among cost analyst and budget accountants, and probably reflects the negative findings in our research. Considered in this light, the supervisors' perceptions described in factor one—budget rigidity—become very important to the accountant. The phenomenon may be detrimental to the accountant's self-esteem and, further, to his own performance. To overcome this negative image, accountants should be encouraged to participate in operating activities, to develop an appreciation for the needs of supervisory personnel, and to exhibit an enthusiasm for meeting their data needs.

Review Performance Evaluation Practices

Our research identified four separate and distinct factors representing ways in which supervisors in industrial organizations perceived that they are evaluated. These factors emphasized the type of data and the way in which the data are used in performance evaluations. They explained 90.4% of the total variation in responses to the survey.

The effectiveness of reward systems probably depends on relevant, accurate, and timely data that are used with some degree of reason, objectivity, and flexibility. Nonaccounting data should be merged with the accounting-related data, and a proper emphasis should be placed

[5]Della A. Pearson, Robert E. Seiler, and Ira A. Weiss, "Why Do Management Accountants Feel Disliked?" *Management Accounting,* March 1982.

on each. The majority of the variance in supervisors' responses was explained by factors related to accounting data that were applied in a rigid manner. Conversely, only a small percentage of the variance was explained by the factor, budget flexibility. These percentages imply that many performance evaluation practices found in industry are undesirable. This finding has implications for supervisors, their superiors, and accountants.

CHAPTER 9 INTRODUCTION TO STANDARD COST ACCOUNTING

REVIEWING THE CHAPTER

Objective 1: Describe the nature and purpose of standard costs (pp. 315-318).

1. **Standard costs** are predetermined costs that are expressed as a cost per unit of finished product. They are used in preparing operating budgets, in identifying production areas that need better cost control, and in simplifying cost accounting procedures for inventories and product costing. In general, standard cost figures are maintained for all manufacturing accounts and are compared with actual cost figures at the end of the period. Any large variances, whether favorable or unfavorable, should then be analyzed.

Objective 2: Describe and differentiate among the three types of standard costs: ideal standards, basic standards, and currently attainable standards (pp. 318-320).

2. Standard costs can be characterized as ideal standards, basic standards, or currently attainable standards. **Ideal standards** are perfection standards because they are based on a maximum efficiency level with no breaks or work stoppages. Materials usage and labor effort are minimal. Because they are so rigid, performance targets established based on ideal standards are almost impossible to attain. In order to be useful, ideal standards must be adjusted downward.

3. **Basic standards** are projections that are seldom revised or updated to reflect current operating costs and price level changes. Such standards remain unchanged after once being computed. They are used to help spotlight trends but must be adjusted to reflect current conditions if they are to be used as targets or goals for managers.

4. **Currently attainable standards** are standard costs that are updated periodically to reflect changes in operating conditions and current price levels for direct materials, direct labor, and factory overhead costs. Normal efficiency is assumed when they are developed. Under these conditions, direct materials standards are based on current market prices and include allowances for normal scrap and spoilage loss. Direct labor standards include allowances for recurring machine downtime and work stoppages by employees.

Objective 3: Identify the six elements of a standard unit cost, and describe the factors to consider in developing each element (pp. 320-322).

5. The standard cost per unit of output is the result of the following standard amounts:
   a. **Standard direct materials cost = direct materials price standard X direct materials quantity standard.**

b. Standard direct labor cost = direct labor time standard X direct labor rate standard.

c. Standard factory overhead cost = (standard variable overhead rate + standard fixed overhead rate) X appropriate application basis.

6. The direct materials price standard is developed from past pricing trends and proposed future price changes. Detailed studies of machine and human performance as well as predictions of performance are used to develop direct material quantity standards. Direct labor time standards result from time and motion studies while job classification analyses and labor contracts often are the source for direct labor rate standards. The standard variable overhead rate and standard fixed overhead rate are computed using predictions of factory overhead costs and allocation base amounts (i.e., direct labor hours).

Objective 4: Compute a standard unit cost (pp. 322-325).

7. A product's standard unit cost is determined by adding together the standard direct materials cost, the standard direct labor cost, and the standard factory overhead cost per unit. Under a standard cost system, the journal entries are similar to those discussed in prior chapters for a manufacturer's accounting system. However, direct materials, direct labor, and factory overhead are entered into Work in Process Inventory at standard (not actual) cost.

Objective 5: Compute and evaluate direct materials and direct labor variances (pp. 325-330).

8. Variances between standard and actual costs are usually determined for direct materials, direct labor, and factory overhead. When standard costs exceed actual costs, the variance is favorable (F). When actual costs exceed standard costs, the variance is unfavorable (U).

9. The total direct materials cost variance consists of the direct materials price variance plus the direct materials quantity variance.

a. The **direct materials price variance** equals the difference between actual price and standard price, times actual quantity of materials purchased.

b. The **direct materials quantity variance** equals the difference between actual quantity of materials used and standard quantity, times standard price.

10. The total direct labor cost variance consists of the direct labor rate variance plus the direct labor efficiency variance.

a. The **direct labor rate variance** equals the difference between the actual labor rate and the standard labor rate, times actual hours worked.

b. The **direct labor efficiency variance** equals the difference between actual hours worked and standard hours allowed, times the standard labor rate.

Objective 6: Prepare journal entries to record transactions involving direct materials and direct labor variances in a standard cost system (pp. 331-333).

11. As was already stated, cost data are journalized at standard cost under a standard cost system. However, when variances exist, they should also be recorded in the general ledger—as a debit to a specific variance account when unfavorable and as a credit when favorable. Separate accounts should be maintained for each variance. At this point, a thorough review of the textbook's standard cost entries involving variances is recommended.

12. When a standard cost system is being used, there will be separate general ledger accounts for the following: direct materials price variance, direct materials quantity variance, direct labor rate variance, and direct labor efficiency variance. The balances in these accounts are closed out at the end of the accounting period.

Testing Your Knowledge

Matching

Match each term with its definition by writing the appropriate letter in the blank.

____ 1. Standard costs

____ 2. Favorable variance

____ 3. Unfavorable variance

____ 4. Direct materials price variance

____ 5. Direct materials quantity variance

____ 6. Direct labor rate variance

____ 7. Direct labor efficiency variance

____ 8. Ideal standards

____ 9. Basic standards

____10. Currently attainable standards

a. Standards that are based on a maximum efficiency level with no breaks or work stoppages.

b. The difference between the standard labor rate and the actual labor rate times actual hours worked.

c. Actual costs exceeding standard costs

d. Standard costs that are updated periodically to reflect changes in operating conditions and current price levels

e. Predetermined costs that are expressed as a cost per unit of finished product

f. The difference between actual price and standard price, times actual quantity of materials purchased

g. Standards that are seldom revised or updated to reflect current operating costs and price level changes

h. The difference between quantity of materials used and standard quantity, times standard price

i. The difference between actual hours worked and standard hours allowed, times standard labor rate

j. Standard costs exceeding actual costs

Completion

Use the lines provided to complete each item.

1. The six standards used to compute total unit cost are

_____

_____

_____

_____

_____

2. A favorable direct materials quantity variance would exist when

_____

_____

_____

3. An unfavorable direct labor rate would exist when

_____

_____

_____

4. The three types of standard costs are

_____

_____

_____

Introduction to Standard Cost Accounting

True-False

Circle T if the statement is true, F if it is false.

T F **1.** One application base used in computing standard costs is actual direct labor hours.

T F **2.** Time and motion studies of workers are used in establishing direct labor rate standards.

T F **3.** Under a standard cost system, all costs that flow through the inventory accounts are at standard.

T F **4.** Computing variances is an essential part of the planning function of budgetary control.

T F **5.** It is impossible to have unfavorable direct materials price and direct materials quantity variances and have a favorable total direct materials cost variance.

T F **6.** The purchasing agent should normally be held responsible for direct materials price variances.

T F **7.** Labor rate variances are normally the responsibility of the production supervisor.

T F **8.** Computing the total direct labor cost variance is more important than computing the direct labor rate and direct labor efficiency variances.

T F **9.** Under a standard cost system, variances would not be recorded in the entry to record the transfer of completed units to Finished Goods Inventory.

T F **10.** Basic standards are updated periodically to reflect changes in operating conditions and current price levels.

T F **11.** If standard costs exceed actual costs, the variance account would be credited to record a favorable variance.

T F **12.** The only use of standard costs is to compare them with actual costs and to analyze the resulting variances.

T F **13.** Ideal capacity is an engineering concept and allows for normal human error, machine downtime, retooling, and maintenance work stoppages.

T F **14.** Standard unit costs are computed by multiplying total standard hours allowed by the standard labor rate.

Multiple Choice

Circle the letter of the best answer.

1. An unfavorable direct labor efficiency variance would probably occur when
a. the workers are overpaid.
b. most workers are inexperienced.
c. the workers are underpaid.
d. most workers are experienced.

2. When there is a favorable direct materials price variance,
a. the purchasing agent has purchased direct materials at below the standard price.
b. the production department has used a smaller quantity of direct materials than is standard.
c. the purchasing agent has purchased more direct materials than is needed.
d. the production department has done a good job at cutting its overhead costs.

3. Worker's wages are all that is needed to compute the
a. direct labor time standard.
b. direct labor rate standard.
c. standard direct labor cost.
d. direct labor cost variance.

4. When recording direct labor costs under a standard cost system,
a. Work in Process Inventory is debited for actual direct labor costs.
b. Factory Payroll is credited for standard direct labor costs.
c. a favorable direct labor efficiency variance would be credited.
d. Factory Payroll is debited for standard direct labor costs.

5. When recording the purchase of materials under a standard cost system,
   a. Materials Inventory is debited for actual quantity purchased times standard cost.
   b. Accounts Payable is credited for actual quantity purchased times standard price.
   c. a direct materials quantity variance might be recorded.
   d. an unfavorable direct materials price variance would be credited.

6. Standard costs for company products are useful for
   a. variance analysis and cost control.
   b. computing production costs in operating budgets.
   c. simplifying the recordkeeping aspects of cost systems.
   d. all of the above.

7. A company employing very tight (high) standards in a standard cost system should expect that
   a. costs will be controlled better than if lower standards were used.
   b. employees will be strongly motivated to attain the standards.
   c. no incentive bonuses will be paid.
   d. most variances will be unfavorable.

8. The difference between actual quantity used and standard quantity multiplied by standard price is the equation for computing the
   a. direct materials price variance.
   b. direct labor efficiency variance.
   c. direct materials quantity variance.
   d. direct labor rate variance.

9. During the current month, Department 727 started 40,000 units of product and transferred 36,000 fully completed units to Finished Goods. The ending Work in Process Inventory was 50 percent complete as to labor operations. There was no beginning Work in Process Inventory, and actual labor hours were 180,000 for the period. Each unit required five standard direct labor hours. Standard hours allowed for the period are
   a. 200,000.
   b. 190,000.
   c. 180,000.
   d. none of the above.

10. If the actual amount of materials used equals the standard amount of materials that should have been used, any difference between the standard direct materials cost and the actual direct materials cost would be labeled
   a. direct materials quantity variance.
   b. direct labor rate variance.
   c. direct materials price variance.
   d. direct labor efficiency variance.

Applying Your Knowledge

Exercises

1. Kranmar Company employs a standard cost system in the manufacture of expensive hand-painted dishes. The standards for the current year are:

Direct materials price standards

Porcelain	$.80/lb
Red paint	$1.00/tube
Blue paint	$1.00/tube

Direct materials quantity standards

Porcelain	½ lb/dish
Red paint	1 tube/20 dishes
Blue paint	1 tube/50 dishes

Direct labor time standards

Molding department	.03 hour/dish
Painting department	.05 hour/dish

Direct labor rate standards

Molding department	$4.00/hour
Painting department	$6.00/hour

Standard factory over-head rates

Standard variable over-head rate	$3.00/direct labor hour
Standard fixed over-head rate	$2.00/direct labor hour

Compute the standard manufacturing cost per dish for direct materials, direct labor, and overhead.

Porcelain	$ _____
Red paint	_____
Blue paint	_____
Molding department wages	_____
Painting department wages	_____
Variable overhead	_____
Fixed overhead	_____
Standard cost of one dish	$ _____

2. The California Peanut Butter Works uses a standard cost accounting system. The standard cost of producing one case of peanut butter is:

Direct material (4lb @ $1/lb)	$ 4.00
Direct labor (2 hr @ $2/hr)	4.00
Manufacturing overhead (2hr @ $3/hr) . .	6.00
	$14.00

During the period, 100,000 pounds of direct materials were purchased. The company produced 25,000 cases of peanut butter during the year and the actual costs per case were:

Direct material (5lb @ $.90/lb)	$ 4.50
Direct labor (2 hr @ $2/hr)	4.50
Manufacturing overhead	
($148,750 ÷ 25,000 cases)	5.95
	$14.95

Write the number of the best answer below.

___ a. The standard quantities allowed for direct materials and direct labor for actual production were
   1. 100,000 pounds of material and 56,250 direct labor hours.
   2. 100,000 pounds of material and 50,000 direct labor hours.
   3. 125,000 pounds of material and 56,250 direct labor hours.
   4. 125,000 pounds of material and 50,000 direct labor hours.

___ b. The material price variance for the period is
   1. $10,000 (F).
   2. $10,000 (U).
   3. $12,500 (F).
   4. $12,500 (U).

___ c. The material quantity variance for the period is
   1. $22,500 (F).
   2. $22,500 (U).
   3. $25,000 (F).
   4. $25,000 (U).

___ d. The labor rate variance for the period is
   1. 0.
   2. $112,500 (F).
   3. $112,500 (U).
   4. $100,000 (F).

___ e. The labor efficiency variance for the period is
   1. 0.
   2. $6,250 (F).
   3. $12,500 (U).
   4. $12,500 (F).

CHAPTER 10 VARIANCE ANALYSIS AND PERFORMANCE REPORTING

REVIEWING THE CHAPTER

Objective 1: Review the principles of performance evaluation (pp. 350-352).

1. The topics of variance analysis and performance evaluation tie two important management accounting concepts together. Clearly, one of the reasons that standard costs are developed is so that operating performance can be measured and controlled. Before continuing our study, it is important to review the performance evaluation principles so they can be applied once standard costs have been developed and variances determined.

2. The following are the behavioral principles of performance evaluation:
   a. Managers should have input into the standards and goals set for their areas of responsibility.
   b. Management support of the evaluation process should be evident.
   c. Only controllable cost and revenue items with significant variances should be included in performance reports.
   d. Opportunity for manager response should be part of the evaluation.

3. The following are the operational principles of performance evaluation:
   a. Providing accurate and suitable measures of performance.
   b. Communicating with appropriate managers and segment leaders to be evaluated.
   c. Identifying the responsibilities of each manager.
   d. Comparing actual performance with a suitable base.
   e. Preparing performance reports that highlight areas of concern.
   f. Analyzing important cause-and-effect relationships.

Objective 2: Prepare a flexible budget (pp. 352-357).

4. A **flexible budget** is a summary of expected costs for various levels of production. For each level of production, budgeted variable and fixed costs and their totals are presented. Also presented is the budgeted variable cost per unit, which of course is the same for all levels of output. Once prepared, the flexible budget is used to determine the flexible budget formula. This formula can then be applied to any level of output to compute its budgeted total cost. This budgeted total cost can then be compared with actual costs to measure the performance of individual workers, managers, and departments.

Objective 3: Compute overhead variances, using both (a) the two-way and (b) the three-way analyses (pp. 357-366).

5. In a standard costing system, the total overhead variance is the difference between the actual variable and fixed overhead costs incurred and the total overhead costs applied during the period using the standard variable and fixed overhead rates.

6. Using the two-way analysis, the total factory overhead variance consists of the controllable overhead variance plus the overhead volume variance.
   a. The **controllable overhead variance** equals actual overhead costs incurred minus budgeted factory overhead for the level of production achieved.
   b. The **overhead volume variance** equals budgeted factory overhead for the level of production achieved minus factory overhead applied using standard variable and fixed overhead rates.

7. Using the three-way overhead variance analysis, the total factory overhead variance is made up of the overhead spending variance plus the overhead efficiency variance plus the overhead volume variance.
   a. The **overhead spending variance** equals actual overhead costs incurred minus budgeted factory overhead for effort expended (actual hours worked).
   b. The **overhead efficiency variance** equals budgeted factory overhead for effort expended minus budgeted factory overhead for the level of production achieved.
   c. The **overhead volume variance** is the same as described in 6b for the two-way overhead variance analysis.
   d. The controllable overhead variance equals the overhead spending variance plus the overhead efficiency variance.

Objective 4: Prepare journal entries involving overhead variances (pp. 366-368.)

8. As was discussed in relation to recording direct materials and direct labor variances, accounts are established in the general ledger for each variance account. Overhead variances are usually computed at period end when the overhead applied and overhead control accounts are closed out. The difference between these two account bal-

ances equals the total overhead variance. The balancing part of this entry is to debit or credit the variance accounts (using either the two-way or three-way approaches) with the favorable or unfavorable variances.

Objective 5: Dispose of variance balances at period end (pp. 368-369).

9. At the end of the accounting period, the variances are closed to the the Cost of Goods Sold account if their balances are small or if all or most of the goods produced during the period were sold. Otherwise, the net variance balance of all but the direct materials price variance is divided among Work in Process Inventory, Finished Goods Inventory, and Cost of Goods Sold based on their relative ending balances. The direct materials price variance must be allocated to these same three accounts *plus* the Materials Inventory account.

Objective 6: Describe the concept of management by exception (pp. 369-372).

10. Variances are differences between actual operating results and budgeted (standard) results. Once variances have been measured, corrective approaches can be taken for those areas that are not operating efficiently.

11. **Management by exception** is an approach to the analysis of variances that locates and analyzes only those areas of unusually good or bad performance. This concept is designed to highlight areas that need management's attention and it helps to utilize a manager's time more effectively.

Objective 7: Evaluate employee performance, using variances (pp. 372-373).

12. Before performance can be evaluated, two parts of the evaluation process must be in place, (1) the responsibility accounting and (2) a system of manager feedback on the variance incurred.

13. Performance reports contain only those cost and revenue items controllable by the manager receiving the report. They should show actual costs, budgeted or standard costs, and the related variances. Space should be provided for manager input as to the causes of the variances.

Testing Your Knowledge

Matching

Match each term with its definition by writing the appropriate letter in the blank.

____ 1. Normal capacity

____ 2. Management by exception

____ 3. Analysis of cause

____ 4. Three-way analysis

____ 5. Controllable overhead variance

____ 6. Overhead spending variance

____ 7. Overhead efficiency variance

____ 8. Overhead volume variance

____ 9. Performance report

____ 10. Flexible budget

a. Locating and analyzing only those areas of unusual performance

b. Actual overhead costs minus budgeted factory overhead for the level of production achieved

c. Expected costs for various levels of anticipated production

d. A written comparison between actual costs and budgeted costs for a segment of the business

e. Budgeted factory overhead for the level of production achieved minus factory overhead applied using the standard overhead rates

f. The overhead variance analysis that yields a spending variance, an efficiency variance, and a volume variance

g. The process of determining what went right or wrong during the period to create a variance

h. The average annual level of operating capacity needed to meet expected sales demands.

i. Actual overhead costs incurred minus budgeted factory overhead for effort expended (actual hours worked)

j. Budgeted factory overhead for effort expended minus budgeted factory overhead for the level of production achieved

Completion

Use the lines provided to complete each item.

1. State the flexible budget formula.

_____

2. A favorable overhead volume variance would occur when

_____

_____

3. An unfavorable overhead spending variance would exist when

_____

_____

4. The overhead efficiency variance is computed by determining the difference between what two flexible budgets?

_____

_____

_____

Circle T if the statement is true, F if it is false.

T F **1.** Management by exception uses the data provided by variances.

T F **2.** The flexible budget includes different sets of both budgeted fixed costs and budgeted variable costs for each level of anticipated activity.

T F **3.** An overhead volume variance will exist only if more or less than normal capacity is used.

T F **4.** To compute the controllable overhead variance, the actual level of production must be known.

T F **5.** The standard fixed overhead rate should be based on practical rather than on normal capacity.

T F **6.** A flexible budget is a summary of estimated overhead costs that is geared to changes in the level of productive activity and is prepared for a range of activity levels.

T F **7.** Multiplying the standard variable and fixed overhead rates by a predetermined allocation base such as direct labor hours or direct labor costs will yield the standard overhead cost of finished products.

T F **8.** Currently attainable standards allow for machine repairs, normal setup time, material waste, and other reasonable operating interruptions.

T F **9.** Performance reports for cost centers and departments should emphasize only the cost factors under the control of individual managers.

T F **10.** The overhead volume variance concentrates on the difference between budgeted and applied variable overhead costs.

T F **11.** The standard fixed overhead rate is computed by dividing normal capacity by total budgeted fixed overhead costs.

T F **12.** Disposing of variance balances to inventories and Cost of Goods Sold prior to preparation of financial statements is generally necessary if the variances are significant in amount or if the variances result from using non-current standards.

T F **13.** An overhead spending variance is computed by determining the differences between two flexible budgets.

T F **14.** The overhead efficiency variance is a byproduct of the computation of the direct labor efficiency variance and is computed at the same time.

Multiple Choice

1. A performance report does not include data for
   a. total direct labor cost variance.
   b. actual costs.
   c. overhead volume variance.
   d. budgeted costs.

2. Management by exception uses which accounting tool to a great extent?
   a. Cost-volume-profit analysis
   b. Product costing procedures
   c. A worksheet
   d. Variance analysis

3. Which of the following items would follow the computation of variances?
   a. Preparing performance reports
   b. Preparing the master budget
   c. Preparing the period budgets
   d. Implementing the budget

4. The successful application of flexible budgets in achieving cost control depends primarily upon
   a. using overhead rates based on normal capacity.
   b. currently attainable standards for prime costs.
   c. precise allocation of overhead variances to inventories.
   d. accurate determination of overhead cost behavior patterns.

5. The primary difference between a fixed (static) budget and a variable (flexible) budget is that a fixed budget
   a. includes only fixed costs, whereas a variable budget includes only variable costs.
   b. is a plan for a single level of sales, whereas a variable budget is really several budgets, one for each of several sales levels.
   c. is concerned only with future acquisitions of fixed assets, whereas a variable budget is concerned with expenses that vary with sales.
   d. cannot be changed after the period begins, whereas a variable budget can be changed after the period begins.

6. When standard hours allowed for good production exceed the capacity measure used in computing the standard fixed overhead rate, the volume variance is
   a. favorable.
   b. unfavorable.
   c. not affected by the difference.
   d. not measurable.

7. A spending variance for variable overhead based on direct labor hours is the difference between actual overhead costs and variable overhead costs that should have been incurred for the actual hours worked and results from
   a. price and quantity differences for overhead costs.
   b. price differences for overhead costs.
   c. quantity differences for overhead costs.
   d. differences caused by variations in production volume.

8. The overhead efficiency variance for factory overhead is an overall indication of the
   a. extent to which capacity was utilized.
   b. extent to which costs were controlled.
   c. efficiency in using variable resources.
   d. absorption of budgeted fixed costs.

9. Which of these variances is least significant for cost control?
   a. Overhead spending variance
   b. Overhead volume variance
   c. Overhead efficiency variance
   d. Controllable overhead variance

10. The Weaver Company uses a standard cost system and a flexible budget. At a normal level of activity of 15,000 units and 45,000 standard direct labor hours, the standard direct labor cost would be $270,000. During July, 44,000 hours were worked to produce 14,000 units at an actual direct labor cost of $308,000. The direct labor efficiency variance in July was
    a. $12,000 (U).
    b. $6,000 (F).
    c. $56,000 (U).
    d. $44,000 (U).

Applying Your Knowledge

Exercises

1. Los Feliz Company expects fixed overhead to total $50,000 for 19xx. In addition, variable costs per unit are expected to be: direct labor, $4.50; direct materials, $1.25; and variable overhead, $2.75. Using these data, prepare a flexible budget for a 10,000-unit, 15,000-unit, and 20,000-unit volume. In addition, determine the flexible budget formula.

Los Feliz Company
Flexible Budget
For the Year Ended December 31, 19xx

2. The Larsen Sporting Goods Company uses a standard cost system for producing 10-pound steel dumbbells. The standard cost for steel is $.60 per pound, and each dumbbell should require .3 standard direct labor hours at a standard rate of $4.50 per hour. The standard variable overhead rate is $2.30 per direct labor hour, and normal capacity was set at a monthly level of 19,000 hours of direct labor. Fixed overhead cost of $3,800 was budgeted for March. During the month of March, 65,000 dumbbells were actually produced, using 657,000 pounds of steel. During the period, 657,000 pounds of steel were also purchased and the cost of the steel was $381,060. Direct labor hours numbered 22,100 at an expense of $100,555. Total overhead expenses came to $57,000. Using the data above, compute the following variances for the month of March. Indicate whether each variance is favorable or unfavorable by writing F or U after each amount.

a. Direct materials price variance =
   $_____

b. Direct materials quantity variance =
   $_____

c. Direct labor rate variance =
   $_____

d. Direct labor efficiency variance =
   $_____

e. Controllable overhead variance =
   $_____

f. Overhead volume variance =
   $_____

g. Overhead Spending Variance =
   $_____

h. Overhead Efficiency Variance =
   $_____

*This exercise is cumulative, covering material studied in Chapters 9 and 10.

Variance Analysis and Performance Reporting

Crossword Puzzle
for Chapters 9 and 10

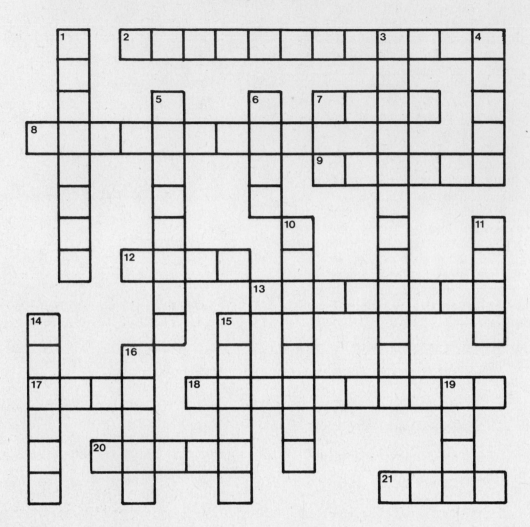

ACROSS

2. Predetermined quantity for materials, labor, and over-head (2 words)
7. Example of a fixed cost
8. Management by ——
9. Operating capacity to meet expected sales
12. Direct labor standard
13. Difference between actual and standard costs
17. Long-term asset
18. Overhead variance
20. Standards that are seldom revised
21. Direct labor standard

DOWN

1. Budget covering a range of activity levels
3. Overhead variance
4. Composite variance
5. Overhead variance
6. Labor measuring unit
10. Direct materials variance
11. Possible materials measuring unit
14. Overhead variance
15. A performance report should consider cause-and- ——factors
16. Performing at maximum efficiency
19. Performance report measuring unit

Measuring Operating Performance Through Cost Accounting

Cost accounting is more than just a traditional means of valuing cost-of-goods-sold and inventory. Today's sophisticated cost accounting systems can help you monitor the effectiveness and efficiency of operating functions in your business.

Business executives are constantly advised of the need for timely and accurate management information. They are told that a new or updated computer system is needed, or that more sophisticated planning or control procedures must be put in place, or even that significant organizational and reporting relationship changes must be made. In short, most of the advice they receive is directed at technical solutions to their current or anticipated business problems.

Certainly, taking the proper technical approach is essential. However, such advice often does not show *how to measure* the benefits that should result from technical changes. This is particularly true of operational or manufacturing information systems.

Cost accounting can be used to measure the improvements brought about by technical changes so that business executives can make more effective use of their operational information systems. In order to take full advantage of this feature of modern cost systems, executives should first understand the role of cost accounting as a management tool.

We shall look briefly at the traditional uses of cost accounting and then contrast that with the experience of two companies utilizing more progressive applications of costing. Both were well managed but were facing increasingly difficult business environments; they profited by enhancing their ability to measure and monitor the uses and effects of technical improvements.

Finally, we shall define the position of cost accounting in the hierarchy of operational information and explain, in specific terms, the form and content of measurement information that a modern cost system should provide. Sophisti-

Source: Article by Edward L. Krommer and William T. Muir, *Price Waterhouse Review* (1983, No. 1). Reprinted by permission.

cated cost accounting, as we have analyzed it, is indispensable for evaluating technical changes and getting the most out of your operational systems.

The Need for Cost Systems

Historical Uses of Cost Systems Traditionally, cost accounting has been associated with the accumulation of historical data on material, labor, and related overhead costs for valuing inventory and cost-of-goods-sold. The data is generally collected on a lot, job order, or process basis and the techniques used to analyze it include the identification of many variance factors and historical cost trends (unadjusted for inflationary impact or changes in production processes). The variances that are developed are usually financial and rarely show operational productivity trends.

In nonmanufacturing industries, cost accounting is often thought of as a special purpose analytical tool, not an ongoing process. Cost data usually is expressed in terms of expense items, such as salesmen's commissions, advertising copy, and research and development. These accounts generally reflect only the actual expenses measured against a budget. If any analysis is performed, it may measure average cost per sales call, cost per copy column inch, or the actual cost for various special projects. It does not address the impact of inflation or changes in the operational side of the business.

Cost accounting often has been left to the accountants as a historical record-keeping system. It generally has not been an integrated and dynamic part of a management control and measurement process.

Modern Uses of Cost Systems Cost accounting should be the primary barometer of the effectiveness and efficiency of the various operating functions of a company. It should help meet the objective of optimizing resource utilization. If used properly, cost accounting is a company's primary operational management information system.

In one sense, cost accounting is the process of connecting the incurrence of costs (that is, labor, material, and equipment) with the recognition of total labor, material, and overhead costs at the end of the general accounting period. The incurrence and recognition of these costs are linked through entries from the payroll, accounts payable, and other accounting feeder systems. This linkage is a basic feature of an effective cost system, but it is one that is often overlooked or not totally achieved. This failure is not one of form but of substance.

In addition to this linkage, a cost system should provide timely, accurate, and complete information about the critical success factors of the company's business. To do this, the purpose of the cost system must be clearly and precisely defined. Special industry factors such as material yield for a chemical process, set-up costs for a customer or small lot machining operation, equipment utilization for a heavily capitalized and automated company, or quality control within a food packing firm should be carefully addressed. These factors then have to be supplemented with considerations of cause and effect variances, such as engineering changes, method changes, labor rates, nonstandard labor costs, alternate sourcing, nonstandard lot sizes, variable crew sizing, and alternate processes. Industry specifics, together with generally accepted variance analyses adjusted for the impact of inflation, provide a basis for management awareness and action.

Because these elements constantly fluctuate, a dynamic and integrated information approach is required. Daily, weekly, and monthly summaries of key data are vital to control a business. Reliable, integrated, and controlled operational systems for inventory, production, and project management planning and control must be in place. Indeed, to consider a cost accounting system as something separate and apart from manufacturing and financial systems completely misrepresents what a cost system is.

Structure of a Cost System

Integration with Support Systems The functions of cost accounting are analogous to threading simultaneously the eyes of several needles. The needles represent the various manufacturing support systems (that is, production and distribution) and the accounting feeder system (that is, accounts payable, payroll, and financial reporting). A cost accounting system depends on substantial, timely, and accurate information from these other systems to achieve its objectives. To perform the cost accounting function separately and apart from these important "support" and "feeder" systems is not only redundant, but also invites a significant loss of data integrity.

A critical element in the development and implementation of a cost system is minimizing and eliminating, wherever possible, redundant transaction processing steps. This begins with inventory record keeping. The use of perpetual inventory records for manufacturing purposes and a different set for accounting purposes should be avoided. The general ledger inventory control accounts should be supported by the manufacturing inventory control system. All transactions which affect the perpetual inventory on-hand records should have a corresponding dollar cost impact on the general ledger inventory accounts. Timing differences must be segregated and physical adjustments to the perpetual records must affect the general ledger.

This isolated example demonstrates a concept that should be applied throughout a cost system. The substance and timing of production efficiency information in the manufacturing system should correspond to financial efficiency information in the cost system. Therefore, reporting efficiencies against current manufacturing standards in the cost system is vital. If the company maintains frozen yearly standards for valuation purposes, then a method variance must be developed to maintain the integrity of the financial statements.

Another example is the way complete units are reported by the production department against an open work-in-process lot as contrasted to the stock-room receipt of completed production. Often the adjustment of work-in-process or inventory dollar transfers to stock is based on reported production. The results in timing differences and possible errors if appropriate recognition is not given to the stock-room receipt transaction. To prevent this, an integrated approach will identify any difference between reported production and stockroom receipt quantities.

Performance Reporting Statistical analysis is a key feature of a responsive cost system. Management has traditionally been interested in key ratios and indices for monitoring and controlling its business. However, the cost system usually has not provided this important data. Unfortunately, various nonintegrated and make-shift special reporting systems have been established to do this. A consistent basis for reporting is often absent and meaningful overall reporting is hampered.

An extensive performance reporting system is mandatory for a cost accounting system to truly measure the efficiency and effectiveness of an organization's overall management of its resources. Labor utilization, equipment used, the ratio of indirect to direct workers, the level of rework labor, material yields, unplanned scrap, manufacturing schedule adherence, and inventory levels are key measurements which the cost system must make.

The manufacturing function is not the only one that requires statistical reporting. Pertinent indices and ratios for research and development, marketing, finance, personnel, and other functional areas should be included in the system. Productivity improvement opportunities and overall control of costs are equally important in these overhead expense areas. This includes such items as the average number of sales calls per salesman, the amount of proposals and contracts per salesman, and the total regular accounts and lost accounts per salesman. Ratios and goals should be established for each organizational unit in the company and actual performance must be monitored. Consideration should also be given to incorporating comparable industry data.

How Two Companies Benefited

We can now look at how two companies applied these lessons to their planning procedures and received immediate benefits.

Case 1: Measuring the Cost Impact of Change

Profitable Company, Inc., processes a variety of consumer products and markets them through food, drug, and discount outlets. Anyone who looked at it two years ago might well have said it was a solid company. It had paid a dividend to its shareholders for many years. Management had established a material management system that was timely and accurate. The company had effective planning and control procedures—its external auditors loved it. The structure of its organization was well conceived and documented, with a clear definition of responsibility and authority.

Unfortunately, many problems lurked beneath this veneer of excellent management information and controls. Profit percentages relative to sales were maintained by constant price increases, but data indicated consumer resistance. A high level of customer service was needed in Profitable's industry, but inventory levels supporting this objective were extremely expensive to maintain. Compounding these problems, consumers were demanding changes in container size and structure, and historical product mixes were continually being altered.

In short, Profitable's business environment was one of constant change that the company's management could not anticipate. This prevented competent action. Because the effectiveness of the planning and control systems could not be measured, management could only wait until a change occurred and then react to it.

This inability to plan for change was directly related to the kind of information that management received, particularly from its cost system. Profitable had an excellent consumer demand forecasting process—rare for most companies. Management could rapidly detect changes in consumer buying habits, but this information was used only to modify the production schedule to fit changing demand. No attempt was made to determine (1) the impact of the change in the schedule on production and distribution costs or (2) whether an operational change to satisfy the revised schedule was cost-effective.

Profitable, like some corporations, had not done a good job of integrating the revenue and the cost sides of the profit/loss equation. Therefore, the cost impact of changes in revenue mix or trends was not determined in time to allow production processes to be effectively controlled. Productivity and resource utilization measurements were not developed from the cost system, financial reporting system, or demand forecasting processes.

Fortunately, this was correct before disaster struck. Armed with a knowledge of the modern concepts of cost accounting, management undertook a detailed study of its information requirements and of the best way to measure the effectiveness of its decisions. As a result, Profitable decided to incorporate resource utilization reporting into its cost accounting process. A mechanism was developed and then integrated with the information captured and processed for the cost accounting system. Several steps were involved:

□ Establishing performance criteria (that is, standards, measures, and ratios).
□ Determining performance standards.
□ Developing product-specific routings and department-specific capacity measures.
□ Improving the methods used to capture actual data.
□ Structuring and formatting output reports so that the operational activity could be monitored frequently.

Implementing this reporting process was not easy. Middle management personnel had always had their performance evaluated against their budget, which had been based on the prior year's results adjusted for inflation. No one ever considered measuring results based on resource utilization (defined as the units of production inputs adjusted for seasonal and volume fluctuations) against usage standards that had been established on the basis of machine, labor, or scheduled capacities. Because management practices had to be changed, there was a significant lapse between the completion of detailed specifications for the measuring processes and their successful and total implementation.

Substantial profits have resulted from this management-oriented cost system. Direct production and warehousing labor costs have been reduced by about 20%. Of course, the resource reporting system did not by itself produce this result. The major reason for the labor cost reduction was the development of labor standards and the adherence to them by middle management. However, the information base that supports the resource reporting system brought to management's attention the resource excesses in the plant warehouse.

Other benefits that have resulted from the system are improved scheduling efficiency and a better understanding of the causes of the substantial operating variances that were reported by the old cost system. It is now possible for Profitable's management to reconcile operating cost variances isolated by the cost accounting system with efficiency levels that are based upon established performance standards. This is done by reporting performance against current standards and against annual standards to identify both efficiency and method change variances.

Equipment utilization is closely monitored to identify productive and nonproductive time and the effect of set-ups on product costs. Signifi-cant costs, such as material yield, scrap, and rework, are specially reported under the resource management system. In all of these areas, key indices and ratios are given for the current period and trends are computed showing progress over time.

Case 2: Identifying True Costs International Manufacturer, Inc., is in some respects quite similar to Profitable. It is a well managed, growing, and highly respected company. International sells products which compete directly and successfully with the Japanese.

International's industry, however, is very different from Profitable's. Its product line consists of many large and different items. They are produced in plants around the world. But, like Profitable, International saw trouble ahead because of changing product mix and demand patterns. Management was disturbed that its inflation-adjusted financial performance was not as good as the company's historical accounting system would lead one to believe.

To correct these problems, International's management initiated a critical examination of its cost accounting approach, including a study of its information systems and its product pricing methods and results. This study showed:

□ Growing sales but diminishing inflation-adjusted profits.
□ Changing manufacturing techniques but overhead allocation formulas that were unchanged for 20 years.
□ An inability to analyze the substantial variance problems that were revealed by the company's financial reporting system.
□ An absence of comprehensive product line profitability information.

These led to the inescapable conclusion that International's cost systems were inadequate.

International, like Profitable, is known for excellence in material planning. Its raw material planning and control systems are state-of-the-art, its data processing support is first-rate, and its products' reputation for quality is without peer. Material control, however, was not enough to reverse the problems disclosed by the management study.

International had not implemented order-specific or department-specific work-in-process control. Its shop floor data capture methods did not include department-to-department transfers or an ability to obtain yield loss information. Its labor costs—and, of more concern, the related direct and indirect overhead costs—were rough estimates based on historical data rather than performance standards.

To resolve the problem of monitoring operating efficiency and to better establish selling prices that related to production costs, management elected to restructure its cost accounting system. The system was redesigned to:

☐ Develop a cost profile for each operating unit so that the sources of cost (direct labor, direct material, and manufacturing and support overhead) could be more precisely established.
☐ Improve shop floor control procedures and associated data capture so that nonstandard activities during the work-in-process cycle could be isolated and analyzed.
☐ Provide a basis of overhead allocation related to the manufacturing process instead of an unrelated method such as a formula based on direct labor dollars.
☐ Provide a basis for the support of the company's LIFO computations (and incidentally retain IRS approval).
☐ Determine the company's overall product line profitability by considering both direct and indirect costs and expenses.

The system's implementation is still in progress. However, benefits have already been derived from the preparation of each operating unit's cost profiles. Management now knows what critical success factors are needed to monitor and control the manufacturing process. Also, management now is committed to attaining real, inflation-adjusted growth for the company. This has made International's employees aware of the need for product quality and personal efficiency.

When an improved shop floor data capture system (which is tightly coupled to, but not part of, the improved cost system project) is implemented, additional cost information benefits are anticipated because management will be able to:

☐ Prepare and analyze meaningful performance variances on both a department and job order basis.
☐ Accurately cost, and thus price, individual products rather than aggregated product families.
☐ Make meaningful make/buy decisions—confident that the cost in both cases can be accurately estimated.

The Importance of Cost Accounting

To gain the most benefit from sophisticated cost accounting systems, management should keep in mind two significant principles:

1. Cost accounting should provide more than just cost-of-goods-sold and inventory valuation information. *It also should provide information measuring the utilization of resources and the impact of anticipated changes to those resources.*
2. Cost accounting is not an isolated system. It is the proper merging of financial, administrative, and operational planning and control systems. *The data produced from any cost accounting process is only as comprehensive, timely, or accurate as the information given it by the operational and administrative support feeder system.*

CHAPTER 11 PRICING DECISIONS, INCLUDING CONTRACT PRICING

REVIEWING THE CHAPTER

Objective 1: Describe traditional economic pricing concepts (pp. 400-402).

1. Traditional economic pricing concepts are based on microeconomic theory. A product's total revenue and total cost curves are projected and plotted. After an initial loss, the lines cross and a profit is realized. At some point, competition causes the revenue and cost lines to approach each other again and finally cross, showing another loss.

2. To determine an optimal product price, the marginal revenue and marginal cost curves are plotted. **Marginal revenue** is the change in total revenue caused by a one-unit change in output. **Marginal cost** is the change in total cost caused by a one-unit change in output. The point where the two lines intersect is projected onto the demand curve, and a price is determined.

Objective 2: Identify external and internal factors on which prices are based (pp. 403-404).

3. Factors external to the company that tend to influence a product's price include (a) the total demand for the product or service, (b) the number of competing products or services; (c) the quality of competing products or services; (d) current prices of competing products or services; (e) customers' preferences for quality versus price; (f) a

sole source versus a heavily competitive market; (g) seasonal demand versus continual demand; and (h) the life of the product or service.

4. Internal factors that influence price include (a) the cost of the product or service, giving consideration to variable costs, full absorption costs, and total costs; (b) price geared toward return on investment; (c) loss leader or a main product; (d) the quality of materials and labor inputs; (e) labor-intensive automated production process; (f) mark up percentage; and (g) usage of scarce resources.

Objective 3: State the company objectives managers use to establish prices of goods and services (pp. 404-405).

5. Managers can use one of several objectives in establishing a price for their products, including (a) identifying and adhering to short-run and long-run pricing strategies; (b) maximizing profits; (c) maintaining or gaining market share; (d) setting socially responsible prices; (e) maintaining a stated rate of return on investment; and (f) ensuring that prices support a trend of total sales increases.

6. Of primary importance in setting company objectives is identifying the market being served and meeting the needs of that mar-

ket. Pricing strategies depend on many factors and conditions. Companies producing standard products for a competitive marketplace have different pricing strategies from firms making custom-designed items. The company making special-order items can be more conservative in its pricing strategy.

Objective 4: Create prices by applying the methods and tools of price determination (pp. 405-412).

7. Pricing is an art, not a science. Pricing is a very subjective problem. Many managers never develop the skills to set correct prices. There are traditional, objective, formula-driven pricing methods that can be used by managers to help set prices. But at some point a manager must deviate from those approaches and rely on his or her experience.

8. The four basic formula-driven pricing methods used in practice are (a) variable cost pricing, (b) gross margin pricing, (c) profit margin pricing, and (d) return on assets pricing.

9. **Variable cost pricing** is a cost-based pricing method that establishes a selling price at a certain percentage above an item's variable production costs. It uses two formulas:

$$\text{Markup percentage} = \frac{\text{Desired profit} + \text{total fixed production costs} + \text{total selling, general and administrative expenses}}{\text{Total variable production costs}}$$

Variable cost-based price = Variable production costs per unit + (markup percentage X variable production costs per unit)

10. **Gross margin pricing** is a cost-based pricing method that establishes a selling price at a percentage above an item's total production costs. It uses the following formulas:

$$\text{Markup percentage} = \frac{\text{Desired profit} + \text{total selling, general and administrative expenses}}{\text{Total production costs}}$$

Gross margin-based price = Total production costs per unit + (markup percentage X total production costs per unit)

11. **Profit margin pricing** is a cost-based pricing method that determines the price at a percentage of the desired profit factor. All costs and expenses are in the denominator of the markup percentage formula.

$$\text{Markup percentage} = \frac{\text{Desired profit}}{\text{Total costs and expenses}}$$

Profit margin-based price = Total costs and expenses per unit + (markup percentage X total costs and expenses per unit)

12. **Return on assets pricing** is a pricing method based on a specific rate of return on assets employed in the generation of the product or service. Assuming that a company has a stated minimum desired rate of return, this formula is used to calculate the return on assets-based price:

Return on assets-based price = Total costs and expenses per unit + (desired rate of return X total costs of assets employed ÷ anticipated units to be produced)

13. **Time and materials pricing** is common practice in service-oriented businesses. Two primary types of costs are used in this method: (a) materials and parts and (b) labor. An overhead rate (which includes a profit factor) is computed for both of these cost categories. When preparing a billing, the total price is determined by adding the following costs: (a) total cost of materials and parts, (b) materials and parts overhead percentage times (a), (c) total labor cost, and (d) labor cost overhead percentage times (c).

Objective 5: Define Defense Acquisition Regulation (DAR) and state the purpose of these guidelines (pp. 412-413).

14. When pricing government contracts, a company should include only appropriate cost and profit elements in the pricing process because it is the taxpayers' money that is being spent. Accordingly, the federal government has established a detailed set of laws and regulations in its attempt to exercise control over the procurement (that is, the acquisition of goods and services) process. In addition, a company that contracts with the federal government must follow the accounting practices and standards that the government has established.

For example, defense contract pricing must be cost based.

15. Two sets of procurement regulations govern most contracting arrangements with the federal government.
   a. **The Defense Acquisition Regulation (DAR)** is a complete set of policies and procedures for contracting with the Department of Defense. The purpose of DAR is to bring together in one publication all prescribed policies, including cost principles, that must be followed in contract pricing with the federal government's defense department.
   b. The Federal Procurement Regulation (FPR) is the primary regulation governing the procurement activities of civilian agencies.

Objective 6: Describe the federal government procurement environment (pp. 413-414).

16. The government procurement process begins with the determination of a need for supplies or services. Typically, inexpensive items are purchased on the open market. However, more expensive items are obtained through a process called *formal advertising.* Here, a government invitation is issued, specifying the need, terms, and conditions. Interested companies then submit bids within the allotted time, and the job usually goes to the lowest bidder.

17. Certain costly, highly complex items (planes, ships, guidance systems) are purchased by negotiating a price with a capable contractor. Where possible, the price is based on the contractor's estimated cost. When costs cannot be estimated reasonably, however, the price is based on the contractor's final cost plus a fee.

Objective 7: Identify and differentiate among the primary types of government contracts (pp. 414-417).

18. Government contracts are negotiated rather than advertised if the government agency is unable to advertise the requirement. These kinds of contracts involve security classifications, difficult-to-measure items such as research and development, and immediate-need items.

19. The two basic types of negotiated contracts used for defense procurement are firm fixed-price and cost-type contracts.
   a. Under firm fixed-price contracts, the contractor assumes the risk of loss because the price cannot be modified.
   b. Under cost-type contracts, the government assumes the risk of loss in that the contractor is reimbursed for costs incurred plus a profit. Variations on this type of contract are fixed-price incentive contracts, cost-plus-incentive fee contracts, and cost-plus-fixed fee contracts.

20. There are some major differences between government contract cost accounting and the cost accounting used for commercial work. For example, the concept of period costs is not applicable to government contract cost accounting. That is, all "allowable costs," whether or not customarily treated as product costs, are assigned to the contract. Thus, a form of full absorption costing is utilized.

Objective 8: State the rules and conditions under which costs are judged unallowable for contract pricing purposes (pp. 417-418).

21. The total cost of a contract is the sum of the **allowable direct costs** (that is, traceable materials and labor costs) and **indirect costs** allocable to the contract, incurred or to be incurred, less any allowable credits. The government disallows those costs that are unreasonable in amount or are otherwise unallowable according to government statutes or regulations. Examples of **unallowable costs** are entertainment, interest costs, advertising costs, and bad debt expenses.

Objective 9: Apply the guidelines and procedures in Cost Accounting Standards 402 and 403 (pp. 418-426).

22. In 1970, Congress established the Cost Accounting Standards Board (CASB) to develop standards for all government-negotiated contracts in excess of $100,000. Although the CASB was disbanded in 1980, all nineteen standards it developed are still in effect. Two of these cost accounting standards are CAS 402 and CAS 403.

a. CAS 402 relates to general cost accounting practices and was designed to prevent the **double counting** of costs. That is, it is illegal to include in an overhead pool any type of cost that already has been charged as a direct cost to a cost objective.

b. CAS 403 relates to specific cost accounting practice, prescribing fair and equitable ways to allocate home office expense to company segments. Created to maximize the costs that are more or less directly allocated, CAS 403 specified the order and manner in which home office expenses are to be allocated to the segments and ultimately to the contracts.

Testing Your Knowledge

Matching

Match each term with its definition by writing the appropriate letter in the blank.

___ 1. Marginal revenue

___ 2. Marginal cost

___ 3. Variable cost pricing

___ 4. Profit margin pricing

___ 5. Gross margin pricing

___ 6. Return on assets pricing

___ 7. Time and materials pricing

___ 8. Defense Acquisition Regulation (DAR)

___ 9. Direct cost

___ 10. Double counting

___ 11. Indirect cost

___ 12. Unallowable cost

a. A pricing approach often used by service-oriented companies

b. Price equals total production costs per unit plus the markup percentage times total production costs per unit

c. A cost not directly identified with a single final cost objective

d. Price equals variable production costs per unit plus the markup percentage times variable production costs per unit.

e. The change in total revenue caused by a one-unit change in output

f. Price equals total costs and expenses per unit plus the desired rate of return times total costs of assets employed divided by anticipated units to be made

g. Price equals total costs and expenses per unit plus the markup percentage times total costs and expenses per unit

h The change in total cost caused by a one-unit change in output

i. Charging the same costs more than once to the same contract

j. A cost that cannot be included in the determination of a government contract price.

k. A cost identified specifically with a particular contract

l. The policies and procedures for contracting with the Department of Defense

Completion

Use the lines provided to complete each item.

1. Explain the traditional economic approach to price determination.

_____

_____

_____

_____

2. Identify four external factors that can influence the pricing decision.

a. _____

b. _____

c. _____

d. _____

3. State four internal factors that can influence the pricing decision.

a. _____

b. _____

c. _____

d. _____

4. Explain the time and materials pricing calculation.

_____

_____

_____

_____

True-False

Circle T if the statement is true, F if it is false.

T F **1.** The process of establishing a correct price is more a science than an art.

T F **2.** Total revenue is defined as the change in revenue caused by a one-unit change in output.

T F **3.** Total demand for a product or service is an external factor that influences the pricing decision.

T F **4.** The long-run objectives of a company need not include a pricing policy because pricing decisions are short-run decisions.

T F **5.** Maintaining or gaining market share is an internal factor that influences pricing decisions.

T F **6.** A price computed using the variable cost pricing method is the same as a price determined using the gross margin pricing approach.

T F **7.** The markup percentage for profit margin pricing is applied to total costs and expenses per unit.

T F **8.** The return on assets pricing method often is used by service-oriented companies.

T F **9.** One objective of the CASB's standards is to improve the comparability and consistency of cost accounting practices.

T F **10.** A logical base for allocating the personnel administration function to a company's segments would be square footage of the segments.

T F **11.** Double counting is illegal in determining a cost-based government contract price.

T F **12.** The General Accounting Office (GAO) is responsible for determining whether the CASB's standards are being met by procurement agencies.

T F **13.** Under firm fixed-price contracts, the government assumes the risk of loss.

T F **14.** Bids must be solicited for all government contracts, with the job going to the lowest bidder.

T F **15.** It is possible that general and administrative expenses could be allowable in determining the price of a government contract.

Circle the letter of the best answer.

1. Establishing a price for an item has been called an art because
   a. the pricing process must be properly displayed.
   b. it takes a creative person with experience in pricing to arrive at a just and fair price.
   c. prices developed without supporting analysis are equally as good as those backed up by cost studies.
   d. prices are developed on an easel.

2. In the traditional economic pricing concept, the history of a product's sales shows two break-even points because
   a. start-up costs double.
   b. after the first break-even point, marginal costs equal marginal revenues.
   c. after the initial break-even point, increased competition tends to increase costs and decrease selling prices.
   d. total revenue always equals marginal cost.

3. Which of the following is *not* an external factor influencing the pricing decision?
   a. Return on investment
   b. Total demand for a product or service
   c. Current prices of competing products or services
   d. Seasonal or continual demand

4. Full absorption cost is an
   a. example of a marginal cost.
   b. opportunity cost.
   c. internal factor that influences price.
   d. unavoidable cost.

5. Which of the following is *not* a pricing policy objective?
   a. Maintaining or gaining market share
   b. Setting socially responsible prices
   c. Ensuring that prices support a trend of total sales increases
   d. Charging unrealistically low prices to eliminate competition

6. Total production costs per unit plus the markup percentage times total production costs per unit is the formula for
   a. variable cost pricing.
   b. gross margin pricing.
   c. profit margin pricing.
   d. return on assets pricing.

7. A common pricing method used by service-oriented businesses is
   a. variable cost pricing.
   b. gross margin pricing.
   c. time and materials pricing.
   d. profit margin pricing.

8. Which of the following costs would *not* normally be allowed in pricing a government contract?
   a. Advertising
   b. Direct labor
   c. Manufacturing overhead
   d. Direct materials

9. The process whereby bids are submitted for a government contract is called
   a. firm fixed-price contracting.
   b. full absorption costing.
   c. formal advertising.
   d. cost-type contracting.

10. The first step in allocating a company's home office expense to its segments is
    a. allocating residual home office expense to all segments.
    b. identifying all costs directly traceable to specific segments.
    c. allocating indirect home office expenses to all segments.
    d. accumulating costs in logical and homogeneous cost pools.

Applying Your Knowledge

Exercises

1. Marty Hi-Tech Corporation is in the process of developing a price for its new product, Triathlon. Anticipated production data reveal the following cost information:

Direct materials costs	$680,000
Direct labor costs	$552,500
Variable factory overhead costs	$204,000
Fixed factory overhead costs	$263,500
Marketing expenses	$238,000
General and administrative expenses	$510,000
Minimum desired profit	$382,500

Management predicts that 850,000 bottles of Triathlon will be produced and sold during the coming year.

From the data presented, compute the selling price per bottle using the following pricing methods:
a. Gross margin pricing
b. Profit margin pricing

2. Guardian Landscaping Company has just completed a major job for a customer. Costs for the job were $46,500 for materials and $32,800 for labor. Overhead and profit percentages developed at the beginning of the year were 40 percent for materials and supplies, 60 percent for labor. Prepare the billing for the customer using the time and materials pricing method. Show the breakdown of all the costs involved.

3. During 19xx, Edtech incurred $800,000 in home office personnel management costs. These costs are to be allocated to the company's five divisions for defense contract pricing purposes. The total square footage and number of employees of each division are listed below.

Division	Square Footage	Number of Employees
A	48,000	100
B	36,000	70
C	20,000	40
D	70,000	130
E	26,000	60

a. Allocate the personnel management costs to the five divisions using the two bases provided.

b. Which allocation base is in accordance with CAS 403?

The Price is Wrong

Base price on value, not cost, consultant says.

When Don Potter counsels companies on pricing products, the San Francisco management consultant sometimes cites this example:

His seven-year old daughter offered to wash his car. He agreed, and his daughter and three friends did the job. They then asked for $4. When Mr. Potter protested that a nearby car wash charged only $2, his daughter countered that she had promised each of her friends a buck for helping, and that she wanted a dollar, too.

"The job cost me $4, so that's what it's going to cost you," she explained.

Don Potter paid up, but afterward it struck him that "pricing decisions at many large, complex corporations are made on a model similar to that devised in the driveway by my daughter. They both use costs to determine what price customers are asked to pay for their products."

That's all wrong, says the one-time McKinsey & Co. partner who three years ago started his own firm, Windermere Associates Inc.

"Customers don't care a bit about a company's costs," he says. They're interested in *value,* he stresses, and prices should be set accordingly. "If prices were set by the relative value of the product offered to the customer, then costs could follow price—a concept I call 'design to price' or 'design to value' rather than the other way around."

GM, IBM Cited

Unfortunately, he charges, some 30% to 40% of U.S. companies continue to base price on costs. As a result, their market share is dropping, and some are even losing money. General Motors Corp. and IBM Corp. are prime examples, he contends.

Source: Article by James Braham. Reprinted with permission from *Industry Week,* December 6, 1986. Copyright, Penton Publishing, Inc., Cleveland, Ohio.

"GM in September announced a 5% average increase in car prices. They said the reason is 'our costs went up.' They don't say anything about price going up because 'our value to our customers would more than support that,' " Mr. Potter notes.

"If you raise prices when costs go up, that's O.K., *providing* somebody else is not able to offer a better-quality product for a lower or the same price. But the Japanese are offering better value. GM [and to a lesser extent other American automakers] is pricing over the value of its products."

As a result, GM's market share has been dropping since 1979, he says. Arvid Jouppi, Detroit auto analyst, says that GM's share of U.S. sales began tumbling in 1978, from 47.8% to 41.7% last year and about 41.3% this year.

IBM's personal computers, Mr. Potter charges, "are not only priced much higher than competing machines that do the same thing, they're priced higher than competing machines that do more."

IBM prices high "to protect its profit margin," but that's shortsighted, he holds. Unless price reflects greater value, more and more consumers will continue to buy from lower-priced competitors. IBM's PC market share already has plunged from about 70% to about half of that.

Cummins Has 'Guts'

As an example of smart pricing, effectively discouraging competition, the consultant cites Cummins Engine Co. Inc. The Columbus, Ind., firm, he explains, watched Japan's Komatsu and Nissan try to invade the U.S. medium-truck engine market with deep discounts from standard pricing.

"Cummins feared that if it let them in, the next thing they'd do is hit the heavy-truck market where Cummins is a major player. So Cummins dropped its prices by about a third. It essentially said, 'I'm going to stop these guys at the shoreline.'

"Now Cummins is going back through its cost structure, dealing with suppliers and other functions, and getting costs down to where it can make a profit with those new prices. And the Japanese are stopped at the beach."

Cummins no doubt felt "uncomfortable" slashing prices, but it was necessary to counter future competition, Mr. Potter believes. "That was a heck of a move. It really took guts."

All of this may sound simplistic, the consultant agrees. However, he says, "It's hard to do this, because you've got to put yourself into your customers' shoes. Most of us don't do that."

Perception

Mr. Jouppi believes that Mr. Potter's criticism of GM pricing is largely a matter of perception of value. "The range of what people perceive to be value [in car prices] ranges from $170,000 down to $30. So if you price purely on what people see as value, you'd have no control over what the cost is. You'd go all over the place."

GM and the domestic auto industry generally base price upon cost and competition, or "cost plus a profit," he says. Even Japan bases its price on costs, he argues. The Japanese simply have lower costs.

"I think we're dealing with a semantics problem," the auto analyst continues. "No manufacturer can go ahead and willy-nilly meet the competition by simply cutting the price. If they do that and costs don't go down," the company would be in serious trouble, he indicates.

What about the Cummins Engine example? This suggests that "all the costs have not been wrung out," Mr. Jouppi replies. "In a highly competitive situation, all the costs have to be wrung out so the manufacturer can make a profit." Even then, he cautions, "it may turn out that your competitor is more efficient than you, or his labor rate is lower, or he's better organized."

Like GM, IBM also realized its pricing predicament. Unlike GM, it has been lowering PC prices; they're still substantially higher than competitor's, however.

IBM's prices on all of its products are generally higher than those of its competitors, observes Steve Josselyn, analyst for International Data Corp. In fact, he says, lower prices are the way rivals compete with IBM.

CHAPTER 12 SHORT-RUN DECISION ANALYSIS

REVIEWING THE CHAPTER

Objective 1: Define and identify information relevant to decision making (p. 450).

1. One important function of the management accountant is to provide management with relevant information supporting decision making. **Relevant decision information** refers to future cost, revenue, or resource usage that will be different for the alternative courses of action under study.

Objective 2: Describe the steps in the management decision cycle (pp. 450-452).

2. The management decision cycle covers (a) discovering the problem or need, (b) identifying the alternative courses of action, (c) analyzing the effects of each alternative on business operations, (d) selecting the best alternative, and (e) judging the success of the decision through post-decision audit analysis.

Objective 3: Calculate unit costs using variable costing procedures (pp. 452-455).

3. Variable costing and incremental analysis are the two most common decision tools used by the management accountant. **Variable costing** (also called direct costing) uses only direct materials, direct labor, and variable factory overhead in product costing. Fixed factory overhead is considered a period cost (expense).

4. Variable costing is very useful for internal management decision making but is not acceptable for tax or financial reporting purposes. Under variable costing, the income statement discloses the contribution margin, a very useful figure for decision analysis. Absorption costing includes fixed factory overhead. This is one more product cost in computing unit cost that variable costing ignores for this process. Therefore, unit cost will vary with volume under absorption costing, whereas it will not vary with volume under variable costing.

Objective 4: Prepare an income statement, using the contribution margin reporting format (p. 455).

5. Unlike the conventional form of income statement based on the absorption costing approach to product costing, the contribution margin reporting format focuses on the difference between fixed costs and variable costs. First, variable cost of goods sold and variable operating and selling expenses are deducted from sales to arrive at a figure called the contribution margin. Second, all fixed costs, operating, selling and administrative, are deducted from the contribution margin to arrive at pre-tax net income.

6. In general, the contribution margin format is more useful for managerial decision making than the conventional format. If a corporate segment, such as a division, department, or product line, is being eval-

uated, preparing an income statement using the contribution margin format pinpoints the ability of the operating unit or product line to absorb its fixed costs and generate a profit. This approach to performance evaluation is not apparent from information on the conventional income statement.

Objective 5: Develop decision data, using the technique of incremental analysis (pp. 455-458).

7. **Incremental analysis** is a decision-making tool that compares cost and revenue data of alternative courses of action. In most cases, only relevant data are included in the analysis. According to the incremental-analysis method, the alternative that results in the highest increase in net income or cost savings is the best alternative. Attention is focused on the difference in the analysis.

Objective 6a: Evaluate alternatives involving make-or-buy decisions (pp. 458-460).

8. Management is continually faced with the **make or buy decision** about parts that go into product assembly. Should the company continue to purchase these parts from outside suppliers or should they be produced internally? The incremental analysis is the best approach to this type of decision, using the relevant costs of the two alternatives. All other things being equal, the alternative resulting in the lowest incremental cost is the one that should be chosen.

Objective 6b: Evaluate alternatives involving special-order decisions (pp. 460-461).

9. Management often must decide whether to accept or to reject special orders of its products. In such cases, only the variable costs become relevant because it is assumed that the fixed costs have been or will be absorbed by normal sales of products or services. In such **special-order decisions**, both incremental analysis and contribution margin reporting can be used to prepare the analysis. In either case, the goal is to compare data that includes the special order with data that does not include the order.

Objective 6c: Evaluate alternatives involving scarce-resource/sales-mix decisions (pp. 462-463).

10. **Scarce-resource decisions** focus on the most effective way to utilize the scarce-resource. Assume that a company has a rare machine that has limited capacity. Three of its products must be processed through this machine center. Each product has an unlimited market demand. The management accountant should compute the contribution margin *per machine hour* for this machine center to determine which of the three products contributes most to fixed costs and company profits. When the product has been identified, produce as much as sales will allow. If demand is reached, then produce quantities of the second biggest contributor.

11. **Sales-mix analysis** is used to find the most profitable combination of product sales when a company is producing more than one product. Generally, the strategy is first to figure the contribution margin for each product. Second, the ratio of contribution margin to capital equipment should be computed for each product to see if some products are more profitable than others. If demand exists, emphasis should be shifted to the more profitable products.

Objective 6d: Evaluate decisions to eliminate unprofitable segments (pp. 463-466).

12. The **analysis of unprofitable segments** compares operating results of the corporation as a whole with operating results for the corporation minus the segment in question. The goal is to isolate the performance of the segment being evaluated. The analysis described below must go beyond the normal contribution margin approach. One must first compute **divisional income**, which equals contribution margin minus traceable fixed costs. A **traceable fixed cost** is one that is clearly associated with a particular segment. Most traceable fixed costs are also **avoidable** costs, in that they will disappear if the segment is eliminated. All unallocated fixed costs (costs not traceable to a segment) should simply be deducted from the "total company" column. Then, incremental analysis will answer the question by comparing income for the company if the segment is kept with income if it is eliminated. Care must be exercised not to treat traceable costs that are *not* also

avoidable as costs that may be saved upon eliminating the segment.

Objective 6e: Evaluating alternatives involving sell or process-further decisions (pp. 466-468).

13. A **sell or process-further decision** centers on the choice between selling a joint product at the split-off point or processing it further. This decision analysis requires an analysis of incremental revenues and costs of the two courses of action. The main objective is to determine if the product's selling price will increase more than the costs incurred to get it to a saleable condition. Key to the decision is the fact that joint cost allocation results are not relevant to the decision. Only the incremental costs and revenues beyond split-off are important.

Testing Your Knowledge

Matching

Match each term with its definition by writing the appropriate letter in the blank.

____ **1.** Variable costing (direct costing)

____ **2.** Incremental analysis

____ **3.** Sales-mix analysis

____ **4.** Relevant information

____ **5.** Decision model

____ **6.** Contribution margin

____ **7.** Special-order decision

____ **8.** Sell or process-further decision

____ **9.** Traceable fixed cost

____ **10.** Make-or-buy decision

a. Fixed costs that are associated with a segment of a business rather than the business as a whole

b. Future cost, revenue, or resource usage data that will be different for the various alternatives being evaluated

c. A symbolic or numerical representation of the variables and parameters affecting a decision

d. The assignment of direct materials, direct labor, and variable factory overhead costs to products

e. A decision analysis in which management is faced with two alternatives, either produce the product or purchase it from an outside vendor

f. The comparison of cost and revenue data that differ among alternatives

g. The decision either to sell a joint product at split-off or to subject it to additional processing

h. Determining the most profitable combination of product sales

i. Sales revenue minus all variable costs

j. The decision to accept an additional sales order beyond normal, anticipated sales

Use the lines provided to complete each item.

1. List the five steps in the management decision cycle.

1. _____

2. _____

3. _____

4. _____

5. _____

2. Distinguish between relevant and irrelevant information.

_____

_____

_____

_____

3. Compare variable costing with absorption costing. Identify the differences.

_____

_____

_____

_____

4. Identify five operating decisions of management.

1. _____

2. _____

3. _____

4. _____

5. _____

True-False

Circle T if the statement is true, F if it is false.

T F **1.** Absorption costing is not acceptable for financial reporting purposes.

T F **2.** Ending inventory is valued higher under variable costing than it is under absorption costing.

T F **3.** Under absorption costing, fixed factory overhead is considered a period cost.

T F **4.** When the contribution margin is less than fixed costs, a net loss has occurred.

T F **5.** When incremental analysis is used, the main concern is with each alternative's net income projection.

T F **6.** Incremental analysis is very useful for make-or-buy decisions.

T F **7.** For special-order analysis, costs that vary because of this special decision are the only relevant costs.

T F **8.** Management decisions require the selection of a course of action from a defined set of alternatives.

T F **9.** Strategic planning involves management decisions concerning company objectives, organizational structure, growth policies, market specialization, and other factors affecting the basic structure of the firm.

T F **10.** If decision alternatives involve both costs and revenues, the typical objective is to maximize annual profits.

T F **11.** Contribution margin is the amount that a segment or product line is contributing to cover the variable costs and profits of the company.

T F **12.** For most special decision reports, there is one correct, set structure to use.

T F **13.** Special-order decision analysis requires determining the most profitable combination of product sales when a company produces more than one product or offers more than one service.

T F **14.** Fixed costs associated with a particular operating segment are commonly called traceable fixed costs.

Multiple Choice

Circle the letter of the best answer.

1. When volume increases,
   a. the unit cost increases under variable costing.
   b. the unit cost decreases under variable costing.
   c. the unit cost increases under absorption costing.
   d. the unit cost decreases under absorption costing.

2. The best method to use in deciding whether to make or buy a product is
   a. variable costing.
   b. equivalent unit analysis.
   c. incremental analysis.
   d. absorption costing.

3. The contribution approach would probably not be used
   a. when deciding whether to discontinue a particular product line.
   b. when performing sales-mix analysis.
   c. when deciding which of two machines to purchase.
   d. when deciding whether to accept a special product order.

4. Products A, B, and C have contribution margins of $3, $5, and $4 per unit, respectively. Granada Company intends to manufacture one of the products and expects sales to be $30,000 regardless of which product is produced. Which product will result in the highest net income for Granada, assuming that the same machinery and workers would be used to produce each?
   a. Product A
   b. Product B
   c. Product C
   d. More information is needed.

5. Which of the following costs is a product cost under absorption costing but not under variable costing?
   a. Variable factory overhead
   b. Fixed factory overhead
   c. Direct materials
   d. Direct labor

6. Estimated future costs that differ between alternative courses of action are termed
   a. relevant costs.
   b. absorption costs.
   c. variable overhead costs.
   d. replacement costs.

7. For several years a company has produced a joint product that is processed after split-off. The product is saleable at the split-off point. To justify additional processing, a decision analysis should demonstrate that
   a. ultimate revenues exceed all joint and separable costs.
   b. additional processing increases the revenue potential.
   c. separable processing costs are less than incremental revenues.
   d. unit production costs after additional processing are lower.

8. The point in the production process when joint products are first identifiable is the
   a. break-even point.
   b. split-off point.
   c. point of indifference.
   d. point of inflection.

9. Costs that can be eliminated if a particular operating segment or activity is discontinued are called
   a. avoidable costs.
   b. fixed costs
   c. historical costs.
   d unnecessary costs.

10. Allocation of joint production costs is of concern to sell or process-further decisions because
   a. allocation method selection is critical to the decision.
   b. assignment of joint production costs can be influenced by the final decision.
   c. such costs are irrelevant to the decision and should be ignored.
   d. such costs must be minimized.

Applying Your Knowledge

Exercises

1. A company must decide whether to purchase machine Q for $10,000 or machine R for $17,000. Machine Q will require the use of two operators, each of whom earns $8,000 per year. It will require maintenance of $300 per year, but will save the company $50 per year in electricity over the machine currently in use. Machine R will require only one operator at $8,000 per year. It will require maintenance of $500 per year, but will cost $80 per year more for electricity over the machine currently in use. In addition, each machine will generate the same amount of revenue. Prepare an incremental analysis to determine which machine to purchase.

2. On June 30, 19x1, Calendars, Unltd., had 100,000 unsold 19x1 calendars. Direct materials costs are $3 per calendar, direct labor is $2 per calendar, variable overhead is $.50 per calendar, and fixed overhead (based on a production volume of 300,000 calendars) is $1 per calendar. Shipping and packaging (paid by the company) is $1.75 per calendar. The normal selling price is $12 per calendar. What is the *minimum* special price that the company could set for the unsold calendars?

3. Harold Enterprises, Inc., processes coconut oil, coconut milk, and edible coconut meat from raw coconuts imported from Hawaii. The products can be sold at point of split-off or processed further into high-quality end products. Selling price information is shown below.

	Unit Selling Price If Sold	
Product	At Split-Off Point	After Additional Processing
Coconut oil	$4.00/gallon	$5.50/gallon
Coconut milk	$1.00/gallon	$1.20/gallon
Coconut meat	$1.50/pound	$1.95/pound

There are 150,000 coconuts to be processed and total production for the year 19x6 is expected to be as follows:

Product	Quantity
Coconut oil	40,000 gallons (25,000 pounds)
Coconut milk	100,000 gallons (25,000 pounds)
Coconut meat	50,000 gallons

The cost accounting department estimates that processing costs beyond split-off will be $40,000 for coconut oil, $25,000 for coconut milk, and $20,000 for coconut meat. Budgeted joint processing costs for 19x6 will be $175,000.

Determine which product(s) should be sold at split-off point and/or which product(s) should be processed further. Justify your answer.

Crossword Puzzle
for Chapters 11 and 12

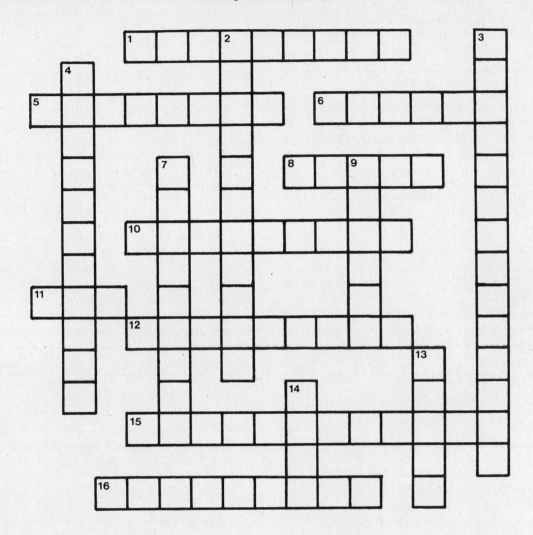

ACROSS

1. Cost that can be eliminated
5. Identified with two or more cost objectives
6. Traceable to a particular contract
8. Special- —— decision
10. Decision that uses 2-Down (hyphenated)
11. Defense contract law (initials)
12. Operating constraint or limitation
15. Pertinent decision information (2 words)
16. Assignable to a government contract

DOWN

2. Analysis focusing on differences between alternatives
3. Price determination basis (3 words)
4. Omitted in determining a government contract price
7. Attributable to a business segment
9. CAS 402 forbids —— counting
13. —— margin pricing
14. Source of government contract standards (initials)

Three-way Path to Fair Analysis of Performance

Is the operating manager being burdened with an unfair share of the company's costs? Clearer performance reporting, measuring his unit's contribution, is needed.

Budgeting gives quantitative expression to plans. Budgetary control involves extracting significant deviations from the budget in the form of variances and analying these in order to assess and control events. Care is needed in the way budget and performance information is presented, because this is likely to influence its reception.

A way of setting out the information, based on its segregation into those items which the operating manager can and cannot control, will help in the appropriate and efficient analysis of various aspects of the organisation's performance.

For simplicity, in the following discussion the word 'unit' will be used to mean either a department or other operating unit or the enterprise as a whole. What is said will be equally applicable to all levels within the organisation.

An initial step in budgetary control concerns the classification of costs. This is because it is important to draw a distinction, for control purposes, between:

> fixed and variable costs,
> indirect and direct costs, and
> controllable and uncontrollable costs.

Fixed costs are those not affected by the level of output over the time period being considered. Examples of fixed costs include the costs of managing a unit, the occupancy costs of rent, rates and so on, all of which tend to remain the same whether the unit produces at 60%, 90% or some other percentage of capacity.

Variable costs are related to the level of output, although not necessarily having a linear relationship with it. Examples of variable costs include the cost of the direct materials used in production, royalty payments and the use of power directly related to the levels of production.

Indirect costs are expenses which are jointly incurred by a number of different cost centres. Thus, for a manufacturer who produces a number of products, at different units but for the same market, an advertising expense[1] incurred by jointly advertising all of those products in a particular publication will have to be allocated between the various units concerned. In the large organisation, the general manager's salary will have to be allocated over a number of departmental cost centres. In the production unit, consumables[1] will be allocated over the different products.

Direct costs are those costs or expenses directly attributable to a cost centre, that is the operating unit, and the 'directness' will depend upon the level of the unit being considered. Direct costs in any factory department will include all costs of production, such as the salary of the managers employed within it, those costs associated with raw materials used, direct expenses and so on. A small firm operating as a single unit would have no indirect costs, all costs being direct.

Controllable costs are those over which the operating manager has some control, although this may be only within certain limits—for example, the power used to heat his department, or the cost associated with substandard production due to insufficient training and supervision of operatives. Uncontrollable costs are those 'imposed' on the operating manager, such as the rent for his unit negotiated by higher management, or the rates dictated by the local authority.

Three points arise from the above classifications:

1. Although the classification of a cost within any of the three goupings—fixed and variable; indirect and direct; controllable and uncontrollable—is mutually exclusive, i.e.

---

[1]These indirect costs may be classified as fixed or variable for other purposes, e.g. advertising and salary will be fixed, and consumables are likely to be variable.

Source: Article by Mike Harvey. Reprinted with permission from the November issue of *Accountancy*.

elements of a cost must be either fixed or variable, there is no mutual exclusivity as far as the classification of a cost as between the three groupings is concerned. A cost can be, for example, fixed, indirect, and uncontrollable at one and the same time.

2. Fixed costs are not necessarily indirect costs, and neither are variable costs always direct.

3. It is crucial in budgetary control, for motivational reasons, to distinguish between whether a cost is controllable or uncontrollable.

Obviously, at the extreme, somebody somewhere, within any business, must ultimately be able to control any cost that the organisation faces. This may be even to the extent of deciding whether to close the firm down, which effectively 'controls' a normally uncontrollable expense such as local authority rates, by stopping the cost from being incurred in the future.

As one goes down the hierarchy of management, it is usual to find that successive managers at lower and lower levels have less and less control over the expenses necessary for the operation over which they are responsible. For example, the manager of a shop floor production unit is unlikely to have control over the rent negotiated by headquarters for the space that his department uses; or the hourly rate paid to employees in his unit, although he may have some control over the number of hours of overtime that he authorises them to work.

All this means that care has to be taken in the classification of costs for control and appraisal—different classifications will be needed for different purposes.

From the foregoing, it can be seen that an operating manager rarely has control over the fixed costs associated with his unit's operations. However, he may have influence over some fixed costs, such as those associated with repairs, through the use of preventive maintenance. It is generally only some aspects of the variable costs of his unit over which he is likely to have significant influence.

Even then, it is only those variable costs which can be classified as direct that are likely to be controllable by him. He is unlikely to be able to influence the indirect costs allocated to his department by headquarters, such as its share of the central and administrative costs that the firm has to pay—other than through protesting about the level of allocation!

The question of allocating indirect costs is important, since each department within an organisation is likely to be faced with an allocation of the group's central costs to its budget. Such an allocation is unlikely to have been made carelessly, and usually will have some apparently logical basis. So one important question about the allocation revolves around whether it has been made using the most appropriate method taking into account the circumstances of the group's cost centres. The only indisputable fact is that any allocation of indirect costs provides an uncontrollable cost for the manager receiving the allocation.

A budgetary control report should be structured in a way which both highlights the performance of the unit and enables an analysis of the unit's overall contribution to the company's performance to be made. The most appropriate layout for providing performance and other information for an operating unit is to use a basically *three-section* approach.[2]

A layout such as that suggested below will help in the analysis of the information by showing a unit's contribution towards central costs and the company's overall profit. It also provides helpful information for comparing performance as between units, and effectively enables the efficiency of the operating manager of the unit to be appraised.

Items are entered in the various sections of the report depending upon their directness and the degree of control that the manager can exert upon them.

The example provided is for a production unit. Although here its manager is unlikely to be able to influence the sales of what his department manufactures, assuming that the product specification is met and there are no capacity constraints, these sales are nevertheless included. This is a common practice because the production manager, who does influence the costs of his unit's production, should know the difference between sales values and production and other costs.

The information in the figure can be analysed as follows. The controllable direct items are shown in the top section of the report. By their very nature, they will also be the direct costs of the unit that is being controlled. The man-

---

[2]It should be noted that in the case of the small enterprise operating as a single unit, with an all-embracing budget and no central costs needing to be allocated, a two-section approach should be used. In such organisations, only the top two sections of the table will be required.

Suggested layout for a unit's contribution to costs and profit

Section		Fixed budget £	Fixed budget £	Actual £	Variance £
Top	*Controllable direct items*				
	Sales	102	106	106	—
	Cost of raw materials	58	60	61	(1)
	Wages and salaries	15	15	14	1
	Occupancy costs (e.g. heat, power, etc.)	2	2	2	—
	Other (e.g. packaging, etc.)	1	1	1	—
	Cost of production	76	78	78	—
	Controllable direct contribution	26	28	28	—
Middle	*Uncontrollable direct items*				
	Occupancy costs (rent, rates, etc.)	8	8	10	(2)
	Other (including depreciation)	4	4	4	—
		12	12	14	(2)
	Direct contribution	14	16	14	(2)
Bottom	*Uncontrollable indirect costs*				
	Marketing and sales costs	10	10	10	—
	Central administration costs	3	3	5	(2)
		13	13	15	(2)
	Profit/loss of unit	1	3	(1)	(4)
Reconciliation with fixed budget	Increase/(decrease) in profit attributed to increase/(decrease) in sales (i.e. flexed budget profit *less* fixed budget profit)				2
		1	**N/A**	**(1)**	**(2)**

Notes:
1. The fixed budget must be flexed to enable variance analysis to take place.
2. Unfavourable variances are shown in brackets.
3. Although the bottom level items concern uncontrollable costs allocated to the unit, they could also be divided into those costs which were, and were not, controllable by higher authorities.
4. In practice, the figure can contain up to some 30 itemised costs appropriate to the cost circumstances of the unit.

ager can use overtime and heating and lighting as economically as possible, and as he has some sort of control over the cost of these and similar items, they will be entered in this section.

Because the manager has a degree of control over items in the top section, it is against the summary of this information—which leads to *the controllable direct contribution*—that his performance should be appraised.

However, the unit itself must make a positive contribution. To appraise performance in this respect, the uncontrollable direct costs incurred, such as rent, rates, the depreciation of the unit's fixed assets, and so on, must be brought into the analysis. These are entered in the middle section of the report. The deduction of the total of the items in this section from the controllable direct contribution leads to the *direct contribution* of the unit towards the group's overall performance.

It is information on this direct contribution that should be used in decisions concerning how viable a production unit really is.[3] The direct contribution must be positive over the

[3] When using the middle section of the report to make a decision as to whether to close the unit down it must be remembered that any reduction in the economic value of fixed assets through using them must be substituted for any depreciation shown in book value terms.

long run if the unit is to be allowed to continue to exist, unless there are special circumstances which necessitate it operating on a negative contribution basis.[4]

The figure arrived at can also be used to rank the direct contributions of the various units operating within the organisation. However, such a simple comparison is not enough: the investment in the unit, and other investment opportunities available to the firm, must also be brought into the analysis before the relative performance of units within the group can be ascertained, and decisions made about the optimum use of the organisation's resources.

Any central costs allocated to the unit go in the bottom section of the report, because such costs must eventually be covered by the group. Their total is deducted from the direct contribution to show the *recorded profit or loss* of the unit, based on the accounting policies used.

However, the result does not necessarily provide a figure upon which decisions about the unit's future should be based. As long as a unit is making some direct contribution towards the group's central costs, which information can be ascertained from the middle section of the report, and while there are no other better investment opportunities open to the enterprise, the unit should be allowed to remain in operation. To close it would cause the organisation to make an even smaller overall profit— *unless the closure enabled a greater reduction in the enterprise's central overheads than the contribution foregone.*

It could be argued that any costs which are likely to be reduced on closedown should have been worked into the middle section of the report. And this is all assuming that the costs in the top two sections can be saved through the closure of the unit.

[4]For example, a component required to make a product may only be available if the firm makes it itself, or the product may be sold jointly with another profitable one which cannot stand alone.

An analysis of the budget and operational results provided in the figure helps in the understanding of the benefits associated with the three-section approach. In the top section, it can be seen that the unit has bettered its budget with sales and controllable direct contribution, but the direct contribution is only as budgeted. The gains from the top section have been 'lost' to rent increases which were at a level beyond that budgeted for. However, the manager was not involved in negotiating rent and so had no control over this or any of the other figures in the middle section.

The bottom section shows that the unit reported an overall loss instead of achieving the overall profit which was budgeted. This was because more headquarters costs had been allocated to it than were originally budgeted for. It is not, however, a signal to close the unit down, but merely points to a need to investigate the level and the allocation of costs from headquarters.

Such an investigation should ask whether central costs give value for money and are necessary at the levels shown. It must be borne in mind that those costs must be covered by the organisation in some way if it is to survive. A futher question to be asked is whether it is necessary to allocate the costs at all and if so, whether the method of allocation is fair. The analysis must always have regard to the fact that if the unit is closed down, and the headquarters costs cannot be reduced, the proportion formerly provided by the unit will still have to be recovered from the units which continue to operate.

In summary, an important aspect of the use of budgetary control concerns its acceptance by operating managers—their acceptance of the technique is strongly influenced by them seeing that it reports their performance in a fair way. The three-section approach does this, and has the added advantage of providing information to management in a way that clearly segregates it for different purposes.

CHAPTER 13 CAPITAL EXPENDITURE DECISIONS

REVIEWING THE CHAPTER

Objective 1: Define and discuss the capital expenditure decision process (pp. 487-488).

1. **Capital expenditure decisions** involve the determination of when and how much to spend on capital facilities for the company. These include but are not limited to decisions about installing new equipment, replacing old equipment, expanding the production area by adding to a building, buying or constructing a new factory or office building, or acquiring another company.

2. The capital expenditure decision process, also referred to as **capital budgeting,** consists of identifying the need for a facility, analyzing courses of action to meet that need, preparing reports for management, choosing the best alternatives, and rationing capital expenditure funds among competing resource needs.

Objective 2: Identify and describe the steps in the capital expenditure decision cycle (pp. 488-493).

3. The capital expenditure decision cycle occurs within a defined time period and under constraints imposed by economic policies, conditions, and objectives originating at corporate, industry, and/or national levels. Steps in the **capital expenditure decision cycle** include (a) detection of capital facility needs; (b) preparation of request for a capital expenditure; (c) pre-liminary analysis of requests; (d) the initial screening process; (e) development of acceptance-rejection standards, including analysis of existing capital mix of the company and determination of the average cost of capital; (f) coordination and formalization of procedures for the remaining requests; (g) final evaluation of proposals, including several methods of evaluation; (h) final selection of alternatives following the determination of funds available for capital expenditures; (i) authorization and appropriation of funds; (j) implementation of projects, and (k) post-completion audit analysis.

Objective 3: Describe the purpose of a minimum desired rate of return, and explain the methods used to arrive at this rate (pp. 493-495).

4. **A minimum desired rate of return** is set by a company's management and identifies the return on investment expected from all operations of the business. Any expenditure proposal that predicts a rate of return below the minimum is automatically refused.

5. The most common measures used to determine a company's minimum desired rate of return are (a) average cost of capital, (b) corporate return on investment, (c) industry's average return on investment, and (d) bank interest rate. The average cost of capital is the primary approach used and consists of computing the average cost of

company debt, preferred stock, equity capital, and retained earnings.

Objective 4: Identify information relevant to the capital expenditure decision process (pp. 496-497).

6. Evaluating capital expenditure proposals requires dealing with large amounts of information, most of which is projected data. Some decision analyses use cost savings as a base while others depend on net cash flow. The book value of assets being replaced often enters the decision analysis. This amount is irrelevant because it is a past cost. Disposal or salvage values of existing assets is relevant because it represents future cash flows. Depreciation expense is relevant to some decision analyses but is irrelevant when dealing with cash flows. However, depreciation does affect taxes paid so it does enter into the determination of net cash flow. Even versus uneven cash flows are a part of capital expenditure decision analyses and must be accounted for properly to assure accurate results.

Objective 5a: Evaluate capital expenditure proposals, using the accounting rate-of-return method (pp. 497-498).

7. The evaluation step of the capital expenditure decision analysis may be accomplished by using the accounting rate-of-return method, the pay-back period method, or the net present method.

8. The **accounting rate of return** equals
$$\frac{\text{project's average annual after-tax net income}}{\text{average investment cost}}$$

The average investment cost equals
$$\frac{\text{total investment + salvage value}}{2}$$

If this method is used, management should think seriously about the investment if the rate of return is higher than the minimum desired rate.

Objective 5b: Evaluate capital expenditure proposals, using the pay-back period method (pp. 498-499).

9. The **pay-back period method** is a tool for finding the minimum length of time it would take to recover an initial investment. When a choice must be made between investment alternatives, the one with the shortest pay-back period is best under this method. The pay-back period is found by dividing the cost of the investment by the projected annual net cash inflow.

Objective 6: Apply the concept of time value of money (pp. 499-501).

10. The **time value of money** implies that cash flows of equal dollar amounts separated by an interval of time will have different current values. This concept is useful in determining the net present value of a series of net cash inflows in capital expenditure decisions.

Objective 7: Evaluate capital expenditure proposals, using the discounted cash flow—present-value method (pp. 501-503).

11. The basis for the **present-value method** is that cash flows from different time periods have different values when measured in current dollars. For example, a dollar that will be received one year from now is currently worth somewhat less than a dollar to be received today. The method is applied by first discounting all cash flows back to the present. (The discount multiplier is based on the minimum desired rate of return and the discount period.) Second, if the net present value of all of the future cash flows exceeds the cost of the asset to be purchased, the expenditure is justified.

Objective 8: Analyze capital expenditure decision alternatives that incorporate the effects of income taxes (pp. 503-506).

12. All capital expenditure analyses should include the effects of income taxes. A company's tax liability will increase as a result of gains or decrease as a result of losses on the sale of assets. Noncash expenses such as depreciation will also affect taxes. Depreciation provides a cash benefit by reducing the amount of taxes to be paid.

13. One important way to keep taxes as low as possible is through careful timing of business transactions. If a company is nearing the top of its tax bracket late in the year,

it may put off an income-producing transaction until the next year. Or it may time the selling of assets in a way that reduces taxes. Other aspects of the tax law offer preferential treatment for certain transactions. It is always considered good management to consider such possibilities.

Objective 9: Rank proposals competing for limited capital expenditure funds (pp. 506-507).

14. One of the most important aspects of the capital expenditure decision process is the determination of the funds available for current expenditure requests. Once this amount has been determined, the management accountant awaits the last screening of the capital expenditure requests. When the final list of acceptable proposals has been identified, each request is ranked by projected rate of return. Requests are then selected based on the funds available.

Testing Your Knowledge

Matching

Match each term with its definition by writing the appropriate letter in the blank.

____ **1.** Capital budgeting

____ **2.** Discounted cash flow

____ **3.** Accounting rate-of-return method

____ **4.** Pay-back period method

____ **5.** Present value method

____ **6.** Capital expenditure decision

____ **7.** Average cost of capital

____ **8.** Time value of money

____ **9.** Cost of retained earnings

____ **10.** Cost of debt

a. The ratio of loan charges to net proceeds of the loan

b. A concept that states that cash flows of equal dollar amounts separated by an interval of time have different current values

c. Determining when and how much to spend on capital facilities

d. The process of identifying the need for a facility, analyzing different actions, preparing reports, choosing the best alternative, and rationing available funds among competing needs

e. The capital expenditure evaluation method that determines the minimum length of time it would take to recover an asset's initial cost

f. The capital expenditure evaluation method that divides a proposed project's net income by the average investment cost

g. The concept applied using the present value method

h. The opportunity cost or the dividends given up by the stockholder

i. The weighted average of the cost of debt, cost of preferred stock, cost on equity capital, and cost of retained earnings

j. The capital expenditure evaluation method that discounts all net cash inflows back to the present

Completion

Use the lines provided to complete each item.

1. List the five steps involved in capital budgeting.

1. _____

2. _____

3. _____

4. _____

5. _____

2. Identify the environmental factors that influence the capital facility decision cycle.

_____

_____

_____

_____

_____

3. List three methods frequently used to evaluate capital expenditure proposals.

1. _____
2. _____
3. _____

4. Identify the four costs that are used to compute the average cost of capital.

1. _____
2. _____
3. _____
4. _____

True-False

Circle T if the statement is true, F if it is false.

T F **1.** Capital budgeting involves the various methods of obtaining cash for business operations.

T F **2.** The simplest method to apply in evaluating a capital investment proposal is the present value method.

T F **3.** The time value of money is ignored in both the accounting rate-of-return and pay-back period methods.

T F **4.** The pay-back period is the maximum length of time it should take to recover in cash the cost of an investment.

T F **5.** The pay-back period equals the cost of the capital investment divided by the annual net cash inflow.

T F **6.** Under the present value method, there is no need for a minimum desired rate of return.

T F **7.** When using the present value method, a negative net present value means that the project proposal should probably be rejected.

T F **8.** A loss on the sale of plant assets could actually provide a cash benefit through a reduction in taxes.

T F **9.** A corporation should always put off income-producing transactions until early the following year if it wants to save on taxes.

T F **10.** Book values of existing assets are relevant considerations when analyzing capital expenditure proposals for replacing facilities.

T F **11.** Tax considerations are not important when evaluating alternative capital expenditure proposals.

T F **12.** The process of screening, evaluating, and selecting capital expenditure projects that satisfy corporate objectives describes the discounted cash flow concept.

T F **13.** Disposal or salvage values are not relevant to capital expenditure proposal evaluations.

T F **14.** Depreciation expense is relevant to all cash-flow-based criteria for decision evaluation.

Multiple Choice

Circle the letter of the best answer.

1. Under the account rate-of-return method, which of the following data is irrelevant?
   a. Salvage value of asset
   b. Annual net cash inflow
   c. Cost of asset
   d. Project's average annual after-tax net income

2. When using the present value method, which of the following net cash inflows will result in the highest amount when discounted to the present period (19x1) at a 10 percent discount rate? (Use the tables in Appendix D.)
   a. $755 received in 19x1
   b. $815 to be received in 19x2
   c. $880 to be received in 19x3
   d. $1,000 to be received in 19x4

3. The earnings lost by not selecting the second best alternative is the definition of
   a. relevant costs.
   b. incremental costs.
   c. sunk costs.
   d. opportunity costs.

4. The method of capital expenditure evaluation that brings the time value of money into the analysis is the
   a. present value method.
   b. accounting rate of return on initial investment.
   c. pay-back period method.
   d. accounting rate of return on average investment.

5. The time value of money is considered in long-range investment decisions by
   a. investing only in short-term projects.
   b. assigning greater value to more immediate cash flows.
   c. weighting cash flows with subjective probabilities.
   d. assuming equal annual cash-flow patterns.

6. The pay-back period method measures
   a. how quickly investment dollars may be recovered.
   b. the cash flow from an investment.
   c. the economic life of an investment.
   d. the probability of an investment.

7. In the capital expenditure evaluation process, the management accountant's responsibilities lie in the area of
   a. detection of facility need.
   b. initial screening.
   c. methods of computation and final screening.
   d. final selection of alternatives.

8. The present value method of evaluating proposed investments
   a. measures a project's time-adjusted rate of return.
   b. ignores cash flows beyond the pay-back period.
   c. applies only to mutually exclusive investment proposals.
   d. discounts cash flows at a minimum desired rate of return.

9. The accounting area in which the only objective of depreciation accounting relates to the effect of depreciation charges on tax payments is
   a. capital expenditure decision analysis.
   b. cost-volume-profit analysis.
   c. income determination.
   d. responsibility accounting.

10. Cost analysis for capital expenditure decisions is best accomplished by techniques that
   a. accrue, defer, and allocate costs to short time periods.
   b. emphasize the liquidity of invested costs.
   c. measure total cash flows over a project's life.
   d. clearly distinguish between different equivalent unit computations.

Applying Your Knowledge

Exercises

1. A company is considering the purchase of a machine to produce plastic chin protectors used in hockey. The machine costs $70,000 and would have a 5-year life (no salvage value). The machine is expected to produce $8,000 per year in net income (after depreciation and taxes). Assume that all income is taxed at 50 percent, that the company uses straight-line depreciation, and that the minimum pay-back period is 3 years.

   a. Using the pay-back approach, determine whether or not the company should invest in the machine. Show all work.

   b. Determine the accounting rate of return.

2. A machine that costs $20,000 will produce a net cash inflow of $5,000 in the first year of operations and $6,000 in the remaining 4 years of use. Present value information for the 16 percent rate of return is as follows:
Present value of 1 due in 1 year = .862
Present value of 1 due in 2 years = .743
Present value of 1 due in 3 years = .641
Present value of 1 due in 4 years = .552
Present value of 1 due in 5 years = .476
Using the present value method, determine whether the company should purchase the machine.

3. Delightful Donut Company is considering the acquisition of a new automatic donut dropper machine that will cost $400,000. The machine will have a life of five years and will produce a cash savings from operations of $160,000 per year. The asset is to be depreciated using the straight-line method and will have no salvage value. The company's income tax rate is 34 percent and management expects a 10 percent minimum after-tax rate of return on all investments.

Write the number of the best answer below.

____ **a.** The depreciation per year on the machine will be
1. $40,000.
2. $48,000.
3. $60,000.
4. $80,000.

____ **b.** The tax shield (increase in cash flow) resulting from the annual depreciation charge will be
1. $16,000.
2. $24,000.
3. $27,200.
4. $32,000.

____ **c.** The accounting rate of return on the machine is
1. 26.4 percent.
2. 52.8 percent.
3. 41.2 percent.
4. 17.7 percent.

____ **d.** The pay-back period, disregarding income taxes, will be
1. 2.0 years.
2. 2.5 years.
3. 4.0 years.
4. 5.0 years.

____ **e.** The present value of future net after-tax cash inflows is
1. $503,444.
2. $303,280.
3. $406,395.
4. $606,560.

____ **f.** After considering all factors, the company
1. should invest in the machine.
2. should not invest in the machine.

Capital Investment Decisions: Sweden and the United States

Decision-making is a universal characteristic of the business world. This analysis takes an international look at one type of decision, that of investing in a capital facility. To be more specific, the study centers on the capital facility decision process in Sweden and the United States and includes a comparative analysis of the responsibilities of the respective managerial accountants. The possible existence of different accounting information needs for the capital facility decision-maker(s) within the two countries provided the impetus for the study. Emphasis is placed on the different economic environments influencing the decision process in the steel industry in each country.

The objectives of this study are two-fold: (1) to analyze the capital facility decision responsibilities of the Swedish and American managerial accountants; and (2) to compare and contrast the decision process used in the two countries.

The data supporting the analyses and conclusions described below were gathered through a combined interview - questionnaire process. A total of eleven accounting executives were interviewed in the two countries. In addition, questionnaires were circulated to all Swedish and American steel firms, usable responses being received from 73 per cent of them. Although Sweden's steel industry contains a small percentage of enterprises owned and operated by the State, this analysis focuses on the dominant private ownership sector of the industry.

The Capital Facility Decision

Most top management personnel have their own idea of the proper approach to the capital facility decision process, but all agree that the success of each decision depends upon a coordinated flow of relevant information from various management functions within the enterprise. The responsibility for this flow generally rests with the managerial accountant. To facilitate a comparative analysis of the capital facility decision responsibilities of the managerial accountant, it was first necessary to construct an all-purpose model flexible enough to be used to examine the decision process in different companies, industries, and countries. The model used, pictured in Exhibit 1, was analyzed by various accounting and long-range planning executives in both Sweden and the United States. As deficiencies were exposed, the model was adjusted. The steps of the capital facility decision process are summarized as follows:[1]

Environmental Factors. The capital facility decision process takes place within a defined time period and under constraints imposed by economic policies and objectives originating at corporate, industry, and/or national levels.

Detection of Facility Need. Ideas for capital investment opportunities may emanate from past sales experiences, company trends, complaints, managerial suggestions, raw material needs, production bottlenecks caused by obsolete equipment, and/or new production or distribution methods.

Request for Capital Expenditures. Depending on the source and size of the proposed expenditure, the request should contain such information as a complete description of the facility under review, reasons for the immediate need of the facility, its estimated costs and related cost savings, engineering specifications, if necessary, and the estimated change in sales demand used to justify the acquisition.

Independent Analysis of Request. The main purpose of this step is to spot computational errors and deficiencies in the informational content of the request prior to the initial screening process.

Source: Reprinted from an article appearing in *Cost and Management* by Henry R. Anderson, October 1973 issue, by permission of the Society of Management Accountants of Canada.

[1] For a detailed explanation, see Henry R. Anderson and Rickard P. Schwartz, "The Capital Facility Decision," *Management Accounting,* National Association of Accountants, (February 1971), pp. 28-32.

Initial Screening. Initial screening processes are used by companies having several branch plants and highly developed capital expenditure programs. The function of initial screening is to identify those proposals that are undesirable or that have no chance of qualifying under capital requirement constraints in the current capital budget.

Acceptance-Rejection Standards. These standards are used to identify projects which offer inadequate or marginal returns, thus enhancing the proposed projects with high demand and return expectancies. In addition to cost of capital figures, a firm may also employ pay-back period standards.

Coordination and Formalization. The coordinating and formalizing steps can occur at several points in the capital facility decision cycle but are most relevant between the first and second screening processes. Coordination involves relating the objectives of the firm with the proposed projects. Formalization is concerned with communicating a project's degree of coordination to the decision-maker.

Computation of Decision Variables. The circular flow diagram of the capital facility decision process, illustrated in Exhibit 1, lists several variables which could be relevant to a particular capital facility decision. However, all may not be relevant to any one proposal.

Final Evaluation of Proposals. The selection process at this stage of the decision process is more refined than in the various preliminary screening areas. Methods of evaluation used in the steel industry include accounting rate of return, pay-back period, and discounted cash flow. The important point to stress for this analysis is that the capital facility decision process demands some method of computing a project's potential to the firm. The approach selected must be used consistently to facilitate project comparison.

Final Selection of Acceptable Alternatives. After the acceptable proposals have passed through the screening processes, they are given to the decision-maker(s) for final review. Before the decision-makers(s) can determine the capital expenditures to be implemented, the dollars available for capital expenditures must be established. Once this amount has been deter-

mined, the decision-maker(s) can prepare the final capital expenditure budget for the period under review.

Authorization, Appropriation, and Implementation. Positive action by the Board of Directors on the proposed capital budget represents formal authorization of the projects and includes formal appropriation of the funds necessary to acquire, construct, and/or install the capital facilities. Implementation of the facilities covers the time period beginning with board authorization and ending with the facility being put into an operable condition.

Post-Completion Audit. The capital facility decision process does not end at the completion of the implementation stage. A post-completion audit of each project should be performed to determine if the forecasted results of the project were accurate. The post-completion audit accomplishes this by: (1) ascertaining the actual performance results of a project; (2) comparing the results with the predicted figures used in the expenditure request; and (3) taking action if correctible differences exist between the actual and predicted figures.

As the capital facility decision process has become more sophisticated, the demands for and the amount of relevant data have increased. This information must originate somewhere and must be gathered, coordinated, and analyzed by various people within management. As the need for information has increased, the responsibilities of the managerial accountant have become more pronounced. Using the decision model described above as a base, the capital facility decision responsibilities of the managerial accountant in Sweden and the United States will now be discussed and compared.

Responsibilities of The Managerial Accountant

Although Sweden is referred to commonly as a socialistic country, over ninety per cent of her enterprises are privately owned. The profit motive exists in Swedish companies much as it does in the free enterprise economy of the United States. As a result, capital spending possesses similar basic characteristics in both countries. However, there are material economic differences between Sweden and the United States and these differences influence the

Exhibit 1
The Capital Facility Decision Process*

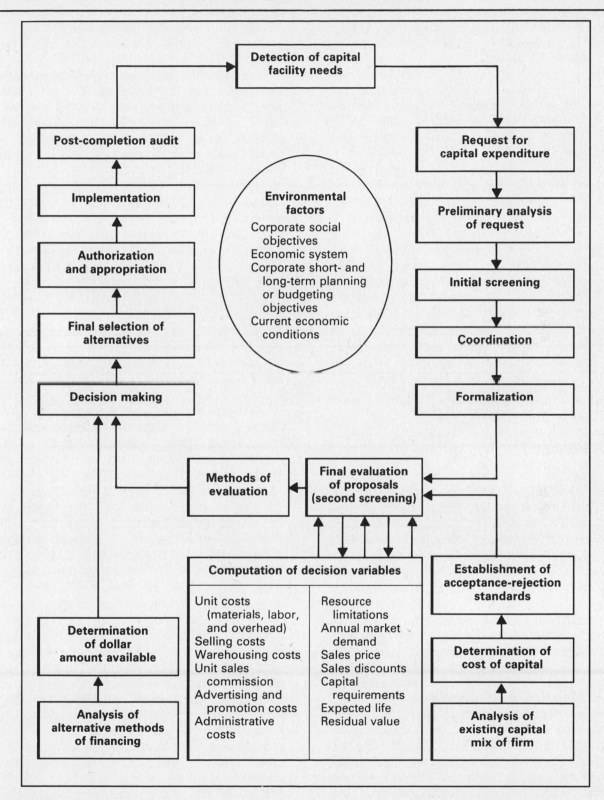

Source: Henry R. Anderson and Rickard P. Schwartz, "The Capital Facility Decision," Management Accounting, February, 1971, p. 30.

capital facility decision process. As the managerial accountant's decision responsibilities in the two countries are reviewed, variations in his duties will be linked to the economic differences. In addition, other environmental factors affecting the decision process will be discussed.

A philosophical look at the capital facility decision process in the two countries will set the stage for the comparative analysis. Not surprising is the fact that the information-supplying function of the managerial accountant is found in the decision processes used in both countries. However, a difference does exist in management's philosophy toward the use of decision manuals. In most steel firms in the United States, management believes that setting standard procedures down in manual form prevents the decision process from maintaining a necessary degree of flexibility. In Sweden, as a firm's decision process matures, standard approaches are incorporated into capital facility decision activities and procedural manuals are created. As a result, the Swedish decision process tends to utilize less sophisticated methods but the managers of the smaller, specialized steel firms consider the advantages of a structured, more controllable process far outweigh those associated with flexibility.

Decision Steps With Similar Accountant Involvement

Five decision steps have a similar degree of managerial accountant involvement in Sweden and the United States. These steps include Request for Capital Expenditure, Independent Analysis of Request, Coordination and Formalization, Final Selection of Acceptable Alternatives, and Authorization, Appropriation, and Implementation.

Request for Capital Expenditures. In both countries, the engineering and/or technical personnel generate the estimated data supporting initial capital expenditure requests. The accountant's duties are limited, consisting mainly of sporadic special request activities.

Independent Analysis of Request. Coincidentally, almost seventy per cent of the firms in both the United States and Sweden reported that the managerial accountant was responsible for conducting an independent analysis on capital expenditure requests. Differences existed on the exact placement of the analysis within the decision's time spectrum, but there was no apparent difference in the extent of the accountant's involvement.

Coordination and Formalization. Results of the study revealed that, in both countries the managerial accountant is responsible for the adequate transmittal of relevant data supporting capital facility expenditure proposals.

Final Selection of Acceptable Alternatives. In Sweden and the United States, the managerial accountant plays, at most, a minor role in the final selection of capital expenditure projects. On an infrequent basis, he serves on the decision-making committee responsible for the final decision.

Authorization, Appropriation, and Implementation. Within this decision step, the accountant's responsibilities in both countries amounted to routine recording procedures of actual operating and purchasing expenditures.

Decisions Steps In Which Swedish Accountant's Involvement Is Greater

The Swedish managerial accountant has a larger role than his American equivalent in the Establishment of Acceptance-Rejection Standards and the Determination of Dollars Available.

Establishment of Acceptance-Rejection Standards. Final determination of acceptance-rejection standards is not the responsibility of the managerial accountant in most steel companies in the United States. However, his Swedish counterpart is either fully or partially responsible for their development in over eighty per cent of the Swedish firms.

Most common among the acceptance-rejection standards used by the steel firms in Sweden and the United States are cost of capital, target rates of return, and minimum pay-back period. In many cases, a combination of these cut-off points is used in decision analyses. If actual cost of capital figures are used as the firm's minimum acceptable rate of return, the managerial accountant is primarily responsible for its calculation and establishment as a minimum cut-off point. In a surprisingly large number of the Swedish steel firms, pay-back period is used exclusively in the capital facility decision process. Here again, the accountant has a major role in selecting the acceptance-rejection standard.

The study of the decision process in the steel firms of the United States revealed that a large number of the companies use minimum rates of return which exceed their cost of capital. Profit and other risk and uncertainty factors are used in the analysis. In these cases, the managerial accountant supplies data on top management but does not participate in the final determination of the acceptance-rejection standards.

Heavy reliance upon cost of capital and/or pay-back period figures by Swedish steel firms is the main reason for the greater involvement by the Swedish accountant in this decision step. Another factor that must be considered is enterprise size. Most of Sweden's steel firms are very small in comparison to the average size of steel companies in the United States. In many of these small firms the Ekonomichefen (Economic Chief) functions as controller, treasurer, and financial vice president. Therefore, his responsibilities can be far more diverse than those of the managerial accountant in the United States and this difference in responsibility may, in part, account for the sporadic nature of the accountant's decision involvement found in the Swedish study.

Determination of Dollars Available. In the steel firms of the United States, the Vice President of Finance is generally responsible for analyzing the alternative methods of financing capital expenditures and determining the dollars available, but the managerial accountant may be called upon to supply a portion of the data used to support the analysis. Within the Swedish decision structure, sources of financing capital expenditures are analyzed by the Managing Director (President). The Economic Chief participates in the determination of kronor (approximately $.2) available for capital spending purposes and this analysis includes a study of the availability of funds from the Swedish Investment Reserve System. This system encourages companies in Sweden to place a portion of their pre-tax profits in a "blocked" reserve fund held by the Riksbank (Bank of Sweden). When the economy needs investment stimulation, these funds are released, resulting in substantial tax privileges to the private companies.[2]

In addition to the normal duties of the accountants in both countries regarding the determination of funds available for capital expendi-

[2]For a complete explanation of the Swedish Investment Reserve System, see Sven-Erik Johansson, "An Appraisal of the Swedish System of Investment Reserves," *The International Journal of Accounting Education and Research*, 1:85-92, Fall 1965.

tures, the Swedish managerial accountant is responsible for continually assessing the possible availability of funds from the Government's reserve system. The primary cause of this variation in decision responsibilities, the existence of the Investment Reserve System, relates directly to a Government fiscal economic policy. At present, the Government of the United States employs the Investment Tax Credit System which acts as a stimulus for investment spending. However, the Swedish system differs in that funds are actually held by the Bank of Sweden for future disposition and subsequent investment spending. Even before the Swedish Government issues a blanket statement for release of the funds, individual companies can petition for use of their "held" funds. So although the two systems have similar objectives, they are not comparable; the Swedish Investment Reserve System demands continuous assessment of possible availability of funds by a firm's managerial accountant.

Decision Steps Containing More Involvement by U.S. Accountants

In the areas of Detection of Facility Need, Initial Screening, Computation of Decision Variables, and Post-Completion Audit, the managerial accountant in the United States has more responsibility than the accountant in Sweden's steel industry.

Detection of Facility Need. Although not a primary responsibility of the managerial accountant in the United States, the survey indicated that in over two-thirds of the participating steel firms, he does gather information which may lead to the discovery of a facility need. This may occur through either his defined accounting responsibilities or specifically requested analyses of operational trouble spots. The same involvement was not found in the Swedish study. Less than forty per cent of the steel firms in Sweden utilize the accountant in this decision step, these positive responses being received mainly from enterprises with large production facilities.

Initial Screening. The major difference disclosed by the surveys conducted in the two countries was that this decision step is relevant only to the capital facility decision processes of large companies with branch plants. Since only a small number of Swedish companies have branch facilities, it is not surprising that results indicated minor involvement of Sweden's managerial accountant. In addition, the study showed that in the United States, the accountant's responsibility for initial screening of capital expenditure requests is defined organizationally while in Sweden, his duties are required only when someone specifically requests his services.

Computation of Decision Variables. Responses to questions concerning the final screening process and computation of decision variables revealed wide differences in the responsibilities of the managerial accountants in the two countries. Exhibit 2 illustrates the fact that more steel firms in the United States than in Sweden utilize the accountant's talents for computing decision variables. For every supporting variable included in the survey, a greater percentage of steel companies in the United States hold the accountant responsible for their compilation and/or verification. Swedish respondents indicated that in the smaller steel companies, technical (engineering) and/or production personnel dominate the capital facility decision process leaving the accountant with more or less clerical duties. Within such an environment, capital facility decisions made are based primarily on the intuition and judgment of the decision-maker.

Post-Completion Audit. Wide disparity is present in the post-completion audit responsibilities of the managerial accountant in the steel industries of the two countries. In the United States, post-completion audit duties are an integral part of the accountant's participation in the capital facility decision-making process. Only accountants in large Swedish steel firms participate actively in post-audit functions. Even in these isolated cases, the accountant's involvement is predicated on a special request from the Managing Director. Survey results illustrated that the managerial accountant in Sweden has very limited contact with production performance evaluations or project replanning activities, areas of primary importance in the post-completion audit responsibilities of the American managerial accountant.

Summary

A combination of factors contributes to the variations in the capital facility decision responsibilities of the managerial accountant in the

---

Exhibit 2
Comparison of Managerial Accountant's Involvement
in Computation of Decision Variables

Proposal's Net Cash Flow:	Managerial Accountant's Total Role				Variances
	United States		Sweden		American Accountant's Role Greater by:
	No.	%	No.	%	
(a) Unit cost of materials	14	87%	11	64%	+23%
(b) Unit Cost of labor	14	93%	11	64%	+29%
(c) Unit cost of overhead	14	100%	0	64%	+36%
(d) Selling costs	11	79%	1	10%	+69%
(e) Warehousing costs	12	93%	10	67%	+26%
(f) Commission on sale of product	6	50%	0	—	+50%
(g) Advertising and promotion costs	6	50%	5	36%	+14%
(h) Administrative costs	13	93%	13	87%	+ 6%
(i) Resource limitations	8	57%	11	55%	+ 2%
(j) Sales (units of)	3	21%	0	—	+21%
(k) Sales price	7	44%	2	15%	+29%
(l) Sales discount amounts	10	77%	0	—	+77%
(m) Life of proposed capital expenditure	12	80%	9	60%	+20%

steel industries of Sweden and the United States. Possible causes for these variations are summarized in Exhibit 3.

Exhibit 3 is based on a comparison of the Swedish managerial accountant's decision role against the decision functions of the accountant in the United States. First, his role is indicated to be either similar, greater, or less than the American managerial accountant. Following the results of the comparative analysis, possible causes are associated with each major difference found in the two accountants' roles. Four possible causes—enterprise size, economic fiscal policies, variations in management structure, and general economic and industry environment—were found to exist during the course of the study.

Sweden's economic environment cannot sustain many steel firms with large production facilities. To compete in world markets, the smaller steel firms have been forced to produce specialty steels, relying heavily on the technical skills and knowledge of production personnel. With research efforts being concentrated on the development of new types of grades of steel, little emphasis has been placed on newer and more effective management decision techniques. Unlike the dynamic nature of the managerial accountant's role in the larger steel firms, the duties and responsibilities of the accountant in the smaller companies have not changed materially in several decades.

The managerial accountant's role in Sweden's larger steel firms equals, and sometimes surpasses, the capital facility decision role of the American accountant. However, most of the firms comprising Sweden's steel industry are very small relative to those in the United States. The influence of these small companies on an empirical survey to develop an industry-wide model of the capital facility decision responsibilities of the managerial accountant causes the Swedish accountant's role to appear smaller than the role of the accountant in the steel industry of the United States.

Some Observations On Decision Effectiveness

The duties and responsibilities of the managerial accountant have now been described and compared but little has been said about their impact on the results of the decisions made. Before the degree of accountant input and the degree of decision effectiveness can be corre-

lated and analyzed, however, final results of a series of decisions must be known. But how do we get such information? This problem has plagued the capital facility decision maker for decades. The post-completion audit step of the decision process has proved to be a headache for many a capital budgeter. If it is of any comfort to those who have made futile attempts at this problem area, Swedish accountants have encountered the same headaches. One Swedish Economic Chief summed up the problem when he said "interaction between different decisions and pieces of equipment makes the post-audit function very difficult."

The problem, then, boils down to the ability to isolate the effects of a particular decision. This is very difficult to do, even for a small firm. Only when an entire plant is constructed is it possible to separate information and measure the performance of the facility being analyzed. One steel firm in the United States may be heading for a solution. The firm is attempting to build a mathematical model of the entire company. If successful, actual data from any capital expenditure can be fed into the model and a "before-and-after" analysis can be undertaken which encompasses the interaction of all relevant variables. To date, however, no results of this endeavor have been made public.

So no one can state specifically that greater involvement of the managerial accountant guarantees greater effectiveness of capital facility decisions. This study did show, however, that company size and accountant involvement are directly related. Small companies that rely heavily on technical people for a major portion of the information required for capital requests have to compete for limited investment funds available, thus, the demand for the services of the managerial accountant increases proportionately.

Conclusions

Even in a socialistically controlled economy, such as that of Sweden, capital facility decision making can still be at the discretion of management, not the Government. It follows, therefore, that the analysis underlying the capital facility decision would utilize somewhat the same approaches in Sweden as would be used in the United States. The mere presence of a socialistic form of government, then, does not alter materially the capital facility decision process. Sweden attempts to stabilize the busi-

| Decision Step | Swedish Accountant's Involvement as Compared to U.S. Standards | | | Possible Causes | | | |
	Similar	Greater	Smaller	Enterprise Size	Economic Fiscal Policies	Variations in Management Structure	General Economic Environment
Detection of Facility Need			X	X		X	X
Request for Capital Expenditure	X						
Independent Analysis of Request	X						
Establishment of Acceptance-Rejection Standards		X		X		X	X
Initial Screening			X	X		X	
Coordination and Formalization	X						
Computation of Decision Variables			X	X		X	X
Determination of Dollars Available		X			X		
Final Selection of Acceptance Alternatives	X						
Authorization, Appropriation, Implementation	X						
Post-Completion Audit		X		X		X	X

ness cycle through the Investment Reserve System, a fiscal measure designed to control private investment spending. This system was found to influence one capital facility decision step, the determination of funds available for investment spending. If other fiscal measures in other economic environments are present, they may influence the data-gathering requirements of other decision steps.

However, where the profit motive exists, whether in a capitalistic or socialistic environment, the decision-maker(s) are interested in maximization of profits or minimization of costs. They are striving for the same objective. Information needs, in addition to being influenced by the Government's attempts to control investment spending, are a function of the types of products manufactured and the market for these products. Product specialization, as was found to exist in Sweden, may dictate the person or persons responsible for collecting and assembling data relevant to the capital facility decision.

Therefore, there exists a universal need for information when a capital expenditure is being contemplated. However, the degree of trust placed in the data supplied by the managerial accountant differs between companies, industries, countries, and economic systems. Under different economic environments, the responsibilities of the managerial accountant will differ but the differences will not be caused entirely by planning policies of the Government.

CHAPTER 14 DECENTRALIZED OPERATIONS AND TRANSFER PRICING

REVIEWING THE CHAPTER

Objective 1: Identify the characteristics of a decentralized organization (pp. 525-526).

1. **A decentralized organization** is one that (a) has more than one operating segment or division, (b) gives each manager complete autonomy over his or her segment, but (c) requires each manager to conform to the company's overall goals, objectives, plans, and policies. In other words, each segment is treated almost as an independent company. On the other hand, a multisegmented organization that maintains control through a central home office is *not* considered decentralized.

2. Manufacturers, merchandisers, and service concerns all can operate as decentralized organizations. The manager of a decentralized division typically has control over all financial and operating aspects of that division. Top management, however, still maintains overall control, and carefully monitors and evaluates each segment's performance.

Objective 2: Describe the four-step performance evaluation process for decentralized operations (pp. 526-529).

3. The management accountant, in cooperation with key employees, is responsible for developing the internal reporting techniques for evaluating segment performance. These techniques are based on the goals and objectives set by top management. There are four steps used to evaluate the performance of decentralized operations:

a. The segments of the company must be determined so that they can be evaluated. When segment determination is difficult, management often relies on either geographic separation or similarity of activities. Once defined, a segment and its manager must be evaluated separately.

b. Revenues and costs that are traceable to, and controllable by, a segment and its manager must be identified. For example, home office costs that do not benefit the segment should be excluded from the performance evaluation. Further, it is possible for a cost to be traceable to a segment but not under the control of its manager.

c. The performance indicators used for each segment must be understood. **Results-achieved indicators** focus on the volume of output or accomplishment. **Costs-incurred indicators** relate to capital expenditures and selected expense items. **Effort-expended indicators** measure input factors, such as sales calls or machine hours. **Resources-employed indicators** center on usage of the company's resources (buildings, equipment, supervisory personnel).

d. Actual operating results must be compared with budgeted amounts, and an explanation should be provided for all significant differences. In addition, a measure must be made of **goal congruence,** the extent to which a manager has achieved both companywide and segment objectives.

Objective 3: Compute the segment performance margin and the margin for decentralized divisions (pp. 529-531).

4. The contribution margin (sales minus variable costs) can be obtained for each segment of a company and has proved to be useful in evaluating divisional performance. Two other useful measures are the segment margin and the performance margin.
   a. The **segment margin** equals the contribution margin minus all fixed costs traceable to the segment. Its purpose is to identify the segment's contribution toward covering the company's unallocated fixed costs, with enough remaining to produce a profit.
   b. The **performance margin** equals the contribution margin minus only those traceable fixed costs controllable by the segment manager. Its purpose is to reflect the effects of divisional management decisions on divisional income. The performance margin minus traceable fixed costs controllable by top management, not by the division manager, equals the segment margin.

Objective 4: Prepare a divisional performance report (pp. 531-534).

5. As described above, each segment margin of a divisional performance report is calculated as follows:

Sales	$XX
− Variable costs	XX
= Contribution margin	XX
− Traceable fixed costs controllable by division manager	XX
= Performance margin	XX
− Traceable fixed costs not controllable by division manager	XX
= Segment margin	XX

Finally, fixed costs that are not traceable to a division (that is, costs that are con-

trolled by top management) should be accounted for as common fixed costs and treated as a cost of the company as a whole.

6. A performance report can be analyzed more easily if each amount is identified as a percentage of division sales. Comparing actual with budgeted data also can help in the evaluation process. And, this contribution approach can be applied if, let's say, a division is further refined into its product line. As a segment is further refined, however, fixed costs become more and more difficult to trace to the segments.

Objective 5: Apply return on investment measures to evaluate divisional performance (pp. 535-540).

7. **Return on investment (ROI)** is a measure of a segment's profitability. It equals income divided by the appropriate investment base. Both income and investment base for a division must be defined and computed in accordance with division or company objectives.

8. **Financial management** is concerned with the acquisition of funds, capital structure, and debt-to-equity relationships. The appropriate ROI measure for evaluating financial management performance is net income after interest and taxes, divided by stockholders' equity.

9. **Operating management** is concerned primarily with the use of available resources to generate the largest income before interest and taxes that is consistent with a company's long-range policies and within social and environmental constraints. Evaluation of operating management must concentrate on the uses of resources and should not be affected by capital structure or the costs of obtaining capital funds.

10. The best measure of investment base is total assets traceable to a particular segment, with such assets as idle facilities, investments, and current assets excluded. The assets included in the investment base should be applied consistently and should be stated at average total cost. Rather than use historical cost, some financial analysts value assets based on general or specific price-level changes.

11. Return on investment also can be defined as profit margin times asset turnover. **Profit margin** equals net income divided by sales; **asset turnover** equals sales divided by average assets. Therefore, action taken to increase sales, reduce costs, or reduce assets employed would cause an increase in return on investment.

Objective 6: Define and discuss transfer pricing (pp. 541-543).

12. A **transfer price** is the price at which goods are exchanged between a company's divisions. This concept is used by large decentralized companies that have production processes utilizing several cost centers. A department does not sell its finished product, but instead transfers it to the next department in the process. By using transfer prices at the point of transfer, performance of the cost center can be measured in terms of return on investment. Transfer prices, then, are artificial prices; they are used internally, *only* to evaluate performance.

Objective 7: Distinguish between a cost-based transfer price and a market-based transfer price (pp. 543-544).

13. A **cost-plus transfer price** is the sum of costs incurred by the producing division plus an agreed-on profit percentage. The weakness of this method is that it guarantees the selling division that its cost will be recovered. Any inefficiencies in the division's operations are not taken into account.

14. A **market transfer price** is a price based on what the product could be sold for on the open market. Because in many cases the product is only partially completed, it is not possible to determine a market price by actual market experience. In such cases, a **negotiated transfer price** is bargained for by the managers involved.

Objective 8: Develop a transfer price (pp. 544-545).

15. To develop a transfer price, the company should (a) compute the unit cost of the item being transferred; (b) include a market price in the price determination process, if the item either has an external market or can be purchased in similar condition by the buying division from an outside source; and (c) negotiate through the managers involved an appropriate price based on the information gathered, taking care that the transfer price negotiated is beneficial to the company as a whole.

Objective 9: Measure a manager's performance by using transfer prices (pp. 545-547).

16. The performance report generated from the use of transfer prices is very similar to a normal performance report. The major difference is that revenue is based on an artificial selling price, not an actual amount. Only controllable costs should be included in the figures for which the manager is responsible.

Testing Your Knowledge

Matching

Match each term with its definition by writing the appropriate letter in the blank.

____ 1. Decentralized organization

____ 2. Segment margin

____ 3. Performance margin

____ 4. Return on investment (ROI)

____ 5. Transfer price

____ 6. Asset turnover

____ 7. Financial management

____ 8. Goal congruence

____ 9. Operating management

____ 10. Profit margin

a. Net income divided by sales
b. The amount charged for goods sold by one division to another
c. A division's overall profitability
d. Those concerned with maximizing income before interest and taxes
e. Sales divided by average assets
f. A business with several operating segments
g. The ratio of an income measure to an investment base
h. The extent to which objectives have been met
i. The contribution margin minus traceable fixed costs controllable by the division manager
j. Those concerned with the acquisition of funds, capital structure, and debt-to-equity relationships

Completion

Use the lines provided to complete each item.

1. List the four steps that should be followed in evaluating the performance of decentralized operations.

   a. _____

   b. _____

   c. _____

   d. _____

2. Briefly distinguish between a cost-plus transfer price and a market transfer price.

   _____

   _____

   _____

   _____

3. Using the mathematical signs provided, list the sequence of items involved in computing the segment margin.

  _____

− _____

= _____

− _____

= _____

− _____

= Segment margin

4. List the four indicators used in evaluating the performance of a segment, and state the significance of each.

a. _____

  _____

b. _____

  _____

c. _____

  _____

d. _____

  _____

True-False

Circle T if the statement is true, F if it is false.

T F 1. Return on investment is a measure of a company's liquidity.

T F 2. As a segment is further refined, fixed costs become easier to trace to the smaller segments.

T F 3. The overall goals and objectives of a decentralized organization are established by top management.

T F 4. If a cost is traceable to a division, it is controllable by its manager.

T F 5. Goal congruence refers to the extent to which a manager has achieved both companywide and segment objectives.

T F 6. The way that return on investment is calculated depends on the type of performance being evaluated.

T F 7. Segment margin minus contribution margin equals traceable fixed costs.

T F 8. A segment and its manager should be evaluated separately.

T F 9. An indicator that measures input factors, such as number of sales calls, is called a results-achieved indicator.

T F 10. The amount that a division contributes to the absorption of companywide fixed costs plus a profit is measured by the divisional contribution margin.

T F 11. In the calculation of return on investment, tangible fixed assets should be entered into the investment base at their existing book value.

T F 12. The return on investment calculation for evaluating operating management should consider income *before* interest and taxes.

T F 13. Transfer prices change cost centers into profit centers for performance evaluation purposes.

T F 14. A cost-plus transfer price is bargained for by the managers of the buying and selling divisions.

T F 15. Market transfer prices are discussed but seldom used without negotiation between managers.

T F 16. When intracompany transfers are priced at amounts in excess of cost to the selling division, total company profits are increased.

Multiple Choice

Circle the letter of the best answer.

1. Return on investment is equal to profit margin
   a. plus asset turnover.
   b. minus asset turnover.
   c. times asset turnover.
   d. divided by asset turnover.

2. Fixed costs that are not traceable to any division should
   a. not be included in a performance report.
   b. be allocated to the segments based on their performance margins.
   c. be allocated to the segments equally.
   d. not be allocated to any segment, but should be included in the performance report.

3. For a given segment, which of the following components would represent the largest dollar amount?
   a. Performance margin
   b. Contribution margin
   c. Segment margin
   d. More information is needed

4. Which of the following is *not* a characteristic of a decentralized organization?
   a. Everyday decisions for each division are made by top management.
   b. Division managers must conform to overall company policies.
   c. Each manager has autonomy over his or her division.
   d. The organization has two or more operating divisions.

5. The extent to which a building is occupied is a(n)
   a. effort-expended indicator.
   b. costs-incurred indicator.
   c. resources-employed indicator.
   d. results-achieved indicator.

6. How well a division manager utilizes the resources under his or her control is measured by
   a. the divisional contribution margin.
   b. sales.
   c. the divisional segment margin.
   d. the divisional performance margin.

7. Return on investment for evaluating financial management's performance should be calculated by dividing net income by
   a. total liabilities.
   b. stockholders' equity.
   c. sales.
   d. total assets.

8. An internal price bargained for by the managers of the buying and selling divisions is known as a
   a. normal transfer price.
   b. cost-plus transfer price.
   c. market transfer price.
   d. negotiated transfer price.

9. Transfer prices allow a decentralized company to
   a. evaluate the performance of cost centers based on return on investment.
   b. increase overall profits.
   c. decrease prices to outside customers.
   d. increase company morale by making the managers happy.

10. In pricing decisions,
   a. external prices are easier to develop than transfer prices.
   b. both external pricing and transfer pricing approaches share many common characteristics and objectives.
   c. transfer pricing policies are taken more seriously than external pricing policies.
   d. the gross margin and profit margin pricing methods are used to develop both external prices and transfer prices.

Applying Your Knowledge

Exercises

1. Below is the income statement for Olsen Company for the year ended December 31, 19xx:

Sales	$900,000
Less variable costs	500,000
Contribution margin	$400,000
Less fixed costs	220,000
Net income	$180,000

In addition, average total assets for the year equaled $600,000.

a. Profit margin = _____ %

b. Asset turnover = _____ times

c. Return on investment (a X b) = _____ %

2. Below is financial information for Divisions A and B of Metal Bellows, Inc., for August 19xx:

	Division A	Division B
Traceable fixed costs not controllable by division manager	$26,000	$16,000
Sales	$200,000	$100,000
Traceable fixed costs controllable by division manager	$18,000	$6,000
Variable costs	$142,000	$65,000

In addition, the company incurred $15,000 in fixed costs that were not traceable to either division.

Prepare a divisional performance report, by amount and percentage of sales, that results in the segment margin for each division and net income before taxes for the company as a whole.

Metal Bellows, Inc.
Divisional Performance Report
For the Month Ended August 31, 19xx

	Division A		Division B		Totals	
	Amount	% of Sales	Amount	% of Sales	Amount	% of Sales

3. For several years, Samuelson Division has produced an electronic component that it sells to Diefenderfer Division at the prevailing market price of $20. Samuelson manufactures the component only for Diefenderfer Division; it does not sell this product to outside customers. The product is available from outside suppliers, who would charge Diefenderfer Division $20 per unit. Samuelson currently produces and sells 20,000 of these components each year and also manufactures several other products. The following annual cost information was compiled after the close of 19xx operations, during which period Samuelson operated at full capacity.

Samuelson Division—19xx

Cost Category	Cost per Component
Direct materials	$ 6.50
Direct labor (hourly basis)	8.60
Variable factory overhead	4.50
General fixed overhead of plant	5.20
Traceable fixed overhead ($60,000/20,000)	3.00
Variable shipping expenses	.25
	$28.05

General fixed overhead represents allocated joint fixed costs, such as building depreciation, property taxes, and salaries of production executives. If production of the components was discontinued, $50,000 of the annual traceable fixed overhead costs could be eliminated. The balance of traceable fixed overhead is equipment depreciation on machinery that could be used elsewhere in the plant.

a. Compute the cost per unit of the electronic component made by the Samuelson Division.

b. The division manager contends that producing the component to accommodate the other division is a sound company policy as long as variable costs are recovered by the sales. Should Samuelson Division continue to produce the component for Diefenderfer Division?

Crossword Puzzle
for Chapters 13 and 14

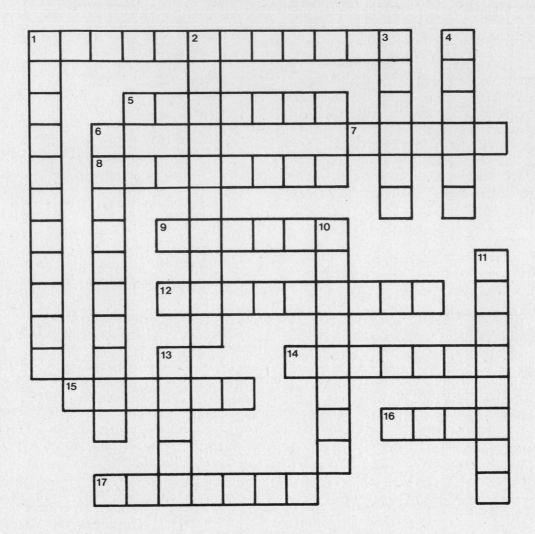

ACROSS

1. Capital budgeting method (2 words)
5. ——— margin
7. ——— -incurred indicators
8. Transfer price with a built-in profit (hyphenated)
9. Transfer price based on external value
12. ——— -employed indicators
14. Descriptive of depreciation expense
15. ROI numerator
16. ——— congruence
17. Period of time to recoup an investment

DOWN

1. ——— margin
2. Transfer price bargained for
3. ——— -expended indicators
4. Average ——— capital
6. ——— rate-of-return method
10. Asset ——— (sales divided by average assets)
11. Discounted ——— (used in 1-Across)
13. Time value of ———

Does Your Transfer Price Make Cents?

If management wanted us to lose money so that the firm as a whole would succeed, how could I fight it?

Mick Anick, our process engineer, entered my office rather jubilantly last week. To say he "floated" in would probably be more accurate. "I think I've solved our problem with the new widget line we started up in the spring for our sister division in East Cow Tail," he beamed.

My wrath was ignited instantly. Not at Mick, but at the policy we were forced to follow. It seems like my predecessor's version of transfer pricing translated into a giveaway. "Better for the company" was his defense. All I know is that "variable plus 10%" didn't cover our fixed costs and we were losing money on this deal. Not wanting to throw cold water on Mick's idea, I subdued my anger as he continued.

"Remember when we first started to look at this job? We really weren't too sure if we could make these things at all. So, rather than invest a lot of capital in tooling and automated equipment, we set it up as manual assembly —individual work stations with each operator building a complete unit."

My solution to the problem had been to ignore it. I figured if management wanted us to lose money so that the company as a whole would succeed, how could I fight it?

Despite my annoyance, Mick persisted. "I think we can save some money on this line," he said, "that is, if we invest some money." I realized Mick wasn't going to go away until I listened to his proposal. So I took a look at his sketch of a new layout.

"Using an assembly line approach," Mick said, "I can eliminate four operators. All we actually need is about $125,000 for the workbenches, jigs, fixtures, and other equipment. What do you think?"

I had to admit that what Mick had in front of me looked good. Doing some quick math,

I realized that the payback had to be great (Table 1).

"This does look like a good investment," I mused. "I suggest you write it up and present it as an expenditure proposal. I'll approve it and talk to the boss."

The Confused Cost Accountant

About a week later, Mick handed me the proposal and I began to read it over. Suddenly an idea occurred to me and I called in my trusted cost accountant, Dan D. Tail.

"Read this, Dan, and tell me what you think." Dan skimmed the proposal and commented favorably.

"It may look good," I said, "But, think about it for a minute. Remember this product is sold to our sister division at variable cost plus 10%."

"Which means below our standard cost," Dan snapped. "All the more reason to be excited about this savings."

"I'm going to have to vote against it, Dan. It's truly not in our best interest."

"What?" He shouted. "You can't be serious! Here's a project that elimintes four operators, saves $100,000 a year, pays back in 1.3 years, and you're against it? What gives?"

I slowly explained my opposition. "Dan, what happens in January when we set new standards?" The expression on his face showed he was with me.

"Look at this, I ran out some numbers." (Table 2.)

"This can't be right!" said Dan. "We reduced our cost by $1.00, but the contribution is $.05 less!"

"I know, that's why I can't approve it. Wait till you see what happens to the ROI."

"Incredible!" Dan sighed. "How can such a good project turn out so bad?" "It's not really so bad," I said.

"Make up your mind," said Dan. "First you're against it and now you're for it!" "I'm still against it," I said. Now totally confused, he slumped into the chair and said "will you

Source: Article by Frederic E. Lesser. From *Management Accounting,* December 1987. Reprinted by permission. Copyright © 1987 by the National Association of Accountants.

please tell me what's going on inside your head?"

To his dismay, I began to chuckle. I could see he was not amused and began to explain: "To the company as a whole, this is a good idea. We save $100,000 and our sister division benefits from our ingenuity by realizing a lower price. But when we project the impact to us on an annual basis, what does it show? Lower profit/unit and lower ROI. Let's be realistic for a minute. Do you think there is any way that the boss is going to be so altruistic? Don't forget, he gets paid a bonus based on profits. In the real world, this project is a dead duck. There's no way I'm going to present this to him. The real loser is the company. But because of our pricing policy, it's actually a disincentive for us to reduce costs."

Dan left my office thinking that he understood my position, but still bewildered that a good investment could be a problem.

I explained this to Mick and his reaction was understandable. "You've got to be kidding! I've put a lot of time into this project, and I'm not going to let some stupid accounting policy stand in my way. If you won't take it to the boss, I will!"

I knew it would be only a short time until the boss would want to see me. How was I going to explain this mess? Here is a basically sound business decision that reduces our income and ROI. I had to agree with Dan—it was incredible.

Facing the Boss

"You know," my boss began, "this is so ridiculous I understand it. But, what I don't understand is how this policy ever got adopted.

Table 1 / The Payback

Four Operators @ $18,750/Year	$75,000.00
Fringes on four operators	25,000.00
Annual Savings	$100,000.00
Pre-tax payback $125,000/ $100,000 = 1.3 years	
Current Volume	100,000 Units
Savings/Unit	$ 1.00
Current Selling Price	12.85
Current Standard Cost	13.20
Less Savings	(1.00)
Gross Profit	.65

Surely the financial wizards who implemented it realized what would happen. What went wrong?"

"The basic policy of variable plus 10% is sound for transfer pricing," I replied. "It's just that. . ."

"What?" he slammed the desk with his hand. "How in the world can you tell me this is a sound policy when it takes a good decision and turns it into a bad one?"

His voice told me I was on thin ice. Choosing my words carefully, I continued. "It is the specific application in this case that presents the dilemma. The policy was intended for products that have an existing external market. Volume from those sales will absorb all the fixed costs. The additional sales to our sister division at variable plus 10% actually gives us a 10% gross profit as long as we don't incur any new fixed costs. So, we benefit by simply producing more of an already established product, and they gain an advantage because they purchase at a price below the competition. Also, under this setup, they ride the coattails of any cost reductions we make for the benefit of our external market. It's what I refer to as 'conflicting goals.' The goals of the corporation—to

Table 2 / Further Analysis

	This Year
Selling Price	$12.85
Variable Cost	11.68
Contribution	$1.17
	Next Year
Variable Cost	$11.68
Cost Reduction	(1.00)
	10.68
5% Inflation	.53
New Variable Cost	11.21
New Selling Price (Variable + 10%)	12.33
Contribution	$ 1.12
Current Net Investment	$5,000,000.00
Addition	125,000.00
	$5,125,000.00
Current Income	$750,000.00
Loss (100,000 Units @ $.05)	(5,000.00)
	$745,000.00
Current ROI $750,000/ $5,000,000 = 15%	
New ROI $745,000/$5,125,000 = 14.5%	

maximize corporate profits—are opposed to the division's goals—to maximize division profits."

Calming down, the boss reflected for a moment. "I see, I see." Unfortunately, the session then ended with his shouting, "But we still end up losing!"

Back in my office, I pondered the situation and convinced myself that there had to be a way to make this work.

"What if," I said out loud to myself, "we had two transfer price policies? Keep the current one for its intended use—products with established external markets. Now, what do we do with products solely for sale to a sister division?" As I wrestled with this problem, I began to focus on the desired end results.

☐ Selling price should be lower than market so that the sister division gains a competitive advantage.
☐ Therefore, our margin will have to be below that of externally marketed products.
☐ All fixed costs must be absorbed. (This conclusion made me realize that any volumes above the full absorption threshold would be marginal income. Therefore, this arrangement will be beneficial as long as volumes are maintained.)
☐ We should keep at least part of any cost reductions. Otherwise there is no incentive to do so.

Putting it all together, I formulated a new policy:

☐ Original price will be established at variable cost plus 10%;
☐ Any new fixed costs must be covered using estimated volumes; and
☐ Cost reductions will be fully retained by selling division.

Now I was stumped! What to do when the costs change next year. Do we use variable plus 10%? No! That defeats the whole objective and in reality, passes the entire cost reduction to the buying division. (See Table 2, "Further Analysis.")

But, if we don't pass along any price decreases, won't the external market price (competition) soon be lower than ours? Certainly they will develop the same technology as ours and cut their prices. I was stuck!

The Solution

Calling in my cost accountant, Dan D. Tail, I reviewed the situation.

"If we don't pass along any cost reductions," said Dan, "these products will have the highest margins in the company, and our sister division will no longer buy from us because the price will be so high that they will be forced to seek other suppliers."

"That's it!" I declared. "We won't let the price get too high for the products we sell to our 'real' customers because we don't want to lose their business. In fact, we are forced to come up with cost savings in order to stay competitive."

"This should give the company the best of both worlds," said Dan.

"Yeah," I replied, "the sister division starts out with a decided edge because we sell at variable plus 10% initially. The price will increase only when we change standards (annually) and then only if the market allows. If the market doesn't allow an increase, we face declining margins and are compelled to cut costs to hold or improve our margins."

"That sounds like nice theory," Dan noted, "but I'm not sure how it improves anything."

"Look, I'll tell you what the biggest obstacle in this whole deal is. Under our present policy, Mick's cost reduction will never get approved. Remember my initial calculations showed a contribution decrease of $.05/each and an ROI reduction of .5%? Well, in reality, that would never occur because the boss wouldn't approve it. Here's what the two scenarios look like." (Table 3.)

"What we end up with is project rejection—no cost savings and a simple inflationary price adjustment. However, we have no room to cut the price if the market demands it! Here's how the new policy would be structured." (Table 4.)

"Now, let's compare what we have," I said. "We should look at what would happen under the old policy—project rejection versus the new policy—project approval. (Table 4.) The net result is that in year 2 the sister division pays the same price, but we realize additional profit of $1.05/unit."

Dan finally was able to get a few words in. "There's a double benefit. First, we get more profit. Second, the company as a whole comes out ahead. We could even pass along some or all of our savings if the market price demanded it."

"Getting back to the original problem," I said, "we now have an incentive for cost reduction, and the policy will do what it's intended to do—increase profits!"

The Moral of the Story

Existing products that have an external market are properly priced at variable cost plus 10% for intercompany sales. What makes this attractive is that all the development and other fixed costs will be covered by profits from the existing external markets. Therefore, 10% above variable cost is all "gravy" to the selling division and represents a real bargain to the buying division.

However, unique products that have no existing external market are different. Under these conditions, variable cost plus 10% is a detriment to the selling division with all the hazards and pitfalls outlined in the dialogue—no incentive for cost reduction.

Companies that do not differentiate their transfer price policies, based on the market products are sold in, may be defeating the purpose those policies are intended for. They may be inadvertently building obstacles in the path of higher earnings.

In this particular case, the policy was designed to yield a price advantage to the purchasing division. The reality was, however, that a disincentive was in place which negated the policy's intent. The moral of this account is—do your policies accomplish what you intend them to accomplish?

Table 3 / Two Scenarios

	Project Gets Approved (Under Old Policy)	Project Doesn't Get Approved (Under Old Policy)
Year 1		
Selling Price	$12.85	$12.85
Variable Cost	11.68	11.68
Contribution	$ 1.17	$ 1.17
Year 2		
Variable Cost	$11.68	11.68
Less: Savings	(1.00)	--
Subtotal	10.68	$11.68
Plus: 5% Inflation	.53	.58
New Variable Cost	11.21	12.26
New Selling Price	12.33	13.48
Contribution	$ 1.12	$ 1.22
Change in Contribution	−.05	+.05

Table 4 / The New Policy

Year 1:		
Variable Cost	$11.68	
Selling Price	12.85	($11.68 x 1.1)
Contribution	$ 1.17	
Cost Reduction	1.00	
New Contribution	$ 2.17	16.9% ($2.17/$12.85)
Year 2:		
Variable Cost	$10.68	(after cost reduction)
5% Inflation	.53	
New Variable Cost	11.21	
Selling Price	13.48	($11.21 @ 16.9% margin)
Contribution	$ 2.27	

. . . AND A COMPARISON

	OLD POLICY	NEW POLICY	
Year 2:			
Selling Price	$13.48	$13.48	No Change
Contribution	1.22	2.27	= $1.05

Measuring Profit Center Managers

Many large companies still measure the financial performance of their profit center managers with techniques developed in the 1920s. They are based on return on investment. In this age of fast-paced change in both technology and management information systems, the attachment to these systems is not only strange but debilitating. Over the past 20 years, I've discussed the problem with senior and division managers both here and abroad and found that, while they recognize the difficulties such systemic rigidities impose, they do not know how to change their systems.

Before management can build a new system, it must understand what is wrong with the old one. I have discovered that the use of return on investment is symptomatic of other, basic conceptual errors in profit center measurement systems. These errors are:

1. The failure to distinguish between techniques used to measure past financial performance and those required to establish future performance objectives.
2. The failure to differentiate between systems that measure the performance of the profit center and those that measure the performance of its managers.
3. The failure to segment variances from the budget by differences in the way that managers can influence them.

In this article I will describe the basis for these conceptual errors, explain how they result in suboptimal measurement systems, and suggest action management can take to correct the problems the systems create.

CONCEPTUAL FLAWS

In using traditional accounting systems to measure organizational units' performance, companies judge the adequacy of profits by

comparing the amounts earned during a series of time periods and calculating the rates of return on the investments made.

Most companies emulate the systems that Du Pont and General Motors developed in the 1920s. Both businesses decentralized profit responsibility to operating units and at the same time began to use ROI to measure their units' financial performance. They expressed future profit objectives in terms of return on divisional assets and began to base projected performance on past results. Later they formalized these ROI objectives into profit budgets.

Measuring vs. Projecting

Return on investment is a valid technique for measuring past profitability. In fact, it is the only technique that allows a company to compare profitability among organizations or investments. But it is not a valid way to set future objectives, because the historical costs of assets—on which it is based—are meaningless in planning future action. Regardless of how much a company pays for a group of assets or what amount of differential cash flow it projects in investment proposals, the only logical thing its managers can do—once the assets are in place—is to use the assets to maximize future cash flow and to invest in new assets when the return from these assets is expected to equal or exceed the company's cost of capital. The failure to make this distinction—between measuring the past and projecting the future—is the principal reason that companies continue to use ROI to measure the financial performance of their managers.

Not making this distinction adds to the undesirable side effects already inherent to ROI as managers try to maximize their return on investment. (For a summary of these side effects, please see the insert "How ROI Can Hurt.")

Not only are historical accounting values of existing fixed assets not relevant, but as soon as a new asset is added, neither the cost nor the projected savings are relevant to future planning except to ascertain how well estimates have been made.

Companies should express profit objectives for both the profit center and its manager in terms of absolute dollars of profit, which are based on the projected potential of existing resources to generate cash flow.

The Manager vs. the Profit Center

Current systems also fail to distinguish explicitly between the measurement of the financial performance of a manager and that of the organizational unit being managed. It is important to make this distinction because:

☐ A company can measure a profit center's financial performance only in absolute terms, while it can measure the unit's head only in relative terms. Managers' performance is limited by their own units' profit potential. Otherwise, managers of high-profit divisions would always be considered successful and managers of low-profit divisions, marginal or unsuccessful.

☐ The extent to which a manager can control an item of revenue or expense is irrelevant to measuring a profit center's performance. For example, the impact of foreign exchange translation gains or losses is important to evaluating a subsidiary's profitability. This impact is entirely irrelevant, however, to judging the performance of that subsidiary's manager.

Many multinationals measure foreign subsidiary managers on the basis of the American dollar, so when the dollar goes up, the performance of the subsidiary goes down. Senior managers believe that tying the foreign subsidiary managers to the dollar forces them to make up for shortfalls in other areas, so that the impact on the corporation as a whole is neutral. But the impact on the manager is very real and demotivating. Managers abroad rightly complain to headquarters that they have no influence on the very factors with which they are being judged.

From the company's point of view, this tie to the dollar may force managers to make up for the problems themselves, but it also gives managers a screen behind which to hide mistakes. When the dollar goes down, the subsidiary's performance goes up, no matter what. Poorly run divisions have been able to hide their failures for years when the dollar has been weak.

☐ The methods used to measure managers affect the way they act. If companies measure

ROI, their managers will do all they can to optimize the ratio, and that may result in suboptimal decisions.

Of course few, if any, companies do measure managers in absolute terms. Almost all companies measure managers against profit budgets, which should take into account the potential profitability of the resources being managed. But by using a single system to measure both the organizational unit and its manager, the company includes items that are irrelevant to management performance and may also exclude items that *are* relevant. The performance criteria for the profit center (return on investment, for example) differ from those for the manager (actual profit compared with budgeted profit, for instance).

I believe that companies should separate their measurement systems and use the traditional accounting system for profit center financial statements and separate profit budget reports to measure managers.

Segmenting Variances from the Budget

Most companies begin the budgeting process by reviewing a strategic plan. The strategic planning process, of course, affects the profit budget. The financial aspects of the strategic plan must be in terms of future cash flow; historical costs are not important to the plan. And the plan is for the profit center, not its manager. Only when the company converts the plan's first year into a detailed profit budget does the manager's responsibility become clear.

In formulating a better profit budget, top management must decide for which items profit center managers are to be held responsible and the degree to which they must meet specific goals. Very few items are entirely controllable by managers, but very few items cannot be influenced by managers. It is important to remember that the distinction is *not* controllability but the ability to influence.

The company should not automatically consider favorable variances good and unfavorable ones bad. It can judge good or poor performance only after it analyzes variances against management explanation.

I propose as a guideline for drawing up the profit budget that the company include only items that managers can influence. Profit center managers are, then, responsible for doing their best to meet or exceed this goal and for explaining the reasons for any variances and what they are doing to correct unfavorable variances.

In general, I believe a profit center manager can influence and thus be held responsible for:

1. All profit and loss items generated directly by the profit center.

2. Any expense incurred outside the center at headquarters or other units for which the center can be billed directly.

3. An expense equal to the controllable working capital (usually receivables and inventories less payables) multiplied by an interest rate (the company's marginal borrowing rate, for instance). I believe such a charge is necessary to take into account trade-offs between the levels of working capital and profits. For example, higher inventories can reduce losses from stockouts, and liberalized credit terms can result in higher sales. Only the profit center manager knows and understands these trade-offs. Because conditions are constantly changing, it is usually not effective to budget working capital levels. The charge will motivate managers to make these trade-offs in the company's best interests. If managers can increase profits above the costs of carrying receivables and inventories, the company will benefit.

In the same spirit, the company would replace depreciation based on historical cost with an amount equal to depreciation based on replacement cost. Depreciation, like the book value of fixed assets, is generally irrelevant to budgeting because a company is primarily concerned with maximizing cash flow. Being a sunk cost, depreciation does not affect the measurement of a profit center's performance.

Depreciation is important in product profitability analysis, however, where management diagnoses areas that are doing well versus those that are doing poorly. Each product varies widely in its use of capital; to gauge profitability, it is necessary to include the replacement costs of the assets used in calculating depreciation.

Under my proposal, the budgeted amount and the actual amount in the budget report would be the same, so depreciation would not affect performance. In fact, managers could omit depreciation from their reports and still calculate their products' profitability. If included, this figure will get greater visibility and consequently will more likely be used.

I advocate a profit budget expressed in terms of dollars to be earned in the budget year. The amount should represent the best estimate of the profit center's potential cash flow as developed through the strategic planning process. The profit budget will include only the parts of the plan a manager can influence. It is the manager's personal financial goal. The manager must explain any deviations from it.

REPORTING AGAINST BUDGET

I would divide the reporting system that accompanies the budgeting system into three parts: (1) an analysis of variances from budget, (2) an explanation of the causes of those variances and any corrective action being taken, and (3) a forecast for the year. Many senior executives have trouble getting realistic (or even honest) explanations and forecasts from profit center managers, especially when the variances are unfavorable. The worse the variance, the greater the danger of cover-up.

This serious problem can be solved if profit center managers know precisely what their financial objectives are and are tested against only the income and expense they can influence. By organizing the analysis to separate variances by the degree of management responsibility, the company will increase the reliability and accuracy of the budget reports.

In most profit budget reporting systems, companies do not classify variances explicitly by the degree of influence management has on them. The practice leads to considerable ambiguity in the explanation of variances and the evaluation of performance. The report should indicate the difference in the degree of influence that a profit center manager can exert on each variance. If a company treats all variances as if they were homogeneous, it may perceive a favorable variance on which the manager has little influence as an offset to an unfavorable variance on which the manager has considerable influence.

Instead, companies should classify variances according to whether they are forecast, performance, or discretionary cost variances.

Forecast Variances

I have found some confusion over the difference between a budget and a forecast, which some managers tend to treat as the same thing. A budget is not a forecast. A budget is a management plan and is based on the assumption that steps will be taken to make events correspond to the plan. A forecast is a prediction of what will most likely happen and carries no implication that the forecaster will attempt to shape events to realize the forecast. A projection is not a prediction but an estimate of what will happen if various conditions and situations exist.

The typical profit budget includes many forecasts. A company should treat them separately because it should judge managers solely on their ability to manage—not on their ability to forecast.

Perhaps the most important forecast in a typical profit budget is that of the total level of sales activity expected in the industry during the budget period. Everybody knows that swings in industry volume can sometimes affect profits to such a degree that all other variances appear minor in comparison.

By isolating the industry volume variance, you can more easily evaluate its impact—see that the volume is going down, for example, but that the manager is increasing market penetration. The industry volume variance allows you to see that the manager is doing well despite adverse conditions.

Each budget also forecasts the level of purchase prices on such costs as raw materials, utilities, supplies, and wages and salaries. The profit center manager normally has little, if any, influence over them. It is also necessary to forecast the level of selling prices, another item over which the manager has limited control. If, however, the budget were to combine purchase and sales price variances, they should offset each other because changes in the purchase prices should affect selling prices. Profit center managers *can* influence the effect of price level cost changes on profitability.

Performance Variances

These variances include market share and operating costs. Because the manager can affect his or her unit's market share and its efficiency, they are the two most important variances a company can use to evaluate the profit center manager. Moreover, they are the most concrete, for they leave the manager little room for ambiguity in explaining them.

In manufacturing profit centers, the most important performance variables are materials usage, direct labor, and overhead. In a service industry like a clothing chain, the actual costs of operating the stores, less the budgeted costs, are important performance variables.

Performance variables measure the profit center's level of efficiency and effectiveness. The profit center manager agrees to go after a given market share and to operate at a certain level of efficiency.

Discretionary Expense Variances

These expenses include administration, marketing, and research and development. Variances in these expenses indicate only whether more or less money has been spent than originally budgeted. They do not indicate efficiency or inefficiency, as other variances do. A company must segregate discretionary expense variances

---

How ROI Can Hurt

I have found that using return on investment to measure profit center managers causes corporate problems because:

☐

The emphasis is on optimizing a ratio, which could discourage growth in the most profitable divisions. Investments in high profit divisions may lower their return, while the same investment in low profit divisions could improve it.

☐

Investments that might earn satisfactory returns will not do so at first because ROI requires that the investments be increased by the total gross book value of the new assets. Managers may not invest if they expect their tenure to be short. Also, their returns will increase over time if they don't make new investments.

☐

All assets in the same division, whether special-purpose assets, general-purpose assets, or working capital, must earn the same rate of return. Moreover, this rate of return is often inconsistent with the company's cost of capital.

☐

The same assets in different divisions may have different implicit interest rates, which may lead to different inventory decision rules in different divisions for identical items of inventory.

☐

Under certain conditions, division managers can increase their rate of return by scrapping perfectly good assets.

---

from the others because managers should not offset unfavorable performance with favorable discretionary expense variances. A company wants to avoid a situation in which a profit center manager takes budgeted objectives so seriously that he or she cuts back on marketing or product development costs to compensate for unfavorable manufacturing cost variances.

THE BOTTOM LINE

In most decentralized companies, managers are under pressure to meet current goals. This pressure influences them to cover up bad news and to take short-term action that is not in the long-run interests of their companies. A system that holds managers responsible for what they really can influence and allows them to explain the reasons they cannot achieve certain goals will relieve some of this pressure. Managers feel freer to communicate bad news if their goals are clear and unambiguous and they know they will be measured on the variances from items for which they are clearly responsible.

The evaluation of subordinates is one of the most important responsibilities of senior management, if not *the* most important one. Evaluation usually involves the observation of a manager's performance over a period normally exceeding the year covered by the typical profit budget. The evaluation also involves measuring managers on several dimensions in addition to their financial performance. Even the best short-term financial measurement systems do not ensure fair evaluation. Without such systems, however, evaluations are much more likely to be unsatisfactory and profit center managers much more likely to take action contrary to the best interests of their companies.

It is difficult to change a financial measurement system that has been in place for a number of years. Generally, almost everyone involved—from the controller to the profit center manager—will resist change. The managers responsible are often reluctant to change because change implies that the current systems are defective. Profit center managers usually believe they can work within the present systems and are unsure of the new. But change is worth the effort necessary to achieve it.

It is quite easy to diagnose the potential problems many current measurement systems create and even easier to decide what corrective actions to take. The problem is not what to do but how to do it.

Companies cannot afford to continue to use the techniques developed in the 1920s to measure the performance of profit center managers in the 1980s. A system of evaluation that is less ambiguous will be more fair to everyone, but it is hard to start the process of change. Unless innovative senior managers begin, however, they will continue to demotivate performance instead of measure it.

CHAPTER 15 THE JUST-IN-TIME PHILOSOPHY

REVIEWING THE CHAPTER

Objective 1: Describe a computer-integrated manufacturing system (pp. 572-574).

1. During the past twenty-five years, the manufacturing environment has changed significantly. The computer slowly has been integrated into the process as isolated machines were equipped with automated devices. Today, companies are installing computer-integrated manufacturing systems in their factories.

2. A **computer-integrated manufacturing (CIM)** system is a fully integrated computer setup in which everything connected with the manufacturing system is performed automatically.

3. CIM is a production process in which all parts of the system are fully integrated through computer technology.

Objective 2: Compare and contrast the traditional manufacturing system with the just-in-time approach to manufacturing (pp. 574-580).

4. The **just-in-time philosophy** is an overall operating philosophy of management in which all resources, including materials, personnel, and facilities, are used in a just-in-time manner.

5. JIT production is based on the objective of continuous flow and requires that each part of the production process work in concert with others.

6. The JIT philosophy has changed the role of the direct labor worker and has significantly reduced waste of labor, space, and production time.

7. In a traditional manufacturing system, raw materials are purchased and stored. They later are requisitioned into production and are routed systematically through departments or functions as various machines and skilled workers shape the product into its final configuration. Between operations, goods in process are stored in bins or containers as work-in-process inventory. When completed, the products are inspected, then packaged and stored in the finished goods inventory until a customer order triggers shipment and delivery.

8. In a just-in-time manufacturing environment, a customer order triggers the purchase of raw materials. Once received, they are put into production immediately. The manufacturing process is structured so that the product flows continuously through the process, resulting in minimal or no work-in-process inventory. Inspection is performed throughout the process by direct labor workers. Goods are shipped to the customer as soon as they are completed. Unlike the traditional manufacturing ap-

proach, the end result of the JIT environment is that very few dollars are tied up in materials, work-in-process, or finished goods inventory. Production throughput is the objective.

Objective 3: Identify the elements that support a JIT operating environment (pp. 580-584).

9. Several concepts support JIT: (a) Simple is better; (b) it is important to emphasize quality and continuous improvement; (c) maintaining inventories wastes resources and often hides bad work; (d) any activity or function that does not add value to the product should be eliminated; (e) goods should be produced only when needed; and (f) workers should be multiskilled and participate in improving efficiency and product quality.

10. Elements that support the JIT philosophy are (a) maintaining minimum inventory levels; (b) developing **pull-through production** planning and scheduling procedures; (c) purchasing materials and producing products as needed in smaller lot sizes; (d) performing simple, inexpensive machine setups; (e) developing a multiskilled work force; (f) creating a flexible manufacturing system; (g) maintaining high levels of product quality; (h) enforcing a system of effective preventive facility maintenance; and (i) encouraging continuous work environment improvement.[1]

11. A **flexible manufacturing system (FMS)** is an integrated set of computerized machines and systems designed to complete a series of operations automatically. An FMS often completes a product from beginning to end without the items being touched or moved by hand. Raw materials are fed in at one end of the FMS cell, and a finished product emerges at the other end.

Objective 4: Analyze the impact of a change from a labor-intensive to a capital-intensive production process on product costing concepts and techniques (pp. 584-585).

12. The JIT philosophy has changed many of the relationships and cost patterns as-

[1]Many of these ideas come from James B. Dilworth, *Production and Operations Management*, 3rd ed. (New York: Random House, 1986), pp. 354-360.

sociated with traditional product costing. New cost allocation techniques, changes in cost traceability, and less reliance on direct labor-based variances are part of these product costing changes.

13. Costs are associated with time elements of the total product manufacturing cycle. These elements include processing time, inspection time, moving time, queue time, and storage time. The emphasis here is on reducing or eliminating all but processing time. The costs associated with and caused by the other time elements (**non-value added activities**) are in turn reduced or eliminated.

Objective 5: Define and give examples of cost drivers (pp. 585-587).

14. A **cost driver** is any activity that causes costs to be incurred.

15. Examples include number of labor transactions, number of material moves, number of schedule changes, number of units reworked, and number of engineering change orders.

Objective 6: Describe how the JIT philosophy and CIM affect the classification of direct and indirect costs (pp. 587-589).

16. In a just-in-time environment and within computer-integrated manufacturing facilities, direct labor is not the main cost driver.

17. Costs are "driven" by engineering, materials handling, actual machine hours of work, and other production activities.

18. Sophisticated computer monitoring of the FMS or production cell allows many costs to be traced directly to the cell and the product being manufactured. Examples include repairs and maintenance, materials handling, operating supplies, utility, and supervision costs.

Objective 7: Record transactions involving the Raw-in-Process Inventory account (pp. 589-590).

19. The **Raw-in-Process Inventory Account** replaces both the Materials Inventory and the Work-in-Process Inventory accounts. Because raw materials are ordered and received just in time for use, there is no need to debit them to a Materials Inventory account.

The Just-In-Time Philosophy

20. All entries previously made by debiting or crediting either the Materials Inventory or Work-in-Process Inventory account are now made to the Raw-in-Process Inventory account.

Objective 8: Use process costing procedures to compute JIT product costs (pp. 590-593).

21. The process costing method can be adapted easily to compute product unit costs in a JIT manufacturing setting. Every manufacturing cost is classified as being either a materials or materials-related cost or a conversion cost (direct labor plus factory overhead costs).

22. Because costs are accumulated by FMS or work cells and production flows continuously in a JIT environment, process costing is used for product costing purposes.

Testing Your Knowledge

Matching

Match each term with its definition by writing the appropriate letter in the blank.

___ **1.** Raw-in-Process Inventory account

___ **2.** Computer-integrated manufacturing (CIM)

___ **3.** Cost driver

___ **4.** Just-in-time (JIT) philosophy

___ **5.** Flexible manufacturing system (FMS)

___ **6.** Pull-through production

___ **7.** Computer numerically controlled (CNC) machine

___ **8.** Non-value added activity

___ **9.** Operating cell (island)

a. A fully integrated computer setup in which everything connected with the manufacturing system is performed automatically

b. An overall operating concept of management in which all resources, including materials, personnel, and facilities, are used in a just-in-time manner

c. An activity that adds costs to the product but does not increase its market value

d. An integrated set of computerized machines and systems designed to complete a series of operations automatically; often completes a product from beginning to end

e. Stand-alone pieces of equipment, including operating machines, computer-assisted design technology, and robots

f. A customer order triggers the purchase of materials and the scheduling of production for the required products

g. Any activity that causes costs to be incurred

h. Contains a complete set of machines that can produce a product from start to finish

i. Replaces both the Materials Inventory and the Work-in-Process Inventory accounts.

Completion

Use the lines provided to complete each item.

1. Briefly define the just-in-time philosophy.

_____

_____

_____

_____

_____

_____

_____

2. What is a cost driver and how is it used by management accountants?

_____

_____

_____

_____

_____

3. Identify and describe the five time elements in a traditional production process.

a. _____

b. _____

c. _____

d. _____

e. _____

4. Just-in-time is not an inventory system. Explain.

_____

_____

_____

_____

_____

_____

True-False

Circle T if the statement is true, F if it is false.

T F **1.** CIM is the acronym for computer intelligence monitor.

T F **2.** Eliminating waste is a key ingredient of the just-in-time operating philosophy.

T F **3.** Computer numerically controlled machines are an integrated set of computerized machines and systems designed to complete a series of operations automatically.

T F **4.** Pull-through production means that a customer order triggers the purchase of materials and the scheduling of production for a product.

T F **5.** A primary goal of the JIT production method is to cut the processing time of a product.

T F **6.** A building's environment is a cost driver.

T F **7.** Queue time is the time spent moving a product from one operation or department to another.

T F **8.** Processing time is the actual time that a product is being worked on.

T F **9.** An engineering change order is a cost driver.

T F **10.** RIP inventory means raw-in-process inventory.

T F **11.** Job order costing can easily be adapted to the just-in-time environment.

T F **12.** JIT is a fully integrated computer setup in which everything connected with the manufacturing system is performed automatically.

T F **13.** Automation and just-in-time are synonymous.

T F **14.** A non-value added activity adds costs to the product but does not increase its market value.

T F **15.** In a JIT operating environment, machinery and equipment are moved into cells or islands, layouts that comprise small autonomous production lines.

T F **16.** Preventive facility maintenance is minimized by a JIT operating system.

Circle the letter of the best answer.

1. A fully integrated computer setup in which everything connected with the manufacturing system is performed automatically is a
   a. flexible manufacturing system.
   b. just-in-time environment.
   c. computer-integrated manufacturing system.
   d. pull-through production system.

2. Which of the following is *not* an element of the just-in-time production philosophy?
   a. Maintaining minimum inventory levels
   b. Developing a multiskilled labor force
   c. Increasing emphasis on direct labor variance analysis
   d. Encouraging continuous improvement in the work environment

3. Pull-through production planning and scheduling means that
   a. automated trucks pull the products through the production process.
   b. a customer order triggers the purchase of materials and the scheduling of production.
   c. A customer complaint triggers the scheduling of rework on the defective product.
   d. the production and scheduling processes are not functioning properly and that a special pull device must be adapted to correct the situation.

4. Maintaining minimum inventory levels is a goal of JIT because
   a. carrying inventory is a waste of working capital.
   b. carrying inventory maximizes the use of factory floor space.
   c. customer needs are no longer a major consideration.
   d. the company's current ratio is increased.

5. Unit costs within a JIT production environment are minimized by
   a. using very inexpensive materials and supplies.
   b. performing quick, inexpensive machine setups.
   c. sacrificing quality for high-speed processes.
   d. using unskilled labor wherever possible.

6. Which of the following is *not* part of the traditional production process?
   a. Storage time
   b. Processing time
   c. Queue time
   d. Decision time

7. Direct costs within the JIT environment are
   a. less important than in a traditional production setting.
   b. higher because of increased traceability.
   c. lower because of reduced production time.
   d. still only associated with materials and labor costs.

8. Within the JIT production setting, the Raw-in-Process Inventory account
   a. replaces the Work-in-Process and Finished Goods Inventory accounts.
   b. is an account used in place of the Work-in-Process Inventory account.
   c. replaces the Work-in-Process and Materials Inventory accounts.
   d. is used in place of the Raw Materials Inventory account.

9. The acronym FMS stands for
   a. flexible materials system.
   b. finite machine setup.
   c. famous manufacturing style.
   d. flexible manufacturing system.

10. Which of the following is *not* a cost driver?
   a. Product inspection
   b. Machine setup
   c. A cutter bolt wrench
   d. Drill press maintenance

Applying Your Knowledge

Exercises

1. The following factory overhead costs were incurred by the Eubanks-Scott Corporation's Component Manufacturing Division:

Engineering labor	$12,750
Setup labor, FMS	$11,420
Electricity, FMS	$1,430
Depreciation, engineering	$4,500
Depreciation, factory building	$10,200
Operating supplies, FMS	$980
Property taxes, factory building	$2,960
Machinery maintenance, FMS	$3,100
Tool and die costs, FMS	$6,210
Electricity, engineering	$1,100
Depreciation, FMS	$8,740
Operating supplies, engineering	$430
Electricity, factory building	$4,200

Divide these costs into separate activity cost pools, then recommend an allocation base for each pool that distributes the costs fairly. Alternative cost drivers or allocation bases include direct labor hours, square footage, engineering hours, machine hours, engineering change orders, and direct labor dollars.

2. Listed below are several commonly incurred costs in a manufacturing environment:

Direct labor	Operating supplies
Depreciation, machinery	Fire insurance, plant
Raw materials	Setup labor
Product design costs	Rework costs
President's salary	Supervisory salaries
Small tools	Utility costs, machinery

Identify each type of cost as being either direct or indirect, assuming the cost is incurred in (a) a traditional manufacturing setting and (b) a JIT flexible manufacturing system environment.

Explain your reasons for any classification changes.

3. Tracy Rosenberg is converting the accounting system of the UCF Manufacturing Company to account for costs related to the company's new JIT/FMS environment. The Raw-in-Process Inventory account has been installed. The following transactions took place last week:

Dec. 22   Metal brackets for Jobs 213 and 216 were ordered and received, $4,890.

Dec. 23   Steel castings for the product's body were received, $13,300.

Dec. 23   Work began on both jobs.

Dec. 24   Both jobs completed, total costs: Job 213, $14,870; Job 216, $17,880.

Dec. 26   Job 216 shipped to customer (the company prices its products using a 60 percent markup over cost).

Using good journal entry form, record these transactions.

	General Journal			
Date		Description	Debit	Credit

How Cost Management Systems Can Support The JIT Philosophy

Traditional measures common in many cost accounting systems may encourage actions contrary to the spirit of JIT.

The Just-in-Time philosophy is reshaping the physical nature of the production environment and changing both the behavioral patterns of production costs and how financial executives must measure and control these costs. Some of the changes that are being applied by financial executives to traditional cost management systems to make them better management tools consistent with the JIT philosophy need to be studied and, perhaps, emulated by others.

Each of the changes discussed have been put into practice by organizations that have had success with applying the JIT philosophies to their business and have realized that changes to their cost management systems were necessary in order to enable them to keep pace with the process changes that result when JIT is adopted.

The JIT philosophies are creating manufacturing environments that require a new, more innovative means of approaching cost management. Traditional methods and procedures for measuring and reporting production costs begin to erode in a JIT environment and require that changes be made to existing cost management systems. For example, the JIT philosophies will significantly impact:

☐ Identification of cost drivers,
☐ Number of product cost elements,
☐ Application of product costs, and
☐ Nature of performance measures.

A number of JIT organizations have enhanced their cost management systems to complement JIT methods. While specific solutions varied from one organization to another, common elements of how change was initiated existed in each of the organizations that successfully

Source: Article by Robert D. McIlhattan. From *Management Accounting,* September 1987. Reprinted by permission. Copyright © 1987 by the National Association of Accountants.

aligned their cost management systems and manufacturing processes.

Identification of Cost Drivers

Perhaps the greatest impact of JIT on an organization and the cost management system is that it focuses management's attention on *nonvalue*-added processes. A nonvalue process is defined as any activity or procedure that is performed within a company that does not add value to a product.

For example, assume that the lead time associated with manufacturing a salable product comprises the following general steps:

☐ *Process Time* is the amount of time that a product is actually being worked on.
☐ *Inspection Time* is the amount of time spent either assuring that the product is of high quality or actually spent reworking the product to an acceptable quality level.
☐ *Move Time* is the time spent moving the product from one location to another.
☐ *Queue Time* is the amount of time the product waits before being processed, or moved, or inspected, or whatever.
☐ *Storage Time* is the amount of time a product spends in stock before further processing or shipment.

Of these five steps, only process time actually adds value to the product. All other activities—inspection time, move time, queue time, and storage time—add cost but no value to the product and therefore are deemed as *nonvalue-added* processes within the JIT philosophy.

In many organizations, the amount of process time is much less than 10% of the total manufacturing lead time and cost (costs associated with longer lead times include shortages, obsolescence, and expediting) associated with manufacturing a salable item. Therefore, over 90% of the manufacturing lead time associated with a product adds cost, but no value to the product. It is this premise that leads to the JIT philosophy that reducing lead time will reduce total cost.

In order to assist in this process, financial executives in JIT environments have begun to identify the causes for the time and cost associated with the nonvalue-added elements of manufacturing a product.

The key impact on traditional cost accounting is that cost management systems now need to identify the cause of costs—the "cost drivers," in addition to capturing the resultant costs. Harley Davidson, Omark Industries, Hewlett-Packard, and other successful JIT users have undertaken studies to define the true "drivers" associated with increasing costs. See Table 1 for a list of "cost drivers."

In all cases the organizations determined that there was a direct correlation between the number of transactions and the cost of production. In addition, Hewlett Packard determined that many of its costs were a direct function of: the number of vendors used, the number of engineering changes to the product, and the total number of part numbers it maintained.

In few cases there is a direct correlation between labor head count and total production costs.

By refocusing the cost management system to identify the true driving force behind nonvalue-added activities, the financial executives were able to assist the manufacturing managers in eliminating the product design and manufacturing process inefficiencies that were at the root of the product cost issues.

Product designs were simplified, reducing engineering changes and part numbers, which

Table 1   Potential Cost Drivers

Number of Labor Transactions
Number of Material Moves
Number of Total Part Numbers
Number of Parts received in a Month
Number of Part Numbers in an average product
Number of Products
Average Number of Options
Number of Schedule Changes
Number of Accessories
Number of Vendors
Number of Units Scrapped
Number of Engineering Change Notices
Number of Process Changes
Number of Units Reworked
Number of Direct Labor Employees
Number of New Parts Introduced

correspondingly reduced financial problems associated with excess stock, obsolescence, storages, rework, and other associated costs. Vendors were reduced, improving quality and delivery schedules; and reporting transactions were either eliminated completely (in the case of direct labor) or reduced to an obsolete minimum, thereby eliminating support costs for clerical activities associated with transaction process, error correction, waiting time, and moving time.

Through the identification of the costs associated with nonvalue-added activities, financial executives in each of these organizations have been able to help identify the true "drivers" of these activities and costs leading to their reduction or elimination.

Number of Product Cost Elements

One of the other impacts that JIT is having on cost management systems is the reduction in the number of cost elements for a product. The philosophies of JIT, while applicable to virtually any industry or process, have had their greatest successes in the industries that, because of the nature of their products and processes, have adopted standard cost systems.

Most traditional standard cost systems maintain standard cost elements for material, direct labor, and manufacturing overhead. More sophisticated standard cost systems often maintained more than these elements. As managers' needs for better cost information increased, overhead costs were typically broken into more finite elements in order to better control production costs. Standard product cost elements associated with variable overhead, fixed overhead, set-up, material acquisition, energy, direct labor overhead, and others were added to cost systems in an effort to obtain better visibility and control over product-related costs.

However, as explained previously, one of the primary philosophies of JIT is to identify the cost drivers associated with production costs. Once identified, the concept of striving for continual improvement in the reduction of product cost through design and process improvements on a daily basis eliminates the need to define multiple cost elements.

Harley Davidson is an example of a JIT-dedicated organization that has reduced the number of standard cost elements associated with its products. It has converted from having five cost elements per part (direct material, direct labor, set-up, variable overhead, and fixed overhead) to just two (direct material and conversion cost). Similar changes have been made by many other JIT organizations including IBM and Caterpillar.

For these organizations, the JIT philosophies have helped them recognize that the issue is the elimination and prevention of costs, not simply the reporting of cost elements. The organizational acceptance and awareness that any cost, regardless of its nature, should be reduced, has focused attention that the design and process improvements necessary to implement JIT successfully will reduce cost through the enhancements themselves. The reduction of cost elements helps people focus on total product cost as opposed to individual elements. Additionally, the reduction of cost elements further reduces the support costs associated with their reporting, calculation, maintenance, and control.

It should be noted that while the number of product cost elements defined within the cost systems for JIT organizations declined, they all retained their standard cost systems. In fact, IBM is in the process of converting some facilities from a weighted average actual cost system to a standard cost system. The application of the standard cost system changed in that it was not longer used as widely to measure performance. Standard cost systems, however, are still important as a tool for valuing inventory and cost of sales and as a tool to estimate potential future costs associated with design and or process changes. Therefore, an additional impact of JIT is that standards are used to a much greater extent as a tool to prevent costs before they arise as opposed to report against once they have incurred. Again, fewer cost elements will suffice in order to meet their purpose.

Application of Product Cost

As stated, one of the key characteristics of JIT is the adoption of manufacturing cells dedicated to the production of single or similar products or major components. In addition to the primary objective of the reduction of manufacturing lead time, manufacturing cells also change the nature of product costs and introduce alternative methods of applying production costs to specific products flowing through each cell.

The vast majority of traditional cost accounting systems in place today apply indirect manufacturing costs to products based upon either the direct labor hours or dollars charged to a specific product. A JIT environment challenges this practice in two significant areas:

1. The vehicle used to charge and collect labor hours (or dollars) to a specific product in most traditional environments is the factory work order. As individuals work on specific jobs, they charge their time to the factory work order that is associated with the item being manufactured. Costs are therefore accumulated as the factory work order travels through the product process. Within a JIT environment, there may be no factory work orders. Daily production schedules are provided for each cell and typically only finished items are reported by the cell over the course of the day. No detail reporting is performed (which again is consistent with the philosophy of reduction of transactions and lead time). Therefore, the total of all related costs is applied to the day's production, not individual jobs and tasks.

2. In a JIT environment, direct labor may not have a correlation to other manufacturing costs and, as previously stated, is usually included in the total conversion costs. Within a JIT environment, alternative methods of applying cost to a product may be more appropriate. For example, many JIT users apply total conversion cost based on velocity through a manufacturing cell. Velocity is based on the theoretical number of units that can be produced within a cell over a given period. Theoretical capacity is used because it is consistent with the JIT philosophy of continual improvement towards perfection with no allowance for inefficiency or downtime. Based on velocity, a cost per hour is computed for a given cell. Therefore, a day's production is costed simply by multiplying the number of units produced by the cost associated with the hours required to produce that day's production. It does not matter whether the hours are direct labor, set-up, queue, or machine hours, the concept is that "time is money" and that the longer it takes to produce something, the more it will cost.

It should be noted that other application methods do exist depending on the nature of the manufacturing cell process. These may include material usage, equipment costs, or more imaginative items identified as true drivers such as number of transactions, quality, or number of engineering change orders.

A second major impact of JIT on the area of

WHAT IS JIT?

The most widely accepted definition of JIT is the constant and relentless pursuit for the elimination of waste, with waste being defined as anything that does not add value to a product—inspection, queue time, and stock. While this definition is true, it is too broad to gain a clear understanding of how JIT might impact today's cost management systems.

The JIT concept is built on the philosophy of lead time reduction from suppliers, through operations, and to customers. The common denominator for this concept is the pursuit of zero inventories, zero defects, flexibility, and zero schedule interruptions.

To accomplish these goals, JIT efforts usually include the following activities and/or attributes:

□ Set-up reduction and introduction of continually smaller lot sizes. This is necessary to help ensure that products move continuously through the process, eliminating queue time and schedule interruptions.

□ Pursuit of improved product quality. Many JIT firms have adopted new quality awareness programs and/or implemented statistical process controls in order to "make it right the first time," and thus help eliminate product defects and the associated costs of scrap, rework, inspection, returns, and other inherent "costs of quality," i.e., production disruption.

□ Continual improvement in some specific element of the production process. An inherent maxim of JIT is that every person should attempt to improve in some dimension of JIT every day. Improvement can be made in many areas: defects, better product design, fewer stoppages in the schedule, more output, or other areas. Many JIT programs have worker involvement programs structured to help motivate and reward workers for making such improvements.

□ JIT firms generally adopt cellular manufacturing techniques. In order to reduce travel distances and inventory between machines, companies set up manufacturing cells that are dedicated to producing a product or major component start to finish without returning to the stockroom. This JIT feature, sometimes referred to as a "factory within a factory," also requires worker involvement and training, and instructing workers on how to move a product through a cell as efficiently as possible.

applying product costs is the increase in the amount of production cost that can be directly applied to a product. This phenomenon is a function of the adoption of manufacturing cells and the dedication of those cells to singular or similar products (Table 2).

Within a JIT environment, a fundamental goal is the reduction of total product cost. In order for the cost management system to measure success in this area, allocations must be eliminated to the greatest extent possible. As most financial executives are well aware, the greater the degree of allocations, the less reliable (or accepted) the information is for decision-making purposes.

As illustrated in Table 2, JIT helps eliminate allocations through the implementation of manufacturing cells dedicated to singular or similar product production. However, many JIT organizations including Caterpillar, Harley Davidson, Omark, and IBM have begun to adopt new cost management methods of associating total production costs, including support function costs, directly to products in an effort to reduce allocations and increase cost information reliability and responsibility; i.e., for "ownership" of product costs.

For example, IBM has adopted a concept of directly charging costs to specific products as a result of their JIT enhancements. Costs are associated to products using one of three methods as follows:

1. Production floor expenses are charged directly to products as they flow through manufacturing cells.

2. Nonoccupancy-related support costs, such as cost accountancy and data processing, are "billed" directly to the products utilizing their services. The billing rates are negotiated between support function managers and product managers before services are rendered and are based on the amount of support given to a specific product.

3. Occupancy-related costs are still allocated to products.

Table 2   Direct vs. Indirect Costs

	Traditional Environment	J-I-T Environment
Direct labor	Direct	Direct
Material handling	Indirect	Direct
Repairs and maintenance	Direct	Direct
Energy	Indirect	Direct
Operating supplies	Indirect	Direct
Supervision	Indirect	Direct
Production support services	Indirect	Largely direct
Building occupancy	Indirect	Indirect
Insurance and taxes	Indirect	Indirect
Depreciation	Indirect	Direct

Through the adoption of its direct charging approach, IBM has significantly increased the amount of support costs that can be directly associated to a product without the need for allocations. Before this process was adopted, only 25% of support costs could be associated to a product. Today, 75% of all support costs can be associated to a product without allocation.

Comments by controllers who have adopted direct charging concepts indicate the benefit of enhancing cost management systems to be more compatible with the philosophies of JIT and resultant process changes. Controllers have commented: "product manager's ownership of expense has improved"; "the accuracy of product cost is better"; "there is an increased visibility and awareness of expense items"; "it allows for flexibility in changing environment, improved sourcing decisions, and competitive analysis"; and "it allows for cost reductions and improves competitiveness."

The Nature of Performance Measures

As organizations begin to adopt a company-wide commitment to total cost management, the performance measurements used to monitor improvement and motivate personnel begin to change. Traditional measures that are commonplace in many cost accounting systems are not appropriate within the JIT philosophy of cost management. In fact, in some cases they may encourage actions that are contrary to the spirit of JIT. Four such examples are:

☐ Direct labor efficiency,
☐ Direct labor utilization,
☐ Direct labor productivity, and
☐ Machine utilization.

These measurements are inappropriate for the following reasons:

1. They all promote building inventory beyond what is needed in the immediate time frame.

2. Emphasizing performance to standard gives priority to output, at the expense of quality. Relatively few companies even adjust results to reflect bad parts. Using standards for performance measurements can be somewhat limiting relative to continuous improvement. Once standards are attained, people usually feel they have "arrived."

3. Direct labor in the majority of manufacturers accounts for only between 5%–15% of total product cost. Traditional cost managers have run with very tight direct labor control and relatively loose overhead control. Frequently, direct labor head count reductions have been more than offset by overhead increases.

4. Using machine utilization is similarly inappropriate because it encourages results in building inventory ahead of needs. Focusing on this measurement has frequently resulted in using expensive equipment and sometimes entire plants around-the-clock, thinking this would maximize ROI. The fact is that under this scenario virtually no time is allowed for preventative maintenance; equipment is run flat out until it breaks down. When it does break down, there is considerable disruption that ripples throughout manufacturing. This results in unnecessary costs and, in fact, reduction in ROI instead of its maximization.

Table 3 highlights some performance measures

The Just-In-Time Philosophy

that may be appropriate for a cost management system that is consistent with the JIT philosophies.

Table 3 lists new JIT performance measures that may be appropriate for inclusion in a cost management system within a JIT environment. Specific performance measures are dependent on the unique business environment and process being managed. For example, Harley Davidson has adopted the following 10 measurements to assess its manufacturing effectiveness:

1. Schedule Attainment,
2. Manning Requirements,
3. Conversion Costs,
4. Overtime Requirements,*
5. Inventory Levels,
6. Material Cost Variance,
7. Scrap/Rework,
8. Manufacturing Cycle Time*
9. Quality Level, and
10. Productivity Improvements.

Measures of flexibility.

Conversely, a different Fortune 100 company has adopted the seven measures and goals listed in Table 4 for measuring its effectiveness in an integrated circuit facility.

While the measures are different for these two organizations, there are similarities. In both cases, non-financial indicators were used to measure performance as part of the cost management system. This is consistent with the identification of true cost drivers outlined earlier in this article and with JIT focuses on quality and lead times.

Both measurement systems were proposed and maintained by the financial executives in these organizations. In each case, the financial executives took the initiative to propose more effective ways of monitoring performance and reducing overall cost and worked closely with manufacturing to refine these proposals and establish a "team approach to performance measurement."

Both performance measurement systems were simplified from their predecessor traditional systems. Simple, easy-to-understand measures were implemented so that everyone in the organization could understand their intent and interpret their results. Additionally, measurement results were posted in the factory so that everyone in the organization could be more aware

Table 3   Performance Measures: Traditional vs. JIT

Traditional	JIT

• Direct Labor
  —Efficiency
  —Utilization
  —Productivity
• Machine Utilization
• Inventory Turnover or Months-on-Hand
• Cost Variances
• Individual Incentives
• Performance to Schedule
• Promotion based on seniority
	• Total Head Count Productivity—Output—Total Head count (direct, indirect, administrative personnel)
	
	• Return on Net Assets
	• Days of Inventory
	• Product Cost, especially relative to competitors' costs
	• Group Incentives
	• Customer Service
	• Promotion based upon increased knowledge and capability
	• Ideas generated
	• Ideas implemented
	• Lead time by product/product family
	• Set-up reduction
	• Number of customer complaints
	• Response time to customer feedback
	• Machine availability
	• Cost of Quality

"The Spirit of Manufacturing Excellence," September, 1986. Ernest C. Huge and Alan D. Anderson

Table 4

Measure	Goal
1. Unit cost—cell $/hr—theoretical units/hr	$1.00
2. Cycle Time = Through cell with no downtime	3 days
3. On-time delivery	100%
4. Quality	0 defects
5. Linearity—Ability to meet daily schedule	0% deviation
6. Inventory turns	75
7. Scrap	0

and in tune to company improvements in these areas.

Focus on Simplification

In each of the major areas of cost management outlined above, specific company solutions differ. The impact of true cost drivers within organizations will differ from one company to another; the number of product cost elements necessary to report and control costs properly may differ between companies. The ability to apply costs directly to products and the types of cost being applied to products will change based on organizational differences and products being manufactured; and, as we have seen, performance measurements differ between companies.

However, without exception, simplification was one of the primary objectives of every financial executive who enhanced his cost management system for JIT. The focus on the two or three true cost drivers within an organization, the reduction in standard product cost elements, the reduction of allocations, and the establishment of fewer, easy-to-understand, key performance measures are all examples of simplification.

JIT strives for design and process simplification because with simplification comes better management. Better management allows for better quality, better service, and less cost. The same principles are true for cost management systems. Traditional cost accounting systems have a tendency to be very complex. Simplification of this process enables the cost accounting system to be used by everyone in an organization, transforming the cost "accounting" system into a cost "management" system.

How to Initiate Change

The management accountant can learn to think "just-in-time accounting." However, he must adjust to changing technology, new management philosophies, and the changing demands of information. Nothing is more discouraging than to hear financial people say "we can't accommodate that change because of our accounting system."

Each organization cited here had its own series of successes and failures before focusing on the cost management direction necessary to support JIT. As financial executives related their stories regarding the cost management changes they made, a set of common steps emerged as to how change occurred:

□ The perception of the accounting function needed to be changed. In each company the accounting function was perceived as a control function, a function that reported when things were bad. This perception (or reality) had to change from one of control of operations to cooperation with operations to reduce costs. The financial executives took the time and effort necessary to understand JIT and joined the operating professionals in an effort to implement its philosophies.

□ The financial executives became an integral part of the manufacturing and engineering project teams. A cost manager sat in on all product design meetings, manufacturing engineering meetings, and production control and planning meetings on a regular basis. This accomplished the following: (a) Accounting personnel learned the key elements of the engineering and manufacturing processes; (b) operating personnel became more aware of the implications of their actions of total cost, raising the total cost awareness throughout the company; and (c) perhaps, most important, it served as the basis for eliminating the communication barriers between accounting and operations. Each objective helped pave the way for obtaining the interfunctional cooperation necessary for the JIT philosophy to work in a company.

□ True cost drivers were identified. Once accounting became more aware of operations and operating personnel became more aware of the cost implications of their actions, those

The Just-In-Time Philosophy

processes or engineering issues that truly determined cost could be identified, segregated, and attacked.

□ Each company re-analyzed its application of costs to products and implemented a higher level of direct charging. The elimination of allocations gave a clearer picture of true product costs and raised the responsibility of costs to managers. Again, this is predicated on accounting's understanding of the engineering and production process.

□ Performance measures were altered to help motivate the entire operating group toward positive results. Individual performance measures were reduced to encourage a team concept. Personnel were trained and informed as to the meaning of performance measures.

□ All systems were simplified. Traditional accounting systems were redesigned to reflect principles of JIT. Information flows and reports were simplified to forcus on the critical processes and measures.

The simplification increased awareness and allowed management to focus on only a few issues that greatly increased the benefits associated with their actions. As process changes took place, cost drivers, and performance measurements changed. Financial executives could change reports and information flows to reflect the new manufacturing process quickly and inexpensively.

Virtually any organization can enhance its cost systems to be more supportive of the JIT philosophy. The first step is for the financial executive himself to adopt the primary JIT principle of continual improvement within the organization and cost management process.

CHAPTER 16 JIT AND AUTOMATION: PRODUCT COSTS, PERFORMANCE MEASURES, CAPITAL INVESTMENTS, AND REPORTING

REVIEWING THE CHAPTER

Objective 1: State the three new areas of emphasis that go hand in hand with the JIT philosophy (pp. 623-624).

1. Significant changes are taking place in the management accounting systems of companies that have adopted automated JIT manufacturing processes. These include (a) a macro versus a micro approach to the control of operations, (b) the increasing importance of nonfinancial data, and (c) the use of theoretical capacity to evaluate actual performance.

2. In a **JIT/FMS environment,** profit is maximized by minimizing the product processing time on each product line. Emphasis is on the entire operation, not departments or cost centers. Time must be minimized, not cost. Cost automatically is reduced as efficiency increases.

3. The JIT environment emphasizes time reduction, product distribution, and customer satisfaction. All of these areas require reports and analyses of a nonfinancial nature, reports and analyses that focus on the causes of excessive processing, waiting and queue time, average delivery time, the number and causes of customer complaints, and other areas.

4. On of the major objectives of the JIT philosophy is to minimize nonproductive time in the total delivery cycle. This means that the company is expected to try to operate at theoretical (ideal) capacity.

Objective 2: Identify the unique aspects of product costing in an automated manufacturing process (pp. 625-629).

5. The degree of factory automation varies from company to company and from process to process. Freestanding **computer numerically controlled (CNC)** machines automate a section or part of a production line and usually represent the starting point of a company's move toward automation. The addition of **computer-aided design and computer-aided manufacturing (CAD/CAM)** is often the second level. The installation of a full flexible manufacturing system (FMS) automates an entire product production line. **Automated material handling systems (AMHS)** can be an integral part of an FMS and are absolutely necessary as the company moves to a complete

computer-integrated manufacturing (CIM) environment. Each of these steps in the factory automation movement influences product costing.

6. The use of inappropriate cost allocation bases is a primary problem of companies that have adopted an automated JIT environment. Direct labor bases are no longer useful. Three machine time expressions should be considered when selecting a cost allocation base for a factory: (a) actual machine hours, (b) run time (total machine hours less setup time), and/or (c) engineered time (standard or predicted machine time for the product).

7. Cost traceability has improved with automated production processes. Costs that traditionally have been treated as indirect (electricity, supplies, setup labor) now can be monitored and traced directly to CNC machines or FMS operating cells.

8. Costs should be grouped by type of activity and allocated using a base that has a causal relationship between the costs incurred and the activity. For example, engineering costs should be allocated based on engineering hours.

9. Because of the wide variety of processes and the varying degrees of automation present in a factory, overhead should be traced to departments or better yet to operating cells before being allocated to products. The use of a plantwide overhead rate should be discouraged.

10. Costs associated with an automated material handling system should be grouped under this activity and allocated to products using a base associated with the cost of materials used in the process.

Objective 3: Compute a product unit cost using data from a flexible manufacturing system (pp. 629-632).

11. The unit cost of an FMS-produced product can be computed using a cell-related overhead rate with many costs formerly treated as indirect being traced directly to the cell before allocation to the product takes place. Activity-based cost allocations, such as materials handling—related overhead costs, should be done before conversion costs are assigned to a product.

Objective 4: Identify the types of financial and nonfinancial analyses used in a JIT environment to evaluate the performance of (a) product quality, (b) product delivery, (c) inventory control, (d) materials cost/scrap control, and (e) machine management and maintenance (pp. 633-638).

12. Performance evaluation measures used to control product quality include analyses of customer complaints, warranty claims, vendor quality records, quality audits, scrap and rework records, product returns and allowances, and lost-business statistics.

13. Measures used to help control and monitor delivery performance include analyses of **delivery time,** setup time, production backlog, **purchase order lead time** (order received to shipment time), order fulfillment rate, **production cycle** time (receipt of materials to product shipment time), and waste time (lead time less processing time).

14. Inventory performance still has some of the measures connected with the traditional manufacturing setting, with a few new approaches added to address the new environment. Measures now used include turnover rates by product, cycle count accuracy, space reduction needs caused by reduced inventory levels, number of inventoried items, and turnover rates by type of inventory (raw in process, finished goods, composite).

15. Emphasis is given to measuring the performance of materials cost and scrap control in the new manufacturing environment. Actual scrap losses are charted; records are kept of scrap by part, product, and operation; and scrap as a percentage of total cost is computed and analyzed. Special attention is placed on measuring the quality of incoming materials because of the critical nature of keeping the JIT/FMS cell in operation. Materials cost as a percentage of total cost is also a good barometer of materials performance.

16. The new manufacturing environment places special attention on machine management and maintenance. Machine availability and its reciprocal, machine downtime, are monitored constantly. Thorough machine maintenance records are kept and policed. Equipment capacity versus utilization is

charted. Measures that plot out equipment experience tell management where present or potential production bottlenecks are located so that corrective action can be taken.

Objective 5: Define full cost profit margin and state the advantages of this measure of profitability (pp. 638-641).

17. A **full cost profit margin** is the difference between total revenue and total costs traceable to the work cell or product.

18. Full cost profit margins are more appropriate than **contribution margins** for measuring profitability in a capital intensive environment. Because the computer has enabled the accountant to trace costs to FMS cells more easily, the JIT/FMS environment can provide data that allow most costs to be treated as direct costs of those cells. With the accuracy problems associated with the allocation of fixed costs no longer a threat, variable costing can give way to full costing. The full cost profit margin becomes the measure to watch when trying to control product costs.

Objective 6: Describe the special costs associated with capital expenditure decisions for automated machines and processes (pp. 641-645).

19. Four characteristics of JIT/FMS capital expenditures make decision making difficult and highlight why the net present value method of analysis is preferred. (a) The expenditures for automated equipment tend to be very high; (b) the useful life of automated equipment tends to be longer, which makes estimating future cash flows more difficult; (c) the equipment is technically and operationally more complex, which makes estimating future operating costs more difficult; and (d) there is an increased amount of uncertainty present in capital expenditure decisions about automated equipment.

20. Three categories of costs are specifically associated with JIT/FMS capital expenditure decisions: (a) cost savings that will result from reducing the amount of direct labor and the labor-related benefits of replaced workers; (b) new costs, which include wages and related costs of workers who maintain and support the robotic/automated equipment, new direct costs such as electrical power and supervision traceable to work cells, and costs associated with scheduling and design; and (3) new costs that need to be capitalized, including engineering design work on the new system, computer programming and software development costs, and machine implementation costs.

Objective 7: Identify the primary areas of management reporting in a JIT/FMS environment and give examples of the reports needed (pp. 645-648).

21. The primary areas of management reporting in a JIT/FMS environment are customer responsiveness, product line profitability, product contribution, operating effectiveness, and asset management. These areas require nonfinancial as well as financial data analyses and reports.

22. Examples of customer responsiveness reports include number and types of customer complaints, returns and allowances by customer, actual versus promised delivery data, backlogged orders, and product shipment tracking.

23. Product line profitability reporting centers on materials purchasing, materials handling costs, conversion costs, and shipping and delivery costs.

24. Product contribution reporting focuses on full cost profit margins and contribution margins of product lines.

25. Reports centering on product cycle times, product lead times, product waste times, scrap/defective units, machine yield rates, and throughput time analyses comprise the operating effectiveness reporting area.

26. Asset management is enhanced by focusing reports around machine maintenance, machine availability/downtime, space utilization, and equipment capacity and experience.

TESTING YOUR KNOWLEDGE

Matching

Match each term with its definition by writing the appropriate letter in the blank.

___ 1. Nonfinancial data

___ 2. Automated material handling system (AMHS)

___ 3. Purchase order lead time

___ 4. Delivery cycle

___ 5. JIT/FMS environment

___ 6. Computer numerically controlled (CNC) machines

___ 7. Full cost profit margin

___ 8. Production cycle time

___ 9. Run time

___ 10. Computer-aided design/computer-aided manufacturing (CAD/CAM)

a. A necessary component of a computer-integrated manufacturing system in which the raw materials and partially completed product handling function is automatic, providing a continuous flow through the process

b. Total machine hours less setup time

c. Stand-alone machines that are computer controlled

d. Using computers in product design, planning and controlling production, and linking CNC machines

e. Information that focuses on time reduction statistics

f. An operating environment created by a flexible manufacturing system functioning within the just-in-time philosophy

g. The difference between total revenue and total costs traceable to the work cell or product

h. The time period between acceptance of the order and final delivery of the product

i. The time it takes for raw materials and parts to be ordered and received so that production can begin

j. The time it takes for the production people to make a product available for shipment to a customer

Completion

Use the lines provided to complete each item.

1. Identify the three new areas of accounting emphasis created by the move to JIT and automated production facilities.

   a. _____

   b. _____

   c. _____

2. What is a JIT/FMS manufacturing environment?

   _____

   _____

   _____

   _____

3. List the five areas of performance measurement required for strong operating control, and identify two nonfinancial data measurements for each area.

a. _____

_____

_____

b. _____

_____

_____

c. _____

_____

_____

d. _____

_____

_____

e. _____

_____

_____

4. Define and discuss the elements of time that are critical to strong product delivery performance.

_____

_____

_____

_____

_____

_____

_____

_____

_____

5. Define full cost profit margin. How is it different from contribution margin?

_____

_____

_____

_____

6. What three special cost categories must be considered when making capital expenditure decisions involving JIT/FMS equipment?

a. _____

_____

b. _____

_____

c. _____

_____

True-False

Circle T if the statement is true, F if it is false.

T F **1.** The JIT management accountant approaches the control of operations by looking at the entire production process rather than small parts or segments of the process.

T F **2.** Nonfinancial data is of little use in controlling the operations of a JIT/FMS−oriented company.

T F **3.** Depreciation expense in a flexible manufacturing system is always an indirect cost.

T F **4.** CNC is the acronym for centralized nonfinancial control.

T F **5.** Engineered time is the standard or predicted machine time for a product.

T F **6.** A computer-controlled production system comprised of several types of machines that perform a series of operations and/or assemble a number of parts in a flexible and automatic fashion is called an AMHS.

T F **7.** CAD/CAM stands for computer-aided design/computer-aided manufacturing.

T F **8.** Plantwide factory overhead rates are encouraged in a JIT/FMS environment because of their flexibility.

T F 9. Customer acceptance controls, among them monitoring the number and types of customer complaints, are a product quality performance measure.

T F 10. Because inventory is no longer an important issue in the JIT environment, inventory performance measures are no longer computed and charted for trends.

T F 11. Purchase order lead time is the period between acceptance of the order and final delivery of the product.

T F 12. One of the objectives of machine management and maintenance measures is to evaluate the performance of maintenance personnel in keeping to a prescribed maintenance program.

T F 13. In the new manufacturing environment, specific records are kept regarding scrap, rework, and defective units.

T F 14. Full cost profit margin is the difference between total revenue and total costs traceable to the work cell or product.

T F 15. Capital expenditure decisions are relatively unimportant in the JIT/FMS environment because everyone connected with the manufacturing process knows how much the equipment is needed.

T F 16. Customer responsiveness reporting is required by the Financial Accounting Standards Board for all manufacturing companies using JIT/FMS work cells.

Multiple Choice

Circle the letter of the best answer.

1. Which of the following is *not* an example of nonfinancial data?
   a. A machine maintenance schedule
   b. Labor cost trend analysis
   c. Delivery cycle analysis
   d. Analysis of the number and types of customer complaints

2. In a JIT/FMS environment, renewed emphasis is placed on operating at
   a. theoretical capacity.
   b. normal capacity.
   c. practical capacity.
   d. excess capacity.

3. In an FMS work cell, which of the following costs is *not* a direct cost of the cell?
   a. Setup labor
   b. Electricity
   c. Supervision
   d. Factory building insurance

4. Detection of design flaws is built into a company's FMS computer program to
   a. do away with the need for the engineering function.
   b. do away with the need for product inspection.
   c. support the engineering design function.
   d. increase the need for direct labor.

5. Which of the following statements concerning the JIT/FMS environment is false?
   a. A JIT company works closely with its vendors to ensure a continuing timely supply of quality raw material inputs.
   b. Many nonfinancial measures have replaced traditional performance measures.
   c. Automated machinery linked into an FMS can easily be programmed with in-process product control mechanisms.
   d. The objective is to have enough inventory on hand to meet any customer need.

6. Which of the following is *not* a quality performance measure?
   a. Equipment capacity/utilization
   b. Warranty claims
   c. Scrap and rework statistics
   d. Customer complaints

7. Inventory performance in a JIT/FMS setting can be measured by
   a. production backlogs.
   b. setup times.
   c. turnover rates by product.
   d. None of the above

8. Which of the following is *not* a characteristic of a JIT/FMS capital expenditure decision?
   a. Payback period is the best decision approach because of the uncertainty involved.
   b. Useful lives are longer, and estimating future cash flows is more difficult.
   c. Expenditures for automated equipment tend to be very high.
   d. There is an increased amount of uncertainty present in capital expenditure decisions about automated equipment.

9. Which of the following statements about reporting in the new manufacturing environment is false?
   a. Continuous records of backlogged orders and delayed delivery dates are critical to maintaining customer satisfaction.
   b. Reports that focus on product cycle times, including process time, lead time, and waste time, are especially helpful in determining operating effectiveness.
   c. An emphasis on direct labor analysis and reporting is the key to effective cost control.
   d. Machine maintenance must be recorded, tracked, and reported on a regular basis.

Applying Your Knowledge

Exercises

1. Rollins Manufacturing Company produces nightstands using an FMS work cell. The wood is shaped and the nightstands are assembled in one continuous operation. The output for December was 5,460 units. Each unit requires three machine hours of effort. Materials handling cost is allocated to the product based on unit materials cost; engineering design costs are allocated based on units produced; and FMS overhead and building occupancy costs are allocated based on machine hours. The following operating data for December has been made available to you:

Materials:		
Wood	$122,850	
Hardware	62,790	$185,640
Materials handling:		
Labor	$46,410	
Equipment depreciation	2,785	
Electrical power	4,650	
Maintenance	1,114	54,949
Direct Labor:		
Machinists		68,250
Engineering design:		
Labor	$3,003	
Electrical power	4,368	
Engineering overhead	2,184	9,555
FMS cell overhead:		
Indirect labor	$56,511	
Repairs and maintenance	9,828	
Supervision	39,312	
Equipment depreciation	18,018	
Operating supplies	4,914	
Electrical power	7,371	135,954
Building occupancy overhead		47,502
Total costs		$501,850

Materials handling cost allocation rate = $\dfrac{\$54,949}{\$185,640}$ = 29.6% per dollar of materials

Engineering design cost allocation rate = $\dfrac{\$9,555}{\$5,460}$ = $1.75 per unit

FMS overhead allocation rate = $\dfrac{\$135,954}{\$16,380}$ = $8.30 per machine hour

Building occupancy allocation rate = $\dfrac{\$47,502}{\$16,380}$ = $2.90 per machine hour

Using this information, compute the unit cost of one nightstand. Identify the six elements of the computation as part of your answer.

2. Grant Rupert, chief operating officer of Natress Company, has led his company to the top spot in the industry with an emphasis on innovation and new production technology. The company's Econo-Quality hand tools have the top market share. Two months ago the company installed a flexible manufacturing system utilizing the JIT philosophy, for its tool line. The goal is to increase product quality and throughput, and to reduce processing time. Management is interested in cutting time in all phases of the delivery cycle.

Below are data gathered by the controller's office for the last four weeks:

	Week			
	1	2	3	4
Average process time (hours)	31.4	31.5	31.7	31.8
Average setup time (hours)	3.3	3.4	3.2	3.1
Customer complaints	11	8	7	4
Delivery time (hours)	49.2	48.4	48.4	48.2
On-time deliveries (%)	96.1	97.7	97.2	98.4
Production backlog (units)	9,480	9,590	9,650	9,870
Production cycle time (hours)	39.1	39.6	39.8	40.2
Purchase order lead time (hours)	27.1	27.2	26.9	26.8
Warranty claims	1	4	2	2

Analyze the performance of the Econo-Quality tool line for the four-week period, centering your analysis on the following areas:
a. Product quality performance
b. Product delivery performance

3. OSU Enterprises is the world's largest producer of running shoes. The company recently installed a flexible manufacturing system for its 19—10 product line, and has recast its accounting system to reflect the new operating process. Monthly operating data for the month before and after the FMS installation are shown below.

	Product 19-10
Average monthly revenue	$690,000
Total operating costs:	
For month before FMS installed:	
Direct materials	$165,600
Direct labor	$227,700
Variable factory overhead	$62,100
Variable selling expenses	$20,700
Variable distribution costs	$27,600
Fixed factory overhead	$456,200
Fixed selling expenses	$132,300
Fixed distribution costs	$189,700
For month after FMS installed:	
Direct materials	$165,600
Materials-related overhead	$24,150
Direct labor	$31,050
Indirect labor	$49,680
Setup labor	$33,120
Electrical power	$12,420
Supervision	$17,940
Repairs and maintenance	$23,460
Operating supplies/lubricants	$5,520
Other traceable indirect costs	$15,180
Traceable selling expenses	26,220
Traceable distribution costs	$28,980
Nontraceable factory overhead	$112,400
Nontraceable selling and distribution costs	$96,500

Using the after-FMS data, compute the full cost profit margin for the 19—10 product line. Include both full cost profit margin and operating profit as a percent of revenue as part of your answer.

Crossword Puzzle
for Chapters 15 and 16

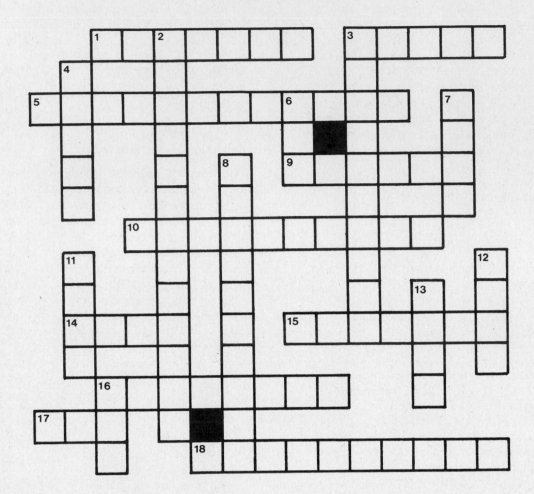

ACROSS

1. One basis for allocating factory overhead (2 words)
3. Delivery —— (time between order acceptance and delivery)
5. JIT inventory account (hyphenated)
9. Use of computers in design and manufacturing (initials)
10. Operating philosophy (hyphenated)
14. With 7-Down, the time it takes to receive materials once ordered
15. With 13-Down, production triggered by customer orders
16. —— manufacturing system (see 16-Down)
17. Manufacturing system run by computers (initials)
18. Standard or predicted machine time

DOWN

2. Activity that increases cost but not price (2 words)
3. Expenditure-producing activity (2 words)
4. What 10-Across and 8-Down help to eliminate
6. Machines controlled by computers (initials)
7. See 14-Across
8. Mechanical production process
11. Autonomous production line
12. Product-handling system (initials)
13. See 15-Across
16. Integrated set of computerized machines (initials)

The New Manufacturing Environment: Major Trends for Management Accounting

U.S. manufacturing is in the midst of dramatic change. From the end of World War II to the mid-seventies, the United States was the most prolific producer in the world. American plants churned out large quantities of goods willingly consumed by an expanding global market. From 1950 to 1979, the U.S. gross national product rose from $641 billion to $1,860 billion (1975 dollars) and foreign consumption of U.S. goods rose from $22 billion to $134 billion. In 1985, U.S. manufacturers exported only $108 billion while U.S. consumers imported $172 billion (1975 dollars), and the U.S. share of total output has dropped from over 40% in 1962 to approximately 25% in 1980.

The shifting competitive balance from domestic to foreign producers commonly is blamed on an expensive labor force, trade barriers to foreign markets, unfavorable exchange rates, and foreign and domestic government interference. These macroeconomic fundamentals are significant, but they are beyond management's direct control. But to say the problem is exogenous to the business community overlooks two serious failures of U.S. manufacturers—the failure to recognize shifts in consumer demands and the complacent acceptance of antiquated manufacturing processes and management philosophies.

Some companies, however, are recognizing what must be done to be competitive in today's global market. These world class manufacturers are using techniques developed both locally and abroad that dramatically change the way they manage their businesses.

Although there are a number of ways to categorize the changes made by these leading U.S. manufacturers, we find it helpful to think in terms of six major trends:

1. Higher quality,
2. Lower inventory,

Source: Article by Robert A. Howell and Stephen R. Soucy. From *Management Accounting*, September 1987. Reprinted with permission. Copyright © 1987 by the National Association of Accountants.

3. Flexible flow lines,
4. Automation,
5. Product line organization, and
6. Effective use of information.

Together they reflect a commitment to producing high quality goods, on time, at the lowest possible cost. These trends also reflect a significant shift in traditional management philosophies. For example, world class manufacturers do not view high quality and low cost as alternative strategies—a popular, but misguided, view of the 1970s. Rather, high quality is viewed as totally consistent with low cost. Nor do world class manufacturers focus on labor utilization or overhead absorption as measures of efficiency or productivity. Measures such as these encourage overproduction and result in excessive inventory balances.

Instead, world class manufacturers strive to eliminate inventory and are introducing new arrangements of equipment, product lines, and organizations. They are breaking with traditional patterns in order to achieve more focus and better results.

It is essential to understand that the resurrection of U.S. manufacturing is a long-term effort.

The management accountant has an opportunity to play a key role in the rebirth of U.S. manufacturing. Understanding how the factory is changing is a start.

The Major Trends

Higher quality is clearly a driving force in the new manufacturing environment. In the 1950s and 1960s, low price served as the primary basis for competition, and quality was defined as a standard level of acceptability.

During the past two decades, foreign competitors have provided markets with higher quality goods at competitive, if not cheaper, prices than their U.S. counterparts. While first ignored by U.S. manufacturers, continual erosion in the export and domestic markets placed pressure on them to either meet the higher quality in the marketplace or drop out.

The electronics and home appliance industries provide a contrasting example of the impact of quality on U.S. manufacturing. In electronics, America's share of the world market has fallen to 10%, less than a third of what it was in 1965. Foreign competitors are providing a higher quality product at a lower cost, forcing U.S. producers to respond in kind. Many have failed to do so. In contrast, the home appliance industry has been nearly impregnable from foreign competition. The industry's success is not the result of quotas, tariffs, or trade agreements, but is due to the high level of quality produced by U.S. manufacturers such as GE, Whirlpool, Maytag, and others.

A second explanation for higher quality is the realization that poor quality is a significant cost driver for the manufacturer. The absence of good materials, highly trained labor, and well-maintained equipment will dramatically increase the costs of nonquality such as scrap, rework, excess inventories, process and equipment breakdowns, field service, and product warranty claims.

For example, purchasing typically has been evaluated on a purchase price variance (actual price versus standard). This motivates purchasers to use suppliers that provide the least expensive material. Yet, low-cost, low-quality materials often result in manufacturing costs such as scrap, rework, and schedule disruptions. Purchasing rarely is accountable for these costs. By motivating purchasers to focus on price, the rest of the company incurs costs of nonquality that often exceed the price "savings" achieved.

Quality is not expensive, nonquality is. Harold K. Sperlich, president of Chrysler, reported that "to put value into the marketplace and meet the competitive challenge, you have to run a cost effective business dedicated to constant, never ending improvement. Quality is the main doorway to improving productivity and running a tighter ship."[1]

Lower Inventories is the second major trend in the new manufacturing environment. Companies are sharply reducing their inventory levels while maintaining delivery schedules and customer service. The impetus behind inventory reduction is threefold. First, inventory requires significant capital and the real cost of capital is dramatically higher today than in the 1950s and 1960s. Secondly, companies are recognizing the tradi-

tional reasons for holding inventory may no longer be valid. Finally, some companies, both foreign and domestic, are obtaining significant cost savings through reductions in inventory.

The cost of inventory traditionally is viewed as a financing cost—the inventory on hand times the cost of capital. While the direct financial cost to carry inventory can be significant, there are other indirect and qualitative costs associated with holding inventory that often are less explicitly identified. Examples include: increased space requirements, increased materials handling costs, increased record-keeping costs, increased insurance and tax obligations, slower throughput, higher scrap and obsolescence, and more costly inventory write-downs.

Efforts to quantify these indirect costs often result in estimates that match or exceed the financing cost of holding inventory. If the financial cost is 10%, then a more accurate estimate of the total cost may be 20 to 25%. By reducing inventory, a company obviously frees up cash to be invested in productive assets, but the savings associated with eliminating the indirect costs can greatly improve a company's short- and long-term profitability performance.

World-class manufacturers also argue that the reasons for holding high inventories are not valid and simply mask organizational deficiencies in sales, engineering, and procurement as well as manufacturing. By reducing the level of inventory, the issues are identified, and with management's effort, resolved.

For example, companies hold raw material inventories because vendor quality and delivery are not reliable. Qualifying vendors on the basis of quality and delivery performance eliminates the need for these buffer stocks. Work-in-process inventory builds up because of schedule changes, production imbalances, worker mistakes, and equipment breakdowns. Tighter process controls eliminate these deficiencies. Sales forecast errors often result in excess finished goods inventory. Shorter production cycles reduce the need for long-term forecasts, which are historically inaccurate.

The final explanation behind the push for lower inventories comes from witnessing the success of manufacturers that sharply lowered their inventory and increased inventory turns. Many Japanese companies are turning their inventories 25 to 30 times a year with some even exceeding 100 times. American companies

[1]Harold K. Sperlich, "The State of Quality in the U.S. Today," *Quality Progress,* April 1985.

also have been very successful in this area. Harley-Davidson increased its annual turns from 3.5 to 20. Ford Motor Co. reduced its inventory by $2 billion from 1979 to 1982. Westinghouse Transportation Division reduced its inventory space requirements from 66% of available space to 15%. Allen-Bradley's World Contactor facility operates with zero end-of-day, work-in-process and finished goods inventory.

Flexible Flow Lines is a third trend in the new manufacturing environment. Flow lines represent the physical path a product takes through the manufacturing process from raw material receipt to product shipment. Companies are redesigning their manufacturing flow lines to shorten cycle time—the length of time it requires to produce a product, and increase product variety.

The trend is to establish multiple product flow lines within a factory as contrasted to functionally organized process flows. A functional plant layout requires products to be moved from one group of like machines to another, oftentimes across the manufacturing plant or even to another building. This results in extensive material handling costs as well as increased work-in-process inventory.

In a product line flow, all the different types of equipment required in the manufacturing process are brought together, splitting up large groups of similar equipment, creating multiple "mini" product line factories. This layout minimizes material handling and inventory. Due to the tightened process flow, it moves the product quickly through the process, reinforces quality, and instills employee identification with the end product.

At AMC Jeep, production lines at its Toledo plant are broken at several places, causing partially assembled car bodies to be dragged manually from one line to the next as the assembly proceeds. By focusing on simplified product flow lines and producing a completed product rather than performing a specific function, world class manufacturers are achieving increased quality, throughput, and productivity, reducing inventory levels, and getting more product and process improvement suggestions from employees.

Once the plant layout is established, management can then leverage its benefits by focusing on the objective of maintaining a continuous flow. This requires that the entire process work in concert. The central idea is that product is pulled through the manufacturing process starting with customer demand and working back to incoming materials. This is in contrast to developing a production plan, buying material, releasing it to the factory floor and pushing it through the plant, and then notifying sales as to what is available to sell or more accurately what there is too much of and needs to be sold.

The "pull" concept is most commonly referred to as just-in-time (JIT) production, but other terms including continuous flow manufacturing (CFM) and pull-through production (PTP) reflect the same objective. Each requires a tremendous amount of discipline because the program is totally dependent upon an effective coordination of the process and the availability of materials.

If machines are not operable, workers are poorly trained, materials are unavailable or of poor quality, the absence of buffer stocks of inventory brings the production line to a halt. Therefore, pull-through production requires a high degree of stability, reliability, and quality in the manufacturing process. This is very much in contrast with the idea that production is a constant crisis environment. For many manufacturers, expediting orders, changing schedules, and fighting fires are virtually standard operating procedures.

The benefits of pull-through production include the elimination of inventories between stages of production, the reduction of space required to accommodate inventories, and low material handling and storage expenses. Because it is so tight a system, it forces all the components of the manufacturing process to work together to produce quality goods.

The trend toward flexible flow lines also reflects the emphasis on making the process more flexible, allowing it to produce more than one product on a production line. The implication of this major trend is that a production process need not be dedicated to any particular product.

Henry Ford's assembly line for the Model T was a product flow line, but it was not very flexible. A customer could have any color provided it was black. Today, Nissan produces both cars and trucks, of different colors, and with some variation of components on the same assembly line. Allen-Bradley can produce hundreds of variations of an electrical contactor on one assembly line in its "factory within a factory."

Automation is probably the most visible

change taking place in the new manufacturing environment. Some large U.S. manufacturers in the automotive, aerospace, heavy equipment, and high technology industries such as GE, Rockwell International, IBM, Apple Computer, and General Motors have invested heavily in automated equipment to increase quality and productivity and meet the competitive challenge of the global market.

While automation provides significant opportunities to manufacturers, companies should not rely on automation to solve their competitive problems. Rather, automation should be used to leverage the progress made in the areas discussed above. Quality, inventory, and flexible flows require management to address the fundamental issues of how business is conducted. Many companies have in fact realized disappointing returns from automation resulting from poor planning, neglect of basic shop floor controls, and unrealistic expectations. A more focused organization and a simpler, more streamlined factory removes the temptation to automate a process that should be eliminated.

A typical example is the automation of material handling. Some companies proudly exhibit highly automated material transfer and storage systems that cost millions of dollars to install but are "reaping" tremendous returns. Other companies, instead, proudly exhibit that they have no inventory to store. For these companies, the returns have been realized without the investment.

The investment in automation can be thought of as consisting of three levels: the stand-alone piece of equipment, the cell, and the fully integrated factory. At each level, automation may allow an organization to increase capacity, reduce inventory and costs as well as contribute to the productive aspects of quality, flexibility, reliability, throughput, and delivery.

Representative stand-alone pieces of equipment include CNC (computer numerically controlled) machines, computer-aided design technology, and robots. The nature of most automated pieces of equipment is that they perform a limited number of tasks (often only one) in repetitive operations and/or undesirable work conditions. Given the limited impact on the factory as a whole, the investment is frequently justified on the basis of labor and materials savings. While the generalization may be reasonable, the introduction of automated equipment often can generate benefits that are qualitatively oriented.

Unfortunately, most capital investment analyses do not attempt to quantify the qualitative benefits. These benefits include improved quality, delivery, service and flexibility, reduced product development time, and improved competitive position and can generate significant cost savings and higher sales. Attributing a value of zero to qualitative benefits is clearly less correct than using a reasonable, well-founded estimate. Companies that are quantifying these benefits assert that it is critical to be generally right than absolutely wrong. The new approach to investment evaluation is undoubtedly an area of significant opportunity for the management accountant.

In one example, the Yamazaki Machinery Company in Japan installed an $18 million flexible manufacturing system. The benefits included: a reduction in machines from 68 to 18, in employees from 215 to 12, in the floor space required for production from 103,000 square feet to 30,000, and in average processing time from 35 days to 1.5.

While traditional capital investment techniques would have considered only the labor savings and the reductions in inventory and equipment, such an analysis would likely provide a return of slightly over 10%, a return unlikely to exceed most companies' established hurdle rates or provide a payback fast enough to justify the investment.[2] Yet, benefits resulting from improved quality, lower process and product variability, greater throughput, and increased schedule attainment clearly need to be considered in an investment of this nature.

Stand-alone pieces of equipment have been steadily introduced into the factory since the seventies. However, the new trend in manufacturing is to integrate machines and systems in an effort to make domestic manufacturing economically viable.

Flexible manufacturing systems, as they commonly are called, produce a particular product or major component from start to finish. A flexible manufacturing system may be a series of electronically interlocked machining centers that perform a set of prescribed operations controlled by a computer using robots or one machine performing a complex series of machining tasks. Flexible manufacturing systems normally provide additional benefits of

[2]Robert S. Kaplan, "Must CIM be Justified by Faith Alone," *Harvard Business Review*, March-April 1986, p. 87. Example cross-referenced to *American Market/Metalworking News*, October 26, 1981.

Chapter 16

reduced material handling and work-in-process, as well as increased quality, flexibility, and throughput.

There are already many examples of flexible manufacturing systms in use. One example is GE's Erie, Pa., locomotive plant. A $16 million FMS produces motor frames and gear boxes and has cut throughput times from 16 days to 16 hours.

The highest level of capital investment is the integrated factory. Examples include Allen-Bradley's World Contactor "factory within a factory" facility in Milwaukee, IBM's Proprinter facility in Charlotte, N.C., Apple Computer's Macintosh plant in Fremont, Calif., and GE's Dishwasher factory in Louisville, Ky.

While automation is not considered the cure-all, neither is the decision to automate a casual alternative. One executive from GE noted that "automation is not a trendy corporate thrust for us. In most of our manufacturing businesses it is survival." GE has realized a competitive advantage through its investments. For example, in its dishwasher plant in Kentucky, management has been able to reduce inventory by 60%, service calls by 53%, cycle time from 5 to 6 days to 18 hours, and increased employee productivity by 25% and production capacity by 20%. Thus, the integrated factory contributes to a company's bottom line on the basis of a significant competitive advantage in terms of product quality, deliverability, and variety, which translates into more sales and lower costs.

Product line organization calls for the scaling down of centralized service departments and reassigning people with specialized skills directly to the product lines. This reorganization results in mini-organizations that focus on a few products.

In contrast, the conventional manufacturing organization structure is characterized by a number of centralized service departments—purchasing, production scheduling, and inventory control, industrial and manufacturing engineering, maintenance, quality control and personnel—providing support to the various production departments.

The rationale for centralized support functions is that maximizing the parts through economies of scale will maximize the whole. According to Harvard Professor Wickham Skinner, however, "the result more often is a hodgepodge of compromises, a high overhead, and a manufacturing organization that is constantly in hot

water with top management." He also noted: "An organization that focuses on a narrow product mix will outperform the conventional plant. Because a focused factory or organization's equipment, supporting systems, and procedures can concentrate on a limited task for one set of customers, its costs and especially its overhead are likely to be lower than those of the conventional plant."[3]

The advantage of a product line organization is the direct identification of the resources required to support a particular product line. Relatively straightforward and easy to manage product lines have limited support resources. Product lines that are more complex have more resources directly assigned to them.

Disaggregating overhead costs helps management understand and control its business better. The typical cost accounting process would have to allocate the service department's costs, by one of several routines, to the production department's. These allocated costs then become a part of the production department's costs. In turn, these costs are assigned to the products going through the department. By the time the allocation process is complete, the final product cost numbers are far removed from the source of the cost and have little value for decision-making purposes.

Unfortunately, these figures often are the basis for out-sourcing production, dropping product lines, or even closing plants. Although product line organizations will not eliminate allocations, they provide a clearer picture of which products use more resources under a disaggregated factory arrangement.

Examples of companies reorganizing their management structure include S.C. Johnson, Hewlett-Packard, and Kollmorgon. S.C. Johnson, the privately held consumer goods company, has increased manufacturing efficiency by dividing its 12,000 person work force in its Racine, Wis. plant into four separate, smaller manufacturing groups concentrating on a limited number of products.

Hewlett-Packard cites people-related factors as a primary reason for going to smaller plants. HP is among a handful of companies that have long held "small is beautiful" and have minimized layers of management, emphasized team approaches to problems, and shortened the lines

[3]Wickham Skinner, "The Focused Factory," *Harvard Business Review,* May-June 1974.

of communication between departments in order to increase efficiency and profitability.

The *effective use of information technology* is the final major trend in the new manufacturing environment. While many companies have been using information technology for years, advancements in integrated systems allow companies to exert greater control over the factory floor through more flexible, real-time, computer-based communications networks. Better information is obtained faster, and often provides the company with a competititve edge.

While systems for operating control and financial/external reporting are traditionally completely separate systems, the world-class manufacturer needs to use technology to create a single database, maintained on a real-time basis, that can be used for both purposes. This capability is not yet a reality because of the incompatibility of most available systems. However, as equipment and systems are purchased with this objective in mind, manufacturing machines and processes are being linked. This enables CNC machines to communicate between each other and with a master control program. It allows a problem arising at one location in the process to be communicated to other operations, thus preventing a build-up of work-in-process inventory until the problem is corrected.

Computers also are being extensively used to monitor and control operations. Computers, using statistical process control, can automatically monitor a process and make adjustments to ensure the consistency and quality of the output.

An integrated factory, such as Allen-Bradley's World Contactor facility, is dependent upon the computer for guidance. As the hardware becomes increasingly integrated, the computer's ability to communicate with multiple systems and between pieces of equipment becomes essential.

The computer also is being used to generate operational and financial data on what is happening on the factory floor and converting it into useful managerial information, such as units produced, material utilized, scrap, cost by operation, and cost by individual product, if appropriate. The computer affords management the opportunity to analyze real-time information regarding the inputs to and outputs of the manufacturing process. Through the application of bar codes and other tracking mechanisms, it is possible to record costs on a unit of one basis.

In a highly competitive environment, managers no longer can wait until the end of the month to get a sense of how things are going. Production managers need to know before the end of a period whether a department's scrap rate is significantly out of line with expectations. Also, strategic decisions are often made using data compiled specifically for financial statement purposes. In most cases, this information fails to reflect these economic realities in ways that enable a manager to make well-informed decisions.

Technology also results in substantial productivity savings as well as financial returns. At Exxon USA, getting the right information to the right person at the right time is a major company objective. According to Michael C. Wilser, Exxon's officer automation coordinator, the company able to do this better than its competitors will achieve a significant strategic advantage in the marketplace.

Implications

Product oriented flow lines, automation, and information technolgy demand that management accountants reassess the traditional method of process control and product cost determination. Automation and increasing reliance on "information workers" in the factory are removing labor and increasing overhead in product costs, pushing labor based overhead rates to extraordinary heights. Product line organizations may bring many overhead costs closer to the product, but flexible flow lines make traditional allocation methods more unworkable. Certainly, methods for allocating costs to products must change.

Automation is increasing the spread between variable costs and full costs, heightening the need to distinguish between contribution margins and full cost profit margins. Decreased labor and increased process reliability will change the shape of traditional, labor oriented variance analysis. Changing management methods for the control of inventory and quality are going to force management accountants to give up labor efficiency oriented performance measures; the search for alternative measures of overall process control has already begun in many plants.

The factory of the future requires the accountant to identify and address many nonfinancial areas of manufacturing performance. Measures such as customer complaints, vendor performance, defect free units, cycle time, schedule attainment and others need to be developed to measure the critical factors of quality, service, and cost.

Capital investments are more complex and expensive. In the new manufacturing environment, investments also improve quality, lower inventory, improve flexibility, and achieve more effective use of information. Greater emphasis must be placed on identifying and including these intangible benefits in the decision-making process.

Traditional methods of analyzing a company's performance need to change to reflect the changing fundamental characteristics of a business. Financial statements provide a fundamental basis for appraising managerial performance as well as establishing security value. The preparers of financial statement information need to spearhead changes in financial statement presentation that reflect the new manufacturing environment.

Management accountants will play a key role in the turnaround of American manufacturing. But they need to get out into the factory and understand what changes are taking place before redesigning and updating the control and reporting mechanisms that will advance their organizations to world-class status.

CHAPTER 17 THE STATEMENT OF CASH FLOWS

REVIEWING THE CHAPTER

Objective 1: Define cash and cash equivalents and describe the statement of cash flows (p. 676).

1. The **statement of cash flows** is considered a major financial statement, as are the income statement, balance sheet, and statement of stockholders' equity. The statement of cash flows, however, provides much information and answers certain questions that the other three statements do not. It replaces the statement of changes in financial position, and its presentation is required whenever an income statement is prepared.

2. The statement of cash flows shows the effects on **cash** and cash equivalents of the operating, investing, and financing activities of a company for an accounting period. **Cash equivalents** are short-term, highly liquid investments such as money market accounts, commercial paper (short-term notes), and U.S. treasury bills. Short-term investments (marketable securities) are *not* considered cash equivalents.

Objective 2: State the principal purposes and uses of the statement of cash flows (pp. 676-677).

3. The principal purpose of the statement of cash flows is to provide information about a company's cash receipts and cash payments during an accounting period. This goal is in accordance with the FASB's "Statement of Financial Accounting Con-

cepts No. 1," which states that financial statements should provide information to investors and creditors regarding the business's cash flows. The statement of cash flow's secondary purpose is to provide information about a company's investing and financing activities during the period.

4. Investors and creditors may use the statement of cash flows to assess such things as the company's ability to generate positive future cash flows, ability to pay its liabilities, ability to pay dividends, and need for additional financing. In addition, management may use the statement of cash flows (among other things) to assess the debt-paying ability of the business, determine dividend policy, and plan investing and financing needs.

Objective 3: Identify the principal components of the classifications of cash flows and state the significance of noncash investing and financing transactions (pp. 677-681).

5. The statement of cash flows categorizes cash receipts and cash payments as operating, investing, and financing activities.
   a. **Operating activities** include receiving cash from customers from the sale of goods and services, receiving interest and dividends on loans and investments, and making cash payments for wages, goods and services purchased, interest, and taxes.

b. **Investing activities** include purchasing and selling long-term assets and marketable securities (other than cash equivalents) as well as making and collecting on loans to other entities.

c. **Financing activities** include issuing and buying back capital stock as well as borrowing and repaying loans on a short- or long-term basis (i.e., issuing bonds and notes). Dividends paid would also be included in this category, but repayment of accounts payable or accrued liabilities would not.

6. The statement of cash flows should include an accompanying schedule of **noncash investing and financing transactions.** Transactions such as the issuance of a mortgage for land or the conversion of bonds into stock represent simultaneous investing and financing activities that do not, however, result in an inflow or outflow of cash.

7. In the formal statement of cash flows, individual cash inflows and outflows from operating, investing, and financing activities are shown separately in their respective categories. To prepare the statement, one needs the assistance of a comparative balance sheet, the current income statement, and additional information about transactions affecting non-current accounts during the period. The four steps to statement preparation are (a) determining cash flows from operating activities, (b) determining cash flows from investing activities, (c) determining cash flows from financing activities, and (d) presenting the information obtained in the first three steps in the form of a statement of cash flows.

Objective 4a: Determine cash flows from operating activities using the direct method (pp. 682-687).

8. Cash flows from operating activities result from converting accrual-basis net income to a cash basis and may be determined by using either the direct method or the indirect method. Under the direct method, Net Cash Flows from Operating Activities is determined by taking cash receipts from sales, adding interest and dividends received, and deducting cash payments for purchases, operating expenses, interest, and income taxes. See table below.

Objective 4b: Determine cash flows from operating activities using the indirect method (pp. 683-687).

9. Under the indirect method, Net Cash Flows from Operating Activities is determined by

Cash Receipts from Sales = Sales
$\begin{cases} + \text{Decrease in Accounts Receivable} \\ \text{or} \\ - \text{Increase in Accounts Receivable} \end{cases}$

Cash Payments for Purchases = Cost of Goods Sold
$\begin{cases} + \text{Increase in Inventory} \\ \text{or} \\ - \text{Decrease in Inventory} \end{cases}$
$\begin{cases} + \text{Decrease in Accounts Payable} \\ \text{or} \\ - \text{Increase in Accounts Payable} \end{cases}$

Cash Payments for Operating Expenses = Operating Expenses
$\begin{cases} + \text{Increase in Prepaid Expenses} \\ \text{or} \\ - \text{Decrease in Prepaid Expenses} \end{cases}$
$\begin{cases} + \text{Decrease in Accrued Liabilities} \\ \text{or} \\ - \text{Increase in Accrued Liabilities} \end{cases}$
$\begin{cases} - \text{Depreciation and Other Noncash Expenses} \end{cases}$

Cash Payments for Income Taxes = Income Taxes Expense
$\begin{cases} + \text{Decrease in Income Taxes Payable} \\ \text{or} \\ - \text{Increase in Income Taxes Payable} \end{cases}$

taking net income and adding or deducting items that do not affect cash flow from operations. Items to add include depreciation expense, amortization expense, depletion expense, losses, decreases in certain current assets (accounts receivable, inventory, and prepaid expenses), and increases in certain current liabilities (accounts payable, accrued liabilities, and income taxes payable). Items to deduct include gains, increases in certain current assets (see above), and decreases in certain current liabilities (see above). The direct and indirect methods produce the same results and are both considered GAAP. The FASB, however, recommends use of the direct method.

Objective 5a: Determine cash flows from investing activities (pp. 689-692).

10. When determining cash flows from investing and financing activities, the objective is to explain the changes in the appropriate account balances from one year to the next. As previously stated, investing activities focus on the purchase and sale of long-term assets and short-term investments.
    a. Under the indirect approach, gains and losses from the sale of the above assets should be deducted from, and added back to, respectively, net income to arrive at net cash flows from operating activities.
    b. Under the direct approach, gains and losses are simply ignored in determining net cash flows from operating activities.
    c. Under both approaches, the full cash proceeds are entered into the Cash Flows from Investing Activities section of the statement of cash flows.

Objective 5b: Determine cash flows from financing activities (pp. 692-694).

11. Financing activities focus on certain liability and stockholders' equity accounts and include short- and long-term borrowing (notes and bonds) and repayment, issuance and repurchase of capital stock, and payment of dividends. Changes in the Retained Earnings account are explained in the statement of cash flows, for the most part, through analyses of net income and dividends declared.

Objective 6a: Prepare a statement of cash flows using the direct method (pp. 695-697).

12. The only difference between the direct and indirect methods of preparing a statement of cash flows is in the structure of the cash flows from operating activities section. Exhibit 17-6 presents a completed statement of cash flows that has incorporated the direct method.

Objective 6b: Prepare a statement of cash flows using the indirect method (pp. 695-697).

13. Exhibit 17-7 presents a completed statement of cash flows that has incorporated the indirect method. As already explained, the essence of the indirect approach is the conversion of net income into net cash flows from operating activities.

Objective 7: Interpret the statement of cash flows (pp. 697-698).

14. When interpreting the statement of cash flows, it is important to examine the items *within* each section and to relate dollar amounts *between* sections. For example, cash flows from operating activities should normally be sufficient to cover dividend payments. In addition, the statement will disclose in what areas the company is expanding or contracting and how. Problems such as the drain of cash caused by overstocking goods might also be uncovered by the statement of cash flows. Finally, the schedule of noncash investing and financing activities should never be overlooked in performing an analysis.

Objective 8: Prepare a work sheet for the statement of cash flows (pp. 698-703).

15. A work sheet for preparing the statement of cash flows is especially useful in complex situations. Using the indirect approach, it essentially allows for the systematic analysis of all changes in the balance sheet accounts.

16. Exhibit 17-8 presents the format of a completed work sheet. To prepare the work sheet, five steps should be followed.
    a. Enter all balance sheet accounts into the Description column, listing debit accounts before credit accounts.

b. Enter all end-of-prior-period amounts and end-of-current-period amounts into the appropriate columns, and foot (add up).

c. In the bottom portion of the work sheet write Cash Flows from Operating Activities, Cash Flows from Investing Activities, and Cash Flows from Financing Activities, leaving sufficient space between sections to enter data.

d. Analyze the change in each balance sheet account using the income statement and other transactions affecting noncurrent accounts during the period. Then enter the resulting debits and credits in the Analysis of Transactions Column, labeling each entry with a key letter corresponding to a reference list of changes.

e. Foot the top and bottom portions of the Analysis of Transactions column. The top portion should balance immediately, but the bottom portion should balance only when the net increase or decrease in cash is entered (credited for an increase or debited for a decrease). The change in cash entered into the top and the bottom of the work sheet should equal each other and should be labeled with the same key letter.

Matching

Match each term with its definition by writing the appropriate letter in the blank.

_____ 1. Statement of cash flows

_____ 2. Cash equivalents

_____ 3. Operating activities

_____ 4. Investing activities

_____ 5. Financing activities

_____ 6. Noncash investing and financing activities

_____ 7. Direct method

_____ 8. Indirect method

a. The items placed at the bottom of the statement of cash flows in a separate schedule

b. The statement of cash flows that most closely relates to net income (loss)

c. In determining cash flows from operations, the procedure that starts with the figure for net income

d. Short-term, highly liquid investments

e. The statement of cash flows section that deals mainly with stockholders' equity accounts and borrowing

f. The financial report that explains the change in cash during the period

g. The statement of cash flows section that deals with long-term assets and marketable securities

h. In determining cash flows from operations, the procedure that adjusts each income statement item from the accrual basis to the cash basis.

Completion

Use the lines provided to complete each item.

1. Give two examples of noncash investing and financing transactions.

_____

_____

_____

_____

2. When preparing the statement of cash flows under the indirect method, why are depreciation, amortization, and depletion expense added back to net income to determine cash flows from operating activities?

_____

_____

_____

3. Which sections of the statement of cash flows are prepared identically under the direct and indirect methods?

_____

_____

_____

_____

4. List three examples of cash equivalents.

_____

_____

_____

True-False

Circle T if the statement is true, F if it is false.

T F **1.** The statement of cash flows must be prepared every time a statement of changes in financial position is prepared.

T F **2.** Payment on an account payable is considered a financing activity.

T F **3.** The proceeds from the sale of investments would be considered an investing activity, whether the investments were classified as short-term or long-term.

T F **4.** To calculate Cash Payments for Purchases, the figure for Cost of Goods Sold must be known, as well as the changes in inventory and accounts payable during the period.

T F **5.** Under the indirect method, a decrease in prepaid expenses would be added to net income in determining Net Cash Flows from Operating Activities.

T F **6.** The Schedule of Noncash Investing and Financing Transactions might include line items for depreciation, depletion, and amortization recorded during the period.

T F **7.** In the Analysis of Transactions columns of a statement of cash flows work sheet, Retained Earnings is credited and Dividends Paid debited for dividends paid during the period.

T F **8.** In the Cash Flows from Operating Activities section of a statement of cash flows work sheet, the items that are credited in the Analysis of Transactions column must be deducted from net income in the statement of cash flows.

T F **9.** It is possible to suffer a net loss for the period but to generate a positive Net Cash Flows from Operating Activities.

T F **10.** A net positive figure for Cash Flows from Investing Activities implies that the business is generally expanding.

T F **11.** The issuance of common stock for cash would be disclosed in the financing activities section of the statement of cash flows.

T F **12.** Under the indirect method, Loss on Sale of Buildings would be deducted from Net Income in the operating activities section of the statement of cash flows.

T F **13.** To calculate Cash Payments for Operating Expenses, operating expenses must be modified by (among other accounts) depreciation, which is treated as an add-back.

T F **14.** In recent years, the cash basis overtook the working capital basis as the more popular form of the statement of changes in financial position.

T F **15.** Cash obtained by borrowing would be considered a financing activity, whether the debt is classified as short-term or long-term.

T F **16.** The purchase of land in exchange for the issuance of common stock in effect represents simultaneous investing and financing activities.

T F **17.** It is possible for the direct and indirect methods to produce a different net-change-in-cash figure on a statement of cash flows.

Circle the letter of the best answer.

1. How would Interest and Dividends Received be included in a statement of cash flows that employs the indirect method?
   a. Included as components of Net Income in the operating activities section
   b. Deducted from Net Income in the operating activities section
   c. Included in the investing activities section
   d. Included in the financing activities section
   e. Included in the Schedule of Noncash Investing and Financing Transactions

2. How would Gain on Sale of Investment be disclosed in a statement of cash flows that employs the indirect method?
   a. Added to Net Income in the operating activities section
   b. Deducted from Net Income in the operating activities section
   c. Included in the investing activities section
   d. Included in the financing activities section
   e. Included in the Schedule of Noncash Investing and Financing Transactions

3. How would an increase in Accounts Payable be disclosed in a statement of cash flows that employs the indirect method?
   a. Added to Net Income in the Operating activities section
   b. Deducted from Net Income in the operating activities section
   c. Included in the investing activities section
   d. Included in the financing activities section
   e. Included in the Schedule of Noncash Investing and Financing Transactions

4. How would the purchase of a building by incurring a mortgage payable be disclosed in a statement of cash flows that employs the indirect method?
   a. Added to Net Income in the operating activities section
   b. Deducted from Net Income in the operating activities section
   c. Included in the investing activities section
   d. Included in the financing activities section
   e. Included in the Schedule of Noncash Investing and Financing Transactions

5. How would Dividends Paid be disclosed in a statement of cash flows that employs the indirect method?
   a. Added to Net Income in the operating activities section
   b. Deducted from Net Income in the operating activities section
   c. Included in the investing activities section
   d. Included in the financing activities section
   e. Included in the Schedule of Noncash Investing and Financing Transactions

6. How would Interest Paid be included in a statement of cash flows that employs the indirect method?
   a. Included as a component of Net Income in the operating activities section
   b. Deducted from Net Income in the operating activities section
   c. Included in the investing activities section
   d. Included in the financing activities section
   e. Included in the Schedule of Noncash Investing and Financing Transactions

7. How would an increase in inventory be disclosed in a statement of cash flows that employs the indirect method?
   a. Added to Net Income in the operating activities section
   b. Deducted from Net Income in the operating activities section
   c. Included in the investing activities section
   d. Included in the financing activities section
   e. Included in the Schedule of Noncash Investing and Financing Transactions

8. All of the following represent cash flows from operating activities except
   a. cash payments for income taxes.
   b. cash receipts from sales.
   c. cash receipts from issuance of stock.
   d. cash payments for purchases.

9. When net income is recorded (debited) in the Analysis of Transactions columns of a statement of cash flows work sheet, which item is credited?
   a. Cash
   b. Income Summary
   c. Net Increase in Cash
   d. Retained Earnings

10. Niemsky Corporation had cash sales of $30,000 and credit sales of $70,000 during the year, and the Accounts Receivable account increased by $14,000. Cash Receipts from Sales totaled
    a. $70,000.
    b. $86,000.
    c. $100,000.
    d. $114,000.

Applying Your Knowledge

Exercises

1. Use the following information to calculate the items below.

Accounts Payable, Jan. 1, 19xx	47,000
Accounts Payable, Dec. 31, 19xx	54,000
Accounts Receivable, Jan. 1, 19xx	32,000
Accounts Receivable, Dec. 31, 19xx	22,000
Accrued Liabilities, Jan. 1, 19xx	17,000
Accrued Liabilities, Dec. 31, 19xx	11,000
Cost of Goods Sold for 19xx	240,000
Depreciation Expense for 19xx	20,000
Income Taxes Expense for 19xx	33,000
Income Taxes Payable, Jan. 1, 19xx	4,000
Income Taxes Payable, Dec. 31, 19xx	6,000
Inventory, Jan. 1, 19xx	86,000
Inventory, Dec. 31, 19xx	74,000
Operating Expenses for 19xx	70,000
Prepaid Expenses, Jan. 1, 19xx	2,000
Prepaid Expenses, Dec. 31, 19xx	3,000
Sales for 19xx	350,000

a. Cash Payments for Operating Expenses =

   $ _____ .

b. Cash Receipts from Sales =

   $ _____ .

c. Cash Payments for Income Taxes =

   $ _____ .

d. Cash Payments for Purchases =

   $ _____ .

e. Net Cash Flows from Operating Activities =

   $ _____ .

2. Use the following information to complete CLU Corporation's statement of cash flows work sheet on the next page for the year ended December 31, 19x9. Make sure to use the key letters in the Analysis of Transactions columns to refer to the following explanation list:

   a. Net income for 19x9 was $22,000.
   b-d. These key letters record changes in current assets and current liabilities.
   e. Sold plant assets that cost $30,000 with accumulated depreciation of $10,000, for $24,000.
   f. Purchased plant assets for $62,000.
   g. Recorded depreciation expense of $26,000 for 19x9.
   h. Converted bonds payable with a $10,000 face amount into common stock.
   i. Declared and paid dividends of $12,000.
   x. This key letter codes the change in cash.

CLU Corporation
Work Sheet for Statement of Cash Flows
For the Year Ended December 31, 19x9

Description	Account Balances 12/31/x8	Analysis of Transactions for 19x9		Account Balances 12/31/x9
		Debit	Credit	
Debits				
Cash	35,000			29,000
Accounts Receivable	18,000			21,000
Inventory	83,000			72,000
Plant Assets	200,000			232,000
Total Debits	336,000			354,000
Credits				
Accumulated Depreciation	40,000			56,000
Accounts Payable	27,000			19,000
Bonds Payable	100,000			90,000
Common Stock	150,000			160,000
Retained Earnings	19,000			29,000
Total Credits	336,000			354,000
Cash Flows from Operating Activities				
Cash Flows from Investing Activities				
Cash Flows from Financing Activities				
Net Decrease in Cash				

"Where's the Cash?"

Savvy investors have long known to keep an eye on how much cash a company takes in, pays out and has in the till rather than net income it reports to shareholders. Now the bankers, sadder but wiser, are using cash flow analysis, too.

"Huge leveraged buyouts, like Metromedia's, are being financed by operating pretax cash flow," says Barre Littel, a bond analyst at Kidder, Peabody. "Reported earnings are becoming less important to the way that corporations are financed and appraised."

Lending officers at commercial banks, too, have learned to look carefully at a prospective borrower's cash flow in more detail than the summary statement in the annual report entitled "changes in financial position." Neil Godfrey, a veteran loan officer at New York's Chemical Bank, says he looks at cash flow for the same reason Littel does: high and continuing leverage. "Nowadays most corporate lending looks like the revolving lines of credit to less-developed countries," Godfrey says.

Loan officer Jan Blackford of North Carolina-based Wachovia Bank & Trust personally attributes the rising importance of cash flow analysis to the trend over the past 20 years toward capitalizing and deferring more and more expenses. Although the practice may match revenues and expenses more closely, a laudable intent, it has also made it harder to find the available cash in a company—and easier for lenders to wind up with a loss, she warns.

Blackford's point that liquidity can be more important than reported profitability is well taken. During the recession five years ago a wave of bankruptcies drew attention to the need for better warning signals of the sort cash flow analysis could provide. The Financial Accounting Standards Board (FASB) looked at improving cash flow disclosure at the time but did

nothing. On Apr. 17 the FASB will probably decide to study three aspects of improved cash flow disclosure.

One of the FASB's considerations is to better define the purpose of cash flow statements in the first place. "Now we have a variety of loosy-goosy statements, such as for 'judging liquidity or financial flexibility' or for 'giving insight into profitability or risks,' " says Halsey Bullen, the FASB staffer who has been doing the preliminary research. The FASB will work on more precise definitions for elements of cash flow—such as cash from operations, cash for or from financings and cash from investments.

Finally, the board will study who should be required to compile cash flow statements and how the information should be presented. Among the currently acceptable ways of reporting are direct and indirect methods. The indirect way starts with a number like net income and adds to it everything that doesn't affect cash, such as depreciation. The direct method starts with sales collections and then subtracts cash outlays.

As ever, the users of financial statements are calling for more information, while those who prepare the statements resist. Since 1981, when the FASB took a fleeting look at the issue, some preparers have been experimenting on their own in the hope of quashing formal rulemaking.

J. W. McAllister, financial vice president of Holiday Inns' Perkins Restaurants, is chairman of an industry group that has been working on cash flow reports for four years. There is "no serious deficiency" in the current form of this section of financial statements, according to McAllister. "I am concerned about FASB getting into cookbook accounting," he says. "We don't want to have to insert numbers with no opportunity to fit the accounting to your line of business."

Source: Article by Jinny St. Goar; edited by Geoffrey Smith. Reprinted with permission of *Forbes* magazine, April 8, 1985. Forbes Inc., 1985.

Meanwhile, cash flow enthusiasts couch their arguments in macroeconomic terms. Improved cash flow disclosure is essential for the health of the economy, they say. Too much emphasis on earnings only encourages managers to limit their investments in order to show "higher" returns. Tom Nourse, publisher of the *Nourse Investor Report,* which analyzes the cash flow of 2,000 industrial companies, is a vocal proponent of this line. "For the last 15 years I have been saying that cash flow is more important than earnings," he says. "In prevailing practice, managers are motivated to take the short-term view."

Although it's unlikely that better cash flow reporting can cure all the ills of the economy, the fact that the most important users of financial statements around—bankers and investment bankers—find it indispensable is persuasive indeed.

Chapter 17

CHAPTER 18 FINANCIAL STATEMENT ANALYSIS

REVIEWING THE CHAPTER

Objective 1: Describe and discuss the objectives of financial statement analysis (pp. 731-732).

1. Decision makers get specific information from general-purpose financial statements by means of **financial statement analysis**.

2. The users of financial statements are classified as either internal or external. The main internal user is management. The main external users are creditors and investors. Both creditors and investors will probably acquire a **portfolio**, or group of loans or investments, because the risk of loss is far less with several investments than with one investment.

3. Creditors and investors use financial statement analysis to (a) assess past performance and the current position, and (b) assess future potential and the risk connected with the potential. Information about the past and present is very helpful in making projections about the future. Moreover, the easier it is to predict future performance, the less risk is involved. The lower risk means the investor or creditor will require a lower expected return.

Objective 2: Describe and discuss the standards for financial statement analysis (pp. 733-735).

4. Decision makers assess performance by means of (a) rule-of-thumb measures, (b) analysis of past performance of the company, and (c) comparison with industry norms.

   a. Rule-of-thumb measures for key financial ratios are helpful but should not be the only basis for making a decision. For example, a company may report high earnings per share, but may lack sufficient assets to pay current debts.

   b. Past performance of a company can help show trends. The skill lies in the analyst's ability to predict whether a trend will continue or will reverse itself.

   c. Comparing a company's performance with the performance of other companies in the same industry is helpful, but there are three limitations to using industry norms as standards. First, no two companies are exactly the same. Second, many companies, called **diversified companies** or **conglomerates**, operate in many unrelated industries, so that comparison is hard. (However, the recent requirement to report financial information by segments has been somewhat helpful.) Third, different companies often use different accounting procedures for recording similar items.

Objective 3: State the sources of information for financial statement analysis (pp. 736-737).

5. The chief sources of information about publicly held corporations are published reports, SEC reports, business period-

icals, and credit and investment advisory services.

  a. A company's annual report provides useful financial information, and includes the following sections: (1) analysis of the past year's operations, (2) the financial statements, (3) footnotes, (4) accounting procedures, (5) the auditor's report, and (6) a five- or ten-year summary of operations.

  b. **Interim financial statements** may indicate significant changes in a company's earnings trend. They consist of limited financial information for less than a year (usually quarterly).

  c. Publicly held corporations are required to file with the SEC an annual report (form 10-K), a quarterly report (form 10-Q), and a current report of significant events (form 8-K). These reports are available to the public and are sources of valuable financial information.

  d. Financial analysts obtain information from such sources as the *Wall Street Journal, Forbes, Barron's, Fortune,* the *Commercial and Financial Chronicle,* Moody's, Standard & Poor's, and Dun and Bradstreet.

Objective 4: Identify the issues related to the evaluation of the quality of a company's earnings (pp. 737-739).

6. The most commonly used predictors of a company's performance are expected changes in earnings per share and in return on equity. Because net income is a component of both of these ratios, the quality of earnings must be good if the measure is to be valid. The quality of earnings is affected by (a) the accounting estimates and procedures chosen when applying the matching principle, and (b) the nature of nonoperating items in the income statement. A different net income figure will result, for example, when different estimates and procedures for dealing with uncollectible accounts, inventory, depreciation, depletion, and amortization are chosen. In general, the method which produces a lower, or more conservative, figure will also produce a better quality of earnings. In addition, nonoperating and nonrecurring items, such as discontinued operations, extraordinary gains and losses, and the effects of accounting changes, can impair comparability if the financial analyst refers only to the bottom-line figure.

Objective 5: Apply horizontal analysis, trend analysis, and vertical analysis to financial statements (pp. 740-747).

7. The most common tools and techniques of financial analysis are horizontal analysis, trend analysis, vertical analysis, and ratio analysis.

  a. Comparative financial statements show the current and prior year's statements presented side by side to aid in financial statement analysis. **Horizontal analysis** shows absolute and percentage changes in specific items from one year to the next. The first of the two years being considered is called the **base year**, and the percentage change is computed by dividing the amount of the change by the base-year amount.

  b. **Trend analysis** is the same as horizontal analysis, except percentage changes are calculated for several consecutive years. For percentage changes to be shown over several years, **index numbers** must be used.

  c. **Vertical analysis** presents the percentage relationship of individual items on the statement to a total within the statement (for instance, cost of goods sold as a percentage of net sales). The result is a **common-size statement.** On a common-size balance sheet, total assets and total equities would each be labeled 100 percent. On a common-size income statement, sales would be labeled 100 percent. Common-size statements may be presented in comparative form to show information both within the period and between periods.

Objective 6: Apply ratio analysis to financial statements in the study of an enterprise's liquidity, profitability, long-term solvency, and market tests (pp. 747-756).

8. **Ratio analysis** determines certain relationships (ratios) between financial statement items, then compares the ratios with those of prior years or other companies. Ratios provide information about a company's liquidity, profitability, long-run solvency, and market strength. The most common ratios are shown in the following table:

Ratio	Components	Use or Meaning
Liquidity Ratios		
Current ratio	$\dfrac{\text{current assets}}{\text{current liabilities}}$	Measure of short-term debt-paying ability
Quick ratio	$\dfrac{\text{cash + short-term investments + receivables}}{\text{current liabilities}}$	Measure of short-term liquidity
Receivable turnover	$\dfrac{\text{sales}}{\text{average accounts receivable}}$	Measure of relative size of accounts receivable balance and effectiveness of credit policies
Average days' sales uncollected	$\dfrac{\text{days in year}}{\text{receivable turnover}}$	Measure of time it takes to collect an average receivable
Inventory turnover	$\dfrac{\text{cost of goods sold}}{\text{average inventory}}$	Measure of relative size of inventory
Profitability Ratios		
Profit margin	$\dfrac{\text{net income}}{\text{sales}}$	Income produced by each dollar of sales
Asset turnover	$\dfrac{\text{sales}}{\text{average total assets}}$	Measure of how efficiently assets are used to produce sales
Return on assets	$\dfrac{\text{net income}}{\text{average total assets}}$	Overall measure of earning power or profitability of all assets used in the business
Return on equity	$\dfrac{\text{net income}}{\text{average owners' equity}}$	Profitability of owners' investment
Earnings per share	$\dfrac{\text{net income}}{\text{outstanding shares}}$	Means of placing earnings on a common basis for comparisons
Long-Term Solvency Ratios		
Debt to equity	$\dfrac{\text{total liabilities}}{\text{owners' equity}}$	Measure of relationship of debt financing to equity financing. A company with debt is said to be **leveraged.**
Interest coverage	$\dfrac{\text{net income before taxes + interest expense}}{\text{interest expense}}$	Measure of protection of creditors from a default on interest payments

Financial Statement Analysis

Price/earnings (P/E) $$\frac{\text{market price per share}}{\text{earnings per share}}$$ Measure of amount the market will pay for a dollar of earnings

Dividends yield $$\frac{\text{dividends per share}}{\text{market price per share}}$$ Measure of current return to investor

Market risk $$\frac{\text{specific change in market price}}{\text{average change in market price}}$$ Measure of volatility (called **beta**) of the market price of a stock in relation to that of other stocks

Chapter 18

Testing Your Knowledge

Matching

Match each term with its definition by writing the appropriate letter in the blank.

_____ 1. Financial statement analysis

_____ 2. Portfolio

_____ 3. Diversified companies (conglomerates)

_____ 4. Interim financial statements

_____ 5. Horizontal analysis

_____ 6. Base year

_____ 7. Trend analysis

_____ 8. Index number

_____ 9. Vertical analysis

_____ 10. Common-size statement

_____ 11. Ratio analysis

_____ 12. Leverage

_____ 13. Beta

a. Debt financing
b. A group of investments or loans
c. A measure of market risk
d. A financial statement expressed in terms of percentages, the result of vertical analysis
e. Limited financial information for less than a year (usually quarterly)
f. The first year being considered when horizontal analysis is used
g. Getting specific information from general-purpose financial statements
h. A presentation of the percentage change in specific items over several years
i. A number used in trend analysis to show changes in related items over several years
j. A presentation of absolute and percentage changes in specific items from one year to the next
k. A presentation of the percentage relationships of individual items on a statement to a total within the statement
l. Companies that operate in many unrelated industries
m. The determination of certain relationships between financial statement items

Completion

Use the lines provided to complete each item.

1. Indicate five ratios that measure profitability.

_____

_____

_____

_____

2. Briefly distinguish between horizontal and vertical analysis.

_____

_____

_____

_____

3. List the three methods by which decision makers assess performance.

_____

_____

_____

4. Why is it wiser to acquire a portfolio of small investments rather than one large investment?

_____

_____

_____

True-False

Circle T if the statement is true, F if it is false.

T F **1.** Horizontal analysis is possible for both an income statement and a balance sheet.

T F **2.** Common-size financial statements show dollar changes in specific items from one year to the next.

T F **3.** A company with a 2.0 current ratio will experience a decline in the current ratio when a short-term liability is paid.

T F **4.** The figure for inventory is not used in computing the quick ratio.

T F **5.** Inventory turnover equals average inventory divided by cost of goods sold.

T F **6.** The price/earnings ratio must be computed before earnings per share can be determined.

T F **7.** When computing the return on equity, interest expense must be added back to net income.

T F **8.** When a company has no debt, its return on assets equals its return on equity.

T F **9.** The lower the debt to equity ratio, the riskier the situation.

T F **10.** Receivable turnover measures the time it takes to collect an average receivable.

T F **11.** A low interest coverage would be cause for concern for a company's bondholders.

T F **12.** A stock with a beta of less than 1.0 indicates a risk factor that is less than that of the market as a whole.

T F **13.** Dividends yield is a profitability ratio.

T F **14.** On a common-size income statement, net income is given a label of 100 percent.

T F **15.** Interim financial statements may serve as an early signal of significant changes in a company's earnings trend.

T F **16.** Probably the best source of financial news is the _Wall Street Journal_.

T F **17.** Return on assets equals the profit margin times asset turnover.

T F **18.** The quality of earnings would be affected by the existence of an extraordinary item in the income statement.

Multiple-Choice

Circle the letter of the best answer.

1. Which of the following is a measure of long-term solvency?
   a. Current ratio
   b. Interest coverage
   c. Asset turnover
   d. Profit margin

2. Short-term creditors would probably be _most_ interested in which ratio?
   a. Current ratio
   b. Earnings per share
   c. Debt to equity ratio
   d. Quick ratio

3. Net income is irrelevant in computing which ratio?
   a. Earnings per share
   b. Price/earnings ratio
   c. Asset turnover
   d. Return on equity

4. A high price/earnings ratio indicates
   a. investor confidence in high future earnings.
   b. that the stock is probably overvalued.
   c. that the stock is probably undervalued.
   d. little investor confidence in high future earnings.

5. Index numbers are used in
   a. trend analysis.
   b. ratio analysis.
   c. vertical analysis.
   d. common-size statements.

6. Which of the following would probably not be found in a company's annual report?
   a. The auditor's report
   b. A five- or ten-year summary of operations
   c. Interim financial statements
   d. Analysis of the past year's operations

7. The main internal user of financial statements is
   a. the SEC.
   b. management.
   c. investors.
   d. creditors.

8. Comparing performance with industry norms is complicated by
   a. the existence of diversified companies.
   b. the use of different accounting procedures by different companies.
   c. the fact that companies in the same industry will usually differ in some respect.
   d. all of the above.

9. A low receivable turnover indicates that
   a. few customers are defaulting on their debts.
   b. the company's inventory is moving very slowly.
   c. the company is making collections from its customers very slowly.
   d. a small proportion of the company's sales are credit sales.

10. In a common-size income statement, net income will be given a label of what percentage?
    a. 0 percent
    b. The percentage that net income is in relation to sales
    c. The percentage that net income is in relation to operating expenses
    d. 100 percent

Applying Your Knowledge

Exercises

1. Complete the horizontal analysis for the comparative income statements shown here. Round percentages to the nearest tenth of a percent.

| | 19x1 | 19x2 | Increase or (Decrease) | |
			Amount	Percentage
Sales	$200,000	$250,000		
Cost of goods sold	120,000	144,000		
Gross profit	$ 80,000	$106,000		
Operating expenses	50,000	62,000		
Income before income taxes	$ 30,000	$ 44,000		
Income taxes	8,000	16,000		
Net income	$ 22,000	$ 28,000		

2. The following is financial information for Lassen Corporation for 19xx. Current assets consist of cash, accounts receivable, short-term investments, and inventory.

Average accounts receivable	$100,000
Average (and ending) inventory	180,000
Cost of goods sold	350,000
Current assets, Dec. 31	500,000
Current liabilities, Dec. 31	250,000
Market price, Dec. 31, on	
21,200 shares	40/share
Net income	106,000
Sales	600,000
Average stockholders' equity	480,000
Average total assets	880,000

Compute the following ratios as of December 31. Round off to the nearest tenth of a whole number for a-i, to the nearest hundredth of a whole number in j-k.

a. The current ratio is _____.

b. The quick ratio is _____.

c. Earnings per share is _____.

d. Inventory turnover is _____.

e. Return on assets is _____.

f. Return on equity is _____.

g. Receivable turnover is _____.

h. Average days' sales uncollected is ____.

i. The profit margin is _____ .

j. Asset turnover is _____ .

k. The price/earnings ratio is _____ .

Crossword Puzzle
for Chapters 17 and 18

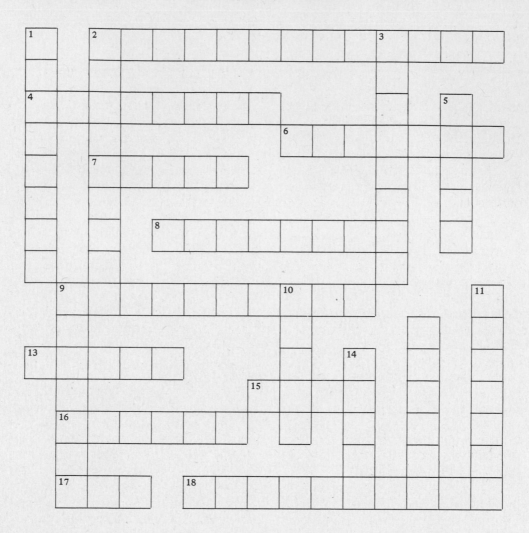

ACROSS

2. Ratio indicating investor confidence in a company (2 words)

4. Analysis resulting in 9-Across

6. Quarterly financial statement, e.g.

7. Statement of cash ——

8. Financial statement ——

9. Statement showing percentage relationships (hyphenated)

13. —— analysis, a variation of horizontal analysis

15. Measure of market risk

16. Debt to —— ratio

17. An Operating-Activity outflow

18. Analysis involving dollar- and percentage changes

DOWN

1. Debt financing

2. Group of investments or loans

3. When received, an Investing Activity

5. Dividends ——

9. With 14-Down, a measure of liquidity

10. Number used in 13-Across

11. Working ——

12. Method of converting income statement from accrual to cash basis

14. See 9-Down

"Rumpelstilzchen Accounting"

Has Standard Oil Co. (Ohio) Chairman Alton W. Whitehouse been rereading the story of Rumpelstilzchen, who spun straw into gold? In Sohio's fourth-quarter 1985 report, just out, Whitehouse says that Sohio's profit ($379 million) "would have increased 11%" over 1984's fourth quarter—only it didn't. Why not? A little matter of a $1.15 billion writeoff. And what's a writeoff among friends? Just a paper entry. An "extraordinary" charge.

Or is it "just" a paper entry? In Sohio's case the writeoff is a confession that Sohio blew well over $1 billion of shareholders' money when it decided to acquire Kennecott, the big copper-mining company. Sohio paid $1.8 billion for Kennecott five years ago. Did its value fall by $1 billion in a single quarter? No. It was a bad deal from the beginning, overpriced and ill-timed.

Hold it: Doesn't this suggest that Sohio was actually overstating its earnings over those five years that the Kennecott investment was deteriorating? Certainly it was evident well before Dec. 31, 1985 that the acquisition was a bad mistake.

Sohio portrays the writeoff as a brave and virtuous step. "We've streamlined the company," explains Sohio spokesman John Andes. "It gets us in shape to deal with the market and proceed as a very healthy company into 1986."

Past sin into future virtue. Bad judgment into praiseworthy realism.

David Hawkins, a finance professor at the Harvard Business School, isn't impressed. "The writedowns are usually taken well after the events actually occurred," says Hawkins, "which makes you think you can't believe any of the numbers over the last few years."

Rumpelstilzchen accounting, also known as Big Bath accounting, was used by dozens of businessmen in 1985's fourth quarter. It seemed a good time to take the hit. The stock market was strong enough to absorb the modestly bad news, and, besides, everyone was doing it.

Why do managers wait so long to take their medicine? Why are they so reluctant to write down assets on a regular basis? "Because it doesn't make them look like very good stewards of shareholders' interests," says a partner at Arthur Young & Co., who asked not to be identified, "particularly if they were the ones who said, 'Let's buy this business.'"

Avon Products' Chairman Hicks B. Waldron took the Big Bath. Waldron recently informed shareholders that he sold Avon's Mallinckrodt, Inc. division and booked a charge of $223 million in last year's fourth quarter. The charge washed fourth-quarter net income from $73.7 million in 1984 to a loss of $149 million in 1985.

Weren't Avon's pretax earnings then overstated by $223 million, up until the writedown? A reasonable question. But Waldron ignored that. Accentuating his "asset redeployment program," Waldron said he expected "earnings to improve steadily in 1986."

An immediate benefit, of course, of a Big Bath is to make your vital return on equity number look better. If you decrease the denominator faster than the numerator, the value of any fraction will grow to the sky.

When T. Boone Pickens was chasing after Unocal, for example, Fred Hartley stoutly defended Unocal's shale oil investment. With Pickens out of the way, Hartley wrote the investment off in last year's fourth quarter, at a cost of $250 million. The beauty of Big Bath accounting is that you decide when to face the music.

A modest proposal: Let managements take their Big Baths subjectively, but make them take the charges against *future* earnings, rather than bunching them up in one quarter's accounts as a special item. Since management

Source: Article by Ben Weberman. Reprinted by permission of *Forbes* magazine, February 24, 1986, pp. 30-31. Copyright © Forbes Inc., 1986.

| | | The Big Hit Parade | | | | | |

The Big Hit Parade

Herewith, some of 1985's more memorable writeoffs. In a few cases, sudden business reverses may have been behind the sudden writeoffs. But, in most cases, managements were simply washing the decks.

Company	Writeoff 1985	Net Income 1984 ($millions)	Net Income 1985	book value 1984	Per share writeoff 1985	net 1985	recent stock price (as of 2/3/86)
Cigna Corp	$1,200.0	$ 100.0	NA	$62.79	$16.60	NA	65 ³/₈
Sohio	1,150.0	1,488.0	$308.0	35.71	4.90	$1.31	47 ³/₄
Phillips Petroleum	342.0	810.0	418.0	14.28	1.23	1.44	10 ⅞
Unocal	250.0	704.0	325.1	32.78	2.54	2.36	24
Avon Products	223.0	181.7	−59.9	18.55	2.82	−0.76	27 ¼
Crown Zellerbach	196.5	86.9	−26.8	36.91	7.14	−1.56	43 ⅛
Gould	175.7	17.8	−175.7	19.59	3.58	−3.94	27 ⅛
Koppers	150.0	28.8	−101.3	19.31	5.51	−3.72	23 ⅝

NA: Not available

overstated past earnings, why not make them understate future earnings to compensate? This is not allowed under current accounting rules, but say this for such a proposal: It would make managements pay for their mistakes where it really hurts.

Nothing wrong with admitting mistakes, but don't expect investors to forget that many of these same managements were responsible for the bad judgment in the first place.

Reading

How Industry Perceives Financial Ratios

There is some agreement on which ratios are important but a lack of consensus on how they should be computed.

Financial statements serve as the primary financial reporting mechanism of an entity, both internally and externally. These statements are the method by which management communicates financial information to stockholders, creditors, and other interested parties. An analysis of this financial information should include the computation and interpretation of financial ratios.

However, at present, comprehensive financial ratio analysis is hampered by the lack of standard computations. Currently, no regulatory agency such as the Securities & Exchange Commission or the Financial Accounting Standards Board gives guidance in this area, except for the computation of earnings per share. As this study will indicate, there is some agreement on which ratios are important, but there is a lack of consensus on the computational methodology of these ratios.

In order to get the views of financial executives on important issues relating to financial ratios, a questionnaire was sent to the controllers of the companies listed in Fortune's 500 Largest Industrials for 1979. Companies that were 100%-owned subsidiaries of another company were excluded, leaving 493 companies to be surveyed. One hundred and three usable responses were received which represents a response rate of 20.9%. Considering both the length of the questionnaire and the amount of detailed questions, the response rate was good.

There were 57 industries represented in the responses; however, three industries had a significantly greater number of responses than the others. These industries were petroleum (10), motor vehicle parts & accessories (8), and chemicals and allied products (9). The other

industries were represented by three or less responses. A separate review of the responses of the more highly represented industries indicated that, in general, their responses were not appreciably different than the summary of the overall responses. Any significant differences will be pointed out.

The questionnaire was designed to accomplish the following objectives: (1) to determine the primary measure that a particular ratio provides, (2) to arrive at the significance of a specific ratio as perceived by financial management, (3) to gather information on the computational methodology used, (4) to find out what use is being made of inflation accounting data in ratio analysis, and (5) to determine which financial ratios are included as corporate objectives and to whom these ratios are reported.

Primary Measure and Significance of Individual Ratios

The first section of the questionnaire was designed to determine the perceived importance of specific financial ratios and what the ratio primarily measured. For this purpose 20 specific ratios were used. Two of these ratios (degree of operating leverage, and degree of financial leverage) proved to be confusing to respondents as indicated by both their lack of response and their written comments. It appears the respondent was not familiar with these ratios; therefore, these two ratios were deleted from the summary.

The 20 ratios were selected based upon a review of textbooks, and discussion with financial executives, and a review of ratios reported in annual reports. It was not considered practical to list all possible ratios nor would it be practical to expect companies to complete an unreasonably long survey. In addition to the 20 specific ratios, the respondents were asked to list other ratios that their company computes.

To determine the primary measure that a particular ratio provides, we asked this question: "Do you perceive this ratio as a primary measure of liquidity, long-term debt paying ability,

Source: Article by Charles H. Gibson. Reprinted from the April 1982 issue of *Management Accounting.* Copyright © 1982 by the National Association of Accountants.

profitability, or other?" The "other" could be anything perceived by the firm. In all probability it would be a measure of activity, or a stock indicator.

Many ratios indicate several measures of a firm. For example, inventory turnover could be an indication of liquidity, profitability, and activity. This question was designed to determine the primary measure indicated by the ratio.

To determine the perceived significance of a ratio, we asked: "How do you rate the significance of this ratio?"

> 0-2 low importance
> 3-6 average importance
> 7-9 high importance

A summary of the perceived primary measure and its significance rating for each of the 18 listed ratios (Table 1) indicates that there is a majority consensus on each ratio as to what the ratio primarily measures—an encouraging result that might help reduce some of the confusion about what a particular ratio is designed to measure. A number of the ratios that were rated primarily as an indication of liquidity were rated by approximately one-fourth of the companies as being a primary measure of something other than liquidity, for example, accounts receivable turnover. Ratios that received relatively high support in the "other" column often are listed in textbooks as activity ratios. Although they are an indication of activity, in my opinion activity is not a logical end objective. Activity is an indication of liquidity, debt, or profitability, depending on the particular ratio. The results of this survey indicate that the financial executives agree that ratios which indicate activity are a primary measure of liquidity, debt, or profitability.

Three ratios—price earnings, dividend payout, and book value per share—were indicated to have a primary measure other than liquidity, debt, or profitability. This result appears to be consistent with the widespread opinion that these ratios are primarily an indication of stock evaluation. A definite conclusion as to what these ratios measure cannot be made because the respondents were not asked to explain their interpretation of "other." This decision was a compromise in the design of the questionnaire in order to keep the response time reasonable.

Liquidity and Debt Ratios

Table 1 indicates the significance rating for each ratio. The significance rating given to the liquidity ratios is repeated below in order of their significance ratings.

Ratio	Rating
Working capital	6.62
Inventory turnover	6.52
Days' sales in receivables	6.46
Current ratio	6.39
Days' sales in inventory	5.31
Accounts receivable turnover	5.05

Note the range of significance does not appear to be material, which suggests that all of these ratios indicate some degree of liquidity. Probably all of these ratios need to be computed in order to get a reasonable view of liquidity based upon the interrelationship of these ratios. For example, accounts receivable turnover and inventory turnover indicate a degree of quality of receivables and inventory, respectively. The perceived quality of receivables and inventory would reflect as to what would be a reasonable current ratio. If the quality of receivables and/or inventory is low, then a higher current ratio would be necessary in order to compensate for a low quality segment that influences the ratio.

The companies responding in the petroleum industry gave three of the liquidity ratios a much lower rating than the overall rating received by the ratio. These ratios were days' sales in accounts receivable, accounts receivable turnover, and inventory turnover. These liquidity ratios were each given a rating of 2.50 by the firms in the petroleum industry. Days' sales in inventory was given a much higher rating of 7.00 by the chemicals and allied products than the overall rating of 5.31.

Working capital was rated 8.70 by the motor vehicle parts and accessories industry which was much higher than the 6.2 overall average.

Although it might be expected that some industries would rate certain ratios much higher or lower than other industries, there were not enough responses by industry to draw any definite conclusion on this point. It is noteworthy that material differences in rating by industry were not indicated for the debt or profitability ratios.

There is a wide range of perceived significance for the debt ratio, as noted on the following page.

Table 1
Primary Measure and Significance of Specific Ratios

Ratio	Primary measure					Significance	
	Liq.	Debt	Profit	Other	No. Responses	Avg. Rating	No. Responses
Days' sales in receivables	**68.0%**	1.0%	7.2%	23.8%	97	6.46	95
Accounts receivable turnover	**67.7%**	2.2%	6.5%	23.6%	93	5.05	88
Days' sales in inventory	**57.8%**	1.1%	12.2%	28.9%	90	5.31	93
Inventory turnover	**52.6%**	1.1%	17.9%	28.4%	95	6.52	91
Working capital	**91.0%**	2.0%	3.0%	4.0%	100	6.62	97
Current ratio	**94.0%**	3.0%	1.0%	2.0%	100	6.39	96
Times interest earned	7.4%	**71.3%**	12.8%	8.5%	94	6.14	96
Fixed charge coverage	7.9%	**69.7%**	15.7%	6.7%	89	5.44	89
Debt to assets	5.8%	**88.4%**	0.0%	5.8%	86	2.96	87
Debt to equity (or debt to capital)	6.2%	**85.6%**	2.1%	6.1%	97	7.48	95
Net profit margin	0.0%	0.0%	**100.0%**	0.0%	102	8.05	99
Total asset turnover	11.6%	2.3%	**51.2%**	34.9%	86	4.50	88
Return on investment (or capital)	0.0%	2.1%	**94.8%**	3.1%	96	8.52	94
Return on equity	1.1%	2.1%	**93.7%**	3.1%	95	8.07	94
Earnings per share	0.0%	0.0%	**98.0%**	2.0%	101	8.63	97
Price earnings ratio	0.0%	1.1%	28.7%	**70.2%**	94	6.12	90
Dividend payout	6.4%	2.1%	9.6%	**81.9%**	94	6.47	95
Book value per share	0.0%	0.0%	4.2%	**95.8%**	96	5.17	96

Ratio	Rating
Debt to equity (or debt to capital) ..	7.48
Times interest earned	6.14
Fixed charge coverage	5.44
Debt to assets	2.96

There are two views on a company's ability to carry debt. One relates to the balance sheet and the other relates to the income statement. The balance sheet view is concerned with how much debt the firm has in relation to funds provided by owners. The income statement view concentrates on the company's ability to service the outstanding debt. Both views are important and both need to be considered when drawing conclusions as to the company's ability to carry debt.

The balance sheet view is expressed with the ratio debt to equity (or debt to capital) and the debt to assets ratio. The debt to equity (or debt to capital) ratios were combined as one alternative because the pretesting of the questionnaire with financial executives and a review of annual reports indicated that there is agreement that a ratio which indicates the degree of debt carried on the balance sheet is needed. However, there is a great deal of disagreement as to the details of the computation. Usually a corporation will compute either the debt to equity or the debt to capital ratio, but not both. There are probably more than 15 different computations used to compute a ratio that indicates the degree of debt on the balance sheet.

The income statement view of debt is reflected by the firm's ability to meet fixed obligations in relation to income. Ratios that are designed to indicate a firm's ability to meet these fixed obligations are times interest earned, and fixed charge coverage. The difference between these ratios is that times interest earned only considers interest in relation to income while the fixed charge coverage considers interest plus other financing obligations a company considers fixed. An example of other fixed obligations would be the use of a portion of rent payments on operating leases.

The times interest earned coverage was rated to be moderately more significant than the

Table 2
Additional Financial Ratios (by Financial Executives)

Ratio	Primary measure					Significance	
	Liq.	Debt	Profit	Other	No. Responses	Avg. Rating	No. Responses
Return on assets	0.0%	3.8%	**96.2%**	0.0%	26	8.33	26
Gross Margin	0.0%	0.0%	**100.0%**	0.0%	11	7.30	12
Quick ratio (acid text)	**80.0%**	0.0%	20.0%	0.0%	10	6.25	9
Cash flow/debt	10.0%	**80.0%**	0.0%	10.0%	10	6.75	9
Sales per employee	0.0%	0.0%	**75.0%**	25.0%	4	6.00	4

fixed charge coverage. A firm probably should consider both of these ratios to get an indication of its income ability to carry debt and related financing commitments.

Profitability and Other Ratios

Four of the profitability ratios received ratings over 8 out of a possible 9:

Ratio	*Rating*
Earnings per share	8.63
Return on investment (or capital) . . .	8.52
Return on equity	8.07
Net profit margin	8.05
Total asset turnover	4.50

These ratios were rated the most significant of all of the ratios used in this study. This result seems to indicate that financial executives pay more attention to profitability than they do to liquidity or debt.

The one profitability ratio that was not given a high significance rating was the total asset turnover. Because the total asset turnover and the net profit margin are integral parts of the return on assets, they are both needed if a company wants to know why the return on assets is going up or down. Return on assets was not included in the list of ratios. It was excluded in an effort to minimize the list of ratios using the reasoning that if either or both net profit margin as total asset turnover were rated high, then the return on assets probably would be rated high.

It is probably necessary to compute all of the profitability ratios to get a reasonable view because each gives a different view of profitability.

As for the ratios rated primarily for other than an indication of liquidity, debt, or profitability, it was interesting that dividend payout (6.47) was rated to be more significant than the price/earnings ratio (6.12). This difference may have resulted because the survey's participants—financial managers—have placed more emphasis on their objective of dividend payout rather than the price/earnings ratio. A review of the financial ratios used in corporate objectives indicates this same point. Book value was rated 7.25 by the motor vehicle parts and accessories industry, which was materially higher than the overall rating for book value of 5.17.

The respondents were asked to list additional ratios that their company computes and to indicate the primary measure and significance of the ratio (Table 2). Many additional ratios were listed by less than four firms, but they are not included in Table 2 because they were not considered representative ratios.

The additional ratios indicate one more liquidity ratio, one more debt ratio, and three more profitability ratios. The liquidity ratio is the quick ratio (acid test), which is similar to the current ratio, except inventory has been removed from the current assets. The rating given to this ratio was approximately the same rating as was given the other liquidity ratios.

The additional debt ratio is the cash flow/debt ratio. The purpose of this ratio is to indicate the cash flow a company is generating in relation to the debt that it is carrying. This ratio first appeared in the literature in 1966 in a bankruptcy study conducted by W.H. Beaver.[1] In his study the cash flow/debt ratio came out as the ratio with the greatest predictive ability

[1] W.H. Beaver, "Financial Ratios as Predictors of Failure," Empirical Research in Accounting: Selected Studies, 1966. Supplement to Vol. 4, *Journal of Accounting Research*, 71-127.

in terms of bankruptcy. The executives who listed this ratio in the survey gave it a relatively high rating of 6.75.

The additional profitability ratios were return on assets, gross margin, and sales per employee. The return on assets ratio was given a relatively high rating and was listed far more times than the other ratios added. The gross margin was listed by several firms as a profitability measure and it was given a relatively high rating by these executives. It appears that this ratio possibly should be considered as an important profitability ratio. The third profitability ratio added was sales per employee. Only four firms added this ratio, but they were all in the retail industry. This ratio is possibly an important profitability measure in the retail industry.

Computational Methodology

The same ratio may be computed in different ways in practice. This is particularly true of the profitability ratios and the debt ratios. These differences essentially are caused by differences of opinion on how to handle special income statement and special balance sheet items. There is a difference of opinion on how to handle these items on the income statement:

1. Unusual or infrequent items,
2. Equity income,
3. Minority share of earnings,
4. Discontinued operations,
5. Extraordinary items, and
6. Cumulative effect of change in accounting principle.

The special income statement items influence most of the profitability measures, and the times interest earned and fixed charge coverage in the debt ratios. To determine how financial management considers the special income statement items when computing these ratios, the question was asked for each special item in relation to a given ratio: "If your firm computes a given ratio, is the indicated special item included in net income in the numerator?" The firms were asked to assume that each item is material and is disclosed separately on the income statement.

Table 3 indicates that approximately 75% of the firms included unusual or infrequent items in the numerator. Whether to include unusual or infrequent items in the numerator is certainly a judgment decision.

A much higher percentage of firms included equity income in the numerator for the profitability ratios than they did for unusual or infrequent items. The percentage of firms that included equity income in the numerator when computing the times interest earned or fixed charge coverage dropped to approximately 70%. This drop in percentage probably was because equity income is a noncash flow item to the extent that actual cash indivdends were not received.

There is a logically correct response when considering equity income. The net profit margin is the relationship between income and net sales. None of the investee's sales are included in the investor's income statement; therefore, equity income should not be included in the numerator. Return on assets expresses the

Table 3
Percentage of Firms Including the Special Item in the Numerator

Special item

Ratio	Unusual or Infrequent Items	Equity Income	Minority Share of Earnings	Discontinued Operations	Extra-ordinary Items	Cumulative Effect of Change in Accounting Principle
Net profit margin	69.3%	81.2%	70.7%	41.0%	29.5%	44.0%
Return on assets	70.3%	85.7%	66.1%	47.6%	26.6%	46.8%
Return on investment	77.6%	90.1%	73.5%	55.1%	32.9%	45.7%
Return on equity	79.8%	91.8%	68.8%	56.2%	38.6%	51.3%
Times interest earned or fixed charge coverage	73.1%	70.1%	70.3%	46.9%	34.3%	48.4%

relationship between income and total assets. Since the investment account is included in the total assets, the equity income should be included in the numerator. Return on investment expresses the relationship between income and long-term sources of funds. Therefore, equity income should be included in the numerator. Return on equity expresses the relationship between income and stockholders' equity. We would want to express the relationship between total income and stockholders' equity; therefore, the equity income should be included in the numerator. Times interest earned or fixed charge coverage ratio indicates the firm's ability to cover the interest or fixed charges; therefore, we would want to exclude the equity income from the numerator because it is a noncash flow item to the extent that actual cash dividends were not received.

Approximately 70% of the firms included minority share of earnings in the numerator when computing the given ratios. Is this a correct response? The net profit margin is the relationship between income and net sales. Since the sales of the subsidiary are consolidated with the parent company's sales, the minority share of earnings should be included with the parent company's income.

Return on assets expresses the relationship between income and total assets. Since subsidiary assets have been consolidated, the minority share of earnings should be included with the parent company's income. Return on investment expresses the relationship between income and long-term sources of funds; therefore, minority share of earnings should be included in the numerator. Return on equity expresses the relationship between income and stockholders' equity. Since the stockholders' equity does not include minority equity, the minority share of earnings should be excluded from the numerator. Times interest earned or fixed charge coverage indicates the firm's ability to cover the interest or fixed charge. The minority share of earnings is available for this coverage; therefore, we would want to include minority share of earnings in the numerator.

Discontinued operations were included in the numerator approximately 50% of the time; however, because discontinued operations are not recurring they should be excluded from the primary ratios. Approximately one-third of the time extraordinary items were included in the numerator. Again, extraordinary items are not recurring; therefore, should be excluded from

the numerator. A little less than 50% of the time firms included the cumulative effect of the change in accounting principle in the numerator, but this item also should be excluded from the numerator because it is not recurring and it applies to prior periods.

Balance Sheet Items

The balance sheet items in the survey were deferred taxes, minority interest, and leases. To determine how deferred taxes are handled, the executives were directed to concentrate on deferred taxes that are presented as liabilities other than short-term. When computing financial ratios, such as the debt to equity ratio (total liabilities divided by shareholders' equity), they were asked: "Are deferred taxes considered to be a long-term liability?" Forty-three out of 101 firms stated that they include deferred taxes as a liability when computing debt ratios such as debt to equity. Twenty-four firms ignored the amount entirely and excluded it from the ratio. Three companies considered the deferred tax amount in equity as a free source of funds. Of the 31 respondents who indicated they did not include deferred tax in liabilities, none explained adequately how they did consider the deferred tax item.

How deferred taxes should be handled is a difficult judgment decision. The deferred tax amount is not likely to result in a cash outlay. But part or all of the deferred tax amount may result in a cash outlay. To be conservative, the deferred tax amount should be included in liabilities. In terms of the probable cash outlay the deferred tax amount should be excluded from liabilities.

When a subsidiary is consolidated in a parent company that owns less than 100% of the stock, an amount results on the balance sheet which is referred to as minority interest. This amount has alternative presentations including presentations with long-term liabilities and presentations between liabilities and stockholders' equity. The executives were asked to assume that they compute the debt to equity ratio. They were asked if the minority interest is included as part of debt, equity, or neither. Ninety-two responses were received on this question with 9.8% including it in debt, 17.4% in equity, and 72.8% not including it in the debt to equity computation.

FASB Statement No. 13 requires the capitalization of some leases on the balance sheet of the lessee. Operating leases are not capitalized but these commitments are disclosed in a footnote. The respondents were asked to consider capitalized leases which are presented as liabilities other than short-term. They were asked the question: "When computing financial ratios, such as the debt to equity ratio, are capitalized leases considered to be debt?" Ninety-two responses out of 97 considered capitalized leases to be part of debt while five did not.

The respondents were asked to consider operating (noncapitalized) leases. The question was: "Do you include the data on operating leases into ratio analysis?" Of the 101 responses, 18 companies indicated that they did include operating leases in ratio analysis. Most of the firms that included operating leases in ratio analysis do so by considering operating leases in the fixed charge coverage. How this is done varies by firm. Some examples of how operating leases are considered in a fixed charge computation are:

1. (a) Fixed charge coverage include 1/3
   (b) Total capital ratios include 7 x subsequent years' operating lease expenses
2. A portion of rent expense is included in the amount of fixed charges used in calculating fixed charge coverage.
3. An interest payment is imputed from the operating lease payment and this imputed interest is included as a fixed charge in determining the ratio of earnings to fixed charges.

One firm responded that operating leases are capitalized at the appropriate cost of debt after deducting implicit operating costs from the lease expense.

Inflation Accounting Data in Ratio Analysis

The respondents were asked if their firm uses any of the data called for in FAS No. 33, "Financial Reporting and Changing Prices," in ratio analysis. One hundred responses were received on this question and 11 answered "yes." Examples of how this data is being used include:

1. Return on equity and return on capital employed are calculated using FAS No. 33 data and historical cost.

2. Income per share calculation only.
3. Ratios are computed on historical cost and inflation-adjusted amounts for comparison.
4. Inflation-adjusted assets are used in calculating the ratios:
   (a) Market value of stock over inflation adjusted assets
   (b) Cash flow return on investment
5. Net income adjusted for general inflation (constant dollar) and changes in specific prices (current cost) is compared to net income on a historical cost basis.
6. When we measure such ratios as return on replacement cost of assets (for internal use only).

In light of the fact that only companies which report inflation accounting data were included in this survey, there does not appear to be much use made of the inflation accounting data in ratio analysis.

Key Financial Ratios as Corporate Objectives

Many firms have selected key financial ratios to be included as part of corporate objectives. Out of 100 respondents 93 indicated that their firms used financial ratios as part of their corporate objectives. Table 4 indicates the ratios that they use and to whom they are reported. Ratios reported by three or fewer firms are not listed.

In Table 4, the profitability ratios, which survey participants rated with the highest significance, were the same ratios used most frequently as corporate objectives. A couple of debt ratios were next in frequency of use. The most popular liquidity ratios were used less frequently than the most popular profitability or debt ratios.

The survey also indicates that a selected ratio is apt to be reported to both the board and to key employees, but a selected ratio is much less likely to be reported to stockholders.

In summary, financial ratios are an important tool in analyzing the financial results of a company and in managing a company. This survey of financial executives indicates the most significant ratios were rated to be profitability ratios. Overall, the debt and liquidity ratios were rated approximately the same.

The computational methodology used by the firms indicates that there is a need for guidance to enable them to compute more uniform

Ratio	No. Using This Ratio	Percentage Reported To:		
		Board	Key Employees	Stockholders
Return on equity	54	53%	51%	42%
Return on assets	53	49%	52%	13%
Net profit margin	43	41%	43%	24%
Earnings per share	38	38%	37%	32%
Return on capital	30	28%	30%	16%
Debt to capital	26	24%	23%	16%
Debt to equity	25	24%	24%	10%
Dividend payout	22	22%	19%	16%
Inventory turnover	18	15%	18%	2%
Days' sales in accounts receivable	13	10%	13%	2%
Current ratio	12	11%	12%	5%
Book value per share	10	10%	10%	9%
Earnings growth	9	9%	9%	6%
Working capital	9	8%	9%	8%
Fixed charge coverage	8	8%	7%	3%
Total asset turnover	7	6%	7%	0%
Accounts receivable turnover	6	4%	6%	0%
Days' sales in inventory	6	4%	5%	1%
Times interest earned	4	4%	4%	2%
Price-earnings ratio	4	3%	4%	2%
Operating margin	4	4%	4%	2%

ratios. This guidance probably should be provided by the Financial Accounting Standards Board.

Based on this survey, there does not appear to be much use made of inflation data in ratio analysis; however, the use of such data may improve as companies become more familiar with it.

Profitability ratios are those most likely to be used as corporate objectives. Ratios used as corporate objectives are as likely to be reported to the board as to key employees. It is much less likely that a key financial ratio will be reported to stockholders.

APPENDIX A ACCOUNTING FOR GOVERNMENT AND NOT-FOR-PROFIT ORGANIZATIONS

REVIEWING THE CHAPTER

Objective 1: Describe the basic concepts related to government and not-for-profit accounting (pp. A-1–A-2).

1. Appendix A deals with accounting for state and local governments, colleges and universities, hospitals, and voluntary health and welfare organizations. The following five paragraphs relate to accounting for state and local governments, and the last paragraph relates to accounting for the other nonprofit groups listed above.

2. The development of governmental accounting standards is currently the responsibility of the Governmental Accounting Standards Board (GASB). Formerly, it was the responsibility of the National Council on Governmental Accounting (NCGA). These standards are developed, not to measure profit, but to measure the changes in the funds available for governmental activities. Of primary importance is the control the governmental unit exercises over the funds made available, many for specific purposes. In governmental accounting, a **fund** is defined as a fiscal and accounting entity, and it is generally based on **modified accrual accounting** (defined in paragraph 5).

Objective 2: Identify and describe the types of funds used in government accounting (pp. A-2–A-3).

3. State and local governments use a variety of funds, each of which must show (a) the financial position and results of operations for the period, and (b) compliance with legal provisions of state and local government.
   a. The **General Fund** accounts for financial resources, such as police, fire, and sanitation, that are not accounted for in any other fund.
   b. **Special Revenue Funds** account for revenues that are legally restricted to specific purposes.
   c. **Capital Projects Funds** account for the acquisition and construction of major capital projects, such as buildings, highways, and sewer systems.
   d. The **Debt Service Fund** accounts for resources to pay principal and interest on long-term debt.
   e. **Special Assessment Funds** account for services or public inprovements to special properties.
   f. **Enterprise Funds** account for activities, such as golf courses and utilities,

which charge the public for goods or services.

g. **Internal Service Funds** account for goods or services that one governmental agency provides to another (within the same governmental unit).

h. **Trust and Agency Funds** account for assets held for individuals, private organizations, or other funds.

4. The funds discussed in paragraph 3a-e are described as **governmental funds;** the Enterprise and Internal Service Funds are described as **proprietary funds;** and Trust and Agency Funds are described as **fiduciary funds.** State and local governments also use a **General Fixed Assets Account Group** and **General Long-Term Debt Group** to account for fixed assets and long-term liabilities, respectively, not related to specific proprietary or trust funds.

Objective 3: Apply the modified accrual basis of accounting used by state and local governments (pp. A-3–A-5).

5. Modified accrual accounting differs from accrual accounting in (a) the method of measuring and recognizing revenues and expenditures, (b) the incorporation of the budget into the accounting records, and (c) the use of **encumbrances** to account for purchases. In governmental accounting, **revenues** are increases in fund resources (other than from interfund transactions or proceeds of long-term debt), and are recognized when measurable and available. **Expenditures** are decreases in fund resources (other than from interfund transfers). Whereas business accounting emphasizes the matching of revenues and expenses to obtain net income, governmental accounting focuses on the inflows and outflows of fund resources. Examples of General Fund journal entries follow.

a. The budget is incorporated into the accounts with a debit to Estimated Revenues, a credit to Appropriations, and a credit to Fund Balance (assuming that revenues are expected to exceed expenditures). The Appropriations account will enable the governmental unit to exercise control over its expenditures. Also, the Fund Balance occupies the equity section of governmental and nonprofit balance sheets.

b. When a governmental unit purchases an asset that is to be received in several weeks or months, the General Fund debits Encumbrances and credits Reserve for Encumbrances. This entry will ensure that the governmental unit adheres to its spending limit.

c. When the above asset is received, two entries are made into the General Fund. First, the encumbrance entry is reversed. Second, a debit to Expenditures and a credit to Cash or Vouchers Payable are made. The encumbered amount will not necessarily be equal to the amount for the expenditure.

Objective 4: Describe the reporting systems used in government accounting (p. A-5).

6. Financial statements of a governmental unit include (a) a combined balance sheet, (b) two types of combined statements of revenues, expenditures, and changes in fund balances, (c) a combined statement of revenues, expenses, and changes in retained earnings (or equity), and (d) a combined statement of changes in financial position.

Objective 5: Identify the various types of not-for-profit organizations and their accounting methods (pp. A-6–A-7).

7. Nonprofit organizations, such as colleges and hospitals, are similar to governmental units in their use of several types of funds and in the absence of the profit motive. However, they differ in their use of full accrual accounting and in their inability to impose a tax as a source of revenue. Also, many of the funds obtained by nonprofit organizations are restricted to specific purposes by the donors.

a. Colleges and universities use an Unrestricted Current Fund, a Restricted Current Fund, Loan Funds, Endowment Funds, Annuity and Life Income Funds, Plant Funds, and Agency Funds. In addition, they prepare (1) a statement of current revenues, expenditures, and other changes, and (2) a statement of changes in fund balances.

b. Nonprofit hospitals use an Unrestricted Fund, a Special Purpose Fund, and Endowment Funds. In hospital accounting, revenues are classified by source, and expenses by function. Statements prepared are the balance sheet, statement of revenues and expenses, statement of changes in fund balance, and statement of cash flows.

c. Voluntary health and welfare organizations, such as the American Cancer Society and the Sierra Club, use funds like those used by colleges and universities. In addition, they prepare a statement of support, revenues and expenses, and changes in fund balances, as well as a balance sheet. As a rule, revenues are classified as public support revenue and revenue from charges for goods and services. Similarly, expenses are classified as program services and supporting services.

Objective 6: Describe the unique aspects of the budgeting process in governmental and not-for-profit organizations (pp. A-7—A-11).

8. Organizations that are not profit-oriented depend heavily on budgeting to maintain control over their funds and to help carry out their goals. The principles of effective budgeting illustrated in Table 8-1 of your textbook (page 288) also apply to not-for-profit and government organizations. However, these organizations concentrate, not on profit or loss measurement, but on cash budgeting techniques as related to changes in the fund balance. Congress, for example, is charged with the enormous task of carefully planning the spending of taxpayers' money. To emphasize the effectiveness of the budgeting process, the resulting statement of revenues, expenditures, and changes in fund balance should include columns

for both actual and budgeted amounts. In addition, expenditures that would exceed the original amount appropriated should normally receive official approval.

Objective 7: Apply and interpret the basic techniques used by government and not-for-profit organizations to control costs of operations (pp. A-11—A-14).

9. The budgets of government and not-for-profit organizations are linked closely with expected revenues for the coming period. The spending limit, or funds appropriated, would be based on such sources of revenues as membership dues, charitable contributions, and tax dollars. Though expenditure budgets are usually prepared independently of revenue budgets, the former must be modified to eventually agree with the latter.

a. Administrative control over government funds is necessary so that government may carry out its mission while covering its day-to-day operations. Each manager is held accountable for the government unit's expenditures as well as for any deviations from budget. In addition, firm fixed-price contracts should be sought, where possible, when dealing with outside contractors.

b. Unforeseen cost overruns can cause a problem for not-for-profit organizations, which normally are subject to spending limits. In such cases, it might be necessary to divert funds (by formal approval, of course) appropriated for other purposes to the items requiring immediate attention.

Matching

Match each term with its definition by writing the appropriate letter in the blank.

_____ 1. Fund

_____ 2. Modified accrual accounting

_____ 3. Governmental Accounting Standards Board (GASB)

_____ 4. General Fund

_____ 5. Specific Revenue Funds

_____ 6. Capital Projects Funds

_____ 7. Debt Service Fund

_____ 8. Special Assessment Funds

_____ 9. Enterprise Funds

_____ 10. Internal Service Funds

_____ 11. Trust and Agency Funds

_____ 12. Proprietary Funds

_____ 13. Fiduciary Funds

_____ 14. Revenues

_____ 15. Expenditures

_____ 16. Appropriations

_____ 17. Fund balance

_____ 18. Encumbrances

_____ 19. Unrestricted Fund

_____ 20. Restricted Fund

_____ 21. Endowment Fund

a. A fund to account for gifts and bequests

b. A fund to account for resources to pay principal and interest on long-term debt

c. The body responsible for developing governmental GAAP

d. The budgetary account used to control or limit expenditures for the period

e. Funds to account for goods or services that one governmental agency provides to another

f. Decreases in fund resources (other than from interfund transfers)

g. Funds to account for services or public improvements to special properties

h. A descriptive term for trust and agency funds

i. The account to reflect anticipated expenditures on the books

j. A fiscal and accounting entity

k. A fund for general operating activities

l. Funds to account for assets held for individuals, private organizations, or other funds

m. The fund to account for financial resources that are not accounted for in any other fund

n. Funds to account for activities that resemble private business activities

o. Increases in fund resources (other than from interfund transactions or proceeds of long-term debt)

p. Funds to account for services or public improvements to special properties

q. The basis of accounting for governmental units

r. In fund accounting, the equity section of the balance sheet

s. Funds to account for the acquistion and construction of buildings, streets, etc.

t. A fund to be used only for a specific purpose

u. A descriptive term for the enterprise and internal services funds

Exercise

1. Transactions for the year ended December 31, 19xx, for the town of Sharon are presented here. For each, prepare the journal entry that would appear in Sharon's General Fund. Omit explanations.

   a. On January 1, the town adopted its budget for the year with estimated revenues of $950,000 and appropriations of $935,000.

   b. On March 15, property taxes of $900,000 were levied. It is estimated that 1% will prove uncollectible.

   c. On March 25, goods were ordered for an estimated cost of $50,000.

   d. On May 9, a new bus was purchased for $30,000 cash.

   e. By June 15, property tax collections totaled $893,000. The remaining $7,000 was written off as uncollectible.

   f. On June 27, the goods ordered on March 25 were received. The supplier's invoice was for $51,000. A voucher was prepared, to be paid next week.

   g. On July 5, the voucher of June 27 was paid.

   h. By December 31, actual revenues totaled $955,000 and actual expenditures totaled $947,000. No encumbrances existed at year-end.

	General Journal			
Date		Description	Debit	Credit

APPENDIX B QUANTITATIVE TOOLS FOR ANALYSIS

REVIEWING THE CHAPTER

Objective 1: Compute the economic order quantity (EOQ) for inventory using a table and formula approach (p. B-1).

1. The optimal inventory level is that level which minimizes carrying costs while avoiding stockouts. To attain this optimal level, management must deal effectively with the delicate balance between inventory ordering costs and carrying costs.
   a. Inventory ordering costs include the costs to place an order, ship the goods, and receive and store the goods.
   b. Inventory carrying costs include storage costs, insurance, property taxes, obsolescence, and interest on investments in inventory.

2. The **economic order quantity (EOQ)** is the quantity of inventory to order that minimizes ordering and carrying costs. Your textbook illustrates two methods for obtaining the EOQ.
   a. One approach is to prepare a table which shows the relevant costs for various order sizes. The optimal order size would be the one which produces the lowest (total) annual cost of ordering and carrying the inventory. This method, however, relies on trial-and-error to obtain an exact answer.
   b. The formula approach will produce an exact answer with the use of calculus.

The EOQ formula is
$$E = \left(\frac{2QP}{AC} \right).$$
E = the economic order quantity in units.
Q = the annual inventory used in units.
P = the cost of placing an order.
AC = the annual carrying cost of one unit of inventory.

Objective 2: Determine the reorder point for inventory when usage is known (pp. B-2 –B-4).

3. Management not only must know how much inventory to order at a time, but also must know **when** to order. The **reorder point,** therefore, is the inventory level that will alert management that inventory needs to be replenished. The reorder point may be calculated by multiplying the lead time by the usage rate. Lead time is the time it takes to receive delivery on an order after it has been placed. So if lead time is expected to be three weeks, and 100 units of inventory are normally used per week, then the reorder point would be when inventory drops to 300 units. At that point, the economic order quantity would be purchased.

Objective 3: Compute safety stock for inventory when usage is unknown (pp. B-4–B-5).

4. In most cases, a company cannot anticipate its exact inventory usage for a given future period. Accordingly, when calculating its reorder point, a company should provide for a **safety stock,** or inventory cushion to help prevent against stockouts. The formulas for safety stock and reorder point (when safety stock is incorporated) are shown below.

a. $\text{Safety Stock} = \left(\text{Maximum Usage} - \text{Average Usage}\right) \times \text{Lead Time}$.

b. Reorder point = (Average Usage X Lead Time) + Safety Stock.

Objective 4: Develop objective function and constraint equations for solving linear programming problems (pp. B-5—B-6).

5. Linear programming is a mathematical technique to maximize profits or minimize costs, within certain constraints that have been imposed. These constraints, or limitations, might be for materials, machine hours, labor, or product demand.

6. The equations used in linear programming are for the objective function (that which is to be maximized or minimized) and for the constraints. While the objective function is normally stated in the form of a straightforward equation, the constraint equations will probably express the unknown quantity as being less than or equal to some known quantity.

Objective 5: Prepare a graphic solution for a linear programming problem (pp. B-7—B-9).

7. Once the constraint equations have been determined, they can be plotted on a graph. To do this, the quantity for each variable must first be obtained (for each equation) with the assumption that the other variable is equal to zero. The points can then be plotted and connected with a line.

8. When all the constraint lines have been drawn, a feasible solution area can then be identified. The optimal point within the feasible solution area will be found at one of the area's corner points (i.e., the point which optimizes the objective function equation).

Testing Your Knowledge

Matching

Match each term with its definition by writing the appropriate letter in the blank.

_____ 1. Economic order quantity (EOQ)

_____ 2. Reorder point

_____ 3. Ordering costs

_____ 4. Carrying costs

_____ 5. Safety stock

_____ 6. Lead time

_____ 7. Linear programming

a. The costs incurred when purchasing inventory

b. How long it takes to receive delivery on an order after it has been placed

c. The costs incurred when holding inventory

d. The optimal amount of inventory to purchase at a given time.

e. A mathematical technique to maximize profit or minimize costs, within constraints that have been imposed

f. Inventory level that triggers replenishment

g. An inventory cushion to help prevent against stockouts

Applying Your Knowledge

Exercises

1. Dolphin Publishing Company uses 1,000 "skids" of paper per year (20 per week), which it purchases for $200 per skid from a paper company. The carrying cost is $4 per skid and the cost to place an order is $25. In addition, the lead time for paper typically is two weeks. *Directions:* Answer the two questions below, rounding amounts to the nearest whole number.
   a. The economic order quantity = ____ skids.
   b. The reorder point = ____ skids.

2. Doherty Products manufactures two products, A and B, which produce contribution margins of $3 and $5, respectively. In addition, the following two constraints exist for the two products:
   a. Demand for product A will not exceed four units per period.
   b. Twenty-four pounds of material is available this period to produce the products. Each unit of A requires 3 lbs., while each unit of B requires 4 lbs.

   Management's objective is to maximize contribution margin.
   a. The objective function equation is ____.
   b. Contribution margin is maximized by producing ____ units of Product A and ____ units of Product B.

APPENDIX C THE USE OF FUTURE VALUE AND PRESENT VALUE IN ACCOUNTING

REVIEWING THE APPENDIX

Objective 1: Distinguish simple from compound interest (pp. C-1–C-2).

1. The timing of the receipt and payment of cash (measured in interest) should be a consideration in making business decisions. Interest is the cost of using money for a specific period of time, and may be calculated on a simple or compounded basis.
   a. When **simple interest** is computed for two or more periods, the amount on which interest is computed does not increase each period (that is, interest is not computed on accrued interest).
   b. However, when **compound interest** is computed for two or more periods, the amount on which interest is computed *does* increase each period (that is, interest is computed on accrued interest).

Objective 2: Use compound interest tables to compute (a) the future value of a single invested sum at compound interest, and (b) the future value of an ordinary annuity (pp. C-2–C-4).

2. **Future value** is the amount an investment will be worth at a future date if invested at compound interest.

   a. Future value may be computed on a single sum invested at compound interest. Table D-1 of the parent text facilitates this computation.
   b. Future value may also be computed on an **ordinary annuity** (that is, a series of equal payments made at the end of equal intervals of time) at compound interest. Table D-2 of the parent text facilitates this computation.

Objective 3: Use present value tables to compute (a) the present value of a single sum due in the future, and (b) the present value of an ordinary annuity (pp. C-4–C-7).

3. **Present value** is the amount that must be invested now at a given rate of interest to produce a given future value or values.
   a. Present value may be computed on a single sum due in the future. Table D-3 of the parent text facilitates this computation.
   b. Present value may also be computed on an ordinary annuity. Table D-4 of the parent text facilitates this computation.

4. All four tables may facilitate both annual compounding and compounding for less than a year. For example, when computing

12 percent annual interest that is compounded quarterly, one would refer to the 3 percent column for four periods per year.

Objective 4: Apply the concept of present value to simple accounting situations (pp. C-7–C-9).

5. Present value may be used in accounting to (a) impute interest on noninterest-bearing notes, (b) determine the value of an asset being considered for purchase, (c) determine the value of a bond, (d) calculate the lease obligation on a capital lease, and (e) determine numerous other accounting quantities, such as pension obligations and depreciation.

Testing Your Knowledge

Matching

Match each term with its definition by writing the appropriate letter in the blank.

_____ **1.** Interest

_____ **2.** Simple interest

_____ **3.** Compound interest

_____ **4.** Future value

_____ **5.** Present value

_____ **6.** Ordinary annuity

a. The amount that must be invested now to produce a given future value

b. The computation whereby interest is computed without considering accrued interest

c. A series of equal payments made at the end of each period

d. The cost of using money for a specific period of time

e. The amount an investment will be worth at a future date

f. The computation whereby interest is computed on the original amount plus accrued interest

Applying Your Knowledge

Exercises

1. Use Appendix D of the parent text to answer the following questions.
   a. What amount received today is equivalent to $1,000 receivable at the end of five years, assuming a 6 percent annual interest rate compounded annually? $ _____
   b. If payments of $1,000 are invested at 8 percent annual interest at the end of each quarter for one year, compute the amount that will accumulate by the time the last payment is made. $ _____
   c. If $1,000 is invested on June 30, 19x1, at 6 percent annual interest compounded semiannually, how much will be in the account on June 30, 19x3? $ _____
   d. Compute the equal annual deposits required to accumulate a fund of $100,000 at the end of twenty years, assuming a 10 percent interest rate compounded annually. $ _____

2. The manager of Foxfield Lanes is considering replacing the existing automatic pinsetters with improved ones that cost $10,000 each. It is estimated that each new pinsetter will save $2,000 annually and will last for ten years. Using an interest rate of 18 percent and Appendix D of the parent text, what is the present value of each new pinsetter to Foxfield Lanes? $ _____ Should the purchase be made? _____

APPENDIX E INTERNATIONAL ACCOUNTING

REVIEWING THE APPENDIX

Objective 1: Define exchange rate and state its significance (pp. E-1—E-2).

1. When businesses expand internationally (called **multinational** or **transnational** corporations), two accounting problems arise. (a) The financial statements of foreign subsidiaries involve different currencies. Thus they must be translated into domestic currency by means of an **exchange rate.** (b) The foreign financial statements are not necessarily prepared in accordance with domestic generally accepted accounting principles.

Objective 2: Record transactions that are affected by changes in foreign exchange rates (pp. E-2—E-5).

2. Purchases and sales with foreign countries pose no accounting problem for the domestic company when domestic currency is being used. However, when the transaction involves foreign currency, the domestic company should record an exchange gain or loss. The exchange gain or loss reflects the change in the exchange rate from the transaction date to the date of payment.

3. When financial statements are prepared between the transaction date and the date of payment, an unrealized gain or loss should be recorded if the exchange rate has changed.

Applying Your Knowledge

Exercise

1. Randy Corporation, an American company, sold merchandise on credit to a Mexican company for 100,000 pesos. On the sale date, the exchange rate was $.05 per peso. On the payment date, the value of the peso has declined to $.045. Prepare the entries in the journal to record Randy Corporation's sale and receipt of payment. Leave the date column empty, as no dates have been specified.

		General Journal		
Date		Description	Debit	Credit

ANSWERS

Chapter 1

Matching

	Financial Accounting	Management Accounting
1.	e	c
2.	g	l
3.	m	b
4.	i	n
5.	a	h
6.	k	f
7.	d	j

Completion

1. Financial accounting reports are used primarily by people outside of the company; i.e., stockholders, bankers, stockbrokers. Management accounting reports are used by managers at all levels inside the company.
2. Financial accounting reports are generally based on historical dollar analyses. Management accounting reports can be based on historical dollars, future dollars, labor hours, machine hours, or whatever unit of measurement is needed.
3. Cost control reports, pricing reports, budgets, cash management reports, capital expenditure analyses, special reports, tax reports.
4. Merchandise-line reports, merchandise inventory control reports.
5. Teller transaction analysis, drive-thru window efficiency reports, time needed to complete a loan transaction.
6. Beginning merchandise inventory
   + Total purchases of saleable goods
   = Cost of goods available for sale
   − Ending merchandise inventory
   = Cost of goods sold
7. Materials costs, labor costs, and various types of factory overhead costs, such as depreciation of machinery, helper labor, supplies, factory rent, and factory insurance costs.
8. For whom the report should be prepared. Who should receive the report (distribution). Who will read the report, if widely distributed.

True-False

1. F The management accountant provides management with information needed for *management* to make the decisions.
2. F They are termed *inventory*.
3. T
4. F The reverse is true.
5. T
6. T
7. F Financial accounting must adhere to GAAP. *Management* accounting has no guides or restrictions.
8. T
9. F It is the *bank* manager who uses all the items listed.
10. F The four W's are Who? What? When? and *Why*?
11. F It is common for the *management* accountant.
12. F It is at least as common for a bank.
13. T
14. F One must satisfy a handful of criteria to become a CMA, one of which is *not* ten years' experience.

Multiple Choice

1. b	**3.** c	**5.** a	**7.** b
2. a	**4.** c	**6.** d	**8.** c

Exercises

1.

Employee	Number of Pizzas Served Per Hour	Employee Rating
P. Porter	22	Excellent
S. White	18	Good
R. Shach	13	Lazy
E. Butterfield	16	Average
B. Kirby	19	Good
B. Worrell	15	Average
G. Johnson	9	The Pits

2. John Madd has answered the who and why questions. Before he can proceed with the analysis, he still must answer the following questions: What kinds of data need to be gathered? When is the report due?

Chapter 2

Matching

1. h	**4.** a	**7.** j	**10.** f	**13.** e
2. c	**5.** g	**8.** k	**11.** i	**14.** n
3. b	**6.** d	**9.** m	**12.** l	

Completion

1. Materials Inventory, Work in Process Inventory, Finished Goods Inventory
2. Direct materials, direct labor, factory overhead
3. A cost is considered direct when it can be conveniently and economically traced to a specific product or other cost objective.
4. Product costing information, planning and control information, special reports and analyses
5. Materials Inventory, beginning of period
   + Materials purchased
   = Cost of materials available for use
   − Materials Inventory, end of period
   = Cost of materials used
6. Cost of materials used
   + Direct labor costs
   + Factory overhead costs
   = Total manufacturing costs

7. Total manufacturing costs
   + Work in Process Inventory, beginning of period
   = Total cost of work in process during the period
   − Work in Process Inventory, end of period
   = Cost of goods manufactured
8. Finished Goods Inventory, beginning of period
   + Cost of goods manufactured
   = Total cost of finished goods available for sale
   − Finished Goods Inventory, end of period
   = Cost of goods sold
9. Gross payroll equals total wages and salaries. Net payroll (i.e. take-home pay) equals gross payroll minus payroll deductions.

True-False

1. T
2. T
3. F   Direct labor data for a particular job can be found on a job card.
4. T
5. T
6. T
7. T
8. T
9. F   Materials Inventory is debited.
10. F   It must be prepared before the income statement can be prepared.
11. T
12. T
13. F   The reverse is true.
14. T
15. F   Neither beginning nor ending Finished Goods Inventory will appear in either column.
16. F   Advertising is an operating expense, and therefore is not included in the cost of goods sold computation.
17. T

Multiple Choice

1. c	**3.** a	**5.** a	**7.** b
2. c	**4.** d	**6.** c	**8.** a

Exercises

1.

Finished goods, Jan. 1	$ 75,000
Add cost of goods manufactured	450,000
Cost of goods available for sale	$525,000
Less finished goods, Dec. 31	80,000
Cost of goods sold	$445,000

2.

Spencer Company
Statement of Cost of Goods Manufactured
For the Year Ended December 31, 19xx

Materials used		
Materials Inventory, Jan. 1	$ 8,700	
Add materials purchased	168,300	
Cost of materials available for use	$177,000	
Less Materials Inventory, Dec. 31	32,600	
Cost of materials used		$144,400
Direct labor		142,900
Factory overhead costs		
Depreciation, factory building and equipment	$ 31,800	
Factory insurance	2,300	
Factory utilities expense	26,000	
Indirect labor	42,800	
Other factory costs	12,600	115,500
Total manufacturing costs		$402,800
Add Work in Process Inventory, Jan. 1		34,200
Total cost of work in process during the year		$437,000
Less Work in Process Inventory, Dec. 31		28,700
Cost of goods manufactured		$408,300

---

3. a. OH   d. DM   g. DM   i. OH
   b. DL   e. OH   h. OH   j. OH
   c. OH   f. DL

Answers: Chapter 2

SOLUTION TO CROSSWORD PUZZLE

(Chapters 1 and 2)

Across:
- 4. PURCHASE ORDER
- 7. INDIRECT
- 9. COST OF
- 12. PERIODIC
- 13. CMAD
- 16. DIRECT
- 17. RAW
- 18. FIXED
- 19. TOTAL

Down:
- 1. P (POUT...)
- 2. RATE
- 3. REQUISITION
- 5. RECEIVING
- 6. WORKING PROCESS
- 8. OVERHEAD
- 9. COST
- 10. FINISHED
- 11. TIME CARD
- 14. RN
- 15. TA

Chapter 3

Matching

1. c   **3.** a   **5.** b   **7.** h
2. e   **4.** f   **6.** d   **8.** g

Completion

1. An underapplication could still occur if the **actual** overhead exceeds the **applied** overhead.
2. Direct materials, direct labor, and applied factory overhead.
3. Close a small difference to Cost of Goods Sold. Divide a large difference among Cost of Goods Sold, Finished Goods Inventory, and Work in Process Inventory.

4. Products such as railroad cars, bridges, wedding invitations, or any other unique or special-order products suggest the use of a job order cost system.

True-False

1. F This can be true only when, in addition, estimated overhead costs equal actual overhead costs for the period.
2. T
3. F It should be divided among Work in Process, Finished Goods, and Cost of Goods Sold.
4. T
5. F A process cost system uses a Work in Process Inventory account for each department.
6. F Indirect costs are charged to Work in Process Inventory through applied overhead.

7. T
8. T
9. F A sale should be recorded when the goods are shipped.
10. F Factory Overhead Control is debited.
11. T
12. F The credit is to Finished Goods Inventory.
13. T
14. F It uses a perpetual inventory system.
15. T

Multiple Choice

1. d   **3.** d   **5.** a
2. c   **4.** b   **6.** d

Exercises

1. a. $1.60/direct labor hour
   b. $.40/direct labor dollar
   c. $240

2.

		General Journal		
\multicolumn{2}{c}{Date}	Description	Debit	Credit
Dec.	23	Materials Inventory Control	2,950	
		Accounts Payable		2,950
		To record purchase of materials		
	26	Work in Process Inventory Control	800	
		Factory Overhead Control	50	
		Materials Inventory		850
		Issued materials and supplies into production		
	26	Factory Overhead Control	1,200	
		Cash		1,200
		Paid telephone, rent, and utilities bills		
	27	Work in Process Inventory Control	1,200	
		Factory Overhead Control	300	
		Factory Payroll		1,500
		To distribute the factory payroll		
	27	Work in Process Inventory Control	3,600	
		Factory Overhead Applied		3,600
		To apply overhead for the week		
		($3 per direct labor dollar X $1,200 direct labor dollars)		
	29	Finished Goods Inventory Control	3,900	
		Work in Process Inventory Control		3,900
		To record completion of goods		
	30	Cost of Goods Sold	2,000	
		Finished Goods Inventory Control		2,000
		To record the shipment of goods		
	30	Accounts Receivable	3,400	
		Sales		3,400
		To record the sale of goods		
	31	Factory Overhead Applied	150,000	
		Work in Process Inventory Control		3,000
		Finished Goods Inventory Control		1,000
		Cost of Goods Sold		16,000
		Factory Overhead Control		130,000
		To divide overapplication of factory overhead for the year among the accounts		

Chapter 4

Matching

1. d		**3.** f		**5.** e	
2. c		**4.** a		**6.** b	

Completion

1. Schedule of equivalent production, unit cost analysis schedule, cost summary schedule.
2. Units started and completed X 100%
   + Units in ending inventory X percentage of completion
   + Units in beginning inventory X 100%
   = Equivalent units

3. Cost of goods transferred out of the department and cost of ending Work in Process Inventory
4. Costs attached to units in beginning inventory
   + Costs necessary to complete units in beginning inventory
   + Costs of units started and completed during the period
   = Cost of goods transferred out of the department

True-False

1. F A Work in Process Inventory account is maintained for each department or operation.
2. T
3. T
4. T
5. F Units started and completed are only part of the computation.
6. T
7. F A combined (conversion cost) unit cost figure is computed for direct labor and factory overhead.
8. F Beginning inventory is multiplied by 100 percent.
9. F There is much overlap between the last two quantities.

10. T
11. F Equivalent units for materials and conversion costs must be multiplied by their respective unit costs.
12. F Work in Process (Department 2) is debited and Work in Process (Department 1) is credited.
13. T
14. F It is made in the cost summary schedule.
15. F Production generally flows in a FIFO manner in manufacturing operations when a process cost system is used.

Multiple Choice

1. d		**3.** d		**5.** c		**7.** b	
2. c		**4.** a		**6.** b		**8.** b	

Exercises

1.

Morris Manufacturing Company
Schedule of Equivalent Production
For the Month Ended May 31, 19xx

Units—Stage of Completion	Units to Be Accounted For	Equivalent Units Materials	Conversion Costs
Beginning inventory	2,000	2,000	2,000
Units started and completed (19,000 - 2,000)	17,000	17,000	17,000
Ending inventory (24,000 - 17,000)	7,000		
(Materials—100% complete)		7,000	
(Conversion costs—30% complete)			2,100
	26,000	26,000	21,100

2.

Morris Manufacturing Company
Unit Cost Analysis Schedule
For the Month Ended May 31, 19xx

	Total Costs Costs from Beginning Inventory	Costs from Current Period	Total Costs to Be Accounted For	+	Equivalent Unit Costs Equivalent Units	= Cost per Equivalent Unit
Materials	$12,000	$114,000	$126,000		26,000	$4.846
Conversion costs	3,000	30,750	33,750		21,100	1.600
Totals	$15,000	$144,750	$159,750			$6.446

3.

Morris Manufacturing Company
Cost Summary Schedule
For the Month Ended May 31, 19xx

	Cost of Goods Transferred to Next Department	Cost of Ending Work in Process Inventory
Beginning inventory		
2,000 units X $6.446 per unit	$ 12,892	
Units started and completed		
17,000 units X $6.446 per unit	$109,582	
Ending inventory		
Materials: 7,000 units X $4.846 per unit		$ 33,922
Conversion costs: 2,100 units X $1.60 per unit		$ 3,360
Totals	$122,474	$ 37,282
Computational check		
Costs to next department		$122,474
Costs to ending Work in Process Inventory		37,282
Total costs to be accounted for (unit cost analysis schedule)		$159,756*

*$6 error due to rounding.

SOLUTION TO CROSSWORD PUZZLE

(Chapters 3 and 4)

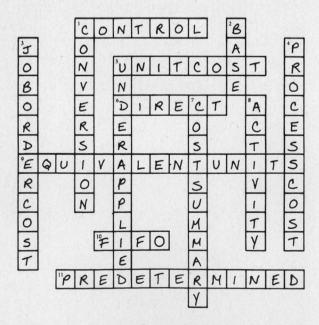

Chapter 5

Matching

1. f	**4.** i	**7.** e	**10.** d	**13.** j
2. k	**5.** o	**8.** b	**11.** m	**14.** c
3. a	**6.** h	**9.** n	**12.** g	**15.** l

Completion

1. Any cost that has both fixed and variable elements, such as telephone expense
2. The high-low method breaks a semivariable cost down to its fixed and variable components.
3. To estimate future costs; To analyze past cost performance
4.

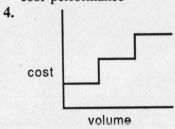

5. Some costs, such as direct materials and direct labor, are easily attributable to a cost objective. Other costs, such as manufacturing overhead, are virtually impossible to trace to specific cost objectives, and must be allocated in some logical manner.

True-False

1. T
2. T
3. T
4. F It is a fixed cost because it does not change with volume.
5. T
6. F They include only costs incurred before the split-off point.
7. F A cost objective is anything that receives an assigned cost.
8. F The reverse is true.
9. T
10. F It would be based on sales dollars expected at the split-off point.
11. T
12. F The objective is to solve for a and b.
13. T
14. F By definition, a supporting service function is not directly involved in production.
15. F The reverse is true.

Multiple Choice

1. c	**3.** b	**5.** a	**7.** b	**9.** c
2. d	**4.** c	**6.** d	**8.** d	**10.** b

Exercises

1. a. Total cost = $800 + $.25/mile
  b. $4,800

2.

Physical Volume Method	Relative Sales Value Method
X = $18,000	X = $4,320
Y = $6,000	Y = $2,880
Z = $12,000	Z = $28,800

3. Dept. 1 = $12,500
    Dept. 2 = $20,000
    Dept. 3 = $10,000
    Dept. 4 = $ 7,500

4. a. Total Cost = $98 + $2.50/direct labor hour
  b. $473

Chapter 6

Matching

1. d	**3.** f	**5.** c	**7.** a
2. b	**4.** h	**6.** g	**8.** e

Completion

1. Sales = VC + FC or Sales − VC − FC = 0
2.

Sales	$XX
− Variable Costs	XX
= Contribution Margin	XX
− Fixed Costs	XX
= Net Income	$XX

3. Sales refers to the gross proceeds realized on the sale of a company's product. Contribution margin, on the other hand, refers to the portion of sales remaining after all variable costs have been deducted. It is the amount available to cover fixed costs plus a profit.

4. a. Behavior of variable and fixed costs can be measured accurately.
   b. Costs and revenues have a close linear relationship.
   c. Efficiency and productivity will hold steady within the relevant range.
   d. Cost and price variables will hold steady during the period being planned.
   e. The product sales mix will not change during the period being planned.
   f. Production and sales volume will be about equal.
5. Shifting production and sales toward those products that promise the highest contribution margin percentages.

True-False

1. F Normal capacity is the most realistic.
2. F Sales = variable costs plus fixed costs, at the break-even point.
3. T
4. T
5. T
6. F A contribution margin is realized from the first unit sold.
7. F The x-axis represents volume.
8. T
9. T
10. F Unless the selling price or variable cost per unit changes, the contribution margin percentage will remain the same.
11. T
12. F The product that promises the highest contribution margin is the best product to sell.
13. T
14. F A weighted average, not a simple average, must be calculated to obtain the average contribution margin percentage.
15. T

Multiple Choice

1. c	**3.** a	**5.** a	**7.** d	**9.** a
2. b	**4.** d	**6.** c	**8.** d	**10.** b

Exercises

1. a. 20,000 units
   b. $260,000
   c. $32,000 loss
   d. $32,500 units

2.

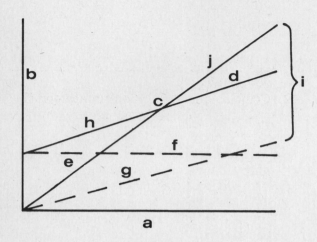

3. a. $20,000 loss.
   b.

Evans Corporation
Projected Income Statement
For the Year Ended December 31, 19XX

Sales (40,000 units X $34)	$1,360,000
Less VC (40,000 units X $24)	960,000
CM (40,000 units X $10)	400,000
Less Fixed Costs	350,000
Net Income	$50,000

4. a. 30.5% ($61,000/$200,000)
   b. $120,000 ($36,600/30.5%)
   c. A = $30,000 ($120,000 X 25%)
      B = $36,000 ($120,000 X 30%)
      A = $54,000 ($120,000 X 45%)

SOLUTION TO CROSSWORD PUZZLE
(Chapters 5 and 6)

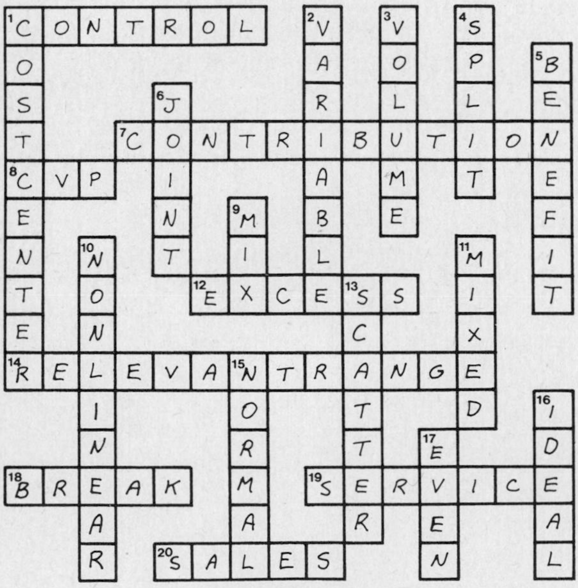

(crossword puzzle grid)

Chapter 7

Matching

1. i	**4.** g	**7.** d
2. h	**5.** b	**8.** f
3. e	**6.** a	**9.** c

Completion

1. Cost/expense center, profit center, investment center.
2. The cafeteria could be a pure profit center if it had profit responsibilities. However, most company cafeterias are subsidized and charge low prices. Such cafeterias would be treated as cost centers.
3. Profit center
4. Cost center
5. $$\text{Return on investment} = \frac{\text{Net Income}}{\text{Dollar value of assets employed in generating that income}}$$

6. 1. Managers should have input into the standards and goals set for their areas of responsibility.
   2. Top management's support of the evaluation process should be evident.
   3. Only controllable cost and revenue items with significant variances should be the focus of performance reports.
   4. Managers should be given opportunities to respond to any part of the evaluation process.

7. 1. Provide accurate and suitable measures of performance.
   2. Communicate expectations to appropriate managers and segment leaders to be evaluated.
   3. Identify the responsibilities of each manager.
   4. Compare actual performance with a suitable base.
   5. Prepare performance reports that highlight areas of concern.
   6. Analyze important cause and effect relationships.

True-False

1. F   It centers on reporting, not on recording.
2. T
3. T
4. F   Allocated costs are not controllable.
5. T
6. F   The manager is also responsible for return on investment.
7. T
8. T
9. F   It is the first step.

Multiple Choice

1. b	**3.** d	**5.** b	**7.** c	**9.** b
2. d	**4.** a	**6.** d	**8.** c	**10.** d

Exercises

1. *Department*   *Contributing Departments*

B	D, E, F, and G
C	H, I, J, and K
H	J and K

2. a.

Performance Report: Profit Center

Company Y
Department X
Performance Report
For the Period Ended —

	Budgeted	Actual	Difference Over (Under) Budget
Controllable by supervisor			
Revenue from sales	$870,000	$900,000	$30,000
Costs:			
Cost of Goods Sold	$700,000	$750,000	$50,000
Storage expenses	49,000	3,000	(46,000)
Selling expenses	900	1,000	100
Totals	$749,900	$754,000	$ 4,100
Controllable departmental income	$120,100	$146,000	$25,900
Uncontrollable by supervisor			
Depreciation	$ 500	$ 500	$ 0
Property tax	1,200	1,000	(200)
Corporate Costs	3,500	4,000	500
Totals	$5,200	$5,500	$300
Net department income	$114,900	$140,500	$25,600

2. b.   Performance Report: Investment Center

Company Y
Department X
Performance Report
For the Period Ended —

	Budgeted	Actual	Difference Over (Under) Budget
Controllable by supervisor			
Revenue from sales	$870,000	$900,000	$30,000
Costs:			
Cost of Goods Sold	$700,000	$750,000	$50,000
Storage expenses	49,000	3,000	(46,000)
Selling expenses	900	1,000	100
Totals	$749,900	$754,000	$ 4,100
Controllable departmental income	$120,100	$146,000	$25,900
Controllable department rate of return	15.01%	18.25%	3.24%
Uncontrollable by supervisor			
Depreciation	$ 500	$ 500	$ 0
Property tax	1,200	1,000	(200)
Corporate Costs	3,500	4,000	500
Totals	$5,200	$5,500	$300
Net department income	$114,900	$140,500	$25,600

Answers: Chapter 7   281

Chapter 8

Matching

1. c	**3.** e	**5.** g	**7.** f
2. h	**4.** b	**6.** a	**8.** d

Completion

1. Long-range goals principles
   Short-range goals and strategies principles
   Human responsibilities and interaction principles
   Budget housekeeping principles
   Follow-up principles
2. Materials usage budget
   Materials purchases budget
   Labor hour requirements budget
   Labor dollars budget
   Factory overhead budget

True-False

1. F It refers to planning and control of operations.

2. F A master budget is a comprehensive budget, usually for a one-year period.

3. T

4. T

5. F The sales budget is in units, whereas the revenue budget is in dollars.

6. T

7. F Depreciation expense does not represent a cash outflow and therefore would not be present in the cash budget.

8. T

9. T

10. F Only cash collected from sales (including prior months' sales) would be included as cash receipts.

11. T

12. T

13. F The reverse is true.

14. T

Multiple Choice

1. d	**3.** c	**5.** d	**7.** b
2. c	**4.** b	**6.** a	**8.** a

Exercises

1.

E & J Company
Production Budget
For the Quarter Ended June 30, 19xx

	April	May	June
Beginning inventory	1,000 units	1,200 units	1,500 units
Add production in units	10,200	12,300	14,400
Units available for sale	11,200	13,500	15,900
Less units sold	10,000	12,000	15,000
Ending inventory	1,200 units	1,500 units	900 units

2.

Rensch Enterprises
Cash Budget
For the Month Ending June 30, 19xx

Cash receipts		
Sales—May	$52,000	
Sales—June	18,000	
Proceeds from loan*	1,000	
Total receipts		$71,000
Cash disbursements		
General and administrative expenses	22,000	
Inventory purchases—May	20,000	
Inventory purchases—June	15,000	
Purchase of office furniture	3,000	
Selling expenses	14,000	
Total disbursements		74,000
Cash increase (decrease)		(3,000)
Cash balance, June 1		7,000
Cash balance, June 30		$ 4,000

* Amount must be derived.

SOLUTION TO CROSSWORD PUZZLE

(Chapters 7 and 8)

```
¹R  E  S  ²P  O  N  S  I  ³B  I  L  I  T  Y
        A              U
   ⁴G      R        ⁵P    D           ⁶A      ⁷D
⁸C  O  S  T        R    G      ⁹S    C      E
   A      I    ¹⁰F  O  R  E  C  A  S  T      C
   L      C        F    T      L    U      E
         I        I    A      E    A      N
   ¹¹R  E  P  O  R  T    R      S    L      T
   E      A        C    Y             R
   C      T        E      ¹²C  A  S  ¹³H      A
   E      I        N          U      L
   ¹⁴I  N  V  E  S  T  M  E  N  T      M      I
   P      E        E             A      Z
   T      ¹⁵P  E  R  F  O  R  M  A  N  C  E
   S                              D
```

284

Chapter 9

Matching

1. e	**3.** c	**5.** h	**7.** i	**9.** g
2. j	**4.** f	**6.** b	**8.** a	**10.** d

Completion

1. Direct materials price standard
   Direct materials quantity standard
   Direct labor time standard
   Direct labor rate standard
   Standard variable overhead rate
   Standard fixed overhead rate
2. A smaller quantity of direct materials is used than was expected for a particular level of volume.

3. A higher wage is paid than is standard for an employee doing a particular job.
4. Ideal standards, basic standards, and currently attainable standards

True-False

1. F The application basis must be in terms of standard measures.
2. F They are used in establishing direct labor time standards.
3. T
4. F It is part of the control function.
5. T
6. T
7. F They are the responsibility of the personnel department.
8. F The individual variances provide more information than the total variance.

9. T
10. F Currently attainable standards are updated.
11. T
12. F Variances are also useful for planning activities and pricing decisions.
13. F Practical capacity is being described.
14. F Standard unit cost is the sum of standard materials, labor, and overhead costs.

Multiple Choice

1. b	**3.** b	**5.** a	**7.** d	**9.** b
2. a	**4.** c	**6.** d	**8.** c	**10.** c

Exercises

1.

Porcelain	($.80 X .5 lbs)	$0.40
Red paint	($1.00/20)	0.05
Blue paint	($1.00/50)	$0.02
Molding department wages	(.03 hr. X $4.00)	0.12
Painting department wages	(.05 hr. X $6.00)	0.30
Variable overhead	(.08 hr. X $3.00)	0.24
Fixed overhead	(.08 hr. X $2.00)	0.16
Standard cost of one dish		$1.29

2. a. 2 (25,000 cases X 4 lb and 25,000 cases X 2 hr)

b. 1 ($.90 − $1.00) X 100,000 = $.10 (F) X 100,000

c. 4 (5 lb − 4 lb) X 25,000 X $1.00

d. 1 No rate variance; actual and standard rates are equal

e. 3 (2.25 hr − 2 hr) X 25,000 X $2.00

Chapter 10

Matching

1. h	**3.** g	**5.** b	**7.** j	**9.** d
2. a	**4.** f	**6.** i	**8.** e	**10.** c

Completion

1. (Variable cost per unit X number of units produced) + budgeted fixed costs =
2. the company operates above normal capacity.
3. actual factory overhead costs exceed the flexible budget for effort expended (actual hours worked).
4. Flexible budget for effort expended (actual hours worked)
   Flexible budget for level of achieved performance (standard hours allowed)

True-False

1. T
2. F Fixed costs are the same for each segment of a flexible budget.
3. T
4. T
5. F It is usually based on normal capacity.
6. T
7. T
8. T
9. T
10. F It concentrates on fixed overhead costs only.
11. F It is computed by dividing total budgeted fixed overhead costs by normal capacity.
12. F All variance balances must be disposed of at period end.
13. F The overhead efficiency variance compares these two budgets; the spending variance is the difference between actual overhead costs and overhead budgeted for actual hours.
14. F The overhead efficiency variance is a separate variance computed with all other overhead variances.

Multiple Choice

1. c	**3.** a	**5.** b	**7.** b	**9.** b
2. d	**4.** d	**6.** a	**8.** b	**10.** a

Exercises

1.

Los Feliz Company
Flexible Budget
For the Year Ended December 31, 19xx

Cost Item	Unit Levels of Activity			Variable Cost per Unit
	10,000	15,000	20,000	
Direct labor	$ 45,000	$ 67,500	$ 90,000	$4.50
Direct materials	12,500	18,750	25,000	1.25
Variable overhead	27,500	41,250	55,000	2.75
	85,000	127,500	170,000	$8.50
Fixed overhead	50,000	50,000	50,000	
Total costs	$135,000	$177,500	$220,000	

Flexible budget formula: ($8.50 X units produced) + $50,000

2. a. $\$13,140 \text{ F} = \left(\$.60 - \dfrac{\$381,060}{657,000} \right) \times 657,000$

b. $\$4,200 \text{ U} = (657,000 - 650,000) \times \$.60$

c. $\$1,105 \text{ U} = \left(\dfrac{\$100,055}{22,100} - \$4.50 \right) \times 22,100$

d. $\$11,700 \text{ U} = [22,100 - (65,000 \times .3)] \times \$4.50$

e. $\$8,350 \text{ U} = \$57,000 - [3,800 + (19,500 \times \$2.30)]$

f. $\$100 \text{ F} = [\$3,800 + (19,500 \times \$2.30)] - \left[19,500 \times \left(\$2.30 + \dfrac{\$3,800}{19,000} \right) \right]$

g. $\$2,370 \text{ (U)} = \$57,000 - [(22,100 \times \$2.30) + \$3,800]$

h. $\$5,980 \text{ (U)} = [(22,100 \times \$2.30) + \$3,800] - [(65,000 \times .3 \times \$2.30) + \$3,800]$

SOLUTION TO CROSSWORD PUZZLE

(Chapters 9 and 10)

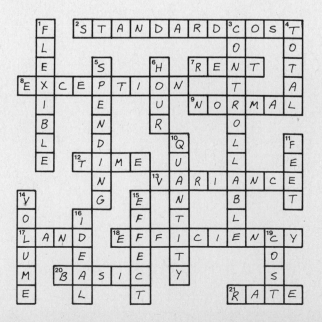

288

Chapter 11

Matching

1. e	**4.** g	**7.** a	**10.** i
2. h	**5.** b	**8.** l	**11.** c
3. d	**6.** f	**9.** k	**12.** j

Completion

1. To determine the optimal price for an item, its marginal revenue and marginal cost curves must be computed and plotted. The point where the two lines intersect is projected onto the demand curve and a price is determined.
2. 1. Total demand for product or service
   2. Number of competing products or services
   3. Quality of competing products or services
   4. Current prices of competing products or services
   5. Customers' preferences for quality versus price
   6. Sole source versus heavy competition
   7. Seasonal demand or continual demand
   8. Life of product or service

3. 1. Cost of product or service (variable costs, full absorption costs, and total costs)
   2. Price geared toward return on investment
   3. Loss leader or main product
   4. Quality of materials and labor inputs
   5. Labor intensive or automated process
   6. Mark-up percentage updated
   7. Usage of scarce resources
4. The sum of the following costs yields the total billing:
   (a) Total cost of materials and parts
   (b) Materials and parts overhead percentage X (a)
   (c) Total labor cost
   (d) Labor cost overhead percentage X (c)

True-False

1. F It is more of an art than a science.
2. F That is the definition for marginal revenue, not total revenue.
3. T
4. F Long-run objective should include a pricing policy.
5. F It is a possible pricing policy objective.
6. T
7. T
8. F No, they often use the time and materials approach to pricing.
9. T

10. F A logical base might be number of employees, labor hours, payroll, or number of hires.
11. T
12. T
13. F The contractor assumes the risk in that the price cannot be modified.
14. F Under certain circumstances, a contractor is chosen and a price is then negotiated.
15. T

Multiple Choice

1. b	**3.** a	**5.** d	**7.** c	**9.** c
2. c	**4.** c	**6.** b	**8.** a	**10.** b

Exercises

1. a.

Mark-up percentage $= \dfrac{\text{Desired profit + total selling, general and administrative expenses}}{\text{Total production costs}}$

$= \dfrac{\$382,500 + \$238,000 + \$510,000}{\$680,000 + 552,500 + \$204,000 + 263,500}$

$= \dfrac{\$1,130,500}{\$1,700,000}$

$= \underline{66.50\%}$

Gross margin-based price $=$ Total production costs per unit + (mark-up percentage X total production costs)

$= (\$1,700,000/850,000) +$
$(\$1,700,000/850,000) \text{ X } .665$

$= \underline{\$3.33}$

b.

Mark-up percentage $= \dfrac{\text{Desired Profit}}{\text{Total costs and expenses}}$

$= \dfrac{\$382,500}{\$680,000 + 552,500 + \$204,000 + 263,500 + \$238,500}$

$= \dfrac{\$382,500}{\$2,448,500}$

$= \underline{15.62\%}$

Profit margin-based price $=$ Total costs and expenses per unit + (mark-up percentage X total costs and expenses)

$= (\$2,448,500/850,000) +$
$(\$2,448,000/850,000) \text{ X } .1562$

$= \underline{\$3.33}$

2. Guardian Landscaping Company

Materials and supplies	$46,500
Materials and supplies-related overhead	
($46,500 X .4)	18,600
Labor cost	32,800
Labor-related overhead	
($32,500 X .6)	19,680
Total billing	$117,580

3. a. Allocation based on square footage:

Div. A = $192,000 ($800,000 X 48,000/200,000)
Div. B = $144,000 ($800,000 X 36,000/200,000)
Div. C = $80,000 ($800,000 X 20,000/200,000)
Div. D = $280,000 ($800,000 X 70,000/200,000)
Div. E = $104,000 ($800,000 X 26,000/200,000)

Allocation based on number of employees:

Div. A = $200,000 ($800,000 X 100/400)
Div. B = $140,000 ($800,000 X 70/400)
Div. C = $80,000 ($800,000 X 40/400)
Div. D = $260,000 ($800,000 X 130/400)
Div. E = $120,000 ($800,000 X 60/400)

b. Allocation based on number of employees
is in accordance with CAS No. 103.

Chapter 12

Matching

1. d	**3.** h	**5.** c	**7.** j	**9.** a
2. f	**4.** b	**6.** i	**8.** g	**10.** e

Completion

1. Discovering the problem or need
   Identifying the alternative courses of action
   Analyzing the effects of each alternative on operations
   Selecting the best alternative
   Judging the success of the decision
2. Relevant information is any decision-related information that is projected or futuristic in nature and that differs between the decision's alternatives. All other information is irrelevant.
3. Both variable costing and absorption costing are approaches to product costing and inventory valuation. Absorption costing bases unit cost on direct materials, direct labor, variable factory overhead, and fixed factory overhead costs. Variable costing treats fixed factory overhead as a period cost rather than as a product cost.
4. Make-or-buy decisions
   Special-order decisions
   Scarce resource/sales-mix decisions
   Decisions to eliminate unprofitable segments
   Sell or process-further decisions

True-False

1. F It is acceptable for financial reporting purposes, but variable costing is not.
2. F The reverse is true.
3. F Fixed factory overhead is a product cost under absorption costing.
4. T
5. F The main concern is with the differences in costs and revenues.
6. T
7. T
8. T
9. T
10. T
11. F *Fixed* costs and profits are what are being covered.
12. F There is no set structure.
13. F Sales-mix analysis is what is being described.
14. T

Multiple Choice

1. d	**3.** c	**5.** b	**7.** c	**9.** a
2. c	**4.** d	**6.** a	**8.** b	**10.** c

Exercises

1.

	Machine Q	Machine R	Difference (Q - R)
Cost of machine	$10,000	$17,000	($7,000)
Direct labor	16,000	8,000	8,000
Maintenance	300	500	(200)
Electricity savings	(50)	80	(130)
Totals	$26,250	$25,580	$ 670

Machine R should be purchased because of the lower incremental cost ($25,580).

2. $1.75 (all other costs are sunk and therefore irrelevant)

3.

		Sales Revenue		
			After Processing	
Product	at Split-off	Sales	Less: Additional Costs	Net Sales
Coconut oil	$160,000	$220,000	$40,000	$180,000*
Coconut milk	$100,000*	$120,000	$25,000	$ 95,000
Coconut meat	$ 75,000	$ 97,500	$20,000	$ 77,500*

*Decisions that will maximize income.

SOLUTION TO CROSSWORD PUZZLE

(Chapters 11 and 12)

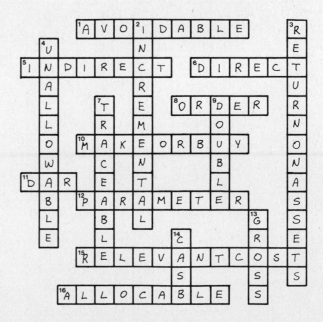

Chapter 13

Matching

1. d	**3.** f	**5.** j	**7.** i	**9.** h
2. g	**4.** e	**6.** c	**8.** b	**10.** a

Completion

1. Identify the need for the facility
   Evaluate different courses of action
   Prepare reports for management
   Choose the best alternative
   Ration available capital expenditure funds
   among competing resource needs
2. Corporate social objectives
   Economic system
   Corporate short- and long-term planning or
   budgeting objectives
   Current economic conditions
3. Accounting rate-of-return method
   Pay-back period method
   Present value method
4. Cost of debt
   Cost of preferred stock
   Cost of equity capital
   Cost of retained earnings

True-False

1. F Capital budgeting does not deal with obtaining cash; it involves the purchase of plant facilities.
2. F Accounting rate-of-return and payback period methods are easier.
3. T
4. F It is the minimum time, not the maximum.
5. T
6. F The desired rate of return must be known.
7. T
8. T
9. F Income would not be put off if the tax rate were higher in the following year.
10. F Book values are past costs and are irrelevant.
11. F Tax considerations may change a decision.
12. F They describe the capital expenditure decision process.
13. F They are a source of cash and therefore relevant.
14. F It is irrelevant to cash-flow-based methods.

Multiple Choice

1. b	**3.** d	**5.** b	**7.** c	**9.** a
2. a	**4.** a	**6.** a	**8.** d	**10.** c

Exercises

1. a. Payback period = $\dfrac{\$70,000}{\$8,000 + \$14,000}$ = 3.2 years

(The $14,000 in the denominator is depreciation.) Since the minimum pay-back period is 3 years, the company should not invest in the machine.

b. Accounting rate of return = $\dfrac{\$8,000}{\$70,000}$ = 11.4%

2.

Year	Net Cash Inflow		Present Value Multiplier		Present Value
1	$5,000	X	.862	=	$ 4,310
2	$6,000	X	.743	=	4,458
3	$6,000	X	.641	=	3,846
4	$6,000	X	.552	=	3,312
5	$6,000	X	.476	=	2,856
Total					$18,782

The company should not purchase the machine, because the present value of future net cash inflows is less than the cost of the machine.

3. a. 4 ($400,000/5 = $80,000)
  b. 3 ($80,000 X .34 = $27,200)
  c. 1 (($160,000 − $80,000 − $27,000/ ($400,000/2))
  d. 2 ($400,000/$160,000 = 2.5 years)
  e. 1 (($160,000 − (80,000 X .34)) X 3.791
  f. 1 Yes, the minimum desired rate of return will be earned

Chapter 14

Matching

1. f	**3.** i	**5.** b	**7.** j	**9.** d
2. c	**4.** g	**6.** e	**8.** h	**10.** a

Completion

1. a. Determine the segments to evaluate.
   b. Identify revenues and costs that are traceable to, and controllable by, each segment.
   c. Communicate to each segment the performance indicator that will be used.
   d. Compare budgeted with actual operating amounts.
2. A cost-plus transfer price is the sum of costs incurred by the producing division, plus an agreed-upon profit percentage. A market transfer price, on the other hand, is a price based on what the product could be sold for on the open market.

3. Sales
   − Variable costs
   = Contribution margin
   − Traceable fixed costs controllable by division manager
   = Performance margin
   − Traceable fixed costs not controllable by division manager
   = Segment margin
4. a. Results achieved indicator−Measures the volume of output or accomplishment
   b. Costs incurred indicator−Measures outlays for capital expenditures and selected expense items
   c. Effort expended indicator−Measures input factors, such as sales calls or machine hours
   d. Resources employed indicator−Measures usage of the company's resources, such as facilities or personnel

True-False

1. F It is a measure of a company's profitability.
2. F Fixed costs would be more difficult to trace to the new segments.
3. T
4. F Some traceable costs are nonetheless uncontrollable by a segment's manager.
5. T
6. T
7. T
8. T

9. F They are called effort-expended indicators.
10. F It is measured by the divisional segment margin.
11. F They should be entered at their total (original) cost, to avoid distortion due to the passage of time.
12. T
13. T
14. F No, a negotiated transfer price is bargained for.
15. T
16. F An artificial price cannot increase total company profits.

Multiple Choice

1. c	**3.** b	**5.** c	**7.** b	**9.** a
2. d	**4.** a	**6.** d	**8.** d	**10.** b

Exercises

1. a. 20 percent
   b. 1.5 times
   c. 30 percent

2.

Metal Bellows, Inc.
Divisional Performance Report
For the Month Ended August 31, 19xx

	Division A Amt.	Division A % of Sales	Division B Amt.	Division B % of Sales	Totals Amt.	Totals % of Sales
Sales	$200,000	100	$100,000	100	$300,000	100
Less variable costs	142,000	71	65,000	65	207,000	69
Contribution margin	58,000	29	35,000	35	93,000	31
Less traceable fixed costs controllable by manager	18,000	19	6,000	6	24,000	8
Performance margin	40,000	20	29,000	29	69,000	23
Less traceable fixed costs not controllable by manager	26,000	13	16,000	16	42,000	14
Segment margin	$14,000	7	$13,000	13	27,000	9
Less fixed costs not traceable to divisions					15,000	5
Net income before taxes					$12,000	4

3. a.

	Volume = 20,000 units	
	Total Cost	Unit Cost
Direct materials	$130,000	$ 6.50
Direct labor	172,000	8.60
Variable overhead	90,000	4.50
Variable shipping expenses	5,000	.25
Total variable	$397,000	$19.85
Avoidable overhead	50,000	2.50
Incremental costs	$447,000	$22.35

b. Unless Diefenderfer Division is willing to pay at least $22.35 per unit, Samuelson Division should not continue to produce this product. Incremental unit costs, considering annual costs and volume, exceed the $20 selling price, and Samuelson is therefore decreasing its profits by continuing to produce the component. The division manager's contention regarding variable cost recovery is not valid. Revenues must recover all incremental costs, both fixed and variable, to avoid an adverse effect on profits.

Sales (20,000 X $20)	$400,000
Less: Variable costs	(397,000)
Contribution margin	$ 3,000
Avoidable fixed costs	(50,000)
Loss ($2.35 X 20,000 units)	$ 47,000

The division manager should also consider the alternative uses to which utilized plant capacity could be applied. This opportunity cost is not included in measuring the $47,000 loss.

SOLUTION TO CROSSWORD PUZZLE

(Chapters 13 and 14)

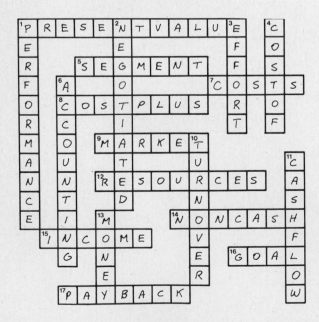

Chapter 15

Matching

1. i	**3.** g	**5.** d	**7.** e	**9.** h
2. a	**4.** b	**6.** f	**8.** c	

Completion

1. Just-in-time is an overall operating philosophy of management in which all resources, including materials, personnel, and facilities, are used in a just-in-time manner.

2. A cost driver is an activity that causes costs to be incurred. In a JIT setting, the objective is to eliminate all unnecessary costs rather than just reducing them through control procedures. But before you can eliminate a cost or account for it properly, you must know what caused the cost—you must know what "drives" the cost. Once the cost driver has been determined, the indirect costs it causes can either be (1) treated as a legitimate product cost and allocated as part of the conversion costs or (2) eliminated by eliminating the need for the cost driver itself.

3. a. Processing time:
   The actual amount of time that a product is being worked on
   b. Inspection time:
   The time spent either looking for product flaws or reworking defective units

   c. Moving time:
   The time spent moving the products from one operation to another
   d. Queue time:
   The time the products spend waiting to be worked on once they arrive at the next operation
   e. Storage time:
   The time the product is either in materials storage, work-in-process inventory, or finished goods inventory waiting to be worked on or sold and shipped.

4. Just-in-time is not an inventory system, JIT is an operating philosophy. One of the goals of a JIT environment is to minimize or eliminate inventory. Unlike the traditional manufacturing approach which requires that inventory be kept on hand to meet customer demands, JIT uses customer orders to trigger production runs. Throughput becomes much more important than the methods of costing inventories.

True-False

1. F   Computer-Integrated Manufacturing
2. T
3. F   They are stand-alone pieces of computerized equipment
4. T
5. T
6. F   A building's environment is not a cost driver because it is not an activity.
7. F   Queue time is time spent by the products waiting to be worked on.
8. T
9. T
10. T

11. F   Process costing can easily be adapted to the just-in-time environment.
12. F   Computer-integrated manufacturing (CIM) is a fully integrated computer setup in which everything connected with the manufacturing system is performed automatically.
13. F   JIT is an operating philosophy; automation is the technology that helps to make JIT happen.
14. T
15. T
16. F   Preventive facility maintenance is an element of the JIT philosophy and is emphasized.

Multiple Choice

1. c	3. b	5. b	7. b	9. d
2. c	4. a	6. d	8. c	10. c

Exercises

1. Separate cost pools recommended:

Engineering Department Cost Pool:

Engineering labor	$12,750
Depreciation, engineering	4,500
Electricity, engineering	1,100
Operating supplies, engineering	430
Total	$18,780

FMS Cost Pool:

Setup labor, FMS	$11,420
Electricity, FMS	1,430
Operating supplies, FMS	980
Machine maintenance, FMS	3,100
Tools and die costs, FMS	6,210
Depreciation, FMS	8,740
Total	$31,880

Factory Building Cost Pool:

Depreciation, factory building	$10,200
Property taxes, factory building	2,960
Electricity, factory building	4,200
Total	$17,360

Possible allocation bases by activity:

Engineering Department Cost Pool:
Engineering hours, engineering change orders
FMS Cost Pool:
Machine hours, number of units produced
Factory Building Cost Pool:
Machine hours, square footage

2. Costs that are classified the same under both the traditional and JIT approaches:

Direct labor—direct cost
Raw materials—direct cost

Costs that are classified as indirect in a traditional system and direct in a JIT environment:

Depreciation, machinery; product design costs; small tools; operating supplies; setup labor; rework costs; supervisory salaries; and utility costs, machinery.

(all of these costs are traceable to a JIT work cell where under a traditional approach, they were all included in a plantwide or departmental overhead cost pool)

The president's salary and fire insurance, plant are indirect costs under both traditional and JIT approaches.

3. The following journal entries would be prepared:

Dec. 22	Raw In Process Inventory	4,890	
	Accounts Payable		4,890
	To record purchase of materials		
Dec. 23	Raw In Process Inventory	13,300	
	Accoaunts Payable		13,300
	To record purchase of materials		
Dec. 23	No entry necessary		
Dec. 24	Finished Goods Inventory	32,750	
	Raw In Process Inventory		32,750
	To record completion of jobs 213 & 216		
Dec. 26	Accounts Receivable	28,608	
	Sales		28,608
	To record sale of Job 216		
	Cost of Goods Sold	17,880	
	Finished Goods Inventory		17,880
	To transfer cost of goods sold		

Chapter 16

Matching

1. e		**3.** i		**5.** f		**7.** g		**9.** b
2. a		**4.** h		**6.** c		**8.** j		**10.** d

Completion

1. a. a macro versus a micro approach to the control of operations.
   b. heavy reliance on the use of nonfinancial data.
   c. to minimize nonproductive time in the delivery cycle, a JIT company is expected to strive to operate at theoretical capacity.
2. An operating environment created by a flexible manufacturing system functioning within the just-in-time philosophy.
3. a. Quality performance measurement
      Customer complaints
      Vendor quality
   b. Delivery performance measurement
      On-time deliveries
      Order fulfillment rate
   c. Inventory performance measurement
      Turnover rates by product
      Space reduction trends
   d. Materials cost/scrap control performance measurement
      Scrap as a percentage of total cost
      Materials cost as a percentage of total cost
   e. Machine management and maintenance performance measurement
      Machine maintenance records
      Equipment capacity/utilization

4. One objective of the JIT philosophy is to minimize the delivery cycle of a product—the time period between acceptance of the order and final delivery. To accomplish this objective, purchase order lead time (the time it takes for raw materials and parts to be ordered and received), production cycle time (the time it takes for the production people to make the product available for shipment to the customer), and the delivery time (the time period between product completion and customer receipt of the item) must be minimized.
5. Full cost profit margin is the difference between total revenue and total costs traceable to the work cell or product. Contribution margin deals only with the difference between total revenues and total variable costs.
6. a. cost savings that will result from reducing the amount of direct labor and the labor-related benefits of replaced workers.
   b. new costs to consider including wages and related costs of workers who maintain and support the robotic (automated) equipment, new direct costs such as electrical power and supervision costs traceable to work cells, and costs associated with scheduling and design.
   c. new costs that need to be capitalized including engineering design work on the new system, computer programming and software development costs, and machine implementation costs.

True-False

1. T
2. F Significant usage
3. F Usually a direct cost
4. F Computer numerically-controlled machine
5. T
6. F Flexible manufacturing system (FMS)
7. T
8. F Departmental or, better yet, FMS cell overhead rates are encouraged.
9. T
10. F Inventory measures such as turnover rates are very important to the control of inventory.

11. F Purchase order lead time is the time it takes for raw materials and parts to be ordered and received so that production can begin. The definition in the question is for the term "delivery cycle."
12. T
13. T
14. T
15. F Very important because they are for very large amounts of money.
16. F Customer responsiveness reporting is required for internal operating and product quality control purposes.

Multiple Choice

1. b	3. d	5. d	7. c	9. c
2. a	4. c	6. a	8. a	

Exercises

1. Unit cost of one wooden nightstand computed.

Materials cost
$185,640/5,460 = $34.00
Materials handling cost
$34.00 X 0.296 =   10.06
Direct labor cost
$68,250/5,460 =   12.50
Engineering design cost
$1.75 per unit   1.75
FMS overhead cost
$8.30 X 3 =   24.90
Building occupancy cost:
2.90 X 3 =   8.70

Manufacturing cost per nightstand $91.91

2. The data given in the exercise was reorganized in the following manner and two additional pieces of information, delivery cycle time and average waste time, were calculated from the given information.

	Weeks				Weekly Average	
	1	2	3	4		
Product quality performance:						
Customer complaints	11	8	7	4	7.50	cmplt.
Warranty claims	1	4	2	2	2.25	claims
Product delivery performance:						
Average process time (hours) (i)	31.4	31.5	31.7	31.8	31.60	hours
Average set-up time (hours) (h)	3.3	3.4	3.2	3.1	3.25	hours
Delivery time (hours) (g)	49.2	48.4	48.4	48.2	48.55	hours
Production backlog (units)	9,480	9,590	9,650	9,870	9,648	units
Production cycle time (hours) (f)	39.1	39.6	39.8	40.2	39.68	hours
Purchase order lead time (hours) (e)	27.1	27.2	26.9	26.8	27.00	hours
On-time deliveries (%)	96.1	97.7	97.2	98.4	97.35	%
Delivery cycle time (e+f+g)	115.4	115.2	115.1	115.2	115.23	hours
Waste time (f-h-i)	4.4	4.7	4.9	5.3	4.83	hours

Product quality performance:

From the data presented, the quality objective seems to be being met. Warranty claims are still averaging a little over two per week. But the number of customer complaints has fallen off significantly from 11 per week to four per week in the past four weeks. This is a very positive sign.

Product delivery performance:

The information on product delivery performance is a bit different. True, average total delivery cycle time is down a fraction of an hour. And set-up time has been reduced from 3.3 hours to 3.1 hours per order. But average processing time has increased as have production backlog and production cycle time. Waste time, the critical element, has increased from 4.4 hours per order to 5.3 hours.

Purchase order lead time and on-time deliveries look good but management should take a careful look at the cause of the increased waste time.

3. Information after FMS installed recast:

	Product 19-10
Total Revenue	$690,000
After FMS installed:	
Traceable costs:	
Direct materials	$165,600
Materials-related overhead	24,150
Direct labor	31,050
Indirect labor	49,680
Set-up labor	33,120
Electrical power	12,420
Supervision	17,940
Repairs and maintenance	23,460
Operating supplies/lubricants	5,520
Other traceable indirect costs	15,180
Traceable selling expenses	26,220
Traceable distribution costs	28,980
Total traceable costs	$433,320
Allocated costs:	
Nontraceable factory overhead	$112,400
Nontraceable selling and distribution costs	96,500
Total nontraceable costs	$208,900
Full cost profit margin:	
Total revenues	$690,000
Less total traceable costs	433,320
Full cost profit margin	$256,680
Less total nontraceable costs	208,900
Operating profit	$47,780
Full cost profit margin as a percent of revenue	37.20%
Operating profit as a percent of revenue	6.92%

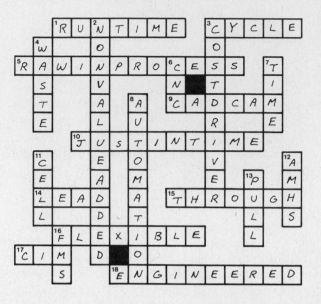

Chapter 17

Matching

1. f	**3.** b	**5.** e	**7.** h
2. d	**4.** g	**6.** a	**8.** c

Completion

1. Issuing capital stock to retire long-term debt
   Purchasing a long-term asset by incurring long-term debt
2. Because they represent noncash expenses that have been legitimately deducted in arriving at Net Income. Adding them back effectively cancels out the deduction.

3. Cash flows from inventing activities
   Cash flows from financing activities
   Schedule of Noncash Investing and Financing Transactions
4. Money market accounts
   Commercial paper (short-term notes)
   U.S. treasury bills

True-False

1. F It must be prepared every time an income statement is prepared.
2. F It is considered an operating activity.
3. T
4. T
5. T
6. F Depreciation, depletion, and amortization would be found in the operating activities section.
7. F The reverse is true.
8. T
9. T

10. F It implies that the business is generally contracting.
11. T
12. F It would be added to Net Income.
13. F Depreciation must be *deducted* from operating expenses in this case.
14. T
15. T
16. T
17. F A change in methods will not produce a different net-change-in-cash figure.

Multiple Choice

1. a	**3.** a	**5.** d	**7.** b	**9.** d
2. b	**4.** e	**6.** a	**8.** c	**10.** b

Exercises

1. a. $57,000
   b. $360,000
   c. $31,000
   d. $221,000
   e. $51,000

CLU Corporation
Work Sheet for Statement of Cash Flows
For the Year Ended December 31, 19x9

Description	Account Balances 12/31/x8	Analysis of Transactions for 19x9		Account Balances 12/31/x9
		Debit	Credit	
Debits				
Cash	35,000		(x) 6,000	29,000
Accounts Receivable	18,000	(b) 3,000		21,000
Inventory	83,000		(c) 11,000	72,000
Plant Assets	200,000	(f) 62,000	(e) 30,000	232,000
Total Debits	336,000			354,000
Credits				
Accumulated Depreciation	40,000	(e) 10,000	(g) 26,000	56,000
Accounts Payable	27,000	(d) 8,000		19,000
Bonds Payable	100,000	(h) 10,000		90,000
Common Stock	150,000		(h) 10,000	160,000
Retained Earnings	19,000	(i) 12,000	(a) 22,000	29,000
Total Credits	336,000	105,000	105,000	354,000
Cash Flows from Operating Activities				
Net Income		(a) 22,000		
Increase in Accounts Receivable			(b) 3,000	
Decrease in Inventory		(c) 11,000		
Decrease in Accounts Payable			(d) 8,000	
Gain on Sale of Plant Assets			(e) 4,000	
Depreciation Expense		(g) 26,000		
Cash Flows from Investing Activities				
Sale of Plant Assets		(e) 24,000		
Purchase of Plant Assets			(f) 62,000	
Cash Flows from Financing Activities				
Dividends Paid			(i) 12,000	
		83,000	89,000	
Net Decrease in Cash		(x) 6,000		
		89,000	89,000	

Chapter 18

Matching

1. g   5. j   8. i   11. m
2. b   6. f   9. k   12. a
3. l   7. h   10. d   13. c
4. e

Completion

1. Profit margin, asset turnover, return on assets, return on equity, earnings per share
2. Horizontal analysis presents absolute and percentage changes in specific financial statement items from one year to the next. Vertical analysis, on the other hand, presents that percentage relationship of individual items on the statement to a total within the statement.
3. Rule-of-thumb measures, analysis of past performance of the company, comparison with industry norms.
4. The risk of total loss is far less with several investments than with one investment because only a rare set of economic circumstances could cause several different investments to suffer large losses all at once.

True-False

1. T
2. F   Common-size financial statements show relationships between items in terms of percentages, not dollars.
3. F   The current ratio will increase.
4. T
5. F   It equals the cost of goods sold divided by average inventory.
6. F   The reverse is true, because the price/earnings ratio depends upon the earnings per share amount.
7. F   Interest is not added back.
8. T
9. F   The higher the debt to equity ratio, the greater the risk.
10. F   Receivable turnover measures how many times, on the average, the receivables were converted into cash during the period.
11. T
12. T
13. F   It is a market test ratio.
14. F   Sales would be labeled 100 percent.
15. T
16. T
17. T
18. T

Multiple Choice

1. b   3. c   5. a   7. b   9. c
2. d   4. a   6. c   8. d   10. b

1.

	19x1	19x2	Increase (or Decrease)	
			Amount	Percentage
Sales	$200,000	$250,000	$50,000	25%
Cost of Goods sold	120,000	144,000	24,000	20%
Gross margin	$ 80,000	$106,000	26,000	32.5
Operating expenses	50,000	62,000	12,000	24%
Income before income taxes	$30,000	$44,000	14,000	46.7%
Income taxes	8,000	16,000	8,000	100%
Net income	$ 22,000	$ 28,000	6,000	27.3%

2. a. 2.0 ($500,000/$250,000)

   b. 1.3 $\dfrac{\$500,000 - \$180,000}{\$250,000}$

   c. $5 ($106,000/21,200)

   d. 1.9 times ($350,000/$180,000)

   e. 12.0% ($106,000/$880,000)

   f. 22.1% ($106,000/$480,000)

   g. 6.0 ($600,000/$100,000)

   h. 60.8 days (365/6.0)

   i. 17.7% ($106,000/$600,000)

   j. .68 ($600,000/$880,000)

   k. 8 times ($40/$5)

SOLUTION TO CROSSWORD PUZZLE

(Chapters 17 and 18)

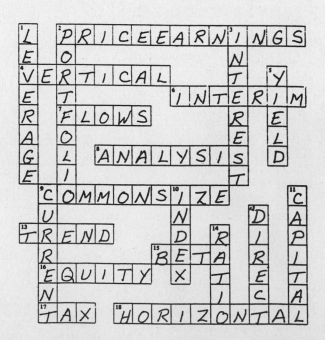

Appendix A

Matching

1. j	8. p	15. f
2. q	9. n	16. d
3. c	10. e	17. r
4. m	11. l	18. i
5. g	12. u	19. k
6. s	13. h	20. t
7. b	14. o	21. a

Exercise

1.

General Journal				
Date		**Description**	**Debit**	**Credit**
Jan.	1	Estimated Revenues	950,000	
		Appropriations		935,000
		Fund Balance		15,000
Mar.	15	Property Taxes Receivable	900,000	
		Revenue		891,000
		Estimated Uncollectible Property Taxes		9,000
	25	Encumbrances	50,000	
		Reserve for Encumbrances		50,000
May	9	Expenditures	30,000	
		Cash		30,000
June	15	Cash	893,000	
		Estimated Uncollectible Property Taxes	7,000	
		Property Taxes Receivable		900,000
	27	Reserve for Encumbrances	50,000	
		Encumbrances		50,000
	27	Expenditures	51,000	
		Vouchers Payable		51,000
July	5	Vouchers Payable	51,000	
		Cash		51,000
Dec.	31	Revenues	955,000	
		Estimated Revenues		950,000
		Fund Balance		5,000
	31	Appropriations	935,000	
		Fund Balance	12,000	
		Expenditures		947,000

Appendix B

Matching

1. d	**3.** a	**5.** g	**7.** e
2. f	**4.** c	**6.** b	

Exercises

1. a. EOQ = 112 skids
   b. Reorder point = 40 skids
2. a. M = $3A + $5B
   b. 0 units of A and 6 units of B

Appendix C

Matching

1. d   **3.** f   **5.** a
2. b   **4.** e   **6.** c

Exercises

1. a. $747 ($1,000 X .747)
  b. $4,122 ($1,000 X 4.122)
  c. $1,126 ($1,000 X 1.126)
  d. $1,745.81 ($100,000/57.28)

2. Present value = $2,000 X 4.494 = $8,988
The purchase should not be made because the present value of future cash savings is less than the initial cost of the equipment.

Exercise

1.

General Journal				
Date		Description	Debit	Credit
		Accounts Receivable, Mexican Company	5,000	
		Sales		5,000
		To record sale of merchandise		
		Cash	4,500	
		Exchange Gain or Loss	500	
		Accounts Receivable, Mexican Company		5,000
		To record receipt of payment		